SCENARIOS OF THE COMMEDIA DELL'ARTE

Portrait of Francesco Andreini, director of I Gelosi from 1578–1604, from his Le Bravure del Capitano Spavento (Venice, 1615).

Scenarios of the
Commedia dell' Arte:
Flaminio Scala's
Il Teatro delle
favole rappresentative

Flaminio Scala

Translated by Henry F. Salerno

With a Foreword by Kenneth McKee

NEW YORK · *New York University Press*

LONDON · *University of London Press Limited*

1967

*Publication of this book was made possible by a partial
subvention from the Purdue Research Foundation, to whom
the publishers are pleased to make acknowledgment.*

© *1967 by New York University*
Library of Congress Catalog Card Number: 67–10693
Manufactured in the United States of America
Designed by Albert Burkhardt

TO MICHELE AND DAVID

ACKNOWLEDGMENTS

I wish to express my appreciation to the following for their invaluable
assistance:

*To the late Professor Marvin T. Herrick for his
advice and guidance; to Elizabeth Grant and Eva
Benton of the University of Illinois Library staff;
to the Purdue Research Foundation for its summer
grants and assistance in publication; to my wife
Nan for her help and encouragement.*

TABLE OF CONTENTS

ILLUSTRATIONS

The *commedia dell'arte* was a unique development in the history of the theater in Western Europe. It flourished in Italy in the second half of the sixteenth century and throughout the seventeenth century. By the middle of the eighteenth century it was a less important factor in the theater, although its influence cannot be said to have died out.

The publication in 1611 of *Il Teatro delle favole rappresentative* by Flaminio Scala was an important event in the history of drama, for not only was it one of the earliest appearances of Harlequin ("Arlecchino") in a printed play, but also it was the first time that anything like a comprehensive collection of the scenarios of the *commedia dell'arte* had been published.

Before *commedia dell'arte* had become a firmly established genre, it had its history of development like any other literary movement. It inherited a fragmentary legacy from many sources: from the *commedia erudita* of the Renaissance; from the clowns and variety artists who entertained at the festivities of the nobles; from the king's jesters; from the minstrels and jongleurs and medicine shows which in Medieval days attracted crowds of spectators on populous streets; from the comedies of Terence and Plautus; from Atellan farces in Rome; and even from Asiatic mimes.

Although all these elements contributed to the formation of the *commedia dell'arte,* the influence of each was completely submerged and scarcely recognizable when the genre reached maturity in the hands of the notable player companies which started to form after 1550.

"Commedia dell'arte" means literally "comedy of the [actor's] guild" and was essentially improvised comedy, which followed a plot outline, called a scenario, rather than written dialogue. The players consisted of a dozen or so stock characters, several of whom wore masks, and two or more *zannis* whose *lazzis* ranged from comic intonations through acrobatics to obscene gestures. This assortment of roles remained almost constant throughout the life of the genre and the types were invariably the same, although the names often changed from troupe to troupe.

Although most of the important actors, save the hero and the ingénue, wore masks, each character was easily identified by his dress: Pulcinella, for example, always had baggy white shirt and trousers, a bulging belly, and a peaked hat, while Arlecchino wore a tight-fitting suit of multicolored diamond design. The mask did not hinder an actor from playing his part—he simply made greater use of bodily movements and inflection of voice. David Garrick, upon witnessing a performance of the *commedia dell'arte,* is said to have remarked: "See how much expression Carlino's back has." Furthermore, when the actors performed indoors by candlelight, it was difficult for spectators to see facial expressions clearly, and the actors had to use every device at their command to interpret their role.

The *zannis* were the buffoons or clowns which were the very embodiment of the spirit of the *commedia dell'arte.* Their names have become bywords in theater history: Brighella, Arlecchino, Pedrolino, Scaramuccia, Pulcinella, Mezzottino, Scapino, Coviello, and a whole brood of slightly less famous cousins. The *zannis* were often the main attraction of the troupe, especially before plebian audiences, and at each performance, they had to dispense a broad sampling of their tricks. Some of the *zannis* were accomplished acrobats: Tomasso Vicentini, who played Arlequin in Paris in the 1720s, could climb the proscenium arch, walk around the railing of the balcony on his hands and descend the other side.

The *lazzis* were the stock in trade of the *zannis.* They included time-honored mock fights, tumbles and falls, disguises and ventriloquism, mistaken identities, and an endless supply of vulgar obscenities.

Shortly after 1550, the players began to organize themselves into companies. One of the earliest to attain recognition was the celebrated company called *I Gelosi* ("The Zealous Ones"), recruited by Francesco Andreini and his talented wife, Isabella. The *Uniti* and the first *Confidenti* soon followed under the patronage of the Duke of Mantua. The *Accesi,* the *Fideli,* and the second *Confidenti* were in operation at the beginning of the seventeenth century, and the tradition continued for many generations. A company was frequently headed by a husband-wife team, and very often the actors intermarried so that in time, as children were added to their numbers, a troupe developed into something like a clan, and created a problem of logistics when they went on tour.

It is regrettable that, although information about the staging of plays is fairly available, records of the troupes' activities are practically non-existent. Unlike the *Comédie Française,* whose archives are almost complete, the Italian troupes left little in the way of authentic documentation: what dates and which plays they performed; how much they collected; what salaries were paid; and other information that gives a true picture of the life of a troupe. Most of our information comes from minutiae found in contracts to perform for royal or noble patrons, licenses to play in various cities, and plans for tours to foreign countries. These items are supplemented by statements made in the correspondence of diplomats who witnessed performances while they were in Italy, and in a variety of diaries and other personal records, often involving the scandalous adventures of some actresses. At the beginning of the eighteenth century, Luigi Riccoboni, who headed a troupe of Italian players sent to Paris at the request of the duc d'Orleans, kept rather complete accounts of both the repertory and the finances of his company. From these scattered details, it has been possible to reconstruct much of the history of the *commedia dell'arte.*

A typical company always included a Pantalone, an elderly parent or guardian; Gratiano, the *dottore,* a doddering and gullible old crony of Pantalone and the butt of much of the comedy of the play; a young hero and an ingénue, the latter usually the daughter of Pantalone or the ward of the *dottore;* a braggart Spanish captain, jealous suitor or other secondary romantic figure; a maid for the heroine who connived with the young couple to outwit their elders; subordinate characters such as servants, nurses or tradespeople; and, most important of all, two or more *zannis* who might be now a clever valet working in the interest of the hero, now a stupid lackey of the *dottore* or Pantalone, but always a buffoon ready to make comedy whenever and wherever the opportunity occurred. Most of the characters were supposed to be natives of a particular city and spoke the local dialect. Pantalone was a Venetian merchant; the *dottore,* a native of Bologna; Arlecchino and Brighella hailed from Bergamo; Scaramuccia and Pulcinella were sons of Naples. The babble of dialects only heightened the farcical elements of the play.

Although Pantalone was the traditional name of the harried parent and Gratiano the name of the pedantic *dottore,* the names of other stock characters varied from company to company. The young hero of *Gelosi* was usually named Flavio or Oratio: of the *Confidenti,* Fulvio or Ortensio: and Lelio was used in a number of other companies. The heroines were frequently Isabella or Silvia, and the names of Flaminia and Rosetta occur in other important feminine roles. Colombine was usually the name of the heroine's servant, with Violetta and Franceschina appearing from time to time. The *zannis,* Pedrolino, Arlecchino, Pulcinella, and the rest, have already been mentioned.

An actor often played a character for so many years and became so famous for his interpretation of the role that he was known to the public, and in subsequent theater history, by his stage name rather than his real name. For instance, Francesco Andreini is called Captain Spavento. He created this enormously popular Spanish captain, who is not unlike the *miles gloriosus* of Plautus, and thereby initiated an enduring vogue for the braggart soldier in other countries. His son, B. G. Andreini, played Lelio until he was seventy-three years old, and is known by that name. Zanetta Benozzi, who played the Silvias in the comedies which Marivaux wrote for the Italian troupe in Paris, is known in the annals of eighteenth-century French theater simply as Silvia. The famous Fiorillo of the Gerhardi troupe is even more renowned as Scaramouche, and the incomparable Biancolelli as Arlequin in France.

The skill of the Italian players is legendary. Since there were no memorized lines for the actors to speak, a performance of a *commedia dell'arte* was an exercise of interplay among the actors, as they improvised the dialogue to suit each occasion. A scene which was glossed over one day might well develop into a climactic moment the next. Each player had to sense the mood of that particular audience and be clairvoyant with respect to his colleagues' intentions so that he could react spontaneously to unforeseen turns in dialogue. The *zannis,* too, took advantage of a responsive audience to indulge in a prolonged interlude of comic antics. Yet the whole had to have dramatic coherence; in fact, each performance was a collective *tour de force* of ingenuity, a demonstration of superb artistry that is rare in the theater.

Of the hundreds of plays used by various companies, only a few scenarios remain. The one rather complete collection is that of Flaminio Scala, who was well acquainted with Francesco Andreini and probably used the scenarios of the *Gelosi* as the basis for his *Il Teatro delle favole rappresentative,* the collection that is here translated. However, enough fragments from other companies remain for scholars to re-establish the pattern of scenarios. In any event, the scenarios were never looked upon as literary pieces; they were merely working documents for the troupe, not worth saving. Here and there, a few lines of set dialogue or specific stage directions have been found, but for the most part the plot outline, such as it was, was all that was ever written down.

Although these troupes excelled in the presentation of *commedia dell'arte,* they took great pride in performing other types of plays with written dialogue: tragedies, pastorals, tragi-comedies, *commedia erudita* and, frequently, parodies or satires of classical masterpieces. With such a diversified repertory and with their dependence on each other to perform the *commedia dell'arte* skillfully, it was well-nigh impossible for actors to shift from one company to another, although there are a few instances in which troupes combined temporarily. Most troupes remained intact for years. Sometimes, as the children matured, they took roles in the company to replace elders who retired.

For two centuries, the player companies toured the length and breadth of Europe. Early in the sixteenth century, individual artists and temporary troupes visited the capitals on occasion. However, after the *Gelosi* started the vogue by appearing at the court of France intermittently from 1571 to 1604, there were few years until the 1750s when one or more companies did not regale the royalty and nobles as well as the general public in other countries. Language seems to have been no barrier, for the Italian actors were excellent mimics and the spectators had little difficulty following the antics on the stage.

France attracted touring companies consistently. After the *Gelosi,* other companies found increasing favor with the French public in 1613–18, 1621, 1625, 1639 and 1644. Finally, in 1660, Louis XIV authorized a troupe, headed by Tiberio Fiorillo and including Dominique Biancolelli, to remain in Paris. The troupe stayed until 1697, when it was expelled for announcing the première of *La finta matrigna,* which purportedly satirized Mme. de Maintenon. After the death of Louis XIV, another company, under the direction of Luigi Riccoboni, was installed on the stage of the Hôtel de Bourgogne, and enjoyed success in the French capital. This troupe adopted the policy of adding comedies by French writers to the repertory, with the result that as time went on the Italian element diminished and eventually, in 1763, when the direction was taken over by Favart and his wife, the theater evolved into the *Opéra Comique*.

Alberto Naseli, known professionally as Zan Ganassa, went to Spain in 1574 and stayed there for several years. Apparently he created quite an appreciation for Italian comedy and won the good will of the Spanish populace, for he built a theater in Madrid and paved the way for the Martinelli brothers, Tristano and Drusiano, to follow him later in the century. Records of other companies are found in Toledo, Seville, Valladolid and Valencia.

The earliest record of Italian players in England, probably only musicians, tumblers, and mountebanks, is an entry in the Chamberlain's accounts in Norwich in 1566. Revels Accounts for 1573–74 indicate that Italian players performed in Windsor and Reading. Drusiano Martinelli was granted permission to appear in England in 1577. By the end of the century, visits of Italian companies to England were fairly common, and in 1602 Flaminio Curtesse played before Queen Elizabeth. Court records show repeated visits in the next hundred years. During the Restoration period, Fiorillo took his troupe to London twice from Paris, and in 1678 Charles II witnessed the performance of a troupe from Modena.

The German kingdoms and Slavic countries received the Italian players frequently. Towards the end of the seventeenth century, the Calderoni couple, noted for their roles of Silvio and Flaminia, took their distinguished company to Munich in 1687, where they played for four seasons; they visited Vienna in 1699 and again in 1703. Warsaw welcomed Tomaso Ristori and his company in 1715 for what turned out to be a fifteen-year run in that city, after which the company journeyed to Russia to entertain the Empress Anna in 1733 and 1735. The Bertoldis, with Andrea playing Pantalone and his wife Marianna playing Rosetta, spent most of their professional careers in Warsaw and Dresden from 1738 to the mid-1750s.

Obviously such widespread and prolonged exposure of the *commedia dell'arte* by the Italian players left its mark on the development of comedy in every country of Europe. The influence is at once self-evident and intangible: self-evident, in that for two centuries dramatists quarried shamelessly in the rich lodes of the *commedia dell'arte;* intangible, in that the usual literary comparisons cannot be made. Since the Italians put no artistic value on their scenarios—indeed, these documents have none—and since they are without stylistic elements, there is no basis for tracing the comparisons of style that one usually expects in literary studies. On the other hand, the comedies of the Elizabethan theater and the French and Spanish classical theaters are replete with parallels in plots, characters and comic tricks drawn from the *commedia dell'arte*.

The innumerable plot devices—mistaken identities; disguises of one or more characters; young people of unknown origin who turn out to be brother and sister of high birth; a friend torn between love and loyalty to his comrade; a lover posing as a servant to be near the girl he adores and hopes to save from marriage to a rich old man; a girl dressed as a man; the use of twins, sometimes two sets of twins (*Zanni Incredible*) and even three (*Li sei Simili*); combinations of the fanciful with reality—all these and a host of other farcical inventions which flooded the stages of Europe in the seventeenth and eighteenth centuries had been exploited ad infinitum by the *commedia dell'arte*. What is lacking in the Italian scenarios, of course, is the soaring poetry of a Shakespeare, the vitality in dialogue of a Molière, and the subtle delicacy of a Marivaux.

Strolling French actors, such as Tabarin and his charlatans, who played on the *tréteaux* of the Pont Neuf, imitated the Italians. There are many analogies between the French and Italian repertories early in the seventeenth century, but the Italians seemed to have a healthier career than the French, who never got beyond the status of disorganized, poverty-stricken actors.

French writers began to find inspiration in the *commedia dell'arte*, particularly in the Spanish captain. Rotrou used several variations of this character in the person of Rhinoceronte (*Clarice*), the extravagant Rosaran (*Agesilan de Colchon*) and the blustering Emile (*Amélie*). Hippocrasse (*Clarice*) is a typical *dottore* from the *commedia dell'arte* and one of the valets (*Agesilan de Colchon*) is labelled "serviteur buffon." Corneille presented the Captain under the name of Matamore, this time a Gascon instead of a Spaniard, in *L'Illusion Comique*. The captain appears again in Maréchal's *Railleur*, and Scarron wrote several burlesques with Matamore as a leading character.

With Molière, the influence of the *commedia dell'arte* becomes more extensive; his theatre abounds in borrowings from the Italians. As a youthful unknown actor touring the provinces, Molière himself acted in Italian plays and it is believed that his early comedies, now lost, were little more than adaptations of *commedia dell'arte*. When Molière was authorized to bring his troupe to Paris in 1659, he was installed in the Hôtel de Bourgogne where he shared the stage for some years with the Italian troupe of Fiorillo.

Molière's comedies are steeped in the Italian tradition. Many of his plays are based on the plot devices just mentioned: the frenetic maneuverings of a crafty servant in the interests of his young master (*Les fourberies de Scapin*); the bewildered elders outwitted by a dashing hero and an intriguing ingénue (*L'école des femmes* and *Le bourgeois gentilhomme*); the pedant doctor (*Le médecin malgré lui* and *Le malade imaginaire*) and all the wily Scapins, Frontins and Sganarelles stem from the *matière* of the *commedia dell'arte*. Needless to say, Molière made the material his own and endowed it with his own genius, but the influence is unmistakable.

The practice of borrowing continued through Regnard and Lesage into the early eighteenth century. Marivaux wrote most of his comedies in the 1720s and 1730s—certainly his best and most successful ones—for Riccoboni's troupe. Hence, the Arlequins, the Silvias, the Lelios and the Colombines which people his plays. Famed though he is for his delicacy of expression, refinement of comedy, finesse in psychological probing and excursions into fantasy, Marivaux projected these qualities through the plot situations and stock characters of the *commedia dell'arte*. His first play, *Arlequin poli par l'amour*, with its flight into Arcadian fantasy, blends the French and Italian elements to perfection; *Le jeu de l'amour et du hasard* and *Le prince travesti* make use of disguises; in *La surprise de l'amour*, conniving servants dominate their masters; and in *La fausse suivante* and *Le triomphe de l'amour*, the heroines pose as men. At the end of the eighteenth century, Bartolo and Basile of *Le barbier de Seville* and *Le mariage de Figaro* might well have stepped out of a number of Italian scenarios.

Elizabethan writers could escape the influence of the visiting Italians no more than the French. Zany, Pantaloon, and Harlakeen appear commonly in Elizabethan comedy. The Italian braggarts were models for the bravos in English drama, and the pedants were fashioned after Gratiano. Even Italian masks were used occasionally.

The echo of the *commedia dell'arte* is heard in several of Shakespeare's plays. The twin brother-sister situation and Viola's masquerade in *Twelfth Night* have their counterpart in a score of Italian scenarios. The trickery of Autolycus in *The Winter's Tale* and the vulgar stage business by Stephano and Trinculo in *The Tempest* are closely related to the bag of tricks of the *zannis*. The Arcadian setting and characters of *As You Like It* parallel the pastorals of the *commedia dell'arte* repertory. *The Merry Wives of Windsor* and the *Comedy of Errors* savor strongly of the materials and methods of the Italian players. The mixture of fantasy and buffoonery in *A Midsummer Night's Dream* can be found repeatedly in Italian scenarios. Like Molière's, Shakespeare's genius transcends and transforms the Italianate material, but the echoes are heard nonetheless.

The influence of the *commedia dell'arte* on the Spanish theater is rather modest by comparison with the French and English theater. Both Ganassa and Bottarga left their mark, since "ganassas" were prominent in Carnaval festivities in the sixteenth century and "botargas" became stock characters in Spanish comedy; the *zannis* were the prototype for the Spanish *graciosos*. While specific influences may be infrequent, the Italian troupes did much to popularize the comedy of intrigue and give direction to the Spanish theater at the moment it was evolving into the *comedia nueva*, which was soon to be perfected by Lope de Vega and the great dramatists of the Golden Age.

As for the impact of the *commedia dell'arte* on the emerging cultures of Eastern Europe, the stimulus was rather direct, since there was little national folklore to draw on. Polish and Russian writers had to imitate Italian comedy openly. According to Allardyce Nicoll, "without a doubt, in these three lands, Germany, Poland and Russia, the Italian comedy was a force leading towards the development of native theaters."

These random samplings show the variety of influences exercised by the

Italians on the theaters in other countries of Europe. Critical opinion has differed on the relative impact of the *commedia dell'arte,* and literary historians have disputed the degree of Italian predominance on one play or another, on one author or another. In most instances, there is some justice on both sides, for basic plots and characters go back far beyond the era of the *commedia dell'arte.* Of course, no one can say just what performances of the Italian troupes were witnessed by Shakespeare, Lope de Vega, Molière and their contemporaries, but it is well known that most playwrights were on friendly terms with visiting Italian companies. The import of these relationships on their writing is manifestly intangible, but one cannot survey the European theater without sensing the strong imprint of Italianate inspiration. Whatever the degree of influence and whatever other sources may be brought into consideration, the undeniable fact remains that the *commedia dell'arte* was one of the potent forces shaping the history of comedy in Europe in the seventeenth and eighteenth centuries.

KENNETH MCKEE
New York University

TRANSLATOR'S NOTE

Scala's text presented some problems involving idiom, format, punctuation, and a few textual errors. His language often included dialect words and, in special instances, the nonsensical talk of mad characters. In each instance an effort was made to work out meaning from the context and to try to find suitable English idioms or expressions to accommodate character and situation. Scala's format was designed principally to meet the demands of the actors. For instance, the placement in the margins of the names of characters entering made it easy for actors to tell at a glance when they were supposed to appear in a scene. He used a kind of elliptical sentence pattern that was sufficient for the actors' purposes. I have tried to make each scenario a readable text and therefore had to fill in the sentence patterns and render punctuation conventional throughout. Some of Scala's errors included the misnaming of characters—that is, indicating an action to be performed or a speech to be spoken by Flavio when Flavio is not onstage. The correct name was, in these instances, worked out from the context.

As Francesco Andreini says, these scenarios were set down pretty much as they were originally written for the stage. As such they were actors' scripts. My principal aim was to make them readers' scripts while maintaining the spirit and integrity of the original.

From the Front Matter of the original book I have omitted two conventional poems by Claudio Achillini addressed to Count Ferdinand Riario (to whom Scala dedicated his book) and seven poems in praise of the book and of Scala by Count Ridolfo Campeggi, Cesare Orsino, Dionysus Lazari, Pietro Petracci, and Ercole Marliani.

H. F. S.

A THEATRICAL

Repertory of Fables

or

Comic, Pastoral, and Tragic

Entertainment

Divided into Fifty Days

Written by Flaminio Scala, known as Flavio

Actor of his most Serene Highness Duke of Mantua

To the Most Illustrious Lord Ferdinand Riario

Marquess of Castiglione di Vald'Orcia

and Senator in Bologna

IN VENICE, PRINTED BY
GIOVANNI BATTISTA PULCIANI
MDCXI

TO THE MOST ILLUSTRIOUS LORD AND PATRON

MY MOST HONORABLE LORD COUNT FERDINAND RIARIO

MARQUIS OF CASTIGLIONE OF VALD'ORCIA AND

SENATOR IN BOLOGNA

That virtue which renders men amiable is disastrous to our souls. Nobility is a quality worthy of esteem: in loving others, we bring greatness out of obscurity and sound the trumpet of fame in praise of others to a world beyond our own. Who will admire your most illustrious self, whose virtue is equal to the nobility and magnanimity appearing in all the nobility, if I yield to my compulsion to dedicate these fifty dramatic outlines to you?

No one, surely, if others do not admire my daring—that is to say, my daring in venturing to address a work so humble to a person so sublime; for I do not fear to be reproached by you who understands that the weight of gratitude counterbalances the spirit of the giver with the smallness of the gift. I do not beseech you to esteem willingly this present, because it would appear to wrong the generosity of your soul which, in the spirit of royalty, can and will anticipate the desires of others. I beseech you, most illustrious lord, to be pleased to allow me to live as your servant under the protection of your famous name, because in this guise I need not fear the outrages of fortune, as I need not fear the sharp tongues of the spiteful over this book which bears that name on its front. With profound reverence I bow, auguring for it every courtly felicity.

THE AUTHOR TO HIS KIND READERS

When I composed these works which now come into your hands, I did not think of offering them to the world in any form other than the one in which they were presented many times in the public theater. Though they have been put to work for me in this form only in the practice of my profession as actor, and for no other purpose, the demands of patrons, the exhortations of friends, and the pleas of the curious brought me to the decision to have them printed. Afterwards, I felt I would be amply repaid, knowing that in this way there would be many opportunities for anyone to procure my works, as I know that they have often been performed on the stage from these dramatic outlines—either in the manner offered here or in some way altered or varied. They are my fruits; mine is the work, whatever it be, and equally mine should be whatever reproach or praise it deserves. Read it, then, kind readers, with an indulgent eye, and remember that there can be no human work without imperfections. I know that if you are inclined to examine it critically, you will be able to find fault with many things—particularly the matter of the use of the language and the spelling, neither of which I have used without some skill. This criticism could be applied to professions other than my own. Likewise, I hold the firm conviction that, in this respect, one cannot fully satisfy all the differences of opinion, of which there are as many as there are fancies. Do not despair, however, of finding some things to your satisfaction; moreover, no work of this kind has, as far as I know, ever been brought to light in this form. It contains such a variety of invention that it would please the appetites and tastes of many minds which find delight in many of the same things, either as entertainment or as part of their vocation. Here I conclude, and because I recognize that this address may only serve to annoy you, I wait for what will soon follow, and in the meanwhile I live in felicity.

By Francesco Andreini

Gelosi Actor, "Captain Spavento"

The Muses lay engulfed in deep oblivion
When you, gentle Flavio, invoked them
With your graceful style, and thus
Awoke your longing for fame:

Because of you the Muses enjoy the stage in all its native honor
And now they fly to Battro and to Thule,
Glorying in your name, while envy,
Wicked and vile, pays the grievous penalty:

The happy Muses now enjoy such honor
That the world, in reward for your labors,
Extends its pleasure to you and to Heaven, its thanks:

From hence, reaffirm every hour
The Muses remain befriended by you,
And full of loving zeal, continue
Giving glory and splendor to the stage.

GENTLE READERS

Man, born in this world, must in his youth take hold of whatever talent he can in order to live virtuously, helping and pleasing others; for man is vicious and ignorant and evil at heart and outwardly dangerous to his neighbor and himself. Therefore, if man is to attain some degree of perfection in his life and, after death, some honor and fame, he must pursue one of the seven liberal arts, and in that pursuit, follow an honorable course. I do not wish to speak of Lisippo, of Roscius, of Socrates, of Tito, of Varo, of Seneca, of Cicero and of many others of rude and little wisdom who lived as if they were at the heart of virtue, and in the knowledge that they would be great and immortal; therefore, it would be superfluous for me to repeat what has many times been said. I will say only this: that Signor Flaminio Scala, known as Flavio in the theater, not to belittle what has already been said and the great praise offered by good philosophers, gave himself in his youth to the noble profession of the theater (let us not forget his noble birth) and in that pursuit made such a great contribution that he deserved to be numbered among the good actors and among the better members of his profession. As man cannot be satisfied with the spoken word alone but must, with all industry and art, leave behind a printed memorial of himself and his work—as so many have already done under my family name—so it is that Signor Flavio, after a long passage of years and after long experience on the stage, wished to leave to the world, not simply his words and his beautiful conceits, but his plays which at all times and in all places brought great honor. Signor Flavio was able to work out his plays (because it was fitting that way) and set them down word for word as they were performed. But because nowadays we only see plays printed with their different speeches, full of bombast in the accepted fashion, he wished, with his new work, to present to the world his plays in their scenario form, leaving to the beauty of the imagination (which thrives on the excellence of its own language) the creation of its speeches. When you no longer disdain to honor his work—which he wrote for no other purpose than to please, allowing the pleasure and the utility to work together, as they do in poetry, to enrich the sensitive and far-reaching spirit—behold this work, which we cannot praise too much, written by your most affectionate Signor Flavio. It will serve, during the leisure hours of day or night, to pass away the tedium and to offer honest and pleasant entertainment to ladies and gentlemen who eagerly seek such spectacles. Because they can the more easily stage their own works, he has for each given his argument, which is not to be spoken, has identified and distinguished the characters, and has indicated all the costumes required in each to avoid any confusion in dress. He has identified the types of plays—comedies, tragedies and pastorals—but because in every good city there is no lack of those who find pleasure in the art of stage craft, and because he did not want to provoke them more than necessary, he allows to each the opportunity to choose his own manner of mounting comedy, tragedy or pastoral. I am quite certain that Signor Flavio will not be able to escape the venomous tongues of bitterly envious persons who are always ready to comfort themselves with the misery of others, so that all who write are submitted to this necessity, and by this enduring law are hindered and lacerated all their lives. In the meantime, receive, gentle readers, the honored works of Signor Flavio and give them all the applause they merit. Resist, as much as you are able, whatever compulsion you feel to find fault with them. In this way you will strengthen your resolve to continue into the following, his representative stage works, not a whit inferior to this opening. Live in happiness.

Your most affectionate servant
FRANCESCO ANDREINI, *Gelosi actor*
known as Captain Spavento

IL TEATRO
delle Fauole rappresentatiue,
OVERO
LA RICREATIONE
Comica, Boscareccia, e Tragica:

DIVISA IN CINQVANTA GIORNATE,

Composte da Flaminio Scala detto Flauio Comico
del Sereniss. Sig. Duca di Mantoua.

ALL'ILL. SIG. CONTE FERDINANDO RIARIO
Marchese di Castiglione di Vald'Orcia, & Senatore in Bologna.

IN VENETIA, Appresso Gio: Battista Pulciani. MDCXI.
Con Licenza de' Superiori, & Priuilegio.

Title page from Flaminio Scala's Il Téatro delle Favole rapprasenta-tive (Venice, 1611). This title page is reproduced from a copy in the Library of Congress that was used in preparing this translation.

The First Day

THE OLD TWINS *

ARGUMENT

There lived in Venice twin brothers. One was named Pantalone de Bisognosi, who had a son named Flavio, and the other was named Tofano de Bisognosi, who had a son named Oratio. Both brothers were very rich merchants who traded with Soria and other parts of the Near East. It happened that both brothers were aboard a ship bound for Alexandria, Egypt, when they were captured by pirates, made slaves, and sold to a Turkish merchant who took them to Persia. Their twelve-year-old sons, Flavio and Oratio, were left to be reared by their mothers. Despite all their efforts, the sons were not able to get news of their fathers for several years. Then, as they were preparing to go to Florence on business, the plague struck and took their mothers, leaving them without parents. When the epidemic subsided, they went on to Florence, for they had received the hopeful news from Soria that a rich Armenian merchant had, in Persia, ransomed two brothers who were slaves, and was taking them to Florence on a business trip. Finally, the Armenian merchant arrived with his slaves. After many unusual events caused by their remarkable likeness, they were finally recognized by their sons, who meanwhile had fallen in love with two beautiful widows. The fathers and sons were reunited and all lived a life of joy and contentment.

CHARACTERS IN THE PLAY

Flavio and Oratio, cousins

Franceschina and Pedrolino, servants

Pasquella, an old witch

Isabella, a noble widow

Doctor Gratiano
Flaminia, his daughter, a widow

* See Appendix p. 395.

Captain Spavento
Arlecchino, his servant

Jewish Merchants Armeno and Christiano

Ramadan, slave, then Pantalone de Bisognosi
Mustaffa, slave, then Tofano de Bisognosi, his brother
[Hibrahim]

PROPERTIES

Two identical slave costumes for the twin brothers
Identical masks and beards for the two brothers
Rich robes for the merchant Armeno
A letter
A paddle
Arms for Pedrolino and Arlecchino

ACT ONE

ORATIO
PEDROLINO

Pedrolino enters reading a letter, and knocks at the door of a house. Meanwhile, Oratio enters dressed in a felt hat and boots. Pedrolino tells Oratio that Flavio wants to go to the villa, but Oratio answers that he has other things to do.

FLAVIO

Just then, Flavio enters dressed for the country and says that one of them must go to Pisa and one to Livorno. He has received a letter from Venice saying that a friend, an Armenian merchant, is to arrive in a month with two brothers who are slaves he has ransomed from the Turks in Persia, and who at last have arrived at Livorno by ship. They have come from Soria and send word they cannot leave. Pedrolino is unhappy because he cannot go to the country. Oratio goes off, announcing that he will leave the following day for Pisa, and Flavio starts into the house to change.

ISABELLA

Isabella, at her window, heard Oratio and Flavio joking with Pedrolino about their going to the villa and having a good time with the courtesans. Now, to make her jealous, Pedrolino tells her that Flavio does not want to go out of respect for her love and her jealousy of the many others who are in love with him. Pedrolino then enters the house, saying, "If it makes me feel bad, I'm sure it makes you feel even worse." Isabella, alone, speaks of her love and of Flavio's cruelty and decides at the first opportunity to tell him she loves him.

PASQUELLA

Pasquella, an old bawd and a dirty witch, now appears. She greets Isabella and asks why she is sad. Isabella tells the bawd that she is

in love with Flavio, but that he loves a courtesan. Pasquella
promises that with her magic, Flavio will fall in love with
Isabella, and that he will not go back to the villa. Isabella gives
her some money and promises much more and, fully consoled,
Isabella goes into the house, leaving Pasquella to boast of her
magic and of the shrewd way she lives.

ORATIO   Oratio enters, saying that he has heard the slaves have arrived from Livorno but cannot remain in Florence. He sees
Pasquella, who tells him she has heard him speak to Flaminia of
his love, and knows that he has found her more cruel than ever;
but she, with her magic, will make Flaminia love him, because it
is impossible for a widow to remain husbandless.

FLAMINIA   Flaminia has heard everything from her window, and she comes
out cursing Pasquella and calling her a witch. Pasquella runs into
her house without a word. Flaminia scolds Oratio for gossiping
with the wicked old woman, and for believing in her fake
witchcraft. Thinking to do himself good, he will do himself
harm, she warns and, enraged, she enters the house. Oratio moans
to himself, and remembers all the times Pedrolino has told him
that Pasquella is a wicked old woman who will gull him.

PEDROLINO   Pedrolino has heard all that has been taking place between
Oratio, Flaminia, and Pasquella, and now he tells Oratio that
although he suspects Flaminia is in love with Captain Spavento,
he wants to help Oratio.

GRATIANO   Gratiano, Flaminia's father, enters now, and Pedrolino quickly
sends Oratio off, saying, "Leave it all to me." Then, greeting the
Doctor, he asks if it is true that he is giving his daughter
Flaminia in marriage to the Captain. When Gratiano says it is
not true, Pedrolino proposes Oratio as a son-in-law. Gratiano
sighs, saying that he loves Franceschina, Oratio's servant, and he
will see that all comes out well.

FLAMINIA   Flaminia appears at her window. She calls to her father to mind
his own business and to come into the house to help. Gratiano
tells Pedrolino that they will see what happens, and he goes into
the house. Pedrolino confesses that he also is in love with
Franceschina, and decides he will play a joke on Gratiano, his
rival.

ISABELLA   Isabella enters. She asks Pedrolino if Flavio has made up with his
lady and if they are going back to the villa. When Pedrolino says
that they are going, Isabella smiles secretively. She says that she
does not want him to make up and go to the villa, and that if her
love for Flavio is not returned, he and Pedrolino will be haunted,

for she has something up her sleeve. She goes into the house, leaving Pedrolino confused by her words.

CAPT. SPAVENTO And now, Captain Spavento enters, exclaiming his love for Fla-
ARLECCHINO minia. Arlecchino says that he suspects that she loves someone else. That is not possible, the Captain says, because he is a man of such perfection. Then he brags of his great strength and valor. Pedrolino informs the Captain that his master Oratio is going to marry Flaminia, and that the following night they will sleep together. The Captain angrily threatens to kill Oratio if he catches him and, with a great display of bravado, leaves with Arlecchino. Pedrolino begins to laugh.

FRANCESCHINA Franceschina bursts into tears in Pasquella's house.

PASQUELLA Pedrolino withdraws to knock at Pasquella's door. Inside, Pasquella is listening to Franceschina tell of being robbed of a piece of linen sixty yards long. Pasquella promises to help her find it, and she sends Franceschina to her room, telling her to wait there while she goes to get something that she needs from the roof of the barn, and she exits. Pedrolino, laughing at Franceschina and Pasquella, plans to play a trick on them.

GRATIANO Gratiano enters, laughing because Flaminia called him to help her pet dog give birth to a litter. Pedrolino immediately tells Gratiano that Franceschina is in Pasquella's house to try to find a certain piece of linen which has been stolen.

PASQUELLA Inside the house, Pasquella is going through some fake conjuring to find the linen, forcing Franceschina to repeat every word. Outside, Pedrolino tells Gratiano that they will have some fun playing a trick on Franceschina. He tells Gratiano to wait until Franceschina comes out and then to go to Pasquella and tell her that he stole the linen and wants to give it to Franceschina himself, that her magic forced him to confess the theft and that the old woman is to call Franceschina; that way Gratiano will have an opportunity to talk to Franceschina and can promise to buy her some linen. Gratiano agrees. They hear the women coming and withdraw.

PASQUELLA Pasquella tells Franceschina that to perform her magic she needs a flask of olive oil and strong vinegar. Franceschina says she will bring it and exits.

GRATIANO Gratiano comes forward, saying that the force of Pasquella's magic has brought him to reveal the theft of the linen and confesses that he himself is the thief. Pasquella is astounded, for she knows that she cannot perform magic. She begins to tremble, and Gratiano shouts, "Call her! Call her!" Pasquella flees into the house with Gratiano behind her, shouting, "Call her!" Pedrolino immediately calls Franceschina.

FRANCESCHINA   Franceschina learns from Pedrolino that someone has gone into Pasquella's house and confessed to the theft of the linen, and Pedrolino urges her to go help Pasquella catch the thief and take him to court. Franceschina goes in, and Pedrolino remains behind, hearing from within a great deal of shouting about the theft.

GRATIANO   The women appear holding Gratiano's arms, calling him a
PASQUELLA   thief and beating him. Gratiano breaks loose and runs off, fol-
FRANCESCHINA   lowed by the two women.

PEDROLINO   Pedrolino exits, laughing, and the first act ends.

ACT TWO

HIBRAHIM   Hibrahim, an Armenian merchant, enters with Ramadan, his
RAMADAN   slave. Ramadan tells briefly how his master ransomed him and of the favors he and his brother, Mustaffa, have received through the great kindness of his master. Hibrahim says that he has some business in Florence he must take care of immediately, because in two days he must leave for Venice, and he exits. Ramadan remains, praising the kindness of the Armenian merchant.

FLAVIO   Flavio now enters with a letter to be sent to his friends who are waiting for him at the villa. He sees the slave, gives him some money, and asks him to take the letter to one Sandrino Tanaiolo of Norcia, at his country house in the old marketplace. The slave says he will do his bidding and exits.

FRANCESCHINA   At that, Franceschina enters, happy that she has found the lost linen. Flavio asks her about Pedrolino, but she says she doesn't know where he is.

PEDROLINO   Just then, Pedrolino enters, laughing at the trick played on Gratiano. Franceschina laughs too and goes into the house, leaving Pedrolino to tell Flavio that he should not go to the villa because of Isabella, and that if Flavio does not return her love, she will haunt both of them. Flavio scoffs, thinking it all a joke.

ORATIO   Thereupon, Oratio enters. Pedrolino tells him that Flaminia is going to marry the Captain, who is looking for him to pick a quarrel, and to mock him. They laugh about this.

ISABELLA	Then, Isabella appears at her window. Flavio greets her and asks how she managed to learn the art of black magic so quickly. He marvels that she could threaten to haunt those who refuse to love her. She says that it was only a joke on Pedrolino and begs for his love, asking him to marry her because he knows they belong to each other. Flavio replies that soon it might come to pass that she will make them all happy. Isabella says that she does not understand him. Oratio marvels at this, and says that if she knows magic, she surely knows everything. He asks her if she will help him win the cruel Flaminia, and in return he will help her win his brother. Isabella agrees to the bargain.
MUSTAFFA	And now, Mustaffa, the slave brother of Ramadan, enters, begging alms. Pedrolino tells everyone to watch his purse, and Flavio, believing the man to be the slave to whom he gave the letter because he looks just like the other, asks him if he delivered the letter to Sandrino Tanaiolo. The slave says he doesn't know what Flavio is talking about, that he has never spoken to him before. Pedrolino drives the slave off.
MUSTAFFA	At that, Ramadan, Mustaffa's brother, enters. He goes over to Flavio to tell him that he gave the letter to Sandrino Tanaiolo. Flavio embraces him, and together with Oratio, they go, leaving Pedrolino by himself.
ISABELLA	Then, Isabella leans out her window to question Pedrolino about what Flavio meant when he said that soon it will come to pass that all will be happy.
PASQUELLA	Pasquella is listening from her window. Pedrolino tells Isabella that twenty years before, Flavio's and Oratio's fathers, who were brothers, were made slaves and never seen again and that the young men decided to leave Venice to live in Florence. He says Oratio received a letter from a friend in Venice who that month had seen an Armenian merchant named Hibrahim. When Hibrahim was in Persia, he had ransomed two Venetian brothers who had been slaves of the Turks. Oratio told Flavio that he hoped one of them might be his father, who had not taken a wife, and who was called Pantalone de Bisognosi of Venice. Pasquella rejoices at the news and withdraws.
FLAMINIA	Thereupon, Flaminia comes to her window and greets Isabella, who invites Flaminia to come and visit at her house. Flaminia says she can't without her father's permission.
GRATIANO	At that, Gratiano arrives and grants Isabella's request to let Flaminia come. After Flaminia and Isabella go into the house, Gratiano sighs that the scheme has gone badly for him. Pedrolino

explains that Franceschina found the linen hidden in the house, but he begs Gratiano to give Flaminia to Oratio, and not to the Captain as rumored. Again Gratiano denies the rumor.

CAPT. SPAVENTO   Captain Spavento enters now, angry because he has not found Oratio, and he sees Gratiano, who tells him that he will not give his daughter to him in marriage. The Captain roars, saying that he knows Gratiano wants to give her to Oratio, and he will kill Oratio and all who depend on him. As Arlecchino begins to roar too, Pedrolino gives him a slap. The Captain draws his sword and gives chase as they all run off.

PASQUELLA   Pasquella enters considering how she might use what she has learned from Pedrolino, and whether or not to tell Isabella Flavio's secret so that Isabella will be more confident.

RAMADAN   Ramadan, the slave, enters. Pasquella sees him, and decides to involve him in her plotting. She fondles him and gives him alms, and tells him that he can earn half a dozen scudi by following her directions. The slave agrees. She explains she wants him to pretend to be the father of a young man in love with a certain girl. The father is a slave like him and the young man has retired in despair and will not come out until he hears his father's name spoken. She wants the slave to pretend to have come from a long way off by means of her magic, and she warns him not to give the name of the father. The slave agrees, and she sends him off up a side street and knocks on Isabella's door.

PEDROLINO   Pedrolino enters, sees Pasquella, and hides to see what she is up to.

ISABELLA   Isabella comes out. Pasquella says she is angry with Flaminia because she does not care about her at all. Instead, she says, she will make Isabella happy. Isabella is grateful, and Pasquella tells her she knows Flavio's secret better than he, and that to help her, she wants Isabella to learn her magic art so they can find out if Flavio's father is alive. If he is, she will make him appear before Isabella. Isabella begs her to do it, so Pasquella pretends to read from her fake conjuring book and mumbles some magic words.

PEDROLINO   Pedrolino, standing off to the side, laughs at the old woman's stupid act and remains to watch. Pasquella ends by calling for Flavio's father, saying in a loud voice, "Pantalone de Bisognosi, now appear before me!"

RAMADAN   At that, Ramadan, amazed to hear himself called by his real name, appears, saying, "I am here; I am Pantalone de Bisognosi." Pedrolino and Isabella are both astonished.

MUSTAFFA	Thereupon, Mustaffa, slave, and brother to Ramadan, appears. "I am here, too, your brother." Pasquella and Isabella, believing them to be conjured spirits, run into their houses. The two slaves turn to Pedrolino who, believing them to be devils, runs off in fright. The slaves follow, and the second act ends.

ACT THREE

FLAVIO ORATIO PEDROLINO	Flavio and Oratio are laughing at Pedrolino, who says that the slave to whom Flavio gave the letter is a devil. Pedrolino swears it's the truth, and that Isabella and Pasquella are both witches who conjured up the spirits with little trouble. He tells them how Pasquella made the two slaves appear. They marvel at Pedrolino's story and wish to speak to Pasquella.
CAPT. SPAVENTO	Captain Spavento arrives. He boasts to Oratio that he will have to stop annoying Flaminia now, because in spite of her father, she is going to be his wife.
ARLECCHINO	Arlecchino, to avenge the slap he received from Pedrolino, beats Pedrolino with his paddle. They all start quarreling and fighting and thus go off down the street.
GRATIANO	Gratiano enters. He decides to give Flaminia in marriage to Oratio to rid himself of all the trouble he's been having and to have his pleasure with Franceschina. He knocks at Franceschina's door.
FRANCESCHINA	Franceschina comes to the door, and she asks Gratiano's pardon for all that happened between them. They make love.
ISABELLA	Isabella, now at her window, again asks Gratiano to send Flaminia out.
FLAMINIA	Flaminia answers Gratiano's call, and she goes with Isabella. Gratiano tries to make Franceschina go into his house to continue their love-making.
CAPT. SPAVENTO	Captain Spavento enters, and they run off. The Captain has written a challenge that he plans to deliver to Flavio and Oratio, and he reads it to Arlecchino.
RAMADAN MUSTAFFA	Ramadan and Mustaffa enter and listen in on the Captain as he reads: "I, Captain Spavento of the region of hell, challenge you, Flavio, and you, Oratio Bisognosi, to a duel with sword and dagger to be fought in shirtsleeves outside the city gate."
RAMADAN	At that, Ramadan crosses and stands between the Captain and his servant. He announces that the young men named in the chal-

lenge are their sons and they are the men who will answer the challenge. The Captain is furious and is about to beat them.

MUSTAFFA   Suddenly, Mustaffa jumps at him with a bat in his hand, and the Captain and Arlecchino, certain that these are two spirits, shout that they refuse to fight with devils and run off. The two old men, rejoicing that they have heard their sons named, go off, each down a different street, to find their Armenian merchant so that he can attend to the matter.

PASQUELLA   Pasquella enters. Believing the two who appeared in the street to be two devils sent to frighten her, she decides that she will no longer do the devil's work, and that she will live as a good woman, no more to pursue the life of a witch or a bawd.

ISABELLA   Isabella sees Pasquella from her window and comes out with Flaminia to ask what happened to the two slaves who appeared. Pasquella tells her that she does not know if they were spirits or live beings.

RAMADAN   Meanwhile the two slaves come in. The women are frightened,
MUSTAFFA   but they try as best they can to reassure themselves that the slaves are not really devils. Pasquella takes courage and stands between Flaminia and Isabella. She begins by asking them who they are, what their names are, how is it they know the names of the fathers of Oratio and Flavio, and what reward will they give for finding their sons. When the slaves reply that the reward is large, Pasquella tells them that they are to embrace the two gentle widows who make their sons happy. The slaves kiss the hands of the two young women, bowing in honorable fashion. Finally, Pasquella tells the young women to take the old men into the house, and the four go into Isabella's house. The women return immediately to make plans. Isabella suggests that Flaminia take Oratio for her husband. Pasquella rejoices and sends them into the house to the old men, saying that she will leave the rest to them.

PEDROLINO   At that, Pedrolino enters. He is covered with weapons, to revenge the beating he got from Arlecchino. Pasquella sends him to find Flavio and Oratio on a matter of great importance. Pedrolino asks her to help him revenge himself on Arlecchino and goes.

ORATIO   Oratio and Flavio enter, laughing about the foolishness of the
FLAVIO   Captain. They meet Pasquella and hear from her what extraordinary things have taken place that day. And, when she tells Flavio that Isabella wants to speak to him on a matter of great importance, the young men clap their hands for joy.

ISABELLA　Isabella comes out to tell Flavio that if he will agree to be her husband, she will give him the dearest thing in the world, and she promises to Oratio two of the dearest things that he desires in the world. The young men, full of happy anticipation, agree.

FLAMINIA
RAMADAN
MUSTAFFA

Isabella goes into the house and, returning with Flaminia, gives her to the happy Oratio to be his wife. Then Isabella returns to the house, leads the two slaves out and, saying to Flavio, "Here is the dearest thing you have in all the world," she presents Flavio to Ramadan, his father, and Oratio to Mustaffa, his father. Fathers and sons recognize one another and joyfully embrace.

HIBRAHIM

At that moment, Hibrahim, the Armenian, arrives. He rejoices with the two slaves when they tell him that they have found their two sons, who are rich merchants, and that here in Florence they will give him anything he desires from them. The old men ask the young men to marry the two widows, and each takes the hand of his lady.

GRATIANO

Gratiano enters now. He is amazed to find so many people in front of his house, and listens as Oratio briefly tells him of all that has taken place—of the two old fathers and the contracted nuptials. Gratiano is satisfied and embraces Pantalone and Tofano, marveling at the great resemblance between them.

FRANCESCHINA

Meanwhile, Franceschina rejoices at the arrival of the two old brothers and bows to them.

CAPT. SPAVENTO

Captain Spavento appears, armed, with Arlecchino. As soon as he sees Gratiano, he tells him Flaminia is to be his wife. Oratio tells him he had better consider otherwise because she is already betrothed to him, and that the two he thought to be devils are really their fathers. The Captain calms down, greets Pantalone and Tofano, and is struck by the great resemblance between the brothers.

PEDROLINO

At that, Pedrolino arrives, covered with weapons. He sees Arlecchino and immediately attacks him, brandishing all his weapons. Arlecchino returns the blows, but the others step between them to make peace. Then they speak of marrying, but Pedrolino and Arlecchino both want to marry Franceschina. Again they begin to fight. The Captain comes between them, urging them to leave the choice to Franceschina. They agree, and Franceschina chooses Pedrolino. Thus Oratio marries Flaminia, Flavio marries Isabella, and Pedrolino, Franceschina. Flavio and Oratio lead the women into the house, leaving Pasquella to swear that for the rest of her life she will never work her magic and her tricks, and the comedy of *The Old Twins* ends.

The Second Day

FLAVIO'S FORTUNE *

ARGUMENT

While at sea, Flavio was captured by pirates and sold as a slave in Constantinople to a Pasha of great wisdom. He lived there for such a long time that the son of the Pasha developed a great affection for him. Realizing the young Turk's feelings, Flavio enthusiastically described to him the grandeur and the marvels of Italy, especially those of Rome. Flavio was so persuasive that the young Turk was determined to go to see them and to become a Christian. Thus agreed, they manned a small galley with a crew of Christian oarsmen and a large escort of Turkish soldiers and seamen, to whom they pretended that they were going only as far as the Strait of Dardanelles. Flavio had spoken often to the young Turk about his beautiful sister who was in Rome, and so the young Turk wanted to see her and woo her. When all was set for sailing and nearly all were aboard, Flavio disguised his lover, the young Turk's sister, in man's clothes, and without his friend's knowledge, hid her in the hold of the ship. They had a full wind in their sails and went at such speed that they sighted the island of Sicily before the Turkish guard discovered the deception. Turning on the son of the Pasha, the Turkish guard shouted violent accusations of treason at Flavio and then drew his sword to kill him. The young Turk, with the help of the Christian oarsmen, immediately turned on the guard who in a short time was disarmed and killed. In the terrible fight that followed, the disguised Turkish girl, frightened by all the commotion, came up out of the hold and immediately attacked her brother, whom in the confusion she took to be one of the Turkish soldiers. Then, after realizing what she had done, she jumped into the sea. They tried vainly to find her, but Flavio, who with the help of the young Turk was freeing the Christian slaves, saw his lover throw herself into the sea and leaped in after to rescue her. So the terrible fight ended. The young Turk looked for Flavio, and

* See Appendix p. 395.

failing to find him, was overcome with grief at the loss of his friend. Finally, all sailed on to Italy and were overtaken by one of Flavio's father's ships and stopped. When they told their story of the escape and of the young Turk's intention to become a Christian, they were taken safely into the ancient port, and with the rest of the crew and all the goods the Turk had taken with him, led to Rome. The young Turk was converted to Christianity, became a close friend of Flavio's father, and fell in love with Flavio's sister, and lived among them without telling of his friendship with Flavio. Meanwhile, Flavio had been washed ashore at Pantelloria, where he was found nearly dead upon the beach by a Christian captain who revived him with food and drink. Grateful to him for having saved his life, Flavio offered to serve the Captain. They sailed together to Bari where the Captain believed he would find his love whom he had left there. Not finding her, he journeyed on with Flavio, desperately looking for her. Finally, on their way to Milan, they arrived in Rome where the Captain fell in love with Flavio's sister. The Captain did not know she was Flavio's sister, for Flavio did not tell the Captain who he was. Meanwhile, the young Turkish girl had been rescued by fishermen. Believing her to be a boy, they took her to Palermo and sold her as a slave to a charlatan. After traveling a long while, the charlatan brought her to Rome where she met her brother, and her lover, Flavio. She became a Christian, and all lived a joyful and happy life.

CHARACTERS IN THE PLAY

Pantalone, a Venetian
Flaminia, his daughter
Franceschina, his servant
Grillo, his servant

Oratio, a Turkish nobleman made Christian
Pedrolino, his servant

Pages

Captain Spavento
Morat, his slave, finally Flavio, son of Pantalone

Gratiano, a charlatan or mountebank
Arlecchino, his companion
Turkish performer and singer, Turchetto, afterward Alissa, sister of Oratio

Waiters
Burattino, host of the inn

Cinthio, nephew of the governor
Servants

Lidia, a pilgrim
Traveling companion

PROPERTIES

A Charlatan's stall
A beautiful traveling bag
A lute
Charlatan's wares
Two flasks of wine
A halberd
A frying pan

ACT ONE

ROME

FRANCESCHINA FLAMINIA A PAGE	Franceschina enters with Flaminia. She is telling Flaminia that she has seen a handsome slave newly come to Rome, and is praising the great generosity of his master, Oratio, a Turk who turned Christian, saying that all of Rome loves and honors him. Flaminia agrees with all this, but she is displeased because her old servant, Pedrolino, has gone to stay with Oratio at her father's bidding.
CAPT. SPAVENTO MORAT, A SLAVE	Then, Captain Spavento enters with his slave, Morat. Seeing Flaminia and taking her for a whore, the Captain salutes her; she returns the greeting and goes quickly into her house. Franceschina looks longingly at the slave, and after making a curtsy, she too goes into the house. The Captain says he likes the young woman and that he is going to woo her while they are in town. The slave tries to talk him out of it.
FRANCESCHINA	Franceschina comes out again to get a cushion she has left at her kinsman's house, and the Captain begins to fondle her. She suddenly hears Pantalone's voice and runs off down the street.
PANTALONE	At that, Pantalone comes out of the house, shouting, "I am not going to argue with this wretch any more. I'm going to rid myself completely of him." Hearing these words, the Captain thinks that

Pantalone is the young woman's lover and tells Pantalone that an old man like him should leave prostitutes alone. Pantalone asks him what he is talking about, and the Captain answers that he is speaking about the whore who lives in the house. The enraged Pantalone calls the Captain a liar, and both draw their swords.

GRILLO

Just then, Grillo, Pantalone's servant, enters with a halberd.

BURATTINO

Burattino, host of the inn, enters with a frying pan. The slave drags the Captain away, and Pantalone, suspecting that his honor is at stake, sends Burattino into the house. Then he tells Grillo, his servant, that he is going to break his word and will not wait for Flavio's return to marry Flaminia. Grillo tells Pantalone that Oratio would be a very good match for Flaminia, and arguing about it, they go off together.

ORATIO
PEDROLINO

Oratio and Pedrolino enter, and Oratio learns from Pedrolino that Pantalone, his first master, is a rich man but distressed by the loss of his son, Flavio, who left home some years before to go to Sicily and has not been heard of since, perhaps, as Pantalone suspects, because he was captured by the Turks. When Oratio begins to weep at this tale, Pedrolino asks him why. Oratio does not reply and instead praises Pantalone for having treated him so generously by giving him his old faithful servant.

BURATTINO

Burattino now enters with two full flasks of Greek wine. He offers them to Oratio, who takes them and gives Burattino some money. Oratio then asks him for news of the town, and Burattino tells him that Pantalone has quarreled with the Captain but that nothing came of it.

GRATIANO

Just then, Gratiano, a charlatan, enters and calls into the inn for his dinner before he mounts his bench with his troupe. Oratio hears that he is the greatest charlatan of all. Burattino offers to grant his every wish and asks him to set up his bench near the inn. Gratiano accepts the offer and enters the inn with Burattino Oratio wants to find out more about Pantalone's quarrel and knocks at his door.

FLAMINIA

Flaminia appears at the window, and Oratio salutes her, asking after her father. When she says he is not at home, Oratio confesses his love for her and says he will ask her father for her hand. She says her father is master of her body and soul, and sighing, she goes back in. Pedrolino begins to tell Oratio that Flaminia is in love with him.

ARLECCHINO WAITERS GRATIANO TURCHETTO	Now Arlecchino enters and mounts the stall the charlatan has set up. After shouting out his wares, he sets up the traveling bag and calls for his troupe, who come out of the inn and mount the stall. Turchetto begins to sing and play.
FLAMINIA	Flaminia appears at her window to hear the troupe perform.
BURATTINO	Burattino comes out to listen.
FRANCESCHINA	Franceschina also enters and stands to watch.
PANTALONE	Pantalone enters, greets Oratio, and they all stand watching. Gratiano advertises his wares and does a good business; Arlecchino follows suit. Turchetto continues to play and sing.
CAPT. SPAVENTO MORAT	Then, Morat and the Captain enter. The Captain spies Flaminia at the window and salutes her; Franceschina greets the slave. The Captain, seeing Arlecchino and recognizing him as the one who had charge of his lady friend, pulls him down from the stall. Pantalone tells Oratio that the Captain is his enemy, and Oratio draws his sword and rushes at the Captain, who turns on Oratio. Arlecchino runs off, the Captain in pursuit. In the melee, the stall is knocked down and everyone rushes into his house. Oratio, Pantalone, and Pedrolino run out after the Captain, and the first act ends.

ACT TWO

CINTHIO ORATIO MORAT CAPT. SPAVENTO	Cinthio, nephew of the governor of Rome, has had Arlecchino imprisoned on the Captain's charges and has made peace between Oratio and the Captain, and now Cinthio asks the Captain why he wants to kill Arlecchino. The Captain tells him that five years ago he had left Arlecchino in Bari, in the custody of his lady, while he went to Malta on important business; returning to Bari six months later, he had found neither his lady nor Arlecchino, and after being told that Arlecchino took her away with him, he looked far and wide for him, not finding him until this day; that is why he attacked him. When Oratio asks the Captain to have Arlecchino released so that he can entertain the people in the neighborhood, the Captain agrees, and Cinthio leaves to arrange for Arlecchino's release. Oratio, the Captain, and Morat remain.
FLAMINIA	Flaminia appears at the window to eavesdrop. Oratio, seeing her there, begins to answer the Captain's request to tell him about himself. He tells his story in great detail as set down in the Argument and also tells the Captain that he had promised to marry the sister of a dear friend who was separated from him by

a strange accident, causing him great sorrow. Suddenly Morat faints, and Flaminia calls Franceschina to fetch some vinegar.

FRANCESCHINA

When Franceschina comes out with the vinegar, all stand around to revive Morat, whose fainting attack was brought on by what he heard from Oratio. Oratio now exits, saying he must find Cinthio to help him release Arlecchino. The Captain asks Morat why he fainted, but he tells the Captain that he cannot answer. The Captain asks Franceschina to kiss the hands of her mistress in his name and leaves. Franceschina flirts with the slave and finally exits, leaving Morat to rail against Love and Fortune—against Love for making him fall in love with Alissa, and against Fortune for taking her from him.

PEDROLINO

Pedrolino has been standing in the shadows listening to what the slave has been saying.

GRATIANO
BURATTINO

Then, Gratiano enters with Burattino, and Morat tells them to go to the Tower of Noon to free Arlecchino, for the Captain has pardoned him for what he had done. Happily, both start off, but as Burattino goes, he spies Pedrolino and calls out to him by name, bids him farewell, and leaves. On hearing Pedrolino's name, Morat looks at him and recognizes him as the old servant of his father. To Pedrolino's bewilderment, Morat embraces and kisses him again and again. Finally, Morat reveals himself to be Flavio, the son of Pantalone. Pedrolino rejoices and asks where he has been all this time, and Flavio tells him the story set down in the Argument, of his great sorrow at the drowning of his lady love, and his promise to give his sister, Flaminia, to Oratio in marriage as soon as Oratio became a Christian. But now there is a dilemma, he says, for the Captain, to whom he owes his life, is in love with Flaminia. He would like to give her to the Captain, but he does not want to betray Oratio, a Turk converted to Christianity and a kind master to him when he was in Constantinople. Pedrolino tells him to leave everything to him, that he will straighten things out, and he will also find out from Oratio if he knows anything about his sister, Alissa. Flavio expresses his gratitude and asks him not to reveal his identity to anyone. At that moment they hear Pantalone coming, and they go off.

PANTALONE

Pantalone enters, speaking of the business brought up by the charlatan, and the charlatan's desire to marry his daughter Flaminia.

TURCHETTO

Turchetto enters from the inn, and Pantalone, seeing his strange dress, asks him why he is in such a getup. Turchetto replies that he must dress this way and that he has been the charlatan's slave for four years. Then he asks Pantalone if he knows a certain

Pantalone de Bisognosi, a Venetian. Pantalone says he is that very man, and Turchetto tells him that he knew his son, Flavio, in Constantinople, where he was the slave of a great Pasha, and he believes Flavio is dead. Pantalone weeps at this and then says he will give Turchetto anything he wishes. He goes into the house, and Turchetto, grief-stricken, follows.

CAPT. SPAVENTO
ARLECCHINO

The Captain enters with Arlecchino, who is explaining to him that he took Lidia, the mistress left in his care, away with him because he suspected that the Captain's relatives wanted to kill her. As they were traveling, he says, they were attacked and robbed by bandits, who then began to quarrel and fight among themselves. When they were about to begin shooting their arquebuses at each other, Lidia fled into the wooded hills, and he never saw her again. The Captain is grief-stricken. To console him, Arlecchino tells him he knows a beautiful Turkish girl near by—Turchetto—who sings on the charlatan's stall; Turchetto, he knows for certain, is a woman, and he offers to buy her for the Captain for a hundred scudi. But the Captain replies that his mind is too full of his former mistress for him to think of another woman.

GRATIANO
MORAT
BURATTINO

At that, Gratiano, Morat, and Burattino enter. Gratiano asks the Captain to let Arlecchino stay with him while they remain in Rome. Morat makes the same request, and Burattino repeats it in the interest of his inn; whereupon the Captain agrees. Then they all go into the inn except the Captain and Morat. When the Captain inquires why he remains behind, Morat replies that he wants to thank him for saving his life on the reef of the Pantallarian Sea. He also tells him that Oratio is in love with Flaminia, whom the Captain loves, and expresses fear that there may be another quarrel. Accordingly he urges the Captain to let Flaminia become a gentlewoman and to accept Gratiano's young Turkish woman. Morat is so persuasive that the Captain agrees, telling Morat to speak to Arlecchino about it, and he exits. Flavio remains, relieved to have removed Flaminia from the Captain's thoughts.

PANTALONE
FLAMINIA

Pantalone and Flaminia enter. Flaminia asks Pantalone why he is weeping. Pantalone replies that Turchetto, the charlatan's servant, disclosed that in Constantinople he knew Flavio as the slave of a grand Pasha but now he believes that Flavio is dead. Flaminia then informs her father that from certain things which she heard Oratio say, she thinks that he was acquainted with Flavio in Turkey. She then urges Pantalone to talk to Oratio and goes into the house. Thereupon Pantalone goes to find Oratio, leaving Flavio by himself.

ARLECCHINO Just then, Arlecchino enters on his way to buy wares to sell at the charlatan's stall. Flavio tells him that the Captain has decided to buy the young Turk, and asks him where he bought their companion. Arlecchino, in a hurry to buy his wares, takes him along to tell him about it, and they leave.

ORATIO
PANTALONE
PEDROLINO

Oratio, Pantalone, and Pedrolino enter. Oratio is telling Pantalone about his son Flavio, relating everything as set down in the Argument, up to the point at which Flavio threw himself into the sea, and of his determination to become a Christian. Oratio says he has heard no more of Flavio and that he did not want to tell him about it and make him more unhappy. Then Pedrolino asks Oratio if he has a sister, and Oratio answers that he does have a sister in Constantinople, a girl named Alissa. Pedrolino tells Pantalone to rejoice, for he thinks that Flavio is alive and that Pantalone will see him soon, and sends him into the house to wait until he returns with good news. When Pantalone is gone, Oratio tells Pedrolino that if he does not marry Flaminia, he will go away to Naples to live. Pedrolino tells Oratio that he will marry Flaminia and takes him off up the street as he tells him of a dream he had in which he had hope of seeing Flavio.

ARLECCHINO
MORAT

Arlecchino and Morat enter. Arlecchino tells the slave that he will send the Turkish woman out immediately, and he goes into the inn, leaving Flavio hopeful that the woman is his Alissa.

TURCHETTO Then Turchetto comes out, and to her amazement, Morat tells her that he knows she is a woman and then asks her where she was made a slave. Flavio rejoices as she tells him her story as set down in the Argument.

CAPT. SPAVENTO The Captain enters. Without a word, he interrupts the slave and begins to fondle the Turkish woman.

GRATIANO Gratiano arrives, and he too, without a word, swaggers up to Turchetto and tries to lead her away into the house. The Captain and Gratiano draw on each other, beginning to shout as they come to blows.

BURATTINO At that, Burattino comes out with the halberd.

ARLECCHINO Then, Arlecchino comes out with a club. The Captain attacks everyone, driving them back into the inn, and Flavio goes off by himself. Staggering, the Captain follows, and the second act ends.

ACT THREE

LIDIA
A PILGRIM

Lidia enters with a Pilgrim; she has arrived safely in Rome; she thanks the Pilgrim for his good company and adds that she wishes to stay in Rome for a few days. When the Pilgrim tells her he will leave Rome immediately, she replies that she will accompany him to the gate, and they go off together.

CAPT. SPAVENTO
MORAT

The Captain and Morat enter. The Captain gives Morat one hundred scudi to purchase the Turkish woman, promising to wait for his return. The Captain professes his great love for Turchetto and exits. Flavio recalls his adventures and says that he surrenders himself to fortune, but he immediately takes it back again. Finally, he ponders the Captain's love for the Turkish woman and his great obligation to give her to the Captain.

PEDROLINO

Pedrolino enters in high spirits. He tells Flavio that Oratio thinks that his sister, Alissa, is still in Turkey. Flavio sadly explains that he has found her, but the Captain, to whom he owes his life, has fallen in love with her. He shows Pedrolino the hundred scudi to ransom Alissa for the Captain, and Pedrolino consoles him by telling him that he will take care of everything; he takes the money from Flavio and tells him to hide. After some thought, Pedrolino knocks at the door of the inn.

BURATTINO

Burattino comes out and sees Pedrolino, who is very excited. Pedrolino tells him that he wants to talk to the charlatan on a matter of great importance, whereupon Burattino calls him.

GRATIANO
ARLECCHINO

Gratiano and Arlecchino come out of the inn, and Pedrolino tells them that by way of secret information the Governor knows they abducted a young Turkish woman four years ago and have kept her dressed as a man. He adds that the Governor has ordered the police to arrest everyone in the inn to clear up the matter. Gratiano replies he knows nothing about the Turk being a woman, but Arlecchino says that he knows for certain she is. Finally, Burattino drives them all out of the inn. Gratiano calls Turchetto.

TURCHETTO

When Turchetto comes out, Gratiano asks him if he is a woman. Turchetto answers that she is, whereupon Gratiano turns her over to Pedrolino. He offers to put her in the care of the women of Pantalone's household where they will hold her until that night to see what must be done. Gratiano and Arlecchino go off. Pedrolino asks her if she knew a slave named Flavio Bisognosi in Turkey. She says she did and that she has seen him here in Rome also. Pedrolino tells her she will become Flavio's wife, and then he knocks at Flaminia's door.

FLAMINIA

At that, Flaminia, accompanied by Franceschina, comes out of the house. Pedrolino tells Flaminia that her father has sent for the Turk because he is to be her husband. He also tells her that the

Turk will tell her about her brother, Flavio. He puts Turchetto in Flaminia's care and rushes off, leaving the astonished Flaminia to wonder over Alissa's story as given in the Argument. Flaminia embraces and kisses her.

ORATIO

Just then, Oratio arrives. He scolds Turchetto and Flaminia for being so bold, and the women laugh.

CAPT. SPAVENTO

At that moment, the Captain enters. He speaks abusively to Oratio and then takes Turchetto off; Oratio pursues him, crying out, "Flavio, come help me!" The unhappy women are soon rejoined by a miserable Oratio.

CINTHIO

Just then, Cinthio enters, sees Oratio, and asks him what's wrong. Oratio rouses himself and says, "Sir, please come with me up the street," and they go off as the women go into the house.

PEDROLINO
MORAT

Pedrolino and Morat enter, and Pedrolino tells Flavio that his Alissa is now with Flaminia, Flavio's sister. But he cannot rejoice, Flavio says, because she belongs to the Captain, to whom he owes his life. Pedrolino laughs at this and knocks at the door.

FRANCESCHINA

Franceschina comes out weeping and tells them that the Captain has abducted Turchetto. Pedrolino is furious at Franceschina, and she runs back into the house. Pedrolino assures Flavio that he will chase after the Captain, tells him not to worry, and then exits. And now, Flavio, feeling miserable, takes out a dagger to kill himself, saying, "Oh Captain Spavento, now you can be happy! I have paid my debt, and now I will end my life!"

LIDIA

Upon hearing the Captain's name, Lidia enters. She grabs Flavio's arms to stop him from killing himself, and then she asks him where the Captain is whose name he just mentioned. Flavio tells her that he is here in Rome, and just then, they hear sounds of fighting.

GRATIANO
CAPT. SPAVENTO

Gratiano and the Captain enter, fighting.

CINTHIO

At that, Cinthio enters, and he and Flavio come between the two men and separate them. Flavio now identifies himself to Oratio as his former slave and friend, and begs his pardon for bringing his sister Alissa to Rome without his knowing it. She is alive and well, he says, and his own sister, Flaminia, is in the house; but Alissa is to become the Captain's wife now because he owes him his life. Thereupon Lidia cries out that the Captain is her husband, and the Captain recognizes her and embraces her, begging her forgiveness. She tells him that she was rescued from bandits and that Arlecchino is also in Rome. The Captain turns to Flavio and releases him from his debt, urging him to take the young Turkish woman.

PEDROLINO
TURCHETTO

Pedrolino leads in Turchetto, who embraces her brother Oratio, and her lover Flavio. Together they call for Flaminia.

FLAMINIA
FRANCESCHINA

Flaminia, followed by Franceschina, comes out to the street to find all has been settled. She takes Oratio for her husband, and the nuptials are arranged: Oratio marries Flaminia, Flavio marries Alissa, the Captain is reunited with Lidia, Pedrolino marries Franceschina, and thus ends the comedy *Flavio's Fortune*.

The Third Day

ISABELLA'S FORTUNE

ARGUMENT

In Genoa lived a well-born and wealthy young man named Cinthio, who was left without father or mother, but who had a sister of great beauty and virtue. It happened that the brother (who thought only of her welfare) became friends with a certain Captain whose one desire was to marry his friend's beautiful sister. After carefully talking it over and finding that she felt as the Captain did, the brother approved the betrothal. Although the Captain had to go to Naples on important business, he promised to return at the first opportunity to marry Isabella, and thus it was all arranged.

But when it happened that the Captain remained in Naples for three years and forgot the promise he made, the brother decided to arrange another and better match for his sister. She, however, told her brother she would marry no other man. Tired of her brother's constant urging, she decided to leave for Rome, dressed as a servant and accompanied by her own servant; there she intended to find her Captain who, however, was looking about for another wife. Thus she went to Rome to reproach the Captain for his faithlessness. When she found him, she spoke her mind to him and then, after a series of adventures, became the wife of another, to the satisfaction of her brother.

CHARACTERS IN THE PLAY

Pantalone, a Venetian
Flaminia, his daughter

Gratiano, a doctor
Oratio and
Flavio, his sons

Pedrolino, the host
Franceschina, his wife

22

Isabella, dressed as a servant
Burattino, her servant

Captain Spavento
Arlecchino

Cinthio

PROPERTIES

A trunk
A traveling bag of hide
A large chest with a lid
A captain's uniform

ACT ONE

ROME

PANTALONE
ORATIO
FLAVIO

Pantalone enters and learns from the two brothers that Gratiano, their old father, is in love with Franceschina and that he is making no effort to find them wives as he should. Suggesting, as a friend, that it is better to marry when old than when young, Pantalone tries to console them. But Flavio complains that his father has kept him in school, not to get a degree, but to prevent him from getting a wife. Then Flavio informs Oratio that they are rivals for the love of Flaminia. Finally they ask Pantalone, as a friend of their father, to divert him from his foolish behavior, and they go off, leaving Pantalone to confess that he is also in love with Franceschina.

DR. GRATIANO

At that, Gratiano, Pantalone's friend, enters. He has returned, he says, to resume his love-making with Franceschina. He refers to the quarrel with his sons, but then says that for the moment he wants to live as he wishes, and laughing, they go off together.

ISABELLA
BURATTINO

Isabella, dressed as a servant, enters with Burattino. They have left Genoa so that Isabella, disguised as a Frenchwoman named Olivetta, can avoid marrying a man her brother has chosen for her, and instead, find the Captain in Rome and reproach him for his faithlessness. They knock at the door of the inn.

PEDROLINO

Pedrolino, the host, comes out and speaks to Olivetta, who replies in French, and joking, they all enter the inn.

FRANCESCHINA

Franceschina, Pedrolino's wife, comes in from the country. She has a chest full of goods on her head.

PANTALONE	Pantalone, who is in love with her, greets her, and expresses his love for her. She replies that she does not love old men and he gives her a pain. Pantalone begins to plead with her.
PEDROLINO	Then, Pedrolino, who has heard all, enters and threatens Pantalone, who apologizes.
BURATTINO	Burattino hears Pedrolino's threat but does not realize that Franceschina is the innkeeper's wife. Franceschina goes into the house.
FLAMINIA	Flaminia appears at her window, calls her father, and tells him that a letter has arrived from Venice. As Pantalone hesitates, not wanting to go in, Pedrolino tells Pantalone that he would like to play the pimp for his daughter. Pantalone laughs and enters his house. Burattino now suggests that he would like very much to have his pleasure with Franceschina, but Pedrolino informs him that she is his wife. Burattino begs ignorance, and together they go into the inn.
ORATIO	Oratio enters. He speaks of his love for Flaminia and his jealousy of his brother Flavio.
FLAMINIA	Flaminia appears at her window.
FLAVIO	Thereupon, Flavio comes down the street and enters so that Oratio stands between him and Flaminia. Oratio greets Flaminia, who pretends to return his greeting, although she really greets her lover, Flavio. She calls, "Signor Oratio, do not be jealous of your brother because I love you and not him."
PEDROLINO	Pedrolino notices that Flaminia pretends to speak to Oratio but really speaks to Flavio. He approaches Oratio, and in a whisper asks him whom Flaminia is speaking to. When Oratio says she's speaking to him, Pedrolino shows him that Flavio is standing behind him. Oratio suddenly realizes what is going on, and he attacks his brother with drawn sword. The two of them go on up the street fighting as Flaminia goes back in, and Pedrolino, laughing, enters the inn.
CAPT. SPAVENTO ARLECCHINO	Captain Spavento enters with Arlecchino, who carries a traveling bag. He has come from Naples to marry Flaminia, Pantalone's daughter, but wanting to go into the inn first, he knocks at the door.
FRANCESCHINA	As soon as Franceschina answers the knock, Arlecchino drops the traveling bag and begins to fondle her.

PEDROLINO | The Captain beats him, and Pedrolino, hearing all the commotion, comes out and sends Franceschina back in. He helps carry the traveling bag, and all go into the inn as the first act ends.

ACT TWO

ISABELLA | Isabella says she has seen the Captain arrive in Rome and has recognized him. She hopes now to carry out her plan.

ORATIO | Oratio enters. He sees the servant and greets her, and she politely returns his greeting in French. Oratio expresses his amazement at hearing her speak Tuscan.

BURATTINO | Burattino enters, and seeing Oratio greet Isabella, explains to him that she is his mistress and a gentlewoman who knows how to speak many languages. Isabella is about to interrupt him.

DR. GRATIANO | Just then, Gratiano arrives and greets Isabella, who again replies in French. Burattino tells him that she is his mistress, and she speaks Tuscan very well. Gratiano starts to flirt with Isabella.

FRANCESCHINA | Franceschina enters, and instantly jealous of Isabella, sends her into the house. Burattino hides to see what goes on. Franceschina pretends to scold Gratiano, and he tries to pacify her with words of love. Burattino goes into the inn, mumbling that Pedrolino is a cuckold and Franceschina a whore.

FLAVIO | Flavio enters now, sees his father making love to Franceschina, and scolds him. Franceschina runs into the house, and Gratiano, enraged that Flavio has interrupted his fun, exits alone.

FLAMINIA | Flaminia appears at her window and greets Flavio, who tells her of his fight with his brother Oratio. If they had not been separated, he says, they would have killed each other.

ARLECCHINO | Arlecchino enters and hides to spy on them as Flaminia, assuring Flavio of her faithfulness, tells him that her father is waiting for the day her Captain comes to Naples to marry her, as arranged in Naples by her uncle.

PEDROLINO | As she names Captain Spavento, Pedrolino enters without making a sound and stands listening.

BURATTINO | Burattino also comes out quietly to listen. Arlecchino, still in hiding, is listening too, as Flavio tells Flaminia that he will take care of everything.

ORATIO | Just then, Oratio arrives. He tells Flavio that he wants to be friends again, to which Flavio responds by offering him his hand;

and Oratio says that he freely renounces Flaminia, not out of disdain, but for a new love. He says that he has seen a most beautiful young lady, dressed as a servant. Having heard all this, Pedrolino promises that he can help him with his love affair, for the girl is staying in his house, and besides, Flavio is to have Flaminia.

ARLECCHINO   Arlecchino speaks up and tells them that such a thing is not possible, because Flaminia is to marry his master, the Captain.

BURATTINO   Burattino also speaks up, saying that the Captain is betrothed to his mistress.

PANTALONE   Pantalone arrives, sees Flaminia at the window, and shouts at her. Arlecchino says, "Don't threaten me, because things will be as I say," and goes. Burattino immediately speaks up, "Don't you believe him, because things will be as I say," and goes. Flavio tells Pantalone, "You prove that you never loved me if you do not help me bring about what I desire," and he goes. Flaminia says, "Dear father, I have great faith that you will do what I wish," and withdraws into the house. Pedrolino immediately speaks up, "Sir, pay no attention to what all the rest say; it will be as I wish it," and he goes. Pantalone is left in complete confusion.

FRANCESCHINA   Franceschina enters just then, and seeing Pantalone, says she wants to tell him something of great importance. She leads him off up the street.

ISABELLA
CAPT. SPAVENTO
ARLECCHINO   Isabella, the Captain, and Arlecchino come out. Isabella reproaches her lover because she remained faithful to him in Genoa. When the Captain says that he can't remember being unfaithful, that she wrongs him, she goes scornfully into the house; Arlecchino warns the Captain that he would be better off with Isabella because Pantalone's daughter is a whore. The Captain is enraged at Pantalone.

PANTALONE   Pantalone arrives just then, and hearing the Captain utter his name, identifies himself. When the Captain calls him a cheat and his daughter a whore, Pantalone yells that he lies and draws his dagger. The Captain runs off up the street, Pantalone at his heels, and Arlecchino says his master is a great coward.

CAPT. SPAVENTO   Just then, the Captain returns. Arlecchino reproaches him, but the Captain orders him to dig a grave for the old man.

FLAMINIA   Pointing to Flaminia, who has just appeared at her window, Arlecchino says, "There is that virtuous lady who is to be your wife." The Captain looks up and speaks scornfully and insultingly to her. Flaminia is shocked at his language and suggests he might speak with more respect to her, to which he replies that he speaks well enough for her.

PEDROLINO
ORATIO
FLAVIO

At that, Pedrolino, Oratio, and Flavio enter, and hearing the Captain speaking insultingly to their friend, approach him from behind, knock him down, and carry him off. Arlecchino is frightened, but when Pedrolino tries to carry him off, he picks Pedrolino up and carries him off, and the second act ends.

ACT THREE

ISABELLA
BURATTINO

Isabella and Burattino enter. Isabella is telling Burattino that now that she has told the Captain off, she feels so good that she has dressed in her own clothes. Also, she says, men prefer women to be clean, well-dressed, and attractive, not dirty and sweaty as she was in her old clothes. Burattino recalls to her her noble rank and that of her brother, Cinthio.

FRANCESCHINA

Then, Franceschina returns and enters the house without recognizing Isabella in her new clothes.

ARLECCHINO

Arlecchino now enters, crying that his master the Captain is dead. Hearing this, Isabella rejoices, and Arlecchino goes into the house.

PEDROLINO

Pedrolino enters. He recognizes Isabella in her new clothes; complimenting her on her appearance, he tells her that Oratio, the gentleman son of Gratiano, is in love with her. She should return his love, he says, and suggests that she humor the gentleman coming, for he is the young man's father.

DR. GRATIANO

At that, Gratiano arrives. He sees Isabella, greets her, and they exchange pleasantries. Isabella tells him that she is a foreigner. Gratiano is delighted at Pedrolino's suggestion that he offer her his hospitality; that way, if she accepts, he will have an opportunity to enjoy her. He invites her into the house, and Isabella accepts. As Burattino exits, she and Pedrolino are waved in by a hopeful Gratiano, who is looking forward to an enjoyable night.

PEDROLINO

Pedrolino soon returns to tell Gratiano that he has taken her to an upstairs room and to urge him to go buy some confections for Isabella. Gratiano goes gladly.

ORATIO
FLAVIO

Oratio and Flavio enter, laughing heartily about the Captain. Pedrolino plans to play a joke on Oratio. He tells Oratio that his father has enjoyed the strange woman and now has her in the house while he, Pedrolino, goes to buy some confections. Enraged, Oratio goes off to find his father, and Pedrolino has a good laugh with Flavio, to whom he confesses that Gratiano has not enjoyed her at all; Isabella is in the house only because she wants to be with Oratio. Flavio goes off to find Oratio and tell him all.

CAPT. SPAVENTO

The Captain enters, completely soaked. He says he was thrown in the Tiber but that he was saved. Wanting to get rid of him, Pedrolino tells the Captain that twenty-five armed men are looking for him, intending to kill him. The Captain, shaking with fear, calls for Arlecchino.

ARLECCHINO

Arlecchino, the servant, enters. The Captain explains that they are in a great hurry and sends him for their traveling bags. Arlecchino returns with the bags, and to Pedrolino's great amusement, they go off in great haste.

FLAMINIA

Flaminia appears at her window. Pedrolino tells her to give up all hope, for Oratio and Flavio, after another fight, have agreed that Flavio is to give Flaminia to Oratio, and that Flavio is to take the beautiful stranger. Flaminia weeps over Flavio.

ISABELLA

Isabella appears at Gratiano's window. Pedrolino says quickly, "Here is the lady who will enjoy the love of Flavio," and he goes. Flaminia greets her, and commenting that she has seen her at the inn, asks what she is doing in the house. Isabella replies that she is there at the command of the master's son but fails to mention the name of Oratio or Flavio. She goes back in, leaving Flaminia to bemoan Flavio's treatment of her.

FLAVIO

Thereupon, Flavio arrives, and Flaminia complains to him about the agreement he made with Oratio which Pedrolino told her about. Flavio bursts out laughing, explaining that his father installed the lady in the house for Oratio and offers to come into her house to tell her all about it. Flaminia says he is to enter as her betrothed, and he goes in.

DR. GRATIANO

Gratiano returns now, bringing confections, flasks of Greek wine, and other things for Isabella.

FRANCESCHINA

Franceschina enters. She says she has heard Pedrolino say that Gratiano has taken the strange woman into his house so he can enjoy her. She complains and weeps, saying that he has stolen her honor only to abandon her for the stranger. She moans at great length, working herself up to such a pitch that Gratiano, to pacify her, takes her into the house to make love to her.

PEDROLINO
BURATTINO

Pedrolino and Burattino enter arguing. Burattino wants to know where his mistress is, and Pedrolino swears that she has been abducted. Crying, Burattino goes off to bring a complaint against the raper of virgins, and Pedrolino bursts out laughing.

ORATIO   At that, Oratio arrives, desperate because he can't find his father, and knocks at the door of his house. Pedrolino hides.

DR. GRATIANO   Gratiano comes out, and Oratio asks him what he has done with the woman in the house. Gratiano, thinking he means Franceschina, can only discuss the matter at cross purposes with Oratio, who is talking of Isabella. Pedrolino laughs through it all. Oratio says that Gratiano is an evil man for stealing his betrothed, to which Gratiano replies that she already has a husband; and he finally makes it clear that he has enjoyed Franceschina, Pedrolino's wife, not Isabella. Pedrolino is enraged and accuses Gratiano of traitorous acts, swearing that he will bring a court action against him, and goes. Gratiano assures Oratio that he will marry Isabella, and he, Gratiano, is going to have a good time with Franceschina. They go into the house.

CINTHIO   Cinthio enters with the Captain and Pantalone, whom he has met
CAPT. SPAVENTO   on his way. He complains of his betrayal to the Captain; he still
PANTALONE   hopes to find his sister. Pantalone reproaches the Captain for wanting to marry his daughter while he is betrothed to Cinthio's sister. Pantalone then knocks on the door of the house.

FLAVIO   Flavio appears at the window with Flaminia and tells Pantalone
FLAMINIA   she is his wife, whereupon Pantalone commands him to bring her outside. Flaminia and Flavio come out, and Flaminia tells the speechless Captain that she has chosen to marry another, for the Captain has wronged both her father and her.

BURATTINO   Just then, Burattino enters, crying, and Cinthio, recognizing him, asks him about his sister. When Burattino tells him she was abducted in Rome by a Roman gentleman, Cinthio laments the loss of his sister's honor.

FRANCESCHINA   Franceschina comes out of Gratiano's house to tell them that the strange woman is doing very well with Oratio, and all hide to see who comes out of Gratiano's house.

DR. GRATIANO   Gratiano, Oratio, and Isabella come out, and Gratiano asks Oratio
ORATIO   who the strange woman is. Oratio replies that she is a noble-
ISABELLA   woman from Genoa, the sister of one called Cinthio, and Gratiano asks who is to bear witness to their marriage. Cinthio comes forth and says, "I will not bear witness, although I am her brother." Isabella kneels before him, begging his forgiveness for running away; she wanted to reproach the Captain for his betrayal, she explains, and now she has found a noble husband who has treated her honorably and in keeping with her brother's dignified position. Cinthio is pacified and agrees to her marriage to Oratio.

ARLECCHINO At that moment, Arlecchino, trying to find his master, enters. He sees him and greets him.

PEDROLINO Pedrolino arrives. He says the lawyers will not bother with cases against cuckolds and whores; he has to take care of it himself. He sees Franceschina and tries to attack her as if he would kill her, but the others come between them. Gratiano explains to Pedrolino that he was not talking about his wife, that he must have misunderstood because he was drunk. Pedrolino agrees that it could be so because he drinks often. All join in calling him a drunkard, and Franceschina, playing the good woman, scolds him for drinking and forces him to beg her forgiveness. Thus the comedy ends.

The Fourth Day

ISABELLA'S TRICK

ARGUMENT

In Perugia lived a gentlewoman, a widow, who urged her brother to invite his mistress to the house. On the pretense of arranging a meeting with his mistress, she put him to bed with a young woman whom he had formerly promised to marry. Thus they lay together. After the brother discovered the truth, he, made aware of his former disdain of her, went along with the jest and finally agreed to marry the girl.

CHARACTERS IN THE PLAY

Pantalone, a Venetian
Pedrolino, his servant

Oratio
Isabella, his sister, a widow
Arlecchino, his servant

Captain Spavento
Flaminia, his sister

Burattino, the host
Franceschina, his wife

Two wily friends of Pedrolino

Two Rogues

PROPERTIES

A great deal of bandage material
Costumes for three rogues
A sign for the inn
A pair of shoes
A sharp knife

A trunk full of food
A frying pan
A long stick

ACT ONE

PERUGIA

CAPT. SPAVENTO   Captain Spavento and Flavio enter. The Captain tells Flavio, his
FLAVIO   friend, of his love for the widow Isabella, his friend Oratio's
sister, and he asks Flavio to speak to Oratio about his desire to
marry her. Flavio promises to help him, then reveals that he too is
in love, and he has written a letter to his love.

FLAMINIA   Flaminia appears at her window with a book in hand; after
telling her brother, the Captain, to come in because a letter has
arrived for him, she goes back into the house. Flavio comments to
the Captain that his sister is always reading, and the Captain
agrees; she has time for nothing else because she reads so many
stories of love and chivalry, he says. Flavio asks the Captain
to deliver the love letter to his sister, for she is the woman he
loves. The Captain takes it, saying that his sister knows more than
he does about the subject of love, and reminding Flavio of his
promise to speak to Oratio, goes into the house. Flavio rejoices at
his good luck in getting his love letter delivered and exits.

PANTALONE   Pantalone and Pedrolino enter. Pantalone tells Pedrolino that he
PEDROLINO   is in love with Isabella and is going to marry her. Then he tells
him that after he had stolen Franceschina's maidenhead, he married her to Burattino with a dowry of 500 scudi; also, he made
out a note promising to give, during his life, a thousand ducats to
the first male child. Pedrolino praises this act of charity and
promises to help him win Isabella, and together they go off up the
street.

FRANCESCHINA   Then, Franceschina and Burattino enter. She is arguing with her
BURATTINO   husband about many different things, but finally she tells him that
if he can make her pregnant with a male child, they would no
longer be poor. Burattino says he knows his duty as a husband.
She answers that he isn't worth much. Each complaining of the
other's faults, they begin a noisy argument.

ISABELLA   At that, Isabella appears at her window. She scolds Franceschina
for arguing with her husband. Burattino tells her to mind her
own business and makes threatening gestures at her.

CAPT. SPAVENTO	The Captain appears and threatens Burattino for shouting at Isabella. Franceschina also begins arguing with the Captain, who gives Burattino some money to buy food for the inn and sends him off. Franceschina goes into the house. The Captain greets Isabella and asks about Flavio. Isabella replies that she has not seen him, and the Captain begins to play the gallant.
ARLECCHINO	Thereupon, Arlecchino, Oratio's servant, enters and scolds Isabella for talking to the Captain. She goes in, and the enraged Captain threatens to beat Arlecchino.
FLAVIO	Just then, Flavio enters and comes between them. He sends Arlecchino away, and Arlecchino leaves, threatening revenge on the Captain. The Captain, enraged at Arlecchino, also leaves, and Flavio speaks of his love for Flaminia.
FLAMINIA	Flaminia appears at her window, and Flavio greets her and asks if she has received the love letter sent by her brother. Answering that it was beautifully written, she wants to know if the letter was truly written by him. Flavio says it was. While they speak of their love, they hear noises of people coming.
CAPT. SPAVENTO ORATIO ARLECCHINO	The Captain and Oratio enter, quarreling, and Arlecchino stands between them with his paddle. Flavio draws his sword to part them, and thus they all go up the street fighting.
BURATTINO	Burattino enters now with a trunk full of food. He says he would like to eat four mouthfuls before he enters the inn, and he sits down in the middle of the stage to eat.
TWO ROGUES	Two rogues enter, greet him, and sit down with him. One of them tells Burattino that he is from the land of Cockaigne, and while he tells his story about the easy life people live in that land, his companion is eating the food. After he finishes eating, the companion begins to lament the torment he suffers for those who have to work for a living. Then the other begins to eat. Between them, one telling a story, and the other eating, they eat up all the food and leave. Burattino suddenly realizes the trick that was played on him, and he goes into the inn crying, and thus the first act ends.

ACT TWO

FLAVIO ORATIO ARLECCHINO	Flavio, Oratio, and Arlecchino enter. Flavio asks Oratio to forget his quarrel with the Captain and make peace with him. He says that the Captain is more a friend to him than he realizes, and Oratio agrees.

CAPT. SPAVENTO	At that moment, the Captain arrives. Arlecchino runs off and climbs up into a window where he feels safely out of his reach. Flavio makes peace between the Captain and Oratio.
PANTALONE PEDROLINO	At that, Pantalone and Pedrolino enter and hide. They wait until the Captain and Oratio go off together, and then Pantalone decides to take this opportunity to talk to Flaminia.
FLAMINIA	Flaminia now appears at her window. She sees Pantalone and tells him she would like to have some fun.
ISABELLA	Just then, Isabella appears at her window, and Flaminia signals to her to come away from the window and down into the street. Flavio exits alone.
FLAMINIA ISABELLA	Flaminia and Isabella come out of their houses. As a joke, Flaminia pretends to be in love with Pedrolino, and Isabella with Pantalone. They talk amorously together. The women ask the men to come that night to serenade them, and they duly promise. The women go into the house, and the men dance for joy.
BURATTINO FRANCESCHINA	Burattino and Franceschina come out and laugh at the two men dancing. Then Franceschina goes back into the house. Pantalone leaves, and Burattino goes on laughing at Pedrolino, who gets angry and says that he will cuckold Burattino. Burattino laughs.
ISABELLA	Then, Isabella appears at her window.
FLAVIO	Flavio arrives. He complains that he does not know whether Flaminia loves him or not, and he says he is going to speak to her again to ask for the return of his letter. Isabella says she has heard everything; she asks Flavio if the Captain and Oratio have found him, for they were looking for him to invite him to the wedding of Oratio to Flaminia, and the Captain to herself. Laughing, she goes into the house. Flavio is stunned.
BURATTINO	Just then, Burattino enters and asks Flavio if he knows the secret for begetting a son. Flavio turns on him angrily and then goes off, and Burattino goes back into the house.
PANTALONE PEDROLINO THREE MUSICIANS	Pantalone and Pedrolino enter, singing and playing with the musicians.
ISABELLA FLAMINIA	Isabella and Flaminia appear at their windows to listen to the music. They thank Pantalone and Pedrolino, who go off with the musicians. The women remain at their windows, and Isabella asks Flaminia to come to the wedding that her brother the Captain has arranged for her and her lover Flavio. Flaminia excuses herself and goes in weeping. Isabella says she has deeply wounded

Flaminia and Flavio, but that she will make things right again, and she goes back in.

BURATTINO   Burattino enters with a urinal containing his wife's urine, which he is taking to the doctor.

PANTALONE   Pantalone and Pedrolino enter. Pantalone is telling Pedrolino that
PEDROLINO   he bought a pair of new shoes for twelve cents. Pedrolino says they look old and that it is a shame that a new pair cost him just as much. Burattino asks Pantalone if he would sell the shoes for twelve cents. Pantalone agrees, and Burattino makes a deal: each will put a penny in Pedrolino's hand and the one who says he is sorry loses the penny. Pantalone agrees. Burattino takes a knife and begins to cut one of the soles, all the time saying, "If one of you says he's sorry, he loses the penny." He cuts one and begins on the other sole; halfway through he asks them if they are sorry, but each says no. Suddenly, he replies that if they are not sorry, he is, and he picks up the urinal and runs off. Pantalone and Pedrolino realize they have been tricked. Marveling at the cunning of Burattino, they go off, and the second act ends.

ACT THREE

ISABELLA   Isabella tells Arlecchino that while she speaks to her brother
ARLECCHINO   Oratio, he is to agree to all she says.

ORATIO   Oratio arrives, and Isabella tells him that Flavio has stayed with her and they have a young woman from Naples who was to marry the Captain. She asks Oratio's cooperation in playing a trick on the Captain. Oratio agrees, and Isabella explains the trick: she will agree to marry the Captain, who is in love with her, and will agree to go into the house to wait for him, but she will send the other young woman in her place. Oratio says he will cooperate and asks her about the young woman. She answers that she has her in the house. Arlecchino confirms this, and Oratio then leaves to fetch the Captain. Isabella and Arlecchino laugh about the joke to be played, and Isabella warns Arlecchino not to say anything about the trick. She goes in, and Arlecchino follows.

PEDROLINO   Pedrolino enters, laughing about the trick Burattino played on them; he says that he has thought of a clever way to cuckold him.

BURATTINO   Burattino enters and says that the doctor has told him his wife is not pregnant. Seeing Pedrolino laughing, he repeats his trick line: "Whoever says he is sorry loses a penny." Pedrolino is enraged, and Burattino, in a very loud voice, calls him Signor Impregnator.

FRANCESCHINA   Franceschina enters and asks her husband what is going on. He tells her he is laughing at Pedrolino, who is Signor Impregnator. They joke about it, then go into the house, and Pedrolino, announcing that he is now ready to make Burattino a cuckold, exits.

FLAVIO   Flavio enters, despairing at what Isabella has told him; he decides to talk to Flaminia and knocks at her door.

FLAMINIA   Flaminia answers the knock and berates Flavio for playing the trick about marrying Isabella. Flavio in turn complains to her about choosing Oratio to marry, and Flaminia says she had never even considered marrying Oratio.

PANTALONE   Pantalone enters, announcing that Flaminia is to be his wife. Flaminia, to spite Flavio, says it is true and that Flavio can just go marry Isabella. Flavio goes off in a rage and Pantalone tries to fondle Flaminia, who, pushing him away and calling him a clod, goes into the house. Pantalone is left in disgrace.

BURATTINO   From his house, Burattino has seen Pantalone rebuffed and now jokes about it. Pantalone goes off in a rage.

PEDROLINO   Pedrolino enters, disguised as a beggar with a false beard and a patch over his eye. He begs alms from Burattino, who tells him to go to work. Pedrolino replies that he was banished from his country for working too hard. Burattino asks how come that happened.

A ROGUE   A rogue, a confederate of Pedrolino's, enters dressed as a merchant. Greeting Pedrolino, he pays him for successfully impregnating his wife with a male child, and then he tells him he must leave the city as soon as possible. Pedrolino says he will do as he says, and the rogue exits. Burattino, having heard their conversation, asks Pedrolino how come he has the power to impregnate women. Pedrolino replies that the power, which will not diminish even when he grows old, was given him by his father.

THE ROGUE   At that moment, the rogue returns and tells Pedrolino that the gentlewoman whom he has impregnated demands that he leave the city immediately or he will be killed. He leaves again, and Pedrolino pretends to be in a hurry to leave. Burattino holds him back and calls Franceschina.

FRANCESCHINA   Franceschina comes out, and Burattino tells her of the man's power to impregnate women. They talk of making use of him to impregnate Franceschina before he leaves, and caressing Pedrolino, they take him into the house.

CAPT. SPAVENTO ORATIO	The Captain and Oratio enter. The Captain agrees to marry Oratio's sister, Isabella, and Oratio calls for her.
ISABELLA	Isabella comes out and agrees to Oratio's proposal. Oratio commands her to take the Captain into the house where she is to have a talk with him. Isabella takes the Captain into the house, and then returning, says that she has put the Captain in her room, and she is going to put the young woman in his room. Oratio laughs at the joke they are about to play and goes to find Flavio. Isabella, saying that she is going to play a joke on Flaminia next, calls her.
FLAMINIA	Flaminia comes out, and seeing that it is dark, says she is surprised to find Isabella in the street at that hour. Isabella tells her that Oratio has been weeping in the house because she does not want to marry him and asks Flaminia to go in to console him. Flaminia says she will—just to spite Flavio—and they go into the house.

NIGHT

FLAVIO	Flavio enters, despairing at the loss of Flaminia, and decides to woo Isabella to spite Flaminia. He hopes that her brother will let him.
ARLECCHINO	At that, Arlecchino returns looking for Flavio on Isabella's orders and, seeing Flavio, he calls for Isabella.
ISABELLA	Isabella comes out and tells Flavio she does not want to marry the Captain, and being a widow, she will marry anyone she pleases. Flavio is happy; they embrace and go into the house.
PANTALONE	Pantalone, on his way home, enters with a lantern.
BURATTINO	Burattino comes out to tell Pantalone to pay up the thousand scudi he promised, because Franceschina is pregnant. Pantalone laughs at him, and Burattino goes happily into the house where his friend is vigorously at work.
ORATIO	Then, Oratio enters and asks Pantalone about Flavio. Pantalone says he has not seen him, and Oratio knocks at the door.
ARLECCHINO	Arlecchino pokes his head out and tells him not to make so much noise because he is disturbing the newlyweds. He comes out holding a lantern and tells Oratio his sister must be a great lady to know how to get a husband for herself and one for Flaminia.
CAPT. SPAVENTO	The Captain enters with a lantern. He thanks the dumbfounded Oratio for giving him his sister in marriage.

FLAVIO
FLAMINIA
ISABELLA

Just then, Flavio comes out laughing about the joke that Isabella played; he is leading Flaminia by the hand. Oratio asks him about the young Neapolitan woman, and Isabella tells him of her love for the Captain and says that she looked for the girl to play a trick on the Captain. Oratio is happy at the way things have turned out. Just then, they hear noises in the inn.

PEDROLINO

Pedrolino comes running out.

BURATTINO
FRANCESCHINA

Burattino is hot on his heels, murderously wielding a frying pan. The others separate them, and Pedrolino begs Burattino's pardon. He says he had promised to cuckold Burattino and tells him of his plan to trick him, but, he confesses, at the last moment he couldn't go through with it and betray his friend. Franceschina says they didn't go through with it because she didn't want to do it either, and they all make peace. Then the Captain marries Isabella, and Flavio marries Flaminia, and thus the comedy ends.

FLAVIO BETRAYED *

ARGUMENT

In Florence lived two young men, Flavio Alidon and Oratio Belmont, who were very fond of each other and true and loyal friends. It happened—as so often happens—that Oratio was enamored of the beautiful daughter of Doctor Gratiano, Isabella, who loved and was loved by, Flavio. Between the two young men in love with Isabella, it was Oratio alone who showed no consideration for their long friendship. Thus he was so deceptive that he made Flavio believe that he was betrayed by his mistress, and that she loved and desired only him. As a result, Flavio lost all hope and spoke of marrying another and of giving up Isabella to his friend. But through a servant's shrewdness, Oratio's betrayal was discovered, and when Flavio came to know of the betrayal, he and Oratio quarreled. However, they continued as friends until the time that the betrayal, as the result of certain strange events, was discovered. Not long after, Oratio fought with an enemy of his and was knocked down and beaten. At that moment, Flavio, who still loved his friend, came to Oratio's aid and rescued him from his enemy. Then Oratio came to recognize the wrong he had done Flavio and begged Flavio's forgiveness, giving Isabella to him in marriage. They became fast friends again and lived with their wives happily ever after.

CHARACTERS IN THE PLAY

Pantalone, a Venetian
Flaminia, his daughter

Doctor Gratiano
Isabella, his daughter
Pedrolino and
Franceschina, servants

* See Appendix p. 396.

Captain Spavento
Arlecchino, his servant

Flavio, a young lover

Oratio, a young lover

Burattino, host

PROPERTIES

Sign for the inn
A large traveling bag
A packet of letters

ACT ONE

FLORENCE

FLAVIO
ORATIO

Flavio enters with his friend Oratio, who tells Flavio that though he is loved by many women, he has fallen deeply in love with the one who, to his great chagrin, is loved by a friend of his. When Flavio asks who the friend is, Oratio replies that he will soon discover his identity.

FRANCESCHINA

At that moment, Franceschina appears at the window and calls to Oratio to catch a letter which Isabella has sent. Flavio, thinking she means him, comes forward. In a loud voice, she says she is speaking to Oratio, and she drops the letter, which Oratio picks up. Franceschina goes back into the house. Oratio reads the letter aloud so that Flavio can hear it. The letter from Isabella commands Oratio to come to see her immediately because she is pregnant by him. Flavio is dumbfounded. Oratio bids him goodbye and goes off in high spirits. Flavio complains bitterly about Isabella and Pedrolino, her confidant, calling them both traitors.

FLAMINIA

At that, Flaminia appears at her window and overhears him. She is fond of Flavio and tries to console him, telling him that those whom we love have no compassion, and he is an abused lover. Flavio turns to her, and still lamenting, begs her pardon. Flaminia also bursts into tears and goes back in. Flavio remains, feeling wretched.

PEDROLINO

Pedrolino comes out of the house with a letter and approaches Flavio. As soon as he sees him, Flavio attacks him with his drawn sword, calling him traitor. With Flavio at his heels, Pedrolino rushes off, and in his haste, drops the letter.

CAPT. SPAVENTO ARLECCHINO	Captain Spavento and Arlecchino enter. The Captain has come from Naples to marry Isabella, daughter of Gratiano. He has in his possession a letter from one of his kinsmen arranging the match. They knock at the door of the inn.
BURATTINO	Burattino, the host, comes out to receive the strangers and sends Arlecchino into the inn with the traveling bag. The Captain asks the host if he knows Doctor Gratiano, to which he replies that he does, and the Captain takes out a packet of letters containing the one for Gratiano. He asks the host to deliver it, and as he goes in, Burattino spies the letter dropped by Pedrolino and picks it up, believing it to be one dropped by the Captain.
PEDROLINO	Pedrolino, realizing he has lost the letter, returns to find it. When he asks the host about the letter, the host gives him both letters, the one meant for Gratiano and the one he picked up, and goes into the inn, leaving Pedrolino exclaiming about Flavio's attempt to kill him.
ISABELLA	Then, Isabella appears at her window and asks Pedrolino if he has given the letter to Flavio. Pedrolino says that he hasn't and tells her what happened. Isabella, having no idea where the other letter came from, puzzles over all this; meanwhile, Pedrolino hides to see what happens.
ORATIO PANTALONE	Oratio and Pantalone enter as Oratio tells Pantalone that as Flavio's friend, he asks that he give his daughter Flaminia to Flavio because he is in love with her. And since they are friends, he says, he will marry Isabella, and the two friends can have a double wedding. Pantalone tells him that Gratiano has arranged to marry Isabella to a Captain Spavento, expected any day from Naples. Oratio says Isabella has to be his wife because she is pregnant by him, and he shows him the letter which Franceschina has given him. Pantalone is puzzled by this, as are Pedrolino and Isabella. Isabella leaves the window to come down as Pantalone says he will discuss it with Gratiano.
ISABELLA	Isabella enters and asks Oratio about the letter he mentioned to Pantalone; she says she never wrote such a letter. Braving it out, Oratio says, "Signora, even if you do not want to, you know our affairs must be kept secret." Isabella, more and more enraged, calls him a traitor and demands to see the letter that dishonors her. Oratio, spying Pedrolino, says, "Signora, pardon me, for I did not see that villain Pedrolino listening to our secrets." Even more enraged, she goes back into the house in tears, and Oratio tells Pedrolino that he, Pedrolino, is the cause of her ruin, and that Isabella did not confide in him.

FRANCESCHINA — Just then, Franceschina arrives. Oratio makes her confess, in the presence of Pedrolino, that Isabella sent him the letter he spoke of, and she is in love with him. Then he sends her off up the street. Oratio turns on Pedrolino threateningly, warns him not to meddle in Isabella's affairs, and goes off up the street, leaving Pedrolino dumbfounded.

FLAVIO — At that, Flavio enters, sees Pedrolino, and calls him a traitor. Without a word, Pedrolino gives him the letter meant for Gratiano, and Flavio takes the letter and leaves.

ARLECCHINO — Arlecchino comes out from the inn and asks Pedrolino where the house of Gratiano is. When Pedrolino does not answer, Arlecchino laughs at him and calls the host.

BURATTINO — Burattino comes out and asks Pedrolino if he has delivered the letter, but Pedrolino does not answer. They joke around, and Arlecchino calls the Captain.

CAPT. SPAVENTO — The Captain comes out and is told that Pedrolino is the one who was to deliver the letter. The Captain asks him what he did with the letter. Still Pedrolino does not answer. The Captain pinches him, and with that, Pedrolino gives such a loud bellow that he frightens all of them into rushing back into the inn. Pedrolino, infuriated, goes off up the street, and the first act ends.

ACT TWO

PANTALONE
DR. GRATIANO — Pantalone and Gratiano enter. Pantalone is urging Gratiano to marry his daughter to Oratio. Gratiano says he cannot even consider it, because he has promised her to Captain Spavento, who is expected any moment. Pantalone tells him that he must marry her to Oratio for the sake of her honor. He says he knows what's cooking and goes, leaving Gratiano puzzled at all this.

PEDROLINO — Pedrolino arrives now, and Gratiano questions him about his daughter, asking him if he has ever seen her make love to anyone. Pedrolino, answering that he is certain there is no one, gives Gratiano the letter Isabella gave him, thinking it is the letter the host asked him to deliver, and leaves. Gratiano reads the unaddressed letter and discovers that his daughter has written to her lover, warning him that her father has betrothed her to a Captain who is expected soon.

ORATIO
FRANCESCHINA — At that moment, Oratio and Franceschina enter, and Gratiano tells them of his worries. "This is my daughter's letter, but I can't imagine to whom she wrote it." Oratio immediately answers, "Sir,

she wrote it to me." Franceschina breaks in with, "I delivered it to him," and Oratio tells him that Isabella is in love with him, and he wants to marry her. Gratiano gives him a piece of his mind, and Oratio leaves. Then Gratiano scolds Franceschina for doing wrong and threatens to turn her out of the house. Then he calls Isabella.

ISABELLA   Isabella comes out, and Gratiano threatens and scolds her for making love to another man, knowing that she was betrothed to the Captain. When she denies having a lover, Gratiano shows her the letter, and shamefacedly, she confesses her love but does not name her lover or tell him that she has sent other letters. Gratiano thinks all the time that she is speaking of Oratio.

PEDROLINO   At that, Pedrolino enters and hears Gratiano tell Isabella that she gave the letter to Franceschina, who has confessed in the presence of Oratio, her lover. Isabella says she has never confided in Franceschina nor written to anyone but Flavio, and that Pedrolino always delivered the letters between them. Gratiano, very unhappy, goes off ranting. Pedrolino, wondering how the letter had been taken out of his hands, tells Isabella that Flavio has been betrayed by Oratio, and he ought to kill Oratio.

CAPT. SPAVENTO   As Isabella begins to cry, the Captain arrives and asks Pedrolino why the young lady is weeping. Pedrolino tells him that someone she hates tried to take her by force; she would willingly give herself to anyone who would beat him and kill him. The Captain offers his services, and Pedrolino takes Isabella aside to explain that she is to promise herself to the Captain and leave the rest up to him. They call the Captain over, and Isabella promises all that Pedrolino suggested and goes into the house alone.

FLAVIO   Thereupon, Flavio enters; he has overheard Isabella say, "I will be yours; no one else's," and thinks she has betrayed him. When he sees the Captain, he looks for an excuse to pick a fight with him. When Pedrolino asks Flavio how things are going, Flavio attacks him, drives him off, and then turns on the Captain and challenges him to a fight. The Captain replies that he never fights unless he has the permission of Mars and the town gallants looking on, and he goes off. Flavio remains, complaining of Isabella's betrayal.

ORATIO   Oratio enters, and Flavio immediately begs his forgiveness for his bad faith. He tells Oratio that it is true that Isabella has betrayed him by giving herself to a certain stranger, even though he knows that her father is waiting for a Captain from Naples who will marry her. Oratio pretends to console him.

PEDROLINO

Pedrolino, in hiding close by, hears all this.

ISABELLA

Just then, Isabella appears at her window; she also listens. Flavio, overcome by grief, says he will marry Flaminia, and Oratio offers to help him by speaking to her father.

PANTALONE

At that moment, Pantalone arrives. Oratio tells him that Flavio has come to marry Flaminia. Pantalone is happy and calls for Flaminia.

FLAMINIA

Flaminia comes out. Pantalone tells her that Flavio wants to marry her. Flaminia, happy at this news, takes Flavio's hand and caresses him and then returns to the house. Pantalone, following her to prepare for the wedding, tells Oratio that he should marry Isabella, and they will have a double wedding. Oratio and Flavio go off together, both very happy, leaving Pedrolino dumbfounded at Oratio's betrayal of his friend.

ISABELLA

Thereupon, Isabella comes down and complains to Pedrolino about Flavio, weeping and calling him a traitor.

FLAVIO

Flavio enters then, and Pedrolino and Isabella call him traitor for marrying Flaminia. Flavio, calling Isabella a shameless and insatiable slut, replies that it is she who is the traitor for making love to Oratio and for chasing a stranger. Isabella says he lies and slaps his face, and Flavio is about to hit her back when Pedrolino steps between them.

CAPT. SPAVENTO
ARLECCHINO

At that moment, the Captain, hearing the noisy argument, enters with drawn sword. As Flavio also draws his sword, Isabella runs back into the house, and the two men move up the street, fighting, as the second act ends.

ACT THREE

PEDROLINO
FLAVIO

As Pedrolino and Flavio enter, Pedrolino reveals to Flavio that he and Isabella, pretending to be friends with the Captain, have arranged for the Captain to fight Oratio for his betrayal of Flavio. Flavio says he is still suspicious, but hearing Franceschina's voice, Pedrolino tells Flavio to hide.

FRANCESCHINA

Franceschina arrives, and Pedrolino tells her that Gratiano has turned him out of the house, and Isabella is a fool for not marrying Oratio. Very cunningly, he leads Franceschina into confessing Oratio's betrayal of Flavio, in which Oratio bribed her to deliver the fake letters. Angered, Flavio draws his dagger to kill her, and Franceschina screams.

BURATTINO	At that, Burattino comes out and tries to stop him, demanding his wife, as Pedrolino, too, pleads for her. Forgiving her, Flavio turns her over to Burattino, who takes her into the inn.
FLAMINIA	Then, Flaminia appears at her window. Pedrolino says he is glad he revealed everything to Flavio, and that he wants to console Isabella. He knocks at Isabella's door as Flavio hides.
ISABELLA	Isabella comes out speaking scornfully of Flavio. Pedrolino tells her that the Captain killed Flavio in a fight, and Isabella begins to weep. Flavio comes out of hiding, and they embrace, each begging the other's forgiveness for the wrongs he has done the other. Pedrolino now tells Flavio to go and find Pantalone and release him from his obligation; then he will send Isabella, who knows from a letter that her fiancé had come from Naples. Everything agreed upon, she goes into the house, and the others leave.
FLAMINIA	Flaminia, who has heard it all from her window, now comes out of the house and weeps about her poor luck.
PANTALONE	Just then, Pantalone enters and asks Flaminia why she is weeping. She replies that Flavio is going to marry Isabella. She reveals all that took place. Enraged, Pantalone sends her into the house; then he goes off angrily to find Flavio.
PEDROLINO	Pedrolino enters, saying that Flavio is in great trouble if he doesn't take Isabella away soon.
CAPT. SPAVENTO	Thereupon, the Captain enters and calls Pedrolino, asking him to show him the enemy of the lady so that he can kill him. Pedrolino replies that he doesn't know who he is but that he is old and lecherous, and the woman is a rich and popular courtesan. Seeing Gratiano coming, he tells the Captain that Gratiano is her chief pimp, and he goes into the house.
DR. GRATIANO	Gratiano arrives. The Captain, taking him for a pimp, tells him he wants to speak to the courtesan who lives in his house. Gratiano, sorely offended, hits him, and the Captain draws his sword.
ORATIO	Just then, Oratio enters and draws his sword on the Captain.
PANTALONE	Pantalone enters and tries to separate them. Oratio falls to the ground in the scuffle, and the Captain jumps on him, threatening to kill him.
FLAVIO	Flavio enters, attacks the Captain, and frees Oratio. Then Flavio knocks the Captain down. When the Captain begs for his life, Flavio lets him go. Oratio, moved by Flavio's great kindness, kneels before him and confesses his betrayal. He asks Pantalone

and Gratiano to call their daughters so that all can be settled. Pedrolino calls them.

ISABELLA
FLAMINIA

Isabella and Flaminia come out of their houses. Oratio asks Isabella to forgive him for his betrayal of Flavio and her, and admitting their great love for each other, he blames love and fortune for all he has done. When he again asks Flavio's forgiveness, they both forgive him and help him up; so everyone is reconciled. But now the Captain jumps up, arguing that Isabella was promised to him. Gratiano begs his pardon, asking him to bear up because she wants to marry Flavio. Just as it is decided that Flavio marry Isabella, and Oratio, Flaminia, they hear noises from the inn.

BURATTINO
ARLECCHINO
FRANCESCHINA

Burattino, Arlecchino, and Franceschina come out fighting because Arlecchino has tried to rape Franceschina. Coming between them, the Captain makes peace. So Burattino marries Franceschina and invites everyone to the wedding, and the play ends.

THE JEALOUS OLD MAN *

ARGUMENT

In Venice lived an old merchant named Pantalone de Bisognosi who had a very beautiful young wife named Isabella. She was in love with a handsome and well-born young man of Venice named Oratio Cortesi. The old merchant was fiercely jealous of his young wife, and to keep her under his watchful eye, he decided to take her to his villa outside Venice. The lady was pursued there by her lover, and they arranged to meet in spite of her husband's vigilance. It happened then that a servant, talking as if in jest to the merchant, told him all that had been going on between the young wife and the young man. Thus, the old man was made to see his own impotence and folly in living a life of jealousy. Finally, in a very generous gesture, he gave his young wife in marriage to the young man.

CHARACTERS IN THE PLAY

Pantalone, the old merchant
Isabella, his wife
Pedrolino, their servant
Gratiano, a friend of the family

Captain Spavento, a hunter
Hunting companions

Oratio and
Flavio, friends

Burattino, a grocer
Pasquella, his wife
Olivetta, his daughter

Cavicchio, peasant pork-butcher

Flaminia, a widow, and sister of Isabella

* See Appendix p. 396.

PROPERTIES

Hunters' costumes, poles, horns, dogs, and
    other hunter's equipment
A trunk
Saucers of silver
Flasks of wine
Drinking glasses
Sweets in silver dishes
Costumes for musicians
Lute or guitar
A dish of figs and other fruits
[Benches and chairs]

ACT ONE

A VILLA NEAR
PADUA

ORATIO — Oratio and Flavio enter. Oratio is telling his friend Flavio that he
FLAVIO — has come to the villa because of his love for Isabella, Pantalone's
wife, who returns his love. Pedrolino, the servant, knows of their
love, he continues, and goes on to say that, although he has not
yet enjoyed her favors, Isabella has promised to find the opportunity while he is there at the villa. Flavio says he does not doubt
that he will find the opportunity.

PEDROLINO — At that, Pedrolino enters wearing a straw hat and carrying a stick.
He tells Oratio that Pantalone has arrived with his wife, Isabella.
Flavio goes immediately to meet them. Pedrolino asks Oratio if
Tofano, who has a villa within two miles of Pantalone's, is a
friend of his. Oratio replies that he is. Pedrolino says he wants to
see him at the house when the time comes; at that moment he
sees Pantalone coming and leaves. Oratio remains.

PANTALONE — Pantalone enters, leading Isabella by the hand, with Flavio lead-
ISABELLA — ing Flaminia, a widow. Oratio greets Pantalone and all the
FLAMINIA — company, expressing his joy at being invited to the villa. A long
FLAVIO — bench has been set up, and all sit down. Gratiano is asked to tell a
GRATIANO — story. Gratiano, after all plead with him, tells a story from
Boccaccio. When he is done, all applaud excitedly, but Pantalone
says it was not a proper story to tell in mixed company.

PEDROLINO — At that moment, Pedrolino enters, out of breath. He tells Oratio
and Flavio that certain Bergamask gentlemen have arrived and

asked about them. They go off to meet them, and the others remain. Just then, singing is heard in the house.

CAVICCHIO

Cavicchio, a peasant, comes out singing; then he sings the song about the martyrdom of the wife with a jealous old husband. All laugh at this song and ask Cavicchio to tell them a story. Cavicchio responds with the tale of the painter who was so inspired he painted a beautiful devil. They are amused by the story, and Cavicchio invites them to a party at his place. All of them accept his invitation. Gratiano takes Flaminia by the hand, making lewd gestures with her, and they go off. Pantalone remains with Isabella, whom he reminds constantly of her honor. She is angry at hearing the same old talk, but Pantalone pacifies her, embraces her, and they go off after the others.

BURATTINO
OLIVETTA

Burattino, a grocer, enters with Olivetta, his daughter. He is scolding her because she does not know how to hoe or plant. She will never get a husband, he says, and he starts giving her lessons on how to hoe.

PEDROLINO

At that, Pedrolino enters, greets Burattino and his daughter, and tells them how they can earn ten scudi. They are to pick a dish of the best Persian figs, bring them to Oratio, and tell him that Tofano has invited them all to his place, and Oratio is to come to talk of an important matter. Pedrolino gives them two scudi in advance and tells Burattino to send out his wife Pasquella. Burattino and Olivetta go into the house while Pedrolino waits.

PASQUELLA

Pasquella comes out of the house, and Pedrolino says for Oratio's sake he asks her to do a great favor. Pasquella replies that Oratio is a fine gentleman, and for him she would do anything. Pedrolino tells her that Oratio is in love with the wife of Pantalone, and to enjoy her, he must be hidden in a room in her house; then, when the occasion arises for Isabella to use the water closet, she is to take Isabella to the room where Oratio is hidden and see to it that no one else comes into the house during that time. Pasquella agrees to do it, and Pedrolino gives her two scudi. Pasquella goes in, and Pedrolino says things have begun very well.

GRATIANO

Gratiano enters and says that the gentlemen have gone. He tells Pedrolino of his love for Flaminia, and Pedrolino promises to help him.

ORATIO
FLAMINIA
FLAVIO
ISABELLA
PANTALONE

Then, Oratio enters, leading Flaminia by the hand, and Flavio leading Isabella. Pantalone follows. After greeting Gratiano and Pedrolino, they ask if dinner is ready. The two answer that all is awaiting their arrival.

BURATTINO	At that, Burattino, the grocer, enters with a dish of beautiful Perisan figs. He presents them to Oratio in the name of his friend Tofano, who requests that he come to his house after dinner. Oratio accepts the gift, gives Burattino a tip, and says he will go at once. Burattino leaves. Pantalone asks for water to wash his hands.
PEDROLINO	Thereupon, Pedrolino enters with a silver wash basin.
GRATIANO	Then, Gratiano enters with towels and a silver jar of water, and they all wash their hands. In gay spirits, they enter the house for dinner, and the first act ends.

ACT TWO

THREE VAGABONDS	Three poorly dressed vagabonds, who have been going from town to town playing and singing to make a living, enter with musical instruments. They begin to play.
PASQUELLA OLIVETTA	At that, Pasquella and Olivetta come out, and the musicians ask them for something to eat and offer to play and sing in return. Pasquella says she will send for some bread and wine.
PEDROLINO	Pedrolino comes out of the house. He tells Pasquella it is nearly time, now that the musicians have come, to arrange the business with Oratio. They send Olivetta into the villa to invite the women out to dance. Promising to pay them well, Pedrolino orders the musicians to begin playing.
OLIVETTA	Thereupon, Olivetta comes out of the villa with the women and their dance partners.
BURATTINO PASQUELLA	Pasquella goes in for benches and chairs, then returns with Burattino, who brings enough benches and chairs to accommodate everyone. Meanwhile, the musicians continue to play.
PANTALONE ISABELLA FLAVIO ORATIO GRATIANO	Pantalone now comes out of the house, followed by all his guests, and sits down among them. Everyone begins to dance, now with one partner, now with another. Oratio excuses himself in the middle of the dance and, explaining that he must go to his friend Tofano's, he leaves. As Burattino goes in for his musical instrument, the musicians are dismissed; Flavio pays them and they begin to leave. Burattino says he will accompany them a short way as they play. They go off together, all except Pasquella, who remains to take care of the house.
ORATIO	Oratio returns and greets Pasquella, who tells him all that Pedrolino has arranged. Then she takes him into the house to the room where he will wait for Isabella.

GRATIANO Gratiano and Pedrolino enter, saying they have drunk a great deal
PEDROLINO at the house of the peasants. Gratiano reminds Pedrolino of his
love for Flaminia, and Pedrolino assures him that he will enjoy
her during the days she is at the villa. At that moment, they hear
the sound of hunting horns and the shouts of approaching hunters.

CAPT. SPAVENTO Captain Spavento, a hunter with dogs and horns, has come to the
HUNTERS villa out of love for Flaminia, Isabella's sister, and now he asks
Gratiano about Pantalone, Oratio, and Flavio. Saying that they
have gone to another villa, Gratiano offers to show him the way.
Pedrolino tells the Captain that Gratiano is his rival in love, and
the Captain laughs.

FLAVIO Flavio arrives with the rest of the company, and they all cheer-
PANTALONE fully greet the Captain. Flavio suggests that after sitting down to
GRATIANO some refreshments, they begin to dance. They all take seats.
ISABELLA
FLAMINIA
BURATTINO

PASQUELLA At that, Pasquella and Olivetta come out and sit among the
OLIVETTA guests.

PEDROLINO Thereupon, Pedrolino, Gratiano, and the servants enter with
GRATIANO dishes of sweets, flasks of wine, fruit, glasses, and saucers. They
SERVANTS serve the refreshments, and all begin eating and drinking. Afterward, they start the dance of the trickster. During the dance,
Isabella makes a sign to Pantalone that she must relieve herself,
and Pasquella, with Pantalone's permission, leads her into the
house. Pantalone, because of his jealous nature, is immediately on
his guard and stands at the door of the house while the others go
on dancing.

FLAMINIA Flaminia also wants to go into Pasquella's house, but to prevent
her from interrupting, Flavio quickly invites her to dance. Then
everyone who tries to go into the house to take care of his needs
is barred by Pantalone, who tells them not to disturb his wife
while she is taking care of her own needs.

ISABELLA Finally, Isabella comes out perspiring. Pantalone quickly dries her
face with his handkerchief, saying, "When desire comes over you,
it is best to give way to it and not hold back." All stop dancing to
seek other amusement, while Pantalone goes off with his wife,
drying her face as she shamefacedly caresses her husband. Thus
the second act ends.

ACT THREE

FLAVIO
PEDROLINO

As Flavio and Pedrolino enter, Flavio says that he would give a thousand scudi to find out how things went with Oratio.

ORATIO

Just then, Oratio comes out of Pasquella's house, and he tells them of his brief enjoyment of Isabella. Pedrolino, saying he wants to play a joke on Gratiano, who is in love with Flaminia, tells them that the Captain is desperately in love with Flaminia, and although it looks like he came to hunt, he has really come for her.

CAPT. SPAVENTO
PANTALONE
ISABELLA
FLAMINIA

The Captain, Pantalone, Isabella, and Flaminia now arrive, and seeing Oratio, they rejoice at his prompt return and kiss one another. Isabella asks Oratio to take up his guitar or his lute and sing one of his Roman songs for the entertainment of the company. Oratio turns to the Captain and asks if he is going to marry. The Captain, looking at Flaminia, says yes. Oratio warns that marriage will bind him; the Captain says he is content.

BURATTINO

Oratio is about to speak to Pantalone about the matter of his marriage, when Burattino arrives. He takes Oratio aside to tell him that he will have to pay for the bedstead he broke when he was enjoying Isabella. Answering that he will pay for it, he sends him away and then asks Pantalone to give Flaminia in marriage to the Captain. Pantalone says he agrees if Flaminia so wishes. Flaminia agrees, and the Captain takes her hand.

PEDROLINO

Pedrolino now enters with the guitar which he gives to Oratio, and everyone sits down.

GRATIANO

Just then, Gratiano arrives. Pedrolino quickly tells him to go into Flaminia's room, lie down on her bed, and close all the windows, explaining that she will soon come to him. Gratiano goes in, and Oratio, beginning to sing and play, sings so softly that Pantalone falls into a deep sleep. Still singing, Oratio leads Isabella off. The Captain, Flaminia, and Flavio follow, leaving Pedrolino by himself.

PASQUELLA

Pasquella comes out, and Pedrolino tells her that Isabella is waiting in Flaminia's room to give her a gift, but she is to go very softly because she is lying on the bed. Pasquella goes happily.

PANTALONE

At that moment, Pantalone wakes up, and seeing only Pedrolino, asks where Isabella has gone. Pedrolino tells him he fell asleep too and does not know. Pantalone begins to worry.

BURATTINO	Burattino enters and asks Pantalone if he has seen his wife Pasquella. In return, Pantalone asks Burattino if he knows where his wife has gone.
ORATIO CAPT. SPAVENTO FLAVIO ISABELLA FLAMINIA	Now, Oratio enters singing, followed by the rest of the company. Seeing Pantalone, they make jokes about his falling asleep. Taunting him, they say what a wife-guard he is, a watcher who hasn't enough spirit to stand on his own guard; think of what might be going on while he sleeps. Pantalone goes off in anger.
PASQUELLA GRATIANO	Pasquella comes out, attempting to escape Gratiano, who is trying to embrace her. As Burattino separates them, Pasquella tells him that Gratiano tried to force himself on her. Gratiano, excusing himself, says that he has been betrayed; he can't speak of it now, but he will avenge himself. Burattino asks Pantalone: if Gratiano had ill-used his wife, would he be a cuckold? Pantalone answers that he would and, hearing that, Burattino says, "Signor Pantalone, you have a wife too. I am not alone. There are other cuckolds about and not far away. I will tell what happened to somebody you know." Then he says that a certain jealous old man came to the villa so that he could keep close watch on his wife. But the wife, who was very much in love with a young man she wanted to enjoy, found a way, with the help of a servant, who arranged to have the young man called away by a friend residing two miles away. Then, while he was free to hide in the house of a woman friend to wait for the lady, the young people began to dance, and so there was a large gathering of men and women dancing to the music of traveling players. While dancing, the wife of the jealous old man pretended to her husband that she had to take care of her needs, and thereupon, the woman in whose house the young man was hiding appeared, and with the husband's permission, took the young lady into the house and into the arms of her lover. Because of his jealous nature, the old man stood at the door of the house to keep all others out, telling them that they were not to disturb his wife who was taking care of her needs. Having finished her love-making, the cunning wife came out, perspiring because of her exertion, and the pitiful husband said to her, "When desire comes over you, it is best to give way to it and not hold back." Then, wiping his wife's face, he kissed her.
PANTALONE	Hearing all this, Pantalone is inflamed with jealousy, shouting that he has been betrayed and destroyed by his wife.
ORATIO	Oratio immediately replies that it was not he but his wife who was destroyed, for in possessing Isabella, Oratio found her to be a virgin; therefore, Pantalone could not really be injured since he is impotent.

PANTALONE   Realizing the truth is known, Pantalone confesses, and says it is
all right for Isabella to marry Oratio. Before beginning to celebrate the wedding of Oratio and Isabella, of the Captain to
Flaminia, and of Pedrolino to Olivetta, they stand in silence at the
dishonor of Burattino. Then all are asked into Pantalone's house
to celebrate the weddings, and the comedy of *The Jealous Old
Husband* ends.

THE LADY WHO WAS BELIEVED DEAD *

ARGUMENT

In Bologna lived a gentleman of good family who had a daughter whom he wished to marry to a worthy youth. However, he betrothed her by letter to a merchant of another city. Meanwhile, the young lady fell in love with a young man of her own city called Oratio, who was as rich and noble as the young lady, and who wanted to marry her. In an attempt to avoid having to marry the man of her father's choice, the young lady conspired with the young man to give her a sleeping potion so that she would appear to be dead. Then he arranged to rescue her from her tomb, as the play will show.

CHARACTERS IN THE PLAY

Pantalone, an old man
Laura, his wife
Flaminia, his daughter believed dead
Arlecchino, a servant of the house

Doctor Gratiano
Isabella, his daughter
Franceschina, his servant
Oratio, son of Gratiano
Pedrolino, a house servant

Flavio, a young lover

Captain Spavento

Many policemen

PROPERTIES

A long cord
A costume of Oratio's clothes
Many lanterns

* See Appendix p. 397.

ACT ONE

BOLOGNA

NIGHT

ORATIO   Oratio and Flavio enter. Oratio hears his friend, Flavio, tell him
FLAVIO   of his sadness over the death of Flaminia, for whom he felt a pure
affection. After Oratio expresses his great compassion, Flavio goes
off sadly up the street. Oratio speaks of his love for Flaminia,
who, because of their love, arranged a feigned death.

PANTALONE   Just then, Pantalone, Flaminia's father, enters with Gratiano and
DR. GRATIANO   the others, who are returning after following the funeral proces-
SERVANTS   sion of the dead Flaminia to the tomb. They pay their respects to
each other, and Pantalone goes into his house. Gratiano goes off
up the street with the servants, leaving Oratio to say that actually
he feels a surge of sorrow at hearing Flaminia's father.

PEDROLINO   Pedrolino enters now to tell Oratio that everything is ready for
the rescue of Flaminia. When Oratio tells him he is to take her to
his house, Pedrolino shows him the cord and other devices for
removing Flaminia from the tomb.

FLAVIO   At that, Flavio arrives, and seeing him, Pedrolino goes quickly
into the house. Flavio, overcome by grief, weeps before Flaminia's house, and Oratio, consoling Flavio, speaks soothing and
sympathetic words.

ISABELLA   Isabella comes out of Pantalone's house with the servant, Frances-
FRANCESCHINA   china, who carries a lighted lantern since it is already night, and
LAURA   Laura, Flaminia's mother, who accompanies them to the door and
then goes back in. Asking Flavio to escort Isabella to her house,
Oratio leaves, and Isabella tells Flavio that she is in love with
him. Flavio speaks sweet words of comfort to her as they arrive at
the door of her house and knock.

DR. GRATIANO   Gratiano comes out and thanks Flavio, who exits, leaving them
grieving at Laura's loss of her daughter.

CAPT. SPAVENTO   Captain Spavento, who is in love with Isabella, enters now, and
seeing her with her father, considers several courses of action and
finally decides to abduct her. He draws his sword, pretending to
start a fight, picks up Isabella in his arms, and forcibly carries her
off up the street as Gratiano and Franceschina shout for help.

PANTALONE   Thereupon, Pantalone, Laura, and Flavio come out to see what all
LAURA   the shouting is about. Gratiano tells them that Isabella has been
FLAVIO   abducted, and Flavio gives chase to rescue Isabella.

PEDROLINO	At that moment, a frightened Pedrolino arrives, and everyone asks him if he has seen her. Thinking they mean Flaminia, Pedrolino says that he has and that the police are after her. Gratiano is worried.
POLICE	Just then, the police arrive, all out of breath, and Gratiano tells them that Flaminia is his daughter. The police tell him that they have not caught up with her, and they go off.
FLAMINIA	Flaminia runs in screaming, "Dear Father, help me!"
POLICE	The police enter chasing her, and she runs off up the street. Gratiano and the others say that it must be the ghost of Flaminia, and frightened, they rush into their houses as the first act ends.

ACT TWO

NIGHT

ARLECCHINO	Arlecchino enters, saying that he comes from Flaminia's tomb, which he found open and strewn with men's clothes and other things; he took the clothes, he says, and after commenting on his master's miserliness—to save money, he buried his daughter at night—he rejoices at having found the clothes.
CAPT. SPAVENTO	The Captain returns to find out what people are saying about the abduction of Isabella. He questions Arlecchino, but they speak at cross purposes, neither understanding the other, and the Captain exits, leaving Arlecchino certain that the Captain is a ghost. Arlecchino now takes off his clothes, puts on those he found in the tomb, and exits, leaving his own clothes behind.
ORATIO PEDROLINO	Oratio and Pedrolino enter. Oratio, unhappy at the way things have turned out, sends Pedrolino up the street to look for Flaminia and remains, despairing.
ARLECCHINO	Just then, Arlecchino enters, dressed in the clothes he found at the tomb, and Oratio, thinking it is Flaminia, plays a scene with him. Finally, Arlecchino reveals his identity. Oratio, thinking him a ghost, runs off in fright.
ISABELLA	Isabella, who has escaped from the Captain, enters now. She sees Arlecchino and takes him for her brother in disguise, and she asks for his help, calling him by her brother's name. The puzzled Arlecchino runs off up the street, while she remains, despairing.
FLAVIO	Then, Flavio enters with a lantern, and Isabella begs him to help her; after they talk over the situation, he takes her to her door and knocks.

DR. GRATIANO	Gratiano, answering the knock, sees his daughter. Overjoyed, he thanks Flavio and takes Isabella into the house; Flavio walks off dejectedly.
FLAMINIA	Flaminia enters. Being a woman, she says, she is afraid to walk around at night for fear of meeting some madman. She admits she regrets doing what she has done, and seeing Arlecchino's clothes, she decides to put them on. While she is taking off her outer garments, she sees a light approaching, and she drops her clothes and hides.
PEDROLINO	Thereupon, Pedrolino enters with a lantern, complaining that he has not been able to find Flaminia. Seeing her clothes, he wonders about them and then decides to put them on.
CAPT. SPAVENTO	Just as he finishes, the Captain arrives, and thinking Pedrolino is a woman, begins to make love to him. Going along with the pretense, Pedrolino responds amorously to his love-making.
ORATIO	At that moment, Oratio appears, and thinking Pedrolino to be Flaminia, hides to see what happens. Having caught sight of Oratio and hoping to anger him, Pedrolino speaks amorously to the Captain, who makes many offers of love. Furious, Oratio comes forward, sword drawn. The Captain runs off, followed by Pedrolino, with Oratio close on their heels, and the second act ends.

ACT THREE

NIGHT

FLAMINIA	Flaminia enters in Arlecchino's clothes. After considering several courses of action, she finally decides to knock at Oratio's door.
DR. GRATIANO	Gratiano calls out, asking who is knocking and what he wants. In a deep voice, Flaminia says she wants Isabella.
ISABELLA	Thereupon, Isabella comes to her window and asks who wants her; she screams in fright and goes back in.
DR. GRATIANO	Inside the house, Gratiano causes an uproar, and then he comes out in his nightshirt, holding a lighted lantern.
ISABELLA FRANCESCHINA	Isabella and Franceschina follow Gratiano in their nightdresses, but as Flaminia turns to them, they run back into the house, screaming in fright. Flaminia is worried because it is nearly dawn.
ARLECCHINO	Just then, Arlecchino arrives, and thinking he is Oratio, she talks amorously to him. Although he recognizes his clothes, it is her

face he sees, and frightened, he pounds furiously on Pantalone's
door.

PANTALONE
LAURA

Then, Pantalone and Laura come out in their nightdresses, and
when Arlecchino tells them that the ghost of their daughter
Flaminia is walking the city, they laugh at him. Flaminia hides,
and Pantalone scolds Arlecchino for making such a racket.

DR. GRATIANO

At that moment, Gratiano appears at his window and threatens
them all for keeping him awake. Arlecchino calls on him as
witness of his story, and Gratiano confirms having seen Flaminia.
Then he comes down into the street, where Pantalone jokes with
him and then goes into his house. Realizing that Arlecchino is
wearing his son's clothes, Gratiano calls him a thief, but Arlecchino denies having stolen the clothes. Gratiano blows out his
lantern and runs into the house as Arlecchino exits.

FLAMINIA

Flaminia enters now, contrite because she has caused so much
trouble.

PEDROLINO

Pedrolino arrives. They watch each other uneasily, then they
reveal their identities. When Flaminia tells him Gratiano has
gone into the house but forgot to lock the door, Pedrolino tries
the door for her; it is unlocked. She goes in with the idea of
revealing her identity to Isabella.

ORATIO
FLAVIO

Then, Oratio and Flavio enter. Oratio tells Flavio the story about
Flaminia and about his having seen her with the Captain. At that
moment he sees Pedrolino; thinking he is Flaminia, he speaks
amorously to him and then scolds him for catching him with the
Captain. Pedrolino begs his forgiveness and then admits who he
is, telling Oratio everything that happened. Just then, they hear a
tremendous uproar in Gratiano's house.

ISABELLA
FLAMINIA

Isabella comes out running, followed by Flaminia.

DR. GRATIANO
PANTALONE
LAURA

Gratiano, Pantalone, and Laura also come out running.

ARLECCHINO
FRANCESCHINA

Then, Arlecchino and Franceschina come out, and the whole story
is finally untangled. Oratio marries Flaminia, Flavio marries Isabella, and the comedy ends.

The Eighth Day

THE FAKE MADWOMAN *

ARGUMENT

In the city of Bologna lived two gentlemen, one named Pantalone and the other Zanobio. Zanobio had two sons, Oratio and Flavio, and Pantalone had a daughter, Isabella. The two brothers were in love with Isabella, and she loved one of them, Oratio. Wishing to marry Isabella off, her father arranged a marriage with a doctor who lived in Pesaro. Having made all the arrangements by letter, he then took his daughter to Pesaro. As a result, Isabella became very melancholy, and looking for a way to stop the marriage, pretended to be mad. The persistent young lover, Oratio, decided to follow her to Pesaro. Flavio, who meanwhile was elsewhere on business, returned to Bologna to find Isabella. Learning that his brother Oratio had pursued her to Pesaro, and being no less convinced that she loved him, he also went to Pesaro. There was in the same city of Bologna another gentleman named Cassandro, who had a daughter who was also in love with Oratio. Hearing of his departure, she disguised herself and went after her lover, as the comedy shows in a nicely worked out plot.

CHARACTERS IN THE PLAY

Pantalone
Isabella, his daughter
Arlecchino, his servant

Zanobio, an old man
Oratio and
Flavio, his sons
Pedrolino, his servant

Gratiano, a doctor
His servant

* See Appendix p. 398.

Cassandro
Bigolo, alias for his daughter, Flaminia
Franceschina, his servant

Francis, friend of Flavio

A Pilgrim

PROPERTIES

A doctor's costume
Two Hungarian costumes
Clothes of a traveler
A small flask
A small box
Costume for Bigolo
Clothes for a lunatic

ACT ONE

THE CITY OF PESARO	
PANTALONE ISABELLA ARLECCHINO	Pantalone arrives in Pesaro accompanied by his daughter, his servant, and porters who are carrying bags. He is going to marry his daughter Isabella to Doctor Gratiano. They knock at the door of Gratiano's house.
THE SERVANT	The servant of Doctor Gratiano comes out and informs them that his master has gone to Ancona to buy some things for the wedding. They go into the house, Isabella complaining about the wedding, and the porters leave.
ORATIO PEDROLINO	Oratio and Pedrolino enter dressed as Levantines. Following his lover, Isabella, Oratio is pretending to be a jewel merchant so that he can get into Doctor Gratiano's house. Pedrolino promises to do all he can to help him, and they go off to find an inn.
PANTALONE ARLECCHINO	Pantalone, followed by Arlecchino, comes out. Pantalone is worried about his daughter's strange behavior and wild talk. Arlecchino says that these fantasies come from her mother.
BIGOLO	Just then, Bigolo, who is Flaminia dressed as a porter, enters. She has been following her lover, Oratio. She recognizes Pantalone and Arlecchino, and she greets them by name. Having overheard them speak of Isabella's ranting, she pretends to be an astrologer.

She tells Pantalone that although his daughter is not mad, she is suffering an attack because he waited too long to get her a husband, and if he delays any longer, Isabella will die; with that, she exits, and they go off to see the city.

THE SERVANT   The Doctor's servant comes rushing out of the house.

ISABELLA   Isabella is at his heels, pretending to be mad. He runs off, and she speaks of her love for Oratio.

PEDROLINO   Then, Pedrolino enters, and seeing the state she is in, realizes the Doctor lives on this street. Reminding her who he is, he tells her that Oratio has come to Pesaro to find her. When she admits that she is pretending to be mad for Oratio's sake, Pedrolino tells her to keep it up and he will do all he can to help.

THE SERVANT   The servant returns and stares in fright at Isabella. Pedrolino leaves, and she caresses the servant, cooing fondly, and they go into the house.

DR. GRATIANO   The Doctor gaily returns from Ancona, hoping that he will find his bride in the house.

PANTALONE
ARLECCHINO   At that, Pantalone and Arlecchino arrive. They introduce themselves to the Doctor, and there is much kissing and embracing. When Pantalone asks about Bigolo, the Doctor replies that he is his servant, and Pantalone praises him as a worthy man. With great ceremony they go into the house to see the bride, and here the first act ends.

ACT TWO

ORATIO
PEDROLINO   Oratio and Pedrolino enter. Oratio tells Pedrolino that he is going to pass himself off as a jewel merchant, and Pedrolino is to follow his instructions. He tells Pedrolino to knock on the door of Doctor Gratiano's house.

ARLECCHINO   Arlecchino answers the knock. When Pedrolino introduces himself as a jewel merchant, Arlecchino calls the Doctor.

DR. GRATIANO   Gratiano comes out. Pedrolino explains that he is a jewel merchant and his companion is a noted man of medicine. Pedrolino shows Gratiano some jewels. Suddenly, there is a great deal of commotion inside the house.

BIGOLO
PANTALONE   Bigolo and Pantalone come running out of the house.

ISABELLA   Isabella comes out chasing them. Then, in front of everyone, she goes through the antics of a lunatic. The amazed Doctor calls on the medical man, and Pantalone implores Oratio to cure his daughter. Then Oratio whispers in Isabella's ear, and she immediately regains her sanity, saying she feels much better, and Oratio announces that he will cure her in three days. They agree that if Oratio goes for some medicine, they will price the jewels on his return. Isabella goes into the house. Bigolo stares at Oratio and Pedrolino, and then he goes into the house with Pantalone and the Doctor. Oratio and Pedrolino leave.

FLAVIO   Flavio and a pilgrim enter. Flavio is lamenting his failure to find
PILGRIM   his lover in Bologna on his return from Florence. So far, he has not been able to find his brother Oratio either, and since he has heard they were both in the city, he has come to Pesaro to find them. The pilgrim expresses his gratitude for all Flavio has done for him; then he gives Flavio an antidote against poison and a cure for madness. Flavio gives him some money and thanks the pilgrim, and they go off together.

FRANCESCHINA   Francheschina enters, disguised as a pilgrim. She says she is Flaminia's nurse, and she is looking for her.

BIGOLO   Just then, Bigolo enters. She is despairing at having recognized Oratio in disguise. She sees her nurse, and she reveals her identity, and they embrace. Franceschina wants to take her away, but she refuses to leave. The nurse says if Flaminia doesn't go with her, she will poison herself; she bought some poison for that purpose. Flaminia very deftly takes the poison from her and reprimands her. Flaminia sends Franceschina back to the inn where they have lodgings and all their clothes. She tells Franceschina that when she gives her the proper signal, she is to come. As Franceschina leaves, Flaminia repeats her oath to kill Isabella, and she goes into the house.

ORATIO   Oratio and Pedrolino enter. They have found a boat in which to
PEDROLINO   take Isabella away. They are returning to the Doctor's house, but they do not want to be seen by the old people in the house, for they want to leave with her immediately.

BIGOLO   Bigolo now enters. She is ecstatic, having managed to put poison in a drink Isabella asked for, and she indicates that she has left her almost dead. She sees Oratio and Pedrolino, and she tells them who she is. She reproaches her lover, Oratio. Then she informs him that she has poisoned his mistress, Isabella, and reviling him, she leaves. They are dumbfounded.

PANTALONE   Then Pantalone and Gratiano come out weeping over the death
DR. GRATIANO   of the bride. They are on their way to ask the physician the cause
of her sudden death. They go off, still weeping. Hearing all this,
Oratio goes mad and rushes off up the street with the desperate
Pedrolino running after him, and the second act ends.

ACT THREE

BIGOLO   Bigolo and Franceschina enter. Bigolo is telling Franceschina she
FRANCESCHINA   has poisoned Isabella. Reprimanding her, Franceschina tells Bigolo not to despair, for if Isabella takes the rest of the poison, she
will recover.

ORATIO   Just then, Oratio enters. He plays a mad scene before them, and
then goes off. Flaminia, weeping for what she has done, starts
after him with Franceschina.

FLAVIO   Flavio enters. He says he has seen and heard that Pantalone and
the Doctor are looking for the physician, but he does not know
why.

PEDROLINO   Just then, Pedrolino enters, weeping because Oratio has gone
mad. He sees Flavio, and they recognize each other. Pedrolino
tells him all that happened with Oratio and Isabella. Very agi-
tated, Flavio goes to remedy the evil that was done. Pedrolino
remains.

ARLECCHINO   Then, Arlecchino comes out, saying he will not stay in the house
because he is afraid of the dead bride.

ORATIO   Thereupon Oratio and Pedrolino enter. Oratio plays a mad scene
PEDROLINO   before them and exits, and Pedrolino follows him. Arlecchino
goes back into the house.

PANTALONE   Pantalone and Gratiano enter and speak of not being able to find
DR. GRATIANO   the physician.

ZANOBIO   At that, Flavio enters, dressed as a physician. He offers to bring
Isabella back to life, on the condition that she is to marry
whomever he chooses. The pact agreed upon, they go into the
house.

ZANOBIO   Zanobio and Cassandro now enter. Zanobio tells Cassandro that
CASSANDRO   he has come after his sons, whom he believes have followed
Pantalone to this city. Then Cassandro says that he himself has
come to find his daughter, Flaminia, who ran away to follow
Oratio.

ARLECCHINO	Just then, Arlecchino comes out of the house shouting, "She is alive! She is alive!" and then he re-enters the house.
PANTALONE DR. GRATIANO FLAVIO	Then, Pantalone and Doctor Gratiano come out of the house. Flavio tells everyone who he is and begs his father's forgiveness. He explains that his love for Isabella made him leave home and put on his disguise. He then asks Pantalone for Isabella's hand, as he rightfully may do, since Pantalone promised to marry her to a person of Flavio's choice. They call her.
ISABELLA	Isabella comes out, but she refuses to fulfill her father's agreement. As she kneels before them, begging the old men not to marry her to Flavio, Flavio falls to his knees, swearing that if he cannot marry Isabella, he will let her die. Everyone pleads with him, but finally she agrees.
ORATIO	Thereupon, Oratio arrives. His father recognizes him, and Oratio plays a mad scene before them, and then runs into the Doctor's house. Promising to make him well, Flavio goes after him. The others wait.
FLAVIO ORATIO	A moment later, the pair return, and Oratio, who is well now, sees Isabella and runs to embrace her. When Flavio tells him that she is to be his wife, Oratio is grief-stricken and falls to his knees, imploring his brother to give her up. Flavio finally gives in, and everyone congratulates him on his generosity.
PEDROLINO	Just then, Pedrolino enters in tears. He announces that Flaminia, grief-stricken over the madness of Oratio, has poisoned herself. He sees that Oratio is well and leaves the dumbfounded group to bring out Flaminia for all to see.
FRANCESCHINA PEDROLINO AND OTHERS	Thereupon, Franceschina, Pedrolino, and others come out carrying the dead Flaminia. Her father begins to weep and Oratio is extremely moved. Flavio then asks Oratio if he would take Flaminia to be his wife if he, Flavio, brings her back to life. Everyone urges the confused Oratio to do as his brother says, and with the potion given him by the pilgrim, Flavio revives her. Oratio then takes Flaminia as his wife and yields Isabella to his brother Flavio, and the comedy ends.

The Ninth Day

THE HUSBAND

ARGUMENT

*In the city of Naples lived two old men, one named Pantalone
and the other, Doctor Gratiano. Pantalone's son, Oratio, and
Gratiano's daughter, Isabella, grew up together as childhood
sweethearts. Pantalone feared that his son would marry Isabella,
for he was very rich, and though she was well-born, she was not
wealthy. Therefore, he pretended to send Oratio on business to
Leone, France, and arranged for his kinsman who lived there to
send for Oratio so that he would be forced to go. Oratio told
Isabella that he would return in three years, and she was not to
marry during that time; but if he did not return, she would
be free to marry another. He assured her that he would return
in time, and with that, he left. The young lady waited for him
to return, and seeing that the time was nearly up, she confided
in her nurse, Franceschina, who told her that it was almost
certain that the delay was Pantalone's fault; he was keeping his
son away so that Isabella would marry someone else. She promised
to help Isabella. She took some gems and some money and bought
from a physician a powerful drug which would deaden her senses
and make her appear to be dead; then she pretended to have herself
buried. Afterwards, with the help of the physician, Franceschina
left during the night for Rome. After living there for one year,
she returned to Naples disguised as a man. She became friends
with Isabella's father and asked for Isabella's hand. Believing her
to be a gentleman from Rome, he married her to his daughter.
As Pantalone no longer stood in the way, Franceschina recalled
Oratio to Naples. What followed, the play shows.*

CHARACTERS IN THE PLAY

Pantalone, an old man
Pedrolino, a servant
Olivetta, a servant
Oratio, his son
Flaminia, Pantalone's ward

66

THE HUSBAND

Doctor Gratiano
Arlecchino, his servant
Isabella, his daughter
Cornelio, her husband, then Franceschina, her nurse

Captain Spavento

PROPERTIES

Many lanterns
Many nightshirts
Woman's clothes for Arlecchino

ACT ONE

THE CITY OF
NAPLES

ORATIO
CAPT. SPAVENTO

Oratio and the Captain enter. Oratio explains to the Captain the reason he remains as a stranger in town is his love of Isabella. He is going to see her without her father discovering it. The Captain tries to talk him out of his love for her because she is a married woman, but Oratio says he can't help himself. The Captain invites him to stay at his house, and the Captain leaves. Oratio speaks of the death of Franceschina, Isabella's nurse.

PEDROLINO

Then Pedrolino enters. He says he has had a dream that Oratio had returned. He sees Oratio, and they embrace. Then, sadly discussing Isabella and Franceschina, they go off together.

PANTALONE
DR. GRATIANO

From inside their houses, Pantalone and Gratiano call for their servants, Pedrolino and Arlecchino, and then come out. Pantalone complains that Pedrolino works too hard, and Gratiano complains that Arlecchino is lazy. Pantalone congratulates the Doctor because he married Isabella to a Roman youth and adds that he wants to find a husband for his ward, Flaminia, who was the daughter of Cassandro. Gratiano offers to take her himself, and Pantalone promises to think it over. Gratiano tells him he will send Arlecchino over for the answer and goes. Pantalone remains and speaks of his love for Flaminia. He hopes to enjoy her himself because the Doctor is poor, and he is rich. Then he calls Flaminia.

FLAMINIA
OLIVETTA

Flaminia, accompanied by Olivetta, comes out, and Pantalone tells her about her future husband. When she says she will think it over, Pantalone replies that she is going to have to accept him and sends her back into the house. Then he asks Olivetta to look after Flaminia, and he exits. She laughs at Pantalone and speaks of her love for Arlecchino.

CAPT. SPAVENTO   Just then, Captain Spavento returns, sees her, and asks her about Flaminia. She says she will be out in a moment and calls her.

FLAMINIA   Flaminia enters and tells the Captain that Pantalone has arranged to marry her to Gratiano. They pledge their faithfulness to each other, and they agree to speak to the old men. Meanwhile, Flaminia is supposed to find the opportunity to speak to Isabella about Oratio, because the Captain has seen him in town and knows everything. The women go into the house as the Captain goes off up the street.

PEDROLINO   Then Pedrolino enters, determined to help Oratio talk to Isabella. He knocks at Isabella's door.

CORNELIO   As Cornelio calls out an answer from within the house, Pedrolino moves into the shadows. Spying him, but pretending not to, Cornelio calls for his wife, Isabella.

ISABELLA   Isabella comes out, and Cornelio and she play a jealousy scene. Cornelio leaves. Pedrolino has seen all, and he begins to weep. Isabella asks him why he is weeping, to which Pedrolino replies that he is reminded of Franceschina. Isabella remarks that we wish no harm to those we once loved, and the perfect love is never forgotten. At those words, Pedrolino informs her of the arrival of Oratio, but Isabella refuses to talk about him. She is married, she says, and she will not stain her honor. Also, she understood that Oratio did not love her.

ORATIO   Just then, Oratio enters, sees her, and approaches. Seeing him approach, she falls in a faint, and Oratio and Pedrolino weep over her.

ARLECCHINO   Arlecchino comes out of the house, sees Isabella, and thinking she is dead, begins to weep over her. As he and Pedrolino carry her into the house, Oratio leaves in tears, and the first act ends.

ACT TWO

OLIVETTA   Olivetta enters. She has been sent by Flaminia to speak to Isabella about Oratio.

PEDROLINO   Then Pedrolino comes out of Isabella's house, and Olivetta tells him that she wants to speak to Isabella about Oratio and the Captain. Pedrolino sends her into the house, saying that he will take care of everything.

CAPT. SPAVENTO ORATIO	Just then, the Captain and Oratio enter, talking over what has taken place. They approach Pedrolino, who tells them that Isabella is not hurt, and they rejoice at the good news. Pedrolino then tells them that when they see Gratiano they must pretend to think that he is to be married so that Pedrolino can play a trick on him.
DR. GRATIANO	Gratiano enters now and speaks of sending Arlecchino for Pantalone's answer. Congratulating him on his coming marriage, Oratio and the Captain now exit, saying that they will announce the event throughout the town. Gratiano is happy, and he calls for Arlecchino.
ARLECCHINO	Arlecchino comes out, and Gratiano sends him to Pantalone for the answer and exits. Arlecchino is happy because now he will have Olivetta.
PEDROLINO	Pedrolino, hiding in the shadows, has heard all. He pretends to be out of breath and tells Arlecchino he has news from Gratiano that Gratiano will give Flaminia in marriage to Pedrolino, and Olivetta will be Arlecchino's. He then asks Arlecchino to do him a favor. Arlecchino says he will do whatever he wishes. Pedrolino replies that he wants only to speak to Isabella, and he tells Arlecchino of Oratio's love for her. Arlecchino agrees to call her because he hates her husband, Cornelio. Arlecchino then calls Isabella.
ISABELLA	Isabella enters. Pedrolino and Arlecchino urge her to make Oratio happy. She is coy at first, but she finally yields to their pleas, and Pedrolino gleefully goes off to find Oratio. Praising love and the life of the courtesan, Arlecchino urges Isabella to make not only Oratio happy, but many other men as well.
CORNELIO	Cornelio, who has been hidden all this time, has heard what Arlecchino has said. Arlecchino, fearing that he has overheard, immediately tells him that he has the most virtuous wife in the whole city. As Cornelio and Isabella go into the house with great formality, Arlecchino says he had to cover up and exits.
PANTALONE	Pantalone enters. He expresses the hope that Olivetta has persuaded Flaminia to accept Gratiano.
OLIVETTA	Olivetta comes in. She tells Pantalone that Flaminia is content to do as he wishes. Pantalone rejoices.
ARLECCHINO	At that, Arlecchino enters and asks Pantalone for his answer to Gratiano's proposal. Pantalone tells him that the bride-to-be accepts, and he will send Olivetta to bring the good news. Pantalone goes back into the house, leaving Arlecchino and Olivetta to speak amorously together.

PEDROLINO   Thereupon Pedrolino enters and rejoices with them. He says they will get married, and when they go to bed that night, they will have their pleasure. He assures them he will find a way to work it out. Then, Pedrolino says that he will arrange to get Gratiano and Cornelio out of the house so that Oratio can talk to Isabella. They knock and Pedrolino hides.

CORNELIO   Cornelio comes out and tells them that Gratiano is not at home.

DR. GRATIANO   Then, Gratiano arrives, and the servants give him Pantalone's answer: the bride-to-be accepts his proposal. They then urge him to give her a beautiful gift, and Gratiano and Cornelio go off to the jeweler's. The servants also exit.

PEDROLINO   Pedrolino and Oratio enter to speak to Isabella, who by now is
ORATIO   alone in the house. They knock.

ISABELLA   Isabella comes out to hear what Oratio has to say. He speaks of his passion for her and offers many reasons for his failure to return when he had promised. She tells him she waited for him a long time praying for his return. She tells him to get out of her sight, because she does not want to make another mistake. Oratio meekly leaves with Pedrolino. Isabella remains, saying that she feels a strong compulsion to clear everything up, knowing that it is not true that Oratio does not love her.

CORNELIO   Just then, Cornelio arrives. Isabella tells him what happened and says it is time to stop the deception. Agreeing that nature will prevail, they embrace and enter the house as the second act ends.

ACT THREE

PANTALONE   Pantalone enters, commenting on how very late Olivetta is in returning home. And then he speaks of the great passion he feels for Flaminia.

PEDROLINO   Just then Pedrolino arrives. Pantalone tells him that since he loves Flaminia, it will do no harm if he has the first taste of her, and Pedrolino urges Pantalone to go ahead and satisfy his desire.

DR. GRATIANO   Gratiano, burdened with jewels and other gifts for the bride,
OLIVETTA   enters with Olivetta. They greet Pantalone; then they send Pedrolino to call Flaminia. Gratiano and Pantalone speak of their kinship and of tomorrow's wedding.

FLAMINIA   Flaminia returns with Pedrolino, who tells her to do as he told
PEDROLINO   her. Flaminia takes the Doctor's hand and accepts the gifts. Then she goes into the house followed by Pantalone and Olivetta. As

she goes, Olivetta tells Pedrolino, "Remember your promise to me." Pedrolino tells Gratiano that the bride will sleep with Gratiano the following night, putting off the time he will enjoy her, and he is to wait until Pedrolino gives him a sign. Then Pedrolino sends Gratiano into the house until he sends Arlecchino for him. Pedrolino says he is going to play a trick on the old men and make the young people happy.

ARLECCHINO   Arlecchino enters now. Pedrolino tells him he is to dress up as a woman, and when he gives the signal, Arlecchino is to come, and he will be taken to Olivetta. Everything agreed, Arlecchino is sent into the house to fetch Isabella so Pedrolino can talk to her.

PANTALONE   At that, Pantalone arrives and pleads with Pedrolino to arrange to have him enjoy Flaminia that very night. Pedrolino says to leave everything up to him. Pantalone is to go into the house and wait until he gives him a certain signal; then he explains that he promised the Doctor he would enjoy Flaminia the following night; but he will send Olivetta to the Doctor and send Flaminia out. At night Pedrolino will send her back to Pantalone, and the following morning Olivetta will leave Gratiano's bed, and Flaminia, Pantalone's. Pedrolino comments that the Doctor is such a muddlehead, he won't know for sure with whom he slept. Pantalone rejoices and goes into the house alone.

ISABELLA   Isabella now comes out. Pedrolino tells her that he wants her to please Oratio. After many entreaties, she agrees to receive Oratio that night, but she says that Pedrolino must come with him so that he can sleep beside her husband while she enjoys Oratio. Pedrolino thinks about it for a moment and finally agrees. Isabella goes into the house and Pedrolino goes to find Oratio.

FLAMINIA   Flaminia appears at her window. She is afraid that Pedrolino is playing a trick on her, and she is sorry she took the Doctor's hand.

CAPT. SPAVENTO   At that, the Captain enters and sees her. She tells him what has been going on and that, although they will be together that night, she doesn't know what will happen. The Captain cheers up.

ORATIO   Thereupon, Oratio arrives, and they embrace. When Flaminia asks about Pedrolino, Oratio replies that soon it will be night, and he still doesn't know where he is. Flaminia goes back in.

NIGHT

PEDROLINO   Just then, Pedrolino enters, sees the two men, and promising them that they will soon be happy, he tells them to hide. They hide. Pedrolino gives the agreed signal.

ARLECCHINO	Arlecchino now enters, dressed in woman's clothes, and Pedrolino hides him in another place. Then Pedrolino gives the signal for Pantalone.
PANTALONE	Pantalone comes out. Pedrolino gives Arlecchino, disguised as Flaminia, to him, and he takes "her" into the house. Pedrolino now gives the signal for the Doctor.
GRATIANO	Gratiano comes out, and Pedrolino has him hide; then he gives the signal for Olivetta.
OLIVETTA	When Olivetta comes out, Pedrolino gives her to the Doctor, who thinks she is Flaminia, and the Doctor takes her into his house. Pedrolino gives the signal for Flaminia.
FLAMINIA	Flaminia comes out, and Pedrolino turns her over to the Captain. Together they go into the house to enjoy themselves.
ISABELLA	And now, Pedrolino gives the signal to Isabella, and she comes out. He turns her over to Oratio. They go into her house to enjoy themselves. Then Pedrolino also goes into the house to lie with Cornelio.
ARLECCHINO PANTALONE	Arlecchino rushes out, pursued by Pantalone, who is in his nightshirt and carrying a lantern and a dagger. Finally, Pantalone says that Pedrolino has betrayed him; he promised to put him to bed with Olivetta. Pantalone, hearing a great deal of noise in his house, goes in. Arlecchino remains.
PANTALONE	Then Pantalone, from within the house, shouts, "To arms, to arms, neighbors!"
CAPT. SPAVENTO	The Captain, in his nightshirt, rushes out with Flaminia, saying that they are husband and wife, married by Pedrolino. At that moment they hear more noise.
OLIVETTA GRATIANO	Olivetta comes rushing out with Gratiano close behind her. They find they have been tricked by Pedrolino. They hear more noise.
ORATIO ISABELLA	Thereupon, Oratio comes out in his nightshirt with Isabella. They blame Pedrolino, but they are reproved by Gratiano. They hear more noise.
PEDROLINO CORNELIO	Then Pedrolino comes rushing out in his nightshirt, followed by Cornelio. Seeing her in her hair curlers, he took her for the ghost of Franceschina. Oratio now reveals all that Isabella has told him. Pantalone begins to threaten his son, Oratio, but is calmed down. Thus Oratio marries Isabella; the Captain marries Flaminia; and Pedrolino discovers Cornelio to be Isabella's fake husband, and the play ends.

The Tenth Day

THE BETROTHED

ARGUMENT

In Venice lived a certain Doctor Gratiano who had a son named Oratio. Oratio loved a young woman named Isabella, who in turn loved him. At the same time, and in the same city, lived a gentleman known as Pantalone, father of a young woman named Flaminia. The equal of Isabella in beauty and nobility, she set out to make Oratio love her so much that he would forget Isabella; so strong was her feeling for him that she was determined to marry him. When Isabella learned of this, she planned her revenge. Disguised as a servant in Pantalone's house, she would do away with Flaminia and cut short the marriage. The outcome is revealed in the play.

CHARACTERS IN THE PLAY

Pantalone, a Venetian
Flaminia, his daughter
Pedrolino, his servant
Franceschina, at the end his niece

Captain Spavento
Isabella, his sister
Arlecchino, his servant

Doctor Gratiano
Oratio, his son

Burattino, found to be brother of Pedrolino

Musicians

Porters

73

PROPERTIES

Marriage costumes for Pedrolino and Franceschina
Two porter's costumes
Costumes to dress the Captain and Arlecchino
Jewels

ACT ONE

MUSICIANS TWO PORTERS PEDROLINO	Musicians enter playing their instruments and followed by two porters, who are leading Pedrolino, the bridegroom.
PANTALONE FRANCESCHINA	Pantalone enters with Franceschina, Pedrolino's bride, on his arm. They come from Padua, where she was a servant of Pantalone's brother, and Pantalone is honoring Pedrolino because he has been a servant in his house for many years. After a great deal of ceremony, they all go into Pantalone's house.
DR. GRATIANO ORATIO	Gratiano enters with Oratio, whom he is taking with him to buy jewels for Oratio's bride, Flaminia, Pantalone's daughter, and they go off.
ARLECCHINO	Arlecchino enters. He comes from Padua in pursuit of Franceschina, whom he loves passionately and jealously.
CAPT. SPAVENTO	At the same time, Captain Spavento enters in despair, for he has heard that Oratio is to marry Flaminia. Seeing Arlecchino, he takes him as his servant, and Arlecchino confesses his love and tells him he is following Franceschina, who is the bride of Pedrolino and servant to Pantalone. The Captain also admits his love. They agree on a plan to go into the house to disrupt the marriage, and they go off to disguise themselves.
ISABELLA	Isabella enters in man's clothes, saying that she is going to disrupt Oratio's and Flaminia's marriage ceremony and kill Flaminia, because she is in love with Oratio.
PEDROLINO PORTERS	Then, Pedrolino comes out with the porters to show them how to act with dignity during the marriage ceremony.
ISABELLA	Isabella, who has been hiding, comes out now and offers herself as a servant for the wedding. Pedrolino looks her over and then calls Pantalone.
PANTALONE	Pantalone comes out and agrees that Pedrolino should hire her. Pantalone sends her into the house with the porters.

DR. GRATIANO ORATIO	Gratiano and Oratio now return from their trip to the jewelers, and greeting Pantalone, they speak of the many relatives gathering for the festivities and then call for the bride.
FLAMINIA FRANCESCHINA	Flaminia and Franceschina come out and, after Oratio presents Flaminia with the jewels, Pantalone invites them all into the house. The old men go in with great ceremony. The married people follow suit, and the first act ends.

ACT TWO

FLAMINIA ISABELLA	Much noise comes from the house of Pantalone. In a moment, Flaminia comes running out, pursued by Isabella, who is brandishing a naked sword and threatening to kill her. They run off up the street.
ORATIO DR. GRATIANO	At that moment, Oratio comes out with a naked sword, but he is held back by Gratiano, his father. Oratio breaks free and chases after Isabella, and Gratiano rushes off after him.
PANTALONE PEDROLINO	Dagger in hand, Pantalone now appears, threatening Pedrolino for hiring the page. Pedrolino is arguing that he himself told him to hire the page.
ISABELLA	Then, Isabella enters and says Flaminia has escaped and run off. Pantalone cries out at her, and she draws her sword threateningly, warning him that Oratio will never marry Flaminia; she exits. Pantalone and Pedrolino go off in great confusion to find Oratio and Flaminia.
FLAMINIA	Flaminia enters, saying she is in terror of Isabella, whom she has recognized. She fears that Isabella has disguised herself because she is in love with Oratio. She then reveals that she is in love with the Captain, Isabella's brother, and she accepted Oratio for her husband against her will.
ISABELLA	Isabella enters and hears Flaminia's confession. She reveals her plan, and they finally come to an agreement: Flaminia is not to marry Oratio, and Isabella is to go find the Captain and tell him everything. Isabella exits alone.
PANTALONE PEDROLINO	Accompanied by Pedrolino, Pantalone enters, sees Flaminia, and learns from her that she was not hurt. But when she tells him she does not want to marry Oratio, Pantalone becomes enraged.
ORATIO	At that, Oratio returns, sees Flaminia, and rejoices. Pantalone immediately tells him that there will be no more talk of what happened. Taking Pedrolino aside, Pantalone tells him that if he

does not make Flaminia take Oratio for her husband, he will never get Franceschina. Then he takes Oratio into the house, saying to Pedrolino, "Do as I have ordered and quickly!" Pedrolino then begs Flaminia to marry Oratio, but she refuses.

CAPT. SPAVENTO
ARLECCHINO

The Captain and Arlecchino enter in disguise and armed with short weapons. Seeing Flaminia and Pedrolino, they tell them that they are musicians who have come to play at their wedding. Flaminia, overjoyed at this, asks Pedrolino to take them into the house and to tell Pantalone she agrees to marry Oratio. Pedrolino knocks and calls Pantalone.

PANTALONE

Pantalone comes out. Rejoicing at the news that Flaminia has agreed to marry Oratio, and relieved that she will be an obedient girl after all, Pantalone takes his daughter into the house, and the second act ends.

ACT THREE

ARLECCHINO
FRANCESCHINA

Noises are heard in the house of Pantalone. Then, out comes Arlecchino with a naked weapon, driving out Franceschina, who comes out screaming.

PEDROLINO

At that moment, Pedrolino comes out with a club. He grabs Franceschina with one hand, and Arlecchino with the other.

PANTALONE
CAPT. SPAVENTO
ORATIO

Then, Pantalone comes out armed, immediately followed by the Captain and Oratio, who enter fighting.

FLAMINIA

Thereupon, Flaminia comes out, and the Captain takes her off with him, still fighting. Everyone rushes off, with Oratio chasing the Captain to try to rescue Flaminia.

PEDROLINO

Pedrolino returns, despairing at having lost Franceschina.

ISABELLA

Isabella comes out to console him, but Pedrolino, enraged at her, tells her that she is the cause of the trouble, and he leaves to find Franceschina. Isabella remains to look for her brother.

DR. GRATIANO

Gratiano, Oratio's father, enters, sees her, and cries out. She reveals herself to be the Captain's sister and tells him that she is in love with Oratio, who was supposed to be her husband. Gratiano wonders about this.

CAPT. SPAVENTO
FLAMINIA

Just then, the Captain enters with Flaminia, who has told him all about his sister. The Captain forgives them and has Gratiano agree to give Oratio to Isabella in marriage.

PANTALONE
ORATIO

Pantalone and Oratio now arrive, and Pantalone is told that Oratio had previously promised to marry Isabella, the Captain's sister. As Isabella comes forward to scold her lover for his bad faith, Oratio begs her forgiveness, and they renew their vow to marry. Stunned at all that has taken place, Pantalone agrees to the marriage of the Captain and Flaminia, and they all go into Pantalone's house.

BURATTINO

Burattino, Franceschina's father, enters. He has just arrived from Bergamo for his daughter's wedding.

PEDROLINO

Pedrolino, desperate to find Franceschina, enters, calling for her. Burattino remains to listen. Pedrolino says he is going to kill himself and calls out his father's name. Burattino comes forth to stop him and speaks to him. They recognize each other and discover that they are brothers. Pedrolino says again that he wants to die because of his love for Franceschina, but Burattino consoles him, saying Franceschina is his daughter, and therefore, Pedrolino's niece. Pedrolino is amazed at this news.

ARLECCHINO
FRANCESCHINA

At that, Arlecchino and Franceschina arrive. Franceschina recognizes her father, who is agreeable to her becoming Arlecchino's wife.

ALL

Thereupon, all come out for the three weddings: the first between Oratio and Isabella, the second between the Captain and Flaminia, and the third between Arlecchino and Franceschina. Thus the play ends.

THE CAPTAIN

ARGUMENT

In the city of Siena lived a gentleman named Cassandro, who had two children, a son named Cinthio and a daughter named Isabella. They lived a virtuous and happy life. At that time, a Captain was marching soldiers through Siena on the way to Naples. The Captain was so pleased by the character of young Cinthio that he wanted to take him with him. Having learned that his son was running off, Cassandro put his daughter in the care of her nurse, Franceschina, and his possessions in the charge of the family friend, Doctor Gratiano, so that he could go after his son, Cinthio. Thus he arrived at Rome, where he saw the Captain and Cinthio embark for Naples. He also set sail for Naples, but it happened that he was captured and enslaved by Monte Cirullo, a Turk. During that time, Franceschina, who was in charge of Isabella, fell in love with a young man who was leaving the city. Inflamed by love, she followed him with Cassandro's daughter, and together they arrived at Bologna. It happened that a gentlewoman saw the young Isabella, and being taken with her, asked Franceschina to let her have Isabella as her waiting woman. Franceschina gave Isabella to her care and immediately left for Milan to find her lover. At the same time, there was in Milan an old man whose son, Oratio, attended the university in Bologna. Pantalone also had a daughter, Flaminia, who had been stolen by the gypsies as a very small child. The gypsies had taken her to Siena and sold her to a doctor, who was so fond of the child he brought her up as his own. Wishing to make a match with a worthy young man, the doctor chose the son of his good friend, Pantalone, and when the match had been arranged by letter, he came to Milan with the young woman. Pantalone wrote his son to return to Milan on an important matter. Meanwhile, in Bologna, Oratio and Isabella had fallen in love with each other. She decided to run away from her mistress, and together they

* See Appendix p. 398.

arrived in Milan. For fear of his father's finding out, Oratio lodged Isabella with Franceschina, who was not recognized. In the same house lodged her brother, who, because of his bravery, had become famous as the companion of the Captain, who supposedly had died fighting for his country. Cinthio had come to Milan to make new friends. Meanwhile, a ship of the Grand Duke captured the Turkish galley that old Cassandro, among many other slaves, was on, and he was freed and went to Siena. Finding neither his daughter nor his friend the Doctor, he wandered about for a long time and finally came to Milan. What happened afterward is revealed in the play.

CHARACTERS IN THE PLAY

Pantalone, a Venetian
Oratio, his son
Pedrolino, his servant

Doctor Gratiano
Flaminia, believed to be his daughter
Arlecchino, his servant

Franceschina, who has a house in the neighborhood
Captain Spavento, afterward Cinthio, son of Cassandro

Cassandro of Siena
Isabella, mistress of Oratio, then daughter of Cassandro

Many soldiers

Isabella's footmen

Musicians

PROPERTIES

A garden at one side of the stage
A small table with chairs
Confections
Covered chests
Soldier's arms
A jewel box

ACT ONE

MILAN

ORATIO ISABELLA PEDROLINO	Oratio, Isabella, and Pedrolino enter; they come from Bologna and are thinking of finding lodgings at a nearby house to hide from Pantalone, Oratio's father. Oratio orders Pedrolino to get them some money so that they can live, and they knock at the door of the house.
FRANCESCHINA	Franceschina comes out. She recognizes Pedrolino, and they embrace. Oratio, Isabella, and Franceschina now go into the house, leaving Pedrolino to think of a way to get some money from Pantalone. Just then, he sees Pantalone coming, and he hides.
PANTALONE DR. GRATIANO	Pantalone and the Doctor enter. Pantalone speaks of the garden he has bought and of the match made between their children. The Doctor goes on into the house, and Pantalone remains, wondering about Oratio's delay and the loss of his daughter many years before.
PEDROLINO	Then, Pedrolino, pretending to be out of breath, rushes out to give Pantalone the bad news that his son Oratio was captured on his way to Milan by bandits who are holding him prisoner at a ransom of a hundred scudi. Pantalone gives him the money to ransom Oratio, and as he goes in; Pedrolino gleefully exits.
CAPT. SPAVENTO	Now, Captain Spavento enters, saying he has come to Milan to be a soldier.
ARLECCHINO	Thereupon, Arlecchino enters, singing. The Captain recognizes him as the man who stole his pay, and they argue. Finally, Arlecchino tells him he is staying with the Doctor. At this point, the Captain forgives him because he is in love with Flaminia, the Doctor's daughter.
FLAMINIA	Flaminia appears at her window. She drops a glove. The Captain picks it up, and when she comes out to get it, they exchange many vows of love and pledge marriage. Flaminia then returns to the house, and the Captain and Arlecchino remain to speak to her father.
PEDROLINO	Pedrolino now enters to look for Oratio.
FRANCESCHINA	Franceschina comes out and reveals that she is in love with Oratio. Pedrolino gives her a piece of his mind and tells her to go in and send Oratio out.

ORATIO — Oratio comes out, and Pedrolino tells him of Franceschina's love for him and confesses that he, Pedrolino, is in love with her. Promising to help him, Oratio sends him in to call Franceschina.

FRANCESCHINA — Franceschina comes out. Oratio pretends to be in love with her, and they make a date to meet in one of the rooms.

ISABELLA — Isabella has heard all of this from her window, and with violent motions she shows her anger and leaves the window. Oratio and Franceschina go on into the house.

DR. GRATIANO — Doctor Gratiano enters, saying that it seems as though Oratio is taking a thousand years to come.

CAPT. SPAVENTO ARLECCHINO — Thereupon, the Captain enters and asks the Doctor for Flaminia's hand. When the Doctor refuses him, the Captain angrily replies that Arlecchino witnessed her promise to marry him. He goes off in anger as the Doctor and Arlecchino knock at Flaminia's door.

FLAMINIA — Answering the knock, Flaminia comes out and confesses to all that the Captain said and adds that for fear of him, she will take care of things in her own way, and she goes back in. The Doctor, satisfied at what Flaminia has said, drives Arlecchino off and goes into the house.

ISABELLA — Isabella comes out and says she knows about Oratio and Franceschina, and then she sadly exits, complaining of Oratio.

PEDROLINO FRANCESCHINA — Just then, Pedrolino comes running out of the house. Franceschina, in hot pursuit, is yelling that he has stolen her honor by pretending he was Oratio.

ORATIO — Then, Oratio enters and pacifies her by promising to marry her. As they all go into the house, the first act ends.

ACT TWO

ORATIO PEDROLINO — Oratio and Pedrolino enter. Oratio is lamenting Isabella's departure; he does not know why she is going.

ISABELLA — Just then, Isabella arrives, sees Oratio, and contemptuously reproaches him for his bad faith. Then, without waiting to hear his reply, she exits, leaving Oratio feeling wretched.

PANTALONE — At that, Pantalone enters and embraces Oratio, grateful for his rescue from the bandits. Oratio does not know what he is talking about, and irritated at his father, leaves with Pedrolino.

ISABELLA   Isabella returns, sorry that she did not wait to hear Oratio's reply. She sees Pantalone and appeals to him. Pantalone questions her, and she reveals everything to him. Then Pantalone reveals himself to be Oratio's father. He calls her a slut and exits, leaving the grieving Isabella.

DR. GRATIANO   Thereupon, the Doctor arrives. Isabella appeals to him, telling him all that has happened to her. The Doctor informs her that he is the father of Flaminia, who is to marry Oratio, and calling her a slut, he too exits, leaving Isabella still grieving.

CAPT. SPAVENTO   Just then, the Captain enters, and hearing her speak Flaminia's name, he befriends her. They make plans to disrupt the marriage of Oratio and Flaminia and leave.

ARLECCHINO   Arlecchino enters, saying he cannot find his master. He knocks at Flaminia's door.

FLAMINIA   Flaminia comes out dressed in man's clothes, and together they go off to find the Captain.

PANTALONE
DR. GRATIANO   Pantalone and the Doctor enter, discussing Isabella.

ORATIO
PEDROLINO   Then, Oratio and Pedrolino enter; Oratio, angry at seeing Isabella speaking with his father, now bows to his father's will and agrees to take Flaminia to be his wife. When she does not come at their call, the Doctor goes into the house and discovers that she has run away; with that, they all go off together to find her.

CASSANDRO   Cassandro of Siena enters now and tells the story of his daughter and son, and of the nurse, as set down in the Argument. He was a slave of the Turks, he says, and when he was freed by a Tuscan galley, he returned to his city; but then finding none of his family there, he has been looking for them ever since.

CAPT. SPAVENTO
ISABELLA   The Captain enters with Isabella, who is dressed as a soldier. When she sees Cassandro, she asks him to become a soldier; he agrees. The Captain signs Oratio up, and in the name of Captain Spavento, he says, Oratio is made a soldier. Then the Captain and Isabella go off.

ARLECCHINO
FLAMINIA   Arlecchino and Flaminia now enter and ask about the Captain, who has become a soldier. Cassandro informs them that he was signed up as a soldier, and he is his lieutenant.

ORATIO
PEDROLINO   At that, Oratio and Pedrolino, who now have money from soldiering, enter in despair at Isabella's running away.

PANTALONE DR. GRATIANO	Thereupon, Pantalone and the Doctor enter. Pantalone sees Oratio dressed as a soldier, and shouts at him. The Doctor, recognizing Flaminia in man's clothes, threatens her and warns her she must keep her word. When she says she wants to marry the Captain, Oratio tells them that the Captain has found another wife, Isabella. Hearing that, Flaminia agrees to marry Oratio. Now recognizing the Doctor, Cassandro comes between them to make the alliance, and they send Pedrolino to buy things for the banquet and Arlecchino to bring the musicians. As Flaminia goes into the house, the others go off up the street, and the second act ends.

ACT THREE

FRANCESCHINA	Franceschina enters, grieving because she will never again see her husband, Pedrolino.
CASSANDRO	Just then, Cassandro enters, looking for the Captain. He sees Franceschina; recognizing her as the nurse, he begins to berate her, and falling to her knees, she tells him all that has happened to his daughter and where she left her.
DR. GRATIANO	At that moment, the Doctor enters, rejoicing about the wedding. He sees Cassandro, who tells him that Franceschina is the nurse and he now hopes to find his daughter. They go into the Doctor's house.
PANTALONE ORATIO	Pantalone and Oratio enter with jewels for the bride.
PEDROLINO PORTERS	Thereupon, Pedrolino enters with porters, who are carrying things for the wedding, and they all go into the Doctor's house.
CAPT. SPAVENTO ISABELLA	Just then, the Captain enters with Isabella, who is dressed as a soldier. They say they want more than anything to stop the wedding, and they hide.
ARLECCHINO MUSICIANS	Arlecchino now enters with the musicians, instructing them that the banquet will be held in a garden at the Tosa Gate. The Captain and Isabella, having heard everything, leave. Arlecchino knocks.
ORATIO FLAMINIA	Oratio comes out, holding Flaminia by the hand.
PEDROLINO FRANCESCHINA	Pedrolino comes out, holding Franceschina by the hand.

PANTALONE DR. GRATIANO	Pantalone comes out, holding the Doctor by the hand. The musicians start playing, and they all dance off to the garden at the Tosa Gate.

THE ROAD TO
THE TOSA GATE

CAPT. SPAVENTO SOLDIERS ISABELLA	The Captain, soldiers, and Isabella enter. The Captain has ordered the kidnapping of Flaminia, designating the garden as the meeting place, and now they hide.
MUSICIANS ALL	Just then, the musicians enter playing, and behind them come all the guests. Everyone comes out of the house together, and they begin to dance. Arlecchino spreads the table.
CAPT. SPAVENTO SOLDIERS ISABELLA	Just then, a footman enters looking for Pantalone de Bisognosi. drawn, and they grab Flaminia and run off with her. The others chase after them. The porters remain and begin eating the confections.
ALL	In a moment, they all return. The Doctor says that Flaminia was destined to be kidnapped by gypsies and soldiers. As he tells what happened, Pantalone gradually realizes that she is his daughter.
CAPT. SPAVENTO ISABELLA	The Captain now enters with Isabella, who accuses Oratio of bad faith and of betraying her. Oratio confesses his wrongs and offers himself to her, and she accepts him as her husband. At the Doctor's request, the Captain goes to get Flaminia and brings her in.
FLAMINIA	When Flaminia arrives, Pantalone recognizes her as his daughter. He says, "At least I should know who the Captain is." The Captain reveals himself to be Cassandro's son and tells his story.
A FOOTMAN	Just then, a footman enters looking for Pantalone de Bisognosi. He sees Franceschina and recognizes her as the person who gave Isabella to his mistress. He tells them that the son of the said Pantalone was led away from Bologna by Isabella and taken with her to Milan. Then Franceschina tells them that Isabella is the sister of the Captain and the daughter of Cassandro.
CASSANDRO	At that moment, Cassandro arrives. He hears all, recognizes his children, and they hold the destined wedding. And here the play ends.

THE DENTIST *

ARGUMENT

In the city of Rome lived a certain Pantalone, father of a young man named Oratio and of a daughter named Flaminia. The young man was in love with a noble widow named Isabella, who returned his love. However, Pantalone himself loved the lady, and meeting only with her scorn, he decided that it was because Oratio was his rival; he planned, therefore, to send his son away to school. The widow found out about it, and not liking the idea, decided she would do something about it. She consulted an old friend who told her she possessed a secret drug which, made up as candy, would deprive whoever tasted it of his reason, and another secret formula which would reverse the effect. Therefore, she thought, if Oratio could be made to believe that Isabella would be his by giving him the secret formula, he would help get rid of his father as a rival. Isabella agreed to give the secret potion to Oratio. That which followed, the play will make known.

CHARACTERS IN THE PLAY

Pantalone
Oratio, his son
Flaminia, his daughter
Pedrolino, his servant

Flavio
Isabella, his widowed sister
Franceschina, her servant
Arlecchino, her servant

The Doctor, alone

Captain Spavento, alone

Pasquella, an old woman by herself

* See Appendix p. 399.

PROPERTIES

Two boxes of candy
A dentist's uniform
A pair of pliers (tinker's tools)
A beautiful chair

ACT ONE

ROME

PANTALONE   Pantalone enters, telling Pedrolino of his love for Isabella, the
PEDROLINO   widow. Fearing his son Oratio is his rival, he says he plans to get
rid of him by sending him away to school. Pedrolino takes
Oratio's side and rebukes Pantalone. They begin to argue, then to
exchange blows, and finally, Pantalone strikes Pedrolino and bites
him on the arm. Threatening to beat him again, Pantalone goes
off saying he will speak to Franceschina about him. Pedrolino
responds by promising to avenge the bite he got from Pantalone.

FRANCESCHINA   Franceschina enters, looking for Oratio on orders from her mistress. She sees Pedrolino, and he tells her about the bite on his
arm. To avenge Pedrolino, they conspire to pretend that Pantalone's breath stinks. Franceschina goes into the house and Pedrolino remains.

FLAVIO   Just then, Flavio enters, and in speaking to Pedrolino of his love,
slaps his wounded arm. Pedrolino cries out, and they also conspire to tell Pantalone that his breath stinks. Flavio exits.

THE DOCTOR   Then the doctor enters on his way to collect his twenty-five scudi
from Pantalone. He grabs Pedrolino by the wounded arm, and
again Pedrolino cries out. The doctor agrees to join in the trick
on Pantalone, and Pedrolino promises to help him get his twenty-five scudi. The doctor exits, and Pedrolino leaves to look for
Oratio.

CAPT. SPAVENTO   Captain Spavento enters, expresses his love for Isabella, and
boasts of his brave exploits.

ARLECCHINO   Thereupon, Arlecchino, Isabella's servant, enters and plays a ridiculous scene with the Captain. Then he goes into the house to call
Isabella as the Captain waits.

FLAMINIA   From her window, Flaminia has seen the Captain, whom she
loves. She pleads for him to return her love.

ISABELLA   At that, Isabella comes out expecting to find Oratio. When the Captain pleads for her love, she scorns him, and he does the same to Flaminia. They play a three-way scene. Finally, Isabella goes into the house scorning the Captain; the Captain does the same to Flaminia and goes. Flaminia remains, lamenting.

PEDROLINO   Just then, Pedrolino enters saying that he has heard everything and threatening to tell her father unless she joins the conspiracy to play the stinking-breath trick on her father. She agrees and goes in. Pedrolino, complaining that his arm hurts even more, swears that if he could become a doctor, he could avenge himself against everyone.

ARLECCHINO   Now Arlecchino arrives. Pedrolino bribes him to masquerade as a dentist and then sends him off to disguise himself.

ORATIO   Oratio enters and learns from Pedrolino that his father, Pantalone, is his rival for Isabella's love, and his father is going to send him away to school. Saddened by the news, Oratio appeals to Pedrolino, who promises to help him in return for Oratio's help in the trick of the stinking breath. Oratio then says that he would like to talk to Isabella, and Pedrolino calls her.

ISABELLA   Isabella comes out, and Oratio tells her he loves her and that he is going away. She becomes sad.

PANTALONE   At that, Pantalone approaches, calling loudly. Isabella hears his voice and goes into the house. Pedrolino tries to argue Oratio out of going to Perugia. Pantalone sees his son, and he orders him to get ready immediately to leave for Perugia. Oratio meekly enters the house to get ready, watching Pedrolino as he tells Pantalone that he has spoken to Franceschina. Then Pedrolino cries out, "Pew, Master, your breath stinks something awful!" Pantalone laughs.

FRANCESCHINA   Then, Franceschina enters and also exclaims about Pantalone's breath. She tells him that if his breath did not stink so, Isabella would love him. Then she goes into the house, and Pantalone begins to wonder about what she has said.

FLAVIO   At that moment, Flavio passes by and is signaled by Pedrolino. He also complains of Pantalone's breath and goes off. By now Pantalone is becoming anxious about these complaints.

THE DOCTOR   The doctor arrives. Pedrolino gives him the sign, and the doctor complains about Pantalone's breath and exits. Pantalone says he is going to ask his daughter if it is true that his breath stinks, and he calls her.

FLAMINIA   Flaminia comes out and tells her father that his breath stinks something awful, and with that, she goes back in.

ORATIO   Then, Oratio comes out of the house and says the same thing as the others have said and goes back in. Pantalone says he is going to have the tooth pulled that is causing the smell. He orders Pedrolino to get a dentist and goes into the house, but Pedrolino remains.

ARLECCHINO   Just then, Arlecchino arrives, dressed as a dentist. Pedrolino tells Arlecchino to pull Pantalone's teeth because they are decayed; then he hides. Arlecchino begins shouting under the windows, calling for those who have bad teeth.

PANTALONE   Thereupon, Pantalone calls down to him from the window and then comes out. Arlecchino takes out his tongs, which are tinker's tools, calling them by ridiculous names. He sits Pantalone down, and with a large pair of pliers, pulls out four good teeth. Crying out in pain, Pantalone grabs the dentist's beard which, being false, comes off in his hand. Arlecchino runs off, and Pantalone throws the chair after him. Complaining of the pain in his mouth, he goes into the house, and the first act ends.

ACT TWO

PASQUELLA   Pasquella, the old woman who is Isabella's friend, comes to visit her; she knocks.

ISABELLA   Isabella comes out and tells Pasquella of Oratio's love and that he must leave at the command of his father. Pasquella consoles her with promises to help with her secret formulas; Isabella says she will send Arlecchino within the hour to fetch the fatal candy, and Pasquella goes. Now Isabella is happy.

PEDROLINO   Pedrolino enters, gleeful about the trick played on Pantalone, and tells Isabella that Pantalone is stubborn and will send Oratio away.

PANTALONE
ORATIO   Pantalone comes to take Oratio away so as to make certain that he would leave immediately. He sees Isabella, greets her, and leaves, followed by Oratio, who makes a sign for her to see Pedrolino. As he exits, Isabella tells Pedrolino that he is to return to her within the hour.

FLAVIO   Just then, Flavio enters. Seeing Pedrolino talking to Isabella, his sister, he suspects something and sends her into the house, threatening Pedrolino. Pedrolino placates him by telling him that he wants to help Flavio marry Flaminia by putting them in the house together. This makes Flavio happy, and Pedrolino sends him off, telling him to disguise himself as a dentist; Flavio goes. Pedrolino, laughing, goes off to find Oratio.

ARLECCHINO | Arlecchino enters, saying that all has gone well with Pantalone.

ISABELLA | At that, Isabella appears at her window, and after sending him to Pasquella's house for the candy, she withdraws. Arlecchino remains.

PEDROLINO | Just then, Pedrolino arrives and begins to laugh at the trick played on Pantalone.

CAPT. SPAVENTO | Thereupon, the Captain arrives. He threatens Arlecchino, who says that his mistress has given orders to Pedrolino about what he must do to get into the house. Then, as the Captain turns to Pedrolino, Arlecchino runs off. Pedrolino says he does not know anything about it; he says he must dress himself as a Venetian like Pantalone and that he will then take him into the house. The Captain is happy and goes off alone to dress himself.

FLAMINIA | At that moment, Flaminia comes out and asks him what is going on, and Pedrolino answers that that evening he will bring her lover, disguised as a woman, and asks for one of her dresses. Flaminia gladly gives him one and goes back into the house.

THE DOCTOR | The doctor enters, saying he intends to have the twenty-five scudi promised by Pantalone, and Pedrolino gives him the dress.

PANTALONE | Then, Pantalone arrives, sees the doctor with the dress, calls him a thief, and hits him. Pedrolino does likewise, paying no attention to the doctor's protests, and then they go into the house as the doctor, in desperation, swears that he will go to court and leaves.

ORATIO | Oratio enters to say farewell to Isabella before he leaves; he knocks on her door.

ISABELLA | Isabella comes out, and they play a love scene. Isabella asks Oratio to eat some candy, which she will give him before he leaves, and he promises to do so. She goes into the house, and Oratio leaves.

FLAVIO | Flavio, dressed as a dentist, now appears and shouts under Pantalone's window.

PANTALONE | At that, Pantalone comes out and beats Flavio, thinking he is Arlecchino disguised as a dentist; he then goes back in, and Flavio runs off.

CAPT. SPAVENTO | The Captain, dressed as Pantalone, enters.

FLAVIO | Then, Flavio returns, and thinking the Captain is Pantalone, gives him a good beating. As they all run off, the second act ends.

ACT THREE

ARLECCHINO	Arlecchino enters with boxes of candy; he knocks.
ISABELLA	Isabella comes out, takes both boxes, and then hands the poisoned candy back to Arlecchino with orders that he give it to Oratio. Keeping the untainted candy for herself, she goes back into the house. Arlecchino remains.
PEDROLINO	Just then, Pedrolino arrives. Arlecchino gives him the candy to give to Oratio and goes into the house. Pedrolino takes some candy and puts it in his pocket.
ORATIO	Then, Oratio enters and takes the candy box. As he leaves, Oratio tells Pedrolino to take Arlecchino with him to deliver something to Isabella. Pedrolino remains, eating the candy he had hidden in his pocket, and immediately he loses his wits.
CAPT. SPAVENTO	At that moment, the Captain enters, swearing that he is going to kill him. When Pedrolino responds nonsensically and acts crazy, the amazed Captain lets him go off.
FLAMINIA	Flaminia enters and pleads her love once again; the Captain turns on her and drives her away. Scorned, she says she is determined to love Flavio and goes in.
THE DOCTOR	The doctor returns, announcing that justice will be done.
PEDROLINO	Then, Pedrolino arrives. The doctor threatens him, but when Pedrolino acts like a madman, the doctor runs off. Pedrolino remains.
FRANCESCHINA	Franceschina enters to speak with him, and Pedrolino acts the same; he leaves. Franceschina follows him up the street.
ARLECCHINO	Arlecchino now enters and, in desperation, knocks at Isabella's door.
ISABELLA	When Isabella answers, he tells her that Oratio, after eating the candy, has gone mad; she says he is to bring him to her, and Arlecchino goes.
FLAVIO	Flavio enters and asks Isabella why she is so pensive. Provoked, she tells him all that has happened with her lover, of Oratio's madness, and of the secret to make him well. Saying that he loves her sister and promising to take care of everything for her, Flavio sends her back into the house and goes to find Pantalone.
PANTALONE	Pantalone enters and says he does not know if Oratio has left.

PEDROLINO	Now, Pedrolino arrives and responds strangely to Pantalone.
ORATIO	Oratio arrives dressed in a long gown. He acts mad and exits. Then Pedrolino does the same and goes off, leaving Pantalone in despair.
FLAVIO	Just then, Flavio returns to console Pantalone with word that Oratio's health is in the hands of his sister. Pantalone asks him to call her.
ISABELLA	Isabella comes out and offers to cure his son Oratio, but she wants two favors: one, that Flaminia marry Flavio, her brother; and the other, that Oratio marry whomever she chooses. Pantalone agrees and calls Flaminia.
FLAMINIA	Flaminia comes out and agrees to marry Flavio.
ORATIO FLAVIO	Thereupon, Oratio, acting the madman and speaking gibberish, enters. Flavio quickly takes him into the house and returns shortly to announce that Oratio has regained his senses.
ORATIO ISABELLA	At that, Oratio enters with Isabella, who asks the other favor of Pantalone. She asks to marry Oratio, and Pantalone consents.
THE DOCTOR	At that moment, the Doctor enters, running from the mad Pedrolino. Flavio takes Pedrolino into the house to cure him, and when he sends him out, Pedrolino reveals to Pantalone the conspiracy to avenge the bite by pretending that Pantalone's breath stank and by pulling his teeth. He confesses his faults and begs pardon of all who were offended by him. All laugh, and here the comedy ends.

THE DESPERATE DOCTOR

ARGUMENT

There was in Bologna a certain doctor, the father of a young man named Oratio. Because his son was in love with a gentlewoman named Flaminia, he decided to send him far away in order to make him forget her. Therefore, he sent him to study in Pavia, where the young man took residence in the house of Signor Cassandro. Signor Cassandro had a son named Flavio, and a daughter named Isabella, who fell in love with Oratio, and he with her. As a result, Oratio forgot Flaminia entirely. While he lived in this carefree fashion, Oratio had news by way of letters from friends that his father, although old, wanted to marry again. Learning this, he returned home to stop the marriage without telling Isabella. Demoralized by the marriage of his father, his dormant love for Flaminia was aroused, and his love for Isabella was forgotten. Isabella, hearing no news of her lover, went with a servant to Bologna. Her old father, Cassandro, and his son, Flavio, followed them. Flavio, as it happened, went to bed with Flaminia and afterward married her.

CHARACTERS IN THE PLAY

Pantalone, a Venetian
Ardelia, his daughter
Pedrolino, his servant

The Doctor
Oratio, his son

Captain Spavento

Cassandro, an old man
Isabella, his daughter
Flavio, his son
Arlecchino, his servant

Flaminia, who is not seen
Franceschina, her servant

Policemen

PROPERTIES

A box with jewels
A ring
A bundle of candles
Two lanterns

ACT ONE

BOLOGNA

ORATIO CAPT. SPAVENTO	Oratio enters, telling the Captain that he has come from Pavia to Bologna to stop the marriage of his father and to see Flaminia, his widowed love, again. The Captain urges him to stop the wedding as he himself is in love with the bride, Ardelia. They come to an agreement and leave.
PANTALONE THE DOCTOR	Pantalone enters with the doctor, Oratio's father, who has come to marry his betrothed, Ardelia; they knock.
ARDELIA	Ardelia comes out and makes fun of the doctor.
PEDROLINO	Pedrolino enters, and knowing all, torments the doctor so much that he leaves in tears. Pantalone and Pedrolino follow the doctor, and Ardelia goes into the house.
ORATIO	Oratio enters and says that he has seen all from hiding. He rejoices and says this is a good opportunity to help the Captain.
ARLECCHINO	Just then, Arlecchino comes to find an inn for Isabella, his mistress. He sees Oratio and asks him where he can find a room, but Oratio torments him, and Arlecchino bursts into tears. Oratio leaves then, commenting that he thinks he has seen the servant somewhere before.
CAPT. SPAVENTO	Thereupon, the Captain arrives. Arlecchino asks him for directions, but the Captain beats him with the flat side of his sword and leaves.
PEDROLINO	Finally Pedrolino arrives. Arlecchino asks him the same question, quickly adding that he has a beautiful mistress. Promising that he will give him a room, Pedrolino shows him Pantalone's house, and Arlecchino leaves to find his mistress. Pedrolino decides to play a trick on him.

ISABELLA	Isabella, who has followed Oratio from Pavia, enters, worried that Arlecchino has played a trick on her. She asks Pedrolino who he is; he answers that he is a relative, and he takes her into Pantalone's house to put her in a separate apartment.
ORATIO CAPT. SPAVENTO	Oratio and the Captain now enter, as Oratio tells the Captain that he will hand over Ardelia to him; they hear Pantalone's voice, and the Captain hides.
PANTALONE	At that moment, Pantalone enters, concerned about the problems that have arisen between the doctor and Ardelia. When Oratio tells him he has come to attend the wedding, Pantalone tells him Ardelia has become peevish. Oratio promises that he will make her satisfied to accept his father. Giving him his ring as a token, Pantalone says he can bring her whenever he wishes, and Oratio exits.
ARLECCHINO	Then, Arlecchino enters and says that he cannot find Isabella, but remembering that he has all the jewelry and money in his possession, he rejoices. Pantalone thinks he is a thief and decides to hire him as a servant in order to steal his wealth from him. He asks Arlecchino, and Arlecchino accepts; each agrees he is not to give his name.
CASSANDRO	Just then, Cassandro, Isabella's father, enters; he has followed her from Pavia. He sees Arlecchino and calls him by name. Arlecchino pretends not to know Cassandro, insisting that this is not his name, and he calls on Pantalone as witness. Pantalone leaves with Arlecchino, and Cassandro follows them off.
ORATIO CAPT. SPAVENTO	Oratio now returns with the Captain to surrender Ardelia; he knocks on the door.
PEDROLINO	Pedrolino comes out. On the pretext of taking her to his father, Oratio asks for Ardelia and shows the ring which Pantalone gave him as a token. Pedrolino takes the ring and calls her.
ARDELIA	Ardelia comes out. Pedrolino turns her over to Oratio, her son-in-law, and exits. Ardelia complains of being wedded to the doctor. Oratio calls the Captain, and he and Ardelia embrace. They all go into the Captain's house, and the first act ends.

ACT TWO

PEDROLINO	Pedrolino enters and says he will persuade Isabella to do as he tells her. He has been given some jewels and plans to frustrate old Pantalone. He calls Isabella.

ISABELLA   Isabella comes out, and Pedrolino places her at the door, telling her that she is not to let anyone in—not even the master. She promises to obey, and Pedrolino leaves. She speaks of her love, Oratio.

PANTALONE   Just then, Pantalone enters with the jewels he has taken from Arlecchino, and seeing Isabella, he asks her what she is doing in the house. She says she is a guest and names the master.

ARLECCHINO   At that moment, Arlecchino arrives, announcing himself as the master, Pantalone; he then attacks Pantalone and takes the jewels from him, calling him thief and forger. Isabella and Arlecchino abuse Pantalone and go into the house. Mocked, Pantalone says he will go to court and leaves.

THE DOCTOR   The doctor enters and announces that he does not want Flaminia any more, but instead he wants Ardelia.

ORATIO   Thereupon, Oratio enters and is immediately recognized by his father, who scolds him for abandoning his studies. Oratio says he is in love with Flaminia and, in turn, scolds his father for wanting to marry at his old age. Enraged, the Doctor curses him, and Oratio exits.

FRANCESCHINA   Just then, Franceschina enters and argues with the doctor, saying that her mistress, Flaminia, will be the wife of his son, Oratio; and with that she goes into the house, leaving the furious doctor.

PANTALONE
PEDROLINO   At that moment, Pantalone enters with Pedrolino, complaining of the woman they found in the house. They offer the doctor their best wishes on his marriage, but the doctor thinks they are making fun of him. Pantalone speaks to him of his daughter, to which the doctor replies that he knows nothing of her. Pantalone turns to Pedrolino, who shows him the ring given as a token to Oratio, the man, he explains, who has taken Ardelia away. Enraged, the Doctor strikes Pedrolino, who runs off with the doctor chasing after him. Pantalone pursues them up the street.

CAPT. SPAVENTO   The Captain enters to tell Pantalone that he has his daughter in his possession; he knocks.

ARLECCHINO   Arlecchino comes out, and the Captain wonders at seeing him. Then the Captain asks after Pantalone. When Arlecchino replies that he does not know him, the Captain mentions Oratio's name, and Arlecchino asks if he means Oratio of Pavia. The Captain replies that he does, and Arlecchino calls Isabella.

ISABELLA   Isabella comes out and is told that the Captain knows Oratio. She talks to him, telling him the story of her love. The Captain promises to help; he will put her in his house with his wife while he goes to find Oratio.

PEDROLINO

At that moment, Pedrolino enters and threatens Isabella for disobeying. The Captain tells him that she is Oratio's, and they finally come to an agreement. Pedrolino goes into the house to get the jewels, and when he returns, they all go into Pantalone's house, the Captain thanking Pedrolino, who remains.

PANTALONE

Thereupon, Pantalone enters, complaining that the doctor has lost his mind. He sees Pedrolino and asks him who all the people are in his house. Pedrolino insists there is no one. Pantalone goes into the house and then returns. Pedrolino tells him he is mad. Pantalone says he saw a woman; Pedrolino says there is no one. Pantalone insists that there is and then cries out, "Is it possible that I saw no one?"

CAPT. SPAVENTO

Just then, the Captain comes out saying, "I have seen her." Pantalone threatens Pedrolino, and they speak at cross purposes. When Pantalone finally hears the Captain name his daughter, Ardelia, he threatens them all and goes off to seek justice. Pedrolino holds his peace, and all exit as the second act ends.

ACT THREE

PEDROLINO

Pedrolino enters, saying that Pantalone has gone for the police.

FRANCESCHINA

At that, Franceschina enters to find Oratio for Flaminia. She sees Pedrolino, and together they speak of their love. Then he tells her that he will take Oratio, dressed as a woman, to Flaminia tonight so they can have their pleasure together.

ARLECCHINO

Arlecchino, who has been hidden all this time, says he has heard all and that he is going to play a trick; he hides again. Franceschina exits and Pedrolino remains.

CASSANDRO

Then, Cassandro enters. He has heard that the old man who was with the Signor is a nobleman called Pantalone de Bisognosi; he sees Pedrolino and asks about Pantalone. Pedrolino replies that he knows him to be a great swindler whom the Chief of Police is after. He persuades Cassandro to give him his clothes to disguise himself, and he then puts Cassandro in Pantalone's house, telling him it is his own house and not to let anyone enter. Cassandro goes in, and Pedrolino, in Cassandro's clothes, goes off to Franceschina's.

ORATIO

Oratio enters, complaining that his father will be the death of him; he laments, calling on Flaminia and Franceschina.

ARLECCHINO	Just then, Arlecchino comes out so he can go for some candles. He hears all and hides, but he is discovered by Oratio. Arlecchino tells Oratio that that night his father will enjoy Flaminia. Oratio leaves in despair, and laughing, Arlecchino exits.
PANTALONE	Pantalone enters with a lighted lantern. He says he has called the police and knocks at his door.
CASSANDRO	From the window, Cassandro argues with Pantalone. He insists that he was placed in that house by the master. When Pantalone says that he himself is master, Cassandro calls him a liar and goes back into the house, and Pantalone goes to the police.
FLAVIO	Flavio, Cassandro's son, enters to look for his father, whom he has followed from Pavia.
FRANCESCHINA	Just then, Franceschina appears at the window watching for Oratio; she gives him a sign, saying, "Is it you? My mistress is waiting." Flavio, following her cue, decides to accept the adventure for the night.
PEDROLINO	At that, Pedrolino arrives and hides.
FRANCESCHINA	Franceschina comes out and leads Flavio, whom she thinks is Oratio, into the house. She then returns and takes Pedrolino into the house, telling her puzzled lover that Oratio is now in the house with Flaminia.
ARLECCHINO	Arlecchino now enters with candles, and saying that he has heard all, goes on into the house.
ORATIO	Oratio enters in despair.
ISABELLA	Just then, Isabella appears at her window. Speaking softly so that no one can hear, they quarrel about their love until finally, Oratio falls to the ground as if dead. Isabella remarks that his voice sounds like Oratio's, and she withdraws.
ARLECCHINO	Arlecchino comes out of the house without seeing Oratio fall; he becomes afraid, and calls out for help.
ISABELLA	At that, Isabella enters; seeing Oratio, she thinks he is dead and begins to cry.
CAPT. SPAVENTO	Thereupon, the Captain enters and also begins to cry.
ARDELIA	Then, Ardelia enters, and she too begins to weep. Oratio regains consciousness, and they all plead with him to marry Isabella. Then all but Arlecchino go into the house.
THE CHIEF OF POLICE POLICEMEN	At that moment, the Chief of Police enters with policemen, and he asks Arlecchino where he can find Pantalone's house. Arlecchino points out Flaminia's house instead. The police go in to catch their man, and Arlecchino bursts out laughing.

FLAVIO
THE DOCTOR

Just then, Flavio comes out in his nightshirt. The doctor asks him what he is doing in his house, so Flavio tells him what happened, adding that he has slept with Flaminia. The doctor, even more unhappy, says he is the son of a cuckold. Arlecchino calls him a liar. All threaten him, and the doctor cries out for help.

THE POLICEMEN
ORATIO
THE CAPTAIN
ARDELIA
ISABELLA

Oratio, the Captain, Ardelia, and Isabella come out of Flaminia's house with the police in the lead. Ardelia asks her father's forgiveness; Isabella asks her brother's forgiveness; and Oratio, his father's. All are satisfied, and the police go into Pantalone's house to lead out the others.

CASSANDRO

Cassandro comes out with the police, and he immediately recognizes his children, who run to embrace him. When Pantalone asks him who placed him in the house, he answers that it was Pedrolino. Arlecchino asks the police to empty out the house, and they go in and bring the others out.

PEDROLINO
FRANCESCHINA

In his nightshirt, Pedrolino comes out with Franceschina, and he confesses to everything. They forgive him; and here the story ends.

THE FAITHFUL PILGRIM LOVER *

ARGUMENT

*In the city of Milan lived a doctor whose daughter, Isabella, was
betrothed to a gentleman of the town named Flavio, who was
very much in love with Isabella. Having arranged the match and
informed his daughter of his plans, the doctor found her entirely
opposed to his desires, for Isabella hated Flavio, but only because
she was contrary and abhorred the idea of marriage and being
ruled by a husband. As she was not afraid to defy her father, she
decided to disguise herself and run away. Having carried out her
plan, she arrived in Genoa, where she became the servant of a
certain Signor Oratio, who was in love with a gentlewoman
named Flaminia. Flaminia, in turn, fell in love with Isabella, who
was disguised as a youth named Fabritio. Flaminia was told
laughingly by Fabritio that he scorned such things. Meanwhile,
Flavio had asked the doctor about his young daughter and learned
that she had run away; he followed her, disguised as a pilgrim,
and after many years he arrived in Genoa. He decided that the
best way to find out about her was to beg alms for the soul of
Isabella. Thus one day they met and recognized each other. Seeing
his fidelity and constancy, she changed her mind about him.
Meanwhile, the doctor also arrived in Genoa; after many unhappy events, he saw his daughter married to Flavio.*

CHARACTERS IN THE PLAY

Pantalone
Flaminia, his daughter
Franceschina, his servant

Oratio, a gentleman
Fabritio, his page, that is, Isabella

Captain Spavento
Pedrolino, his servant

* See Appendix p. 399.

Pilgrim, that is, Flavio
Arlecchino, his servant

The Doctor
Isabella, his daughter

Policemen

PROPERTIES

Pilgrim's costume
Beggar's costume
Many lanterns

ACT ONE

CITY OF GENOA

ORATIO FABRITIO	Oratio enters, telling Fabritio, his servant, how much he loves Flaminia. Fabritio tries to talk him out of it by telling him how many have come to grief because of Love; after a lengthy discourse, they go off.
CAPT. SPAVENTO PEDROLINO	Captain Spavento enters, telling Pedrolino, his servant, how much he loves Flaminia. Pedrolino urges the Captain to pursue his love. The Captain is uncertain about pursuing her, afraid of being caught chasing after Love, but Pedrolino tells him of all the famous men of arms who have loved and served Love. Then they leave and go off up the street.
PANTALONE	Pantalone enters, telling Flaminia, his daughter, that he wants her to marry and be happy, and that she should tell him what she thinks. She says she wants an educated man; Pantalone tells her he wants her to marry a military man. They have a long talk on various professions; then they call Franceschina.
FRANCESCHINA	Franceschina comes out, and they ask her opinion as to whom Flaminia should marry. She sides with Pantalone, who finally suggests that they leave it up to the first one who passes; all agree, and they wait.
PEDROLINO	At that moment Pedrolino arrives and is made to be judge of the two professions; he decides that every woman should marry a military man, not an educated man. Pantalone is happy at this, and leaves with Pedrolino. Flaminia complains to Franceschina and sends her into the house while she remains, and once alone, she speaks of her love for Oratio.

ORATIO
FABRITIO

Just then, Oratio and Fabritio enter. Oratio sees Flaminia, greets her, and then hears from her that her father has decided to marry her to a military man; they speak of their love. Fabritio begins to laugh, and when Oratio scolds him, he tells Oratio that Flaminia does not love him but simply pretends to, and he will prove it. Oratio, to remove all doubt, tells Flaminia that he has only pretended to love her. Flaminia quarrels with him and calls him a false and traitorous lover, until finally, she bursts into tears and goes into the house. Sorry for what he has said, Oratio threatens Fabritio, and scorning him, goes off. Fabritio laughingly speaks of the misery of lovers.

ARLECCHINO

Then, Arlecchino enters, dressed as a rogue. He calls Fabritio a liar and runs off. Fabritio continues with his comments on love's miseries. Arlecchino reappears and again calls him a liar and runs. Fabritio draws his sword and chases him, and the first act ends.

ACT TWO

CAPT. SPAVENTO
PEDROLINO

The Captain and Pedrolino enter. Pedrolino tells the Captain all that happened between Pantalone and Flaminia.

PANTALONE

Just then Pantalone arrives. Seeing him, Pedrolino tells the Captain not to choose Flaminia for a wife, and that if he wishes to marry, he ought to marry the Queen, for that way he will be rich. Pantalone hides, but when the Captain tells Pedrolino that the King of Morocco sent the Captain a letter offering his daughter in marriage, Pantalone comes out of hiding to implore him to marry Flaminia. Pedrolino promises that the Captain will marry her, and the agreement is made. Pantalone goes to give orders to prepare the wedding banquet. Pedrolino tells the Captain he knows that he made up the story of the letter to make Pantalone believe he is an important person, so he would agree to his marrying Flaminia.

FRANCESCHINA

At that, Franceschina arrives. Pedrolino tells her what has taken place between Pantalone and the Captain.

ARLECCHINO

Thereupon, Arlecchino enters and hides to hear what they say. When Franceschina tells the Captain that Flaminia loves Oratio, who lives in that city, and it is impossible for the Captain to marry her, the Captain says he will kill Oratio. Then he sees Arlecchino and threatens him, making a great deal of noise. Franceschina goes off, and the frightened Arlecchino exits.

ORATIO
FABRITIO

Oratio enters, arguing with Fabritio. The Captain and Pedrolino leave, and Oratio, after denouncing Fabritio as the cause of his ruin, speaks eloquently under Flaminia's window.

ARLECCHINO

Arlecchino enters, still afraid; he asks them for alms for the soul of Isabella Aretusi, but Oratio drives him off. Fabritio wonders about it, and again, Arlecchino begs from Oratio, who drives him away again, shouting his own name. Hearing the name, Arlecchino tells Oratio that if he gives him alms, he in turn will reveal to Oratio the name of a person who wants to kill him. Oratio exits with Arlecchino, and Fabritio remains, puzzling about what the beggar had said.

A PILGRIM

Just then, a pilgrim enters and asks for alms for the soul of Isabella Aretusi. When Fabritio asks him about this Isabella of whom he speaks, the pilgrim tells the story of his love for Isabella. Believing her dead, he asks alms for her soul. Fabritio recognizes him as Flavio in disguise, and giving him alms, asks the identity of the other man who asks alms for Isabella. The pilgrim replies that the other man is a servant who did not want to desert him. Fabritio tells him that he can find news of Isabella very easily. The pilgrim is happy to hear the good news.

ORATIO

Oratio enters, very troubled, takes Fabritio by the arm, and goes off with him. Disappointed by the sudden departure of Fabritio, the pilgrim exits.

ARLECCHINO

Arlecchino enters, saying that the gentleman gave him much money to show him the man who wants to kill him; then, concluding that he will never find his mistress, he decides to become Oratio's servant, and he pretends to look for Oratio's house. Wondering who lives there, he knocks at Flaminia's door.

FLAMINIA

Flaminia comes out, and Arlecchino informs her that he has saved her lover, Oratio, from the Captain who wanted to kill him. Arlecchino assures her that the Captain will not succeed. She agrees, but she says Franceschina is watching her. Knowing that she loves Oratio, he has come to take her to see him.

FRANCESCHINA

Franceschina is watching.

PANTALONE

Just then, Flaminia's father, Pantalone, enters, pleased about the match with the Captain. Arlecchino asks him for alms, and Pantalone gives him some money and sends him into Flaminia's house.

PEDROLINO

Pedrolino enters and tells Pantalone that his daughter is dishonored and Franceschina has heard that the coming night she plans to run off with her lover. Pantalone calls Franceschina.

FRANCESCHINA

Franceschina comes out to confirm all, and she tells Pantalone that it is Oratio with whom Flaminia is going to run off. The enraged Pantalone calls Flaminia.

FLAMINIA
Flaminia enters and is scolded by her father, but she boldly tells him she does not want to marry the Captain. Angrily, he orders her into the house and takes the others to court with him as witnesses.

FABRITIO
Fabritio enters, tells his story, and speaks on the power of Love; he begs for victory and praises his lover.

THE PILGRIM
Just then, the pilgrim arrives. To assure herself of his love, Fabritio says Isabella is dead. Flavio almost goes out of his mind; he swears that he is going to kill himself and draws his sword from the scabbard.

ARLECCHINO
At that moment, Arlecchino enters and jumps on him.

THE POLICE
Thereupon, the police enter, and thinking they are fighting, try to arrest them. All run off, and here the second act ends.

ACT THREE

ARLECCHINO
Arlecchino enters, crying, because he fears his master is dead.

FLAMINIA
Just then, Flaminia enters and asks why he is weeping, and Arlecchino tells her that he is weeping for the death of the most faithful lover in the world. Thinking he means Oratio, she begins to cry too, and Arlecchino exits, still in tears.

PANTALONE
Pantalone now enters, sees her, and scolds her. She tells him that his stubbornness is the cause of Oratio's death.

PEDROLINO
Thereupon, Pedrolino enters and hears the accusation and Flaminia's angry threat that the Captain's servant will pay dearly. With that she goes into the house, leaving Pantalone to wonder what she meant. Pedrolino says he knows nothing about it.

FABRITIO
At that moment, Fabritio enters and says to Pantalone: "Because of your bad judgment, you have caused a death. But do not fear because you will also die—you who have been cruel—you will die the father of a loved one who will reveal all, and the servant who has proved unfaithful will also die." Enraged, he exits, leaving Pantalone and Pedrolino grief-stricken.

CAPT. SPAVENTO
Then, the Captain arrives. They ask him if he knows anything of the death of Oratio. Thinking he actually is dead, the Captain cries out, "The Captain has killed him!"

ARLECCHINO
Just then, Arlecchino enters and calls him a liar. The Captain draws his sword, and Arlecchino runs off with the Captain at his heels. Pantalone and Pedrolino chase after them.

THE DOCTOR	The doctor, Isabella's father, enters disguised as Fabritio and tells his story.
THE PILGRIM	The pilgrim enters, weeping over the death of Isabella, whom he calls by name. The doctor identifies himself, and after each has told the other all he knows, the grief-stricken doctor falls to the ground as if dead. The pilgrim grieves.
FABRITIO	At that, Fabritio enters. When he sees the pilgrim alive, he rejoices. Then, seeing his father lying as if dead, he begins to weep, whereupon the doctor regains consciousness. Fabritio falls to his knees before him, begging forgiveness and revealing himself to be Isabella. As the doctor embraces her, the pilgrim reveals himself to be Flavio, and all rejoice.
ARLECCHINO	Hearing all this rejoicing, Arlecchino enters and joins them in rejoicing, and all go into Oratio's house.
FLAMINIA	As they exit, Flaminia enters, crying that she wants to die because of Oratio's death.
FRANCESCHINA	At that moment, Franceschina comes out to console her.
ORATIO	Thereupon, Oratio arrives, saying he has given orders to kill the Captain, and now, seeing Flaminia, he embraces her, assuring her that he really is alive.
PEDROLINO	Pedrolino now enters, but seeing Oratio, he is frightened and runs off, yelling for the Captain.
PANTALONE	Pantalone arrives. He is frightened at the sight of Oratio but is assured that he is alive. Then he is told that Flaminia wants to marry Oratio. Pantalone says he does not want to be forced to fight Oratio, to which Oratio replies that he does not want to have to fight Pantalone.
CAPT. SPAVENTO PEDROLINO	Just then, the Captain arrives and moves between Pantalone and Oratio. When Pantalone says he wants Flaminia to marry the Captain, Oratio draws his sword on him, and without a fuss, the Captain and Pantalone yield.
FABRITIO THE DOCTOR PILGRIM ARLECCHINO	At that, Fabritio enters, and to his amazement, reveals herself to Oratio as a woman, and the pilgrim reveals himself as her lover. They all embrace one another. Arlecchino asks for Franceschina, but Pedrolino challenges him, replying that he will have to win her in a fight. Arlecchino quickly gives her up, and Pantalone does the same. The wedding is held, and here the comedy ends.

The Fifteenth Day

THE TRIALS OF ISABELLA *

ARGUMENT

*In the city of Venice lived a gentleman of great fortune named
Pantalone, who lived with his daughter, Flaminia. While he was
away from home attending to some business, bad fortune descended upon him and made his life miserable in the form of a
certain Captain Spavento, brother of one Fabritio, both of whom
were noble and rich and in love with Flaminia. They had begun
to stop often under her window and thus became a great nuisance
to her father. Finally, her father told the young men not to
compromise his honor and publicly ordered them to go home and
not bother his daughter again. The young men not only laughed
at him and paid no attention to the old man, but they came more
and more often. Although they were also warned by others, the
young men ignored everyone, especially the Captain, who saw
from the beginning that the young woman loved him. To put a
stop to the trouble, Pantalone put his affairs in order and then put
his daughter in the charge of Flavio and Pedrolino, his servants,
with these instructions: "To free myself of the shame forced on
me by the Captain and his brother, I have decided to fight and to
kill them; I will go to Rome until things quiet down, or I will
visit my friend, the doctor. When you see that things have
reached a bad state, you will come to Rome with Flaminia." After
giving these commands, the old man, with the help of some
ruffians, attacked the brothers and left them for dead. Then he left
for Rome. Soon after, the servants followed him. After they
recovered, the brothers determined to avenge themselves—each
on his own, not knowing of the other's plan. What followed is
revealed in the play.*

CHARACTERS IN THE PLAY

Pantalone
Flaminia, his daughter

* See Appendix p. 400.

Flavio, a dealer (agent)
Pedrolino, his servant

Captain Spavento
Fabritio, his brother
Arlecchino, his servant

The Doctor
Oratio, his son
Franceschina, his servant

Flavia, a noblewoman, by herself

PROPERTIES

A felt hat
A stick
A faggot for Pantalone
Two loaves of bread
A piece of cheese
A glass of wine
A dish with seven fried cakes
Material to make a bundle

ACT ONE

ROME

PANTALONE

Pantalone enters with a pack and stick. He is glad to have arrived in Rome, where now, pretending to beg alms, he knocks at all the doors.

FRANCESCHINA

Finally, Franceschina answers her door and gives him alms. When Pantalone asks for the doctor's house, Franceschina says that it is this very one.

ORATIO

Just then, Oratio, the doctor's son, enters and learns that he is Pantalone; he embraces him as a friend of his father, and they go into the house.

PEDROLINO

Pedrolino, Pantalone's servant, enters next; he is in beggar's clothes, asking for alms in a high-pitched voice.

FLAVIA

Flavia throws him a loaf of bread from her window, and he starts eating it.

ORATIO

Oratio comes out of the house to find his father. Seeing Flavia, he greets her, and they speak amorously. Pedrolino interrupts them repeatedly to request alms from Oratio, who finally calls Franceschina.

FRANCESCHINA	Franceschina comes out, and after being ordered to get Pedrolino something to eat, she goes back into the house. As Oratio returns to talk with Flavia, proposing they enjoy each other, Pedrolino comes between them, offering to serve them.
FRANCESCHINA	Franceschina comes out with a dish of food and a glass of wine.
CAPT. SPAVENTO	At that, Captain Spavento enters dressed as a beggar; he asks for his share, eats and drinks at his ease without speaking to anyone, and then leaves. Pedrolino sees that the Captain has eaten everything, and he begins to cry amid the laughter of the bystanders. As Flavia withdraws from the window, Oratio exits, and Franceschina takes Pedrolino into Flavia's house to give him something to drink.
THE DOCTOR CAPT. SPAVENTO	The doctor walks in now, followed by the Captain, who begs alms and offers to kill anyone at his bidding. The doctor agrees, and then knocks at the door.
PANTALONE	Pantalone appears at the window, recognizes the doctor, and comes out to embrace him. Then he tells the doctor his story, while the Captain, off to one side, hears part of it and leaves. Pantalone says he wants to hire someone to protect him because he has powerful enemies. The doctor promises to send him a man if he thinks of one. Pantalone goes into the house, and the doctor goes to find a bodyguard.
PEDROLINO	Then, Pedrolino comes out of Flavia's house, eating; he complains, however, that the wine is bad and says that he is going to get something to drink at Franceschina's. The Doctor asks him what he wants in the house, to which Pedrolino replies that, in short, he is the master of the house, and repeats all that he has heard Oratio and Flavia say. Enraged, the doctor beats him, and Pedrolino runs up the street.
FLAVIA	From the window Flavia has heard all, and she is despondent.
ORATIO SERVANT	Oratio enters with a servant, who is carrying a suit of man's clothes, and sees Flavia. When she comes out to tell what she heard, Oratio gives her the clothes to put on so that they can go off as arranged. As she goes into the house to dress, Oratio sends his servant away and then goes into his house.
CAPT. SPAVENTO	Hidden in the shadows, the Captain has heard all, and now he plots to take the clothes given to Flavia.
ARLECCHINO	Just then, Arlecchino, the Captain's servant, enters dressed as a beggar. They embrace, and after discussing their narrow escape, they complain of how they are dying of hunger. Suddenly they see the doctor coming, and they hide.

THE DOCTOR	The doctor enters with a dish of seven fried cakes, which he has received from a client. He begins to count and divide them, saying, "Three for me, two for the stranger, and two for my son." Then, saying that the servant will be angry if she does not get one, he divides them again in this way, saying, "Three for me, two for the stranger, one for my son, and the other for the servant." Then he reconsiders, saying that it is not a good idea to make the servant equal to the son. Arlecchino makes a sign to the Captain, who now comes up behind the doctor. Arlecchino comes out and kneels, begging for alms, saying he was forced to leave home. The doctor has him tell the story of his disgrace, and Arlecchino begins: "Sir, my father had a guest for breakfast one morning; at breakfast, much food was brought to the table, including a dish with seven fried cakes. Being very fond of all kinds of pastry, I was contemplating how delicious they looked with their golden brown crusts dripping with honey when, at that moment, the guest stretched out his hand, took one, and ate it." Here, the Captain, who is behind the doctor, reaches out, takes one, and eats it at once. One by one, the moment Arlecchino says the number of the fried cake, it is taken and eaten by the Captain, Arlecchino saying all the time, "I watched with fascination the actions of this greedy guest. Finally, seeing the last one and hoping to take it, I saw even that one eaten; then I took out my sword and striking a blow, cried, 'God give you joy!' " Then he leaves with the Captain, and the doctor, realizing that he has been tricked, says he is going to feed the guest on what is left and goes into the house, and here the first act ends.

ACT TWO

FLAMINIA	Flaminia enters, wearing the ragged clothes left behind by Flavio, her servant, lamenting the disgrace of her father, of her lover, and of herself.
FLAVIO	Flavio, also dressed in ragged clothes, follows to console her, saying that there is hope of finding Pedrolino and Pantalone.
THE DOCTOR ORATIO	Just then, the doctor enters, and referring to Pedrolino, argues with Oratio because of what he said about the poor. When Oratio denies it, Flavio and Flaminia step forward to beg alms; the doctor, suddenly becoming enamored of Flaminia, sends Oratio away and then embraces the beggars and calls his servant.
FRANCESCHINA	As Franceschina enters, the doctor gives her orders to entertain the two beggars and then confesses that he has a mind to enjoy

the beggar woman. Franceschina laughs, saying she knows from experience that he is not a very good lover.

CAPT. SPAVENTO — At that, the Captain enters, and seeing Flaminia, stops to admire her. Flavio, Franceschina, and the doctor think he is the ghost of the Captain, and run off up the street in fright. The Captain takes Flaminia away up the street.

PEDROLINO — Pedrolino enters with Flavio, who tells him that he just saw the
FLAVIO — Captain. Pedrolino tells him that it is impossible because he saw him dead in Venice.

ARLECCHINO — Thereupon, Arlecchino arrives. They recognize one another, embrace, and begin to speak of their masters.

CAPT. SPAVENTO — The Captain arrives and joins Flavio and Pedrolino, who run off frightened. The Captain tells Arlecchino that he has Flaminia. Taking him aside, he says that he has much to tell him; then he knocks on Flaminia's door.

FLAVIA — Flavia comes out and learns that he is a friend of Oratio, and that they have found a way to escape; he has her give him a suit and two of her dresses, all by order of Oratio, and says soon they will come for her.

PEDROLINO — Just then, Pedrolino arrives with Flavio; when they see the Captain, they drop to their knees and beg his forgiveness; he says he does not want to offend them because he has Flaminia in his possession, but then, angered, he says he has killed Pantalone and goes, leaving Flavio and Pedrolino in tears at the death of their master.

PANTALONE — At that moment, Pantalone appears at the window, calling in a low voice, first Flavio and then Pedrolino; when they see him at the window, the terrified pair think he is a ghost and run off up the street. Pantalone goes back in.

THE DOCTOR — The doctor enters saying that he has not found one soldier in any of the streets who can act as a bodyguard; then he comments that he has seen someone carry off a woman—not knowing that it was Flaminia.

PEDROLINO — Pedrolino enters now and walks back and forth in front of the house several times, all the time watching the window where he saw Pantalone; finally he leaves. The doctor becomes suspicious.

ARLECCHINO — Then, Arlecchino enters, does the same, and leaves. The doctor becomes even more suspicious.

CAPT. SPAVENTO | Just then, the Captain enters, in disguise. The doctor wonders about him, but then tells him that Pantalone needs someone to guard him against his enemies. Hearing the name of Pantalone, the Captain tells the doctor that Pantalone's enemy is in Rome, and for that reason, advises that he get out into the country for a few days, offering to accompany him. When the doctor says he will tell Pantalone, the Captain leaves. The doctor calls Pantalone and knocks at the door.

PANTALONE | Pantalone comes out, and hearing from the doctor that the soldier has agreed to accompany him to the country, he gives the doctor his golden neckchain to sell and goes back into the house alone.

PEDROLINO
FLAVIO
ARLECCHINO | Pedrolino arrives with Flavio and Arlecchino, and seeing the neckchain, he makes plans to steal it; he orders Flavio and Arlecchino to hide. Then he steps up to the doctor and tells him who he is. The doctor recognizes him and learns that Pedrolino has stolen a bundle of silk worth 500 scudi from some mule drivers, and he wants to sell it to go back to his province; he takes the bundle and puts it in the middle of the stage.

FLAVIO | Thereupon, Flavio comes forth, threatening Pedrolino and calling him a thief for having stolen his bundle. He demands a hundred scudi, or else he will have him put in prison. The doctor comes between them, and handing over the chain to Pedrolino to sell, he gives Flavio 100 scudi. As they exit, the doctor remains, guarding the bundle, saying that he is going to cheat the thief by putting it in his house; then he sees the bundle move.

ARLECCHINO | At that moment, Arlecchino jumps out of the bundle. The frightened doctor runs off, and Arlecchino bursts out laughing and then exits as the second act ends.

ACT THREE

FLAMINIA | Flaminia enters, dressed in Flavia's clothes, which the Captain gave her, and complains that he left her alone at the inn.

ARLECCHINO | Arlecchino comes on next and recognizes her. She confesses that she has been the cause of the death of Fabritio, the Captain's brother. To her questions about the Captain himself, Arlecchino answers that he thinks he is in love with a woman who gave him the dresses which she wears, and he is delighted when Flaminia believes him and begins to weep.

ORATIO | Just then, Oratio enters, and seeing her dress, but not her face, runs to embrace her, saying, "Flavia, my soul!" She faints in

Oratio's arms, and Arlecchino exits, laughing at the amazed Oratio.

FLAVIA

Flavia enters now, and seeing Flaminia in Oratio's arms, and in Flavia's own clothes, she becomes jealous. Flaminia revives, saying, "Is this how you betray me, my handsome one?" Hearing that, Flavia disdains even scolding Oratio, and goes into the house without saying a word. The confused Oratio exits, leaving behind the weeping Flaminia.

PEDROLINO

Pedrolino enters, sees her dressed in other clothes, and taunts her. Finally he tells her he has a gold chain for her.

CAPT. SPAVENTO
ARLECCHINO

At that moment, the Captain enters with Arlecchino, who is telling him that he saw Flaminia in the arms of another man. The Captain says that such a thing is impossible, for Flaminia is his.

FLAVIA

Immediately after, Flavia enters, saying, "Sir, it is true. I myself saw her in the arms of that traitor Oratio, acting wantonly." The Captain swears that he will take revenge on one or the other, to which Flavia replies with an offer of herself, and with amorous words, she walks off boldly.

FLAMINIA

Flaminia, who has seen the Captain speaking with Flavia and has heard the last amorous words, now comes forward and calls him a traitor; they begin a hot quarrel. Worked up to a fury, the Captain says he will kill Oratio and goes, leaving the tearful Flaminia.

THE DOCTOR

Then the doctor enters, recognizes her, and greets her with an amorous speech and the suggestion that he can give her a good time. Still weeping, she accepts, and the doctor calls his servant.

FRANCESCHINA

Franceschina comes out. The doctor tells her about the young woman and asks her to call for Pantalone, saying he wants to give him a good time.

PANTALONE

When Pantalone comes out, the doctor tells him that he wants to go with him to the country, adding that they will take along a fine wench. The doctor shows Flaminia to Pantalone who, in embracing her, discovers that she is his daughter. The doctor asks him how the girl looks to him.

FLAVIO

Thereupon, Flavio enters and embraces Pantalone. The doctor recognizes him and then asks him about the neckchain, and he replies that Pedrolino has it. Pantalone says it is safe there, and the doctor sends all of them into the house as he goes off to find his bodyguard.

ORATIO

Oratio enters, and chastising himself, calls himself by name. He looks up at Flavia's house and sighs, "Alas, my Flavia."

ARLECCHINO	Arlecchino, who has heard all, enters immediately and tells him that she is no longer his, but his master's, who is looking for Oratio to kill him. Oratio draws his sword, and Arlecchino runs off. Angry, Oratio knocks on Flavia's door.
FLAVIA	Flavia answers the door immediately and calls him a traitor. When he tries to explain, she refuses to listen to him. Oratio calls her faithless, and says that she gave a stranger the order to kill him, and for that reason, he is going to kill himself. He begins to weep.
PANTALONE	At that, Pantalone arrives. He tries to console Oratio, but he falls into deeper despair.
FLAMINIA	Flaminia comes out now and asks her father to explain what is going on. Flavia immediately turns on Oratio and says, "Ah, traitor, how can you deny it now. You have kept her in your own house!" Oratio asks Pantalone who the woman is. He replies that she is his daughter. Flaminia, seeing that the two lovers are embroiled in a misunderstanding, reveals all that happened to the Captain and asks her father's forgiveness. He forgives her, and Oratio and Flavia are reconciled.
PEDROLINO	At that, Pedrolino enters with the neckchain and embraces Pantalone, who now promises to arrange with the doctor that Flavia and Oratio marry. He sends everyone into the house to wait for him.
THE DOCTOR CAPT. SPAVENTO ARLECCHINO	The doctor enters, accompanied by the Captain and the disguised Arlecchino. Telling them to follow at a distance, he knocks at the door.
ALL	They all come out of the house, and the doctor wonders about Flavia. Pantalone requests that Oratio be married to Flavia, and the doctor agrees. The doctor recognizes Pedrolino; then all want to go out to the villa. But just then, the Captain, drawing his sword, reveals his identity to Pantalone, who is so frightened he drops to his knees. Although everyone pleads for Pantalone, the Captain says he is going to kill him to avenge the death of his brother Fabritio.
FABRITIO	At that moment, Fabritio, the Captain's brother, enters. To the wonder of all, he announces that he has been hiding all this time and knows all that has been going on. The brothers forgive Pantalone, and everyone is reconciled. Flaminia asks Pantalone to marry her to the Captain, and when he agrees, she tells the Captain of the mistake he had made. They marry, and the play ends.

THE MIRROR

ARGUMENT

There was in Naples, on business, a Venetian widower named Pantalone, who, while attending his affairs by himself, fell in love with a gentlewoman named Olympia and promised to marry her one day; she became pregnant and gave birth to a daughter, who was named Isabella. Meanwhile, Pantalone had to return to his own city and came to Rome, where he forgot his love and his promise to Olympia, and fell in love with a young woman named Flaminia. After some years, still living in Naples, Olympia decided to go to Rome to look for him; she came to Rome, where Pantalone heard she was looking for him. She took her daughter with her and dressed her as a manservant to work for her own father. He did not realize who she was, but her father was well known to her. What followed will be revealed in the play.

CHARACTERS IN THE PLAY

Pantalone, a Venetian
Flavio, his son
Fabritio, a page, then Isabella, his daughter
Arlecchino, his servant

Laura, a widow
Flaminia, her daughter-in-law
Oratio, her son
Pedrolino, friend of the family

Doctor Gratiano

Captain Spavento
Companions

Two Ghosts

Many Policemen

PROPERTIES

Two flasks of wine
A large mirror which stands on its own feet
A stool
Two low chairs
Identical rings

ACT ONE

ROME

FLAVIO
FABRITIO
ARLECCHINO

Flavio enters with a dagger, chasing Fabritio, who enters with a bat, chasing Arlecchino and calling him traitor. Flavio comes between them, and the angry Fabritio, saying that he is going to tell Pantalone they planned to put him to sleep, exits alone, leaving the pair sad and dejected. Flavio laments the fact that his father has removed him from the management of his affairs, and then he speaks of his love for Flaminia. Arlecchino promises to help him, and Flavio has him knock at Flaminia's door.

FLAMINIA

Flaminia comes out and she tells Flavio that her stepmother wants to marry her to Oratio, her stepmother's son, so that the dowry can remain within the family; they agree to elope and plan to take the diamond from the hand of Pantalone, Flavio's father. As Flaminia goes into the house, Flavio and Arlecchino go off to the goldsmith's to find a ring like his father's with a fake diamond.

ORATIO
PEDROLINO

Oratio enters with Pedrolino; he tells Pedrolino that he is sad because Laura, his mother, wants to marry him to Flaminia, and he knows that his friend Flavio is in love with her, and he does not want to betray his friend. He tells Pedrolino he wants him to help set things straight. As Oratio leaves, Pedrolino promises to do everything he can and goes off to find Flavio.

PANTALONE
DR. GRATIANO

Pantalone and Gratiano now enter. Pantalone wants to take a wife, and urging Gartiano to marry Laura, says he will take Flaminia. When Gratiano says he wants the daughter and not the mother, each discovers the other to be a rival for the love of Flaminia, and they come to blows.

CAPT. SPAVENTO	At that, the Captain, Pantalone's friend, comes between them. Gratiano leaves, and Pantalone tells the Captain he has relieved his son Flavio of the management of his affairs and that he himself wants to marry Flaminia. The Captain then offers to marry Laura, and Pantalone shows him the diamond which is to be Flaminia's wedding ring. They go to find Pedrolino, who is part magician, to help them.
FLAVIO ORATIO	Flavio enters, telling his friend that he is much obliged to him for refusing to marry Flaminia for the sake of their friendship and thanks him and offers to do as much for Oratio. Just then, hearing people coming, they hide.
LAURA FLAMINIA	Laura enters, asking Flaminia to take Oratio, her son, for a husband. Flaminia replies that she is satisfied if he wants her; they see the two young men.
CAPT. SPAVENTO	Now the Captain enters, walks around the two women, then goes to stand at a distance. When Laura sends Flaminia into the house, she stays to have some fun with the Captain; they play a love scene, and finally, Laura tells him to find Pedrolino, who will tell him what he must do. The Captain leaves, and Laura says she is going to play a trick on the Captain.
PEDROLINO	Just then, Pedrolino arrives, and she asks him to play a trick on the Captain. Pedrolino agrees and explains that he is going to play a trick on Pantalone also, and for that reason, some ghosts will appear; she goes into the house and Pedrolino exits.
FLAVIO FABRITIO	Flavio and Fabritio enter, and Flavio asks Fabritio not to say anything to his father about the whole matter. Fabritio replies that he is as much her father as his and reveals herself to be a woman, the daughter of Pantalone and Olympia Belmonti; she tells him that Olympia had exchanged marriage vows with Pantalone in Naples, but then, realizing Pantalone had betrayed her, Olympia took her daughter and came to Rome where she had Isabella play a servant in Pantalone's house. Flavio embraces her and accepts her as his sister. She tells him where their mother, Olympia, is. When Fabritio then reveals that she is in love with Oratio, and she would like to marry him, Flavio promises to help her, telling her to go into the house to dress herself in woman's clothes. She goes in.
PANTALONE ARLECCHINO	Pantalone enters, asking Arlecchino what he was doing at the goldsmith's. Arlecchino excuses himself to go over to show the hidden rings to Flavio. Seeing his son, Pantalone tells him he is going to marry Flaminia, but Flavio scolds him and leaves in anger. Pantalone and Arlecchino now knock at Flaminia's door.

FLAMINIA Flaminia comes out, loudly announcing to Pantalone that she is not going to marry him. When Pantalone says she does not realize the power of Pedrolino's magic, she laughs and goes into the house, leaving Pantalone to grumble that he will be the one to do the laughing when he has given commands to Pedrolino.

PEDROLINO Pedrolino enters, telling Gratiano that he is to bring a flask of
DR. GRATIANO wine, and the first person he meets with a flask of wine like his will be Flaminia; by his magic, she has taken the form of a person who loves her, and by drinking a little at a time, she will be transformed back into Flaminia. He then tells Gratiano to do it immediately. Gratiano exits.

PANTALONE Pantalone comes out with a flask of wine according to Pedrolino's commands. Pedrolino silently makes conjuring gestures and then, hearing Gratiano coming, he exits, leaving Pantalone alone.

DR. GRATIANO Gratiano now comes out of his house with a flask of wine. When he sees Pantalone, he tells him he is Flaminia transformed, and Pantalone says that it is true. They begin to drink to transform the other into Flaminia. They complain of the delayed reaction.

GHOSTS Just then, ghosts come out of the house, take away their flasks, beat them soundly, and everybody runs off up the street as the first act ends.

ACT TWO

FLAVIO Flavio comes out of the house with the fake diamond rings
ARLECCHINO similar to Pantalone's; he gives one to Arlecchino and keeps the other. Together they arrange to give a sleeping drug to his father and then to take off the genuine ring and replace it with a fake one. Then saying that he has spoken to his mother-in-law, who has given her permission for him to give his sister in marriage to anyone he pleases, he tells Arlecchino that he is going to give her to Oratio and leaves. Arlecchino thinks he is crazy, saying that he knows that Flavio has no sisters.

ORATIO Thereupon, Oratio enters, telling Laura he is not going to marry
LAURA Flaminia. The angry Laura lectures him, giving him a piece of her mind, and as Oratio leaves, she swears that she will go to her lawyer. When Arlecchino tells her that Oratio does not want Flaminia because he is going to marry Flavio's sister, she is even more enraged, thinking for sure that Pantalone has daughters.

PANTALONE Pantalone now arrives, complaining of the devilish beating, and Laura immediately reproaches him because he wants to marry his daughter to Oratio. Pantalone laughs; denying he has any daughters, he orders Arlecchino to get some wine to make a punch and invites Laura to have a drink. Enraged, she goes to find her lawyer. Pantalone says he must refresh himself, being parched after so much chasing about, and he goes into the house.

PEDROLINO   Pedrolino enters, laughing about the trick he played on the old men.

CAPT. SPAVENTO   At that moment, the Captain enters and tells Pedrolino that Laura has sent for him to give him certain instructions. Pedrolino pretends to understand it all; then he asks the Captain if he is at all talented, because Laura likes men who are talented. He sends him to dress himself up and to get a companion who plays, sings, and dances, or who has some talent, and to return in about half an hour with him. When the Captain leaves, Pedrolino says that if possible, he is going to send him off as a galley slave.

ORATIO   Then, Oratio enters and says he wants to make peace with his mother. When he appeals to Pedrolino for help, Pedrolino promises to help him and then, seeing Laura coming, tells him to hide.

LAURA   Laura now enters, complaining that she has not found a notary. Pedrolino tells her that he has seen her son weeping, sorry for having made her angry; he is now resolved to marry Flaminia to please her. Oratio comes out of his hiding place, weeping, and she gives him her blessing and goes into the house. Oratio marvels that Pedrolino made her behave in that way, and Pedrolino tells him to think no more about it, but to go find Flavio.

FABRITIO   Fabritio enters, dressed in woman's clothes, pretending to weep. His mother has driven him out of the house, he says, whereupon Pedrolino shows pity for him.

LAURA   At that, Laura and Flaminia come out, happy because Oratio is
FLAMINIA   going to marry Flaminia. Fabritio, still pretending to be a woman, drops to his knees and tells of his mother's anger and the wrong she had done him by driving him from the house. The women say they will take him into the house to right the wrong done him. Pedrolino tells them that some talented person will be coming to see them. The women go into the house, and Pedrolino leaves to play a trick on the Captain.

FLAVIO   Flavio returns to find out what Arlecchino has done.

ARLECCHINO   Then Arlecchino enters and happily tells Flavio that he has given the sleeping potion to Pantalone when he demanded something to drink on his return home, and he has exchanged the diamonds;

he gives the real diamond to Flavio. Just then they hear Pantalone coming, and Flavio leaves.

PANTALONE

Pantalone enters and tells Arlecchino he slept too long and asks him to take a look at his ring, explaining that it does not seem like the same one. Arlecchino blames it on his oversleeping.

DR. GRATIANO

At that moment, Gratiano enters and wrangles over Flaminia with Pantalone, and swearing at him, finally exits, leaving Pantalone furious at Pedrolino for having tricked him.

PEDROLINO

Now Pedrolino arrives. Pantalone threatens him, but Pedrolino explains that Gratiano has ruined everything by not knowing how to work the enchantment, and Pantalone is pacified. Pedrolino then asks for the ring so he can take care of some business, and Pantalone gives it to him.

CAPT. SPAVENTO
COMPANIONS

The Captain, dressed as a beggar, enters next with his companions, playing, dancing, and singing.

DR. GRATIANO
POLICE

Dr. Gratiano arrives, with the police. In a very clever move, Pedrolino puts the ring that Pantalone gave him in the Doctor's sleeve; then he comes forward and tells Pantalone that they are all thieves, Gratiano is the chief one, and he saw him steal a ring from Pantalone. On Pantalone's order, the Police grab Gratiano, search him, and find the ring. Then everyone jumps on the Doctor and beats him. When Gratiano appeals to Arlecchino and Pedrolino for help, they free him, and all go off as the second act ends.

ACT THREE

CAPT. SPAVENTO

The Captain enters, enraged at what happened.

PANTALONE

Then, Pantalone comes in. He taunts the Captain about his profession, saying that he learned it by rote; he tells him that Pedrolino tricked him. When Pantalone shows him the ring, the Captain tells him it is false, and together they go off to the jeweler's to find out.

ORATIO

Oratio now enters, saying that he has heard that Flavio wants to give him his sister for a wife, but he doesn't know who the girl is.

FABRITIO

Just then, Fabritio enters in woman's clothes and says she is Flavio's sister. Oratio accepts her for his wife, pledging his faith, and Fabritio goes into the house while Oratio leaves to find Flavio.

PEDROLINO	Pedrolino enters, laughing about the trick played on the Doctor.
FLAVIO	At that, Flavio arrives, and Pedrolino gives him the good ring, with which Flavio, in Pedrolino's name, is to marry Flaminia and then leave town with Arlecchino. Flavio exits.
FLAMINIA	Flaminia comes out, and Pedrolino tells her of Flavio's desire. He starts to put the ring on her finger.
ORATIO	At that moment, Oratio arrives, and he gives her the other ring, saying he wants to marry her.
LAURA	Thereupon, Laura enters, and thinking that Oratio marries her for himself, rejoices and sends him to invite the relatives. Oratio leaves, the women go into the house, and Pedrolino remains.
FLAVIO ARLECCHINO	Flavio now enters, and Pedrolino tells him of Oratio's betrayal, saying that he took the ring and married Flaminia himself. Enraged, Flavio goes to look for him, and all leave.
PANTALONE CAPT. SPAVENTO	Pantalone and the Captain return; they have found that the ring is false and the good one has been stolen. The Captain says that Laura has a secret method of finding stolen goods.
DR. GRATIANO	Gratiano arrives. When he learns about the ring, they all make peace and agree to call Laura.
LAURA	Laura comes out, and they ask her to help them find Pantalone's ring with her secret method. After making them pray, she has them bring a seat, a large mirror, and two low chairs. Putting the mirror on the seat, she calls the women out of the house.
FLAMINIA FABRITIO	Flaminia and Fabritio come out of the house and are made to sit down and look into the mirror. Flaminia says she sees the face of Pedrolino and tells all about the trick that Pedrolino played on the old men with the flasks of wine.
PEDROLINO	Just then, Pedrolino comes out of hiding and looks into the mirror. Flaminia says, "Look at him, look at him!" All look into the mirror. Pedrolino exits, laughing, and Laura has Fabritio look into the mirror. He says that he sees Arlecchino making soup for Pantalone, that he is putting a potion into it, and as Pantalone falls asleep, Arlecchino removes the ring from his finger, and putting another in its place, gives the original to Flavio.
ARLECCHINO	Arlecchino comes out of hiding now, and he too looks into the mirror. Fabritio says, "Look at him, look at him!" As they all look into the mirror, Arlecchino laughs and exits. Flaminia turns to look into the mirror, saying that she sees Pedrolino taking Pantalone's ring and hiding it in Gratiano's sleeve.

PEDROLINO
ARLECCHINO

Thereupon, Pedrolino and Arlecchino come forth, whirl in front of the mirror, and leave. Then Pantalone asks Fabritio what else he sees in the mirror. Fabritio says he sees a young man like Pantalone, in a city that looks like Naples, make love to a woman, enjoy her, and the young woman is left pregnant by him. Then he says he sees Pantalone leave for Rome and sees the young woman give birth to a daughter who, being grown up, is dressed as a boy and taken to Rome. Here she becomes a servant in her father's house. He sees the daughter reveal to Flavio that she is his sister, and sees her dressed as a woman and being ordered by her father to look into a mirror. Then Isabella turns and exclaims, "Father mine, I am she, and Olympia is my mother!" Pantalone, weeping for joy, embraces her and receives her as his daughter.

PEDROLINO
ARLECCHINO

At that, Pedrolino and Arlecchino enter and kneel, begging Pantalone's pardon for all the tricks they played. Pantalone pardons them.

FLAVIO
ORATIO

At that moment, Flavio and Oratio enter fighting, but all come between them. Oratio says he married Flaminia only for Flavio's sake, and thus they make peace. Oratio marries Fabritio, that is, Isabella, and Flavio marries Flaminia; and here the play ends.

The Seventeenth Day

THE TWIN CAPTAINS *

ARGUMENT

There lived in Rome a certain doctor who was of a noble and wealthy family. He had only one heir, a daughter named Isabella, whom he wished to marry to a certain Captain before he died. He believed the Captain would make her a good husband, but things turned out quite differently. At the time the Captain was born, a twin brother, who looked exactly like him, was also born. They could not be told apart. It happened that the Captain wished to visit his brother, whom he had not seen for a long time, so he left his wife in Rome and went to Naples to find him. In Naples his brother had also become a Captain. From there he went to Sicily, then to Malta, and for six years he did not return to Rome. Meanwhile, Isabella fell in love with a gentleman named Oratio. When the Captain, after his years of traveling, was unable to find his brother, he decided to return to Rome to find out if his wife remained faithful. On the day of his return, his brother whom he was seeking also arrived in Rome. Because of their remarkable resemblance, many things happened, which the comedy will reveal.

CHARACTERS IN THE PLAY

Pantalone, a Venetian
Flaminia, his daughter

Doctor Gratiano
Isabella, his daughter
Franceschina, his servant

Oratio, a gentleman

Pedrolino, owner of the inn

* See Appendix p. 400.

Captain Spavento
Flavio, his friend

The Stranger-Captain, twin brother of Captain Spavento
Arlecchino, his servant

PROPERTIES

A sign for the inn
A bat
Much bandage material

ACT ONE

THE CITY OF
ROME

ISABELLA Isabella enters with Franceschina, complaining to her servant that
FRANCESCHINA she is neither widowed nor married, for it is seven years since her
father, Gratiano, married her to a captain. After six months, she
says, the Captain left, saying he was going to Naples to find his
brother. From that time she has heard nothing of him. She has
become melancholy because of that, and because she has fallen in
love with a gentleman named Oratio. Franceschina commends her
love and praises Oratio, saying she knows him well.

FLAMINIA Just then, Flaminia, who has heard all, comes out and says,
"Signora Isabella, I advise you for your own good to put all
thoughts of Oratio out of your mind." When Franceschina scolds
her, Flaminia angrily calls her a slut, and after exchanging angry
words, they come to blows.

ORATIO At that, Oratio enters and forces them apart, showing tender
feeling for Isabella. When Flaminia angrily turns on Oratio and
gives him a tongue lashing, he reproves her; but she, only made
more angry, says to him, "Oh, traitor, so you leave me for a slut."
Franceschina calls her a liar and attacks her again.

PANTALONE Then Pantalone, Flaminia's father, arrives, and Flaminia tells him
she has been fighting with that crazy Isabella. Isabella responds
that Flaminia herself is crazy, and full of rage, she turns on
Flaminia, striking her repeatedly like a mad woman. All the
others standing about are dumbfounded. Finally, Flaminia escapes
into the house, and Isabella, nearly out of her mind, goes into her
house. Franceschina, as if possessed, also goes into the house. The

frightened Oratio goes off up the street, leaving only the thunder-struck Pantalone.

DR. GRATIANO   Gratiano, Isabella's father, enters, and Pantalone immediately tells him to go for a physician to cure his daughter, who has gone mad. Gratiano thinks he is joking, and tells him to mind his own business.

FRANCESCHINA   At that, Franceschina comes out and tells Gratiano that Isabella has smashed all the dishes, the glassware, and whatever was breakable in the house. Gratiano, desperate, goes into the house. Franceschina makes a face at Pantalone, and she goes into the house. Pantalone goes into his own house to find out from Flaminia the cause of all the trouble.

THE STRANGER-CAPTAIN ARLECCHINO   The Captain, a stranger, now enters with Arlecchino. He says he has come from Spain to find his brother, married to a woman in Rome these many years. They knock at the door of the inn.

PEDROLINO   Pedrolino, owner of the inn, comes out to welcome him, and the Captain asks him if he knows a captain who was married here in Rome. Pedrolino says no, and speaking of different things, they go into the house.

ORATIO   Oratio, who is in love with Flaminia, enters and says he is afraid she is jealous of Isabella.

FRANCESCHINA   At that, Franceschina comes out and tells Oratio that Isabella has gone mad for love of him, and he must come dressed as a physician and try to make her well again. Persuaded by the servant, Oratio promises to come as a physician and goes to dress himself. Franceschina says she is going to start trouble between the two women.

DR. GRATIANO   When Gratiano enters and asks Franceschina if she has gone to get a physician, she says she has sent for him, and Gratiano asks the cause of Isabella's madness. Franceschina says it comes from her mother and from being too long without a husband.

ORATIO   Now Oratio enters, dressed as a physician. Franceschina, recognizing him, tells Gratiano he is the physician. Gratiano begs him to help cure his daughter.

FLAMINIA   Then, Flaminia appears at her window and recognizes Oratio. She comes out, takes Gratiano aside, and tells all, calling Franceschina a slut. Oratio keeps his face muffled in his false beard to keep Flaminia from recognizing him, but Flaminia pulls it off and strikes him. Gratiano runs into the house, and Oratio runs off. Flaminia returns to her house, calling Franceschina dirty names.

Franceschina shouts back at her, "If that's where you itch, scratch it," and she goes off up the street. Here the first act ends.

ACT TWO

CAPT. SPAVENTO
FLAVIO

Captain Spavento enters, telling Flavio, his friend, the reason for his long stay away from the city. Then, taking him into his confidence, he asks him if he knows anything about his wife. Flavio says no.

ORATIO

Oratio enters, lamenting to himself over his love for Flaminia. "I know very well that you love me, but what can I do if Isabella is also in love with me?" The Captain Spavento and Flavio, standing in the shadows, hear all.

PEDROLINO

Pedrolino now comes out and asks Oratio if he knows to whom Isabella is married. Oratio replies that her husband is a captain who has been away for six years and that nobody has heard anything from him. Pedrolino comments that the Captain who is in his house is a sly fellow. Then he tells Oratio that the Captain has come, but he does not tell him he is staying in his house, and then adds that he does not know why he has not gone straight to his wife. "Perhaps he first wants to find out if his wife has been faithful," he says. Oratio wonders about that, asking Pedrolino where the Captain is. Pedrolino turns away, and seeing the stranger and thinking he is the same person as the captain in his house, says no more and goes. Oratio follows him. The Captain speaks to Flavio about the things they overheard and asks him to find out from Pedrolino what is going on. Flavio sends him into the house and goes after Pedrolino.

PANTALONE

Pantalone enters, desperate because he cannot discover from Flaminia the cause of the trouble. He goes to ask Franceschina.

FLAMINIA

Thereupon, Flaminia, having heard all from her window and suspecting Franceschina, comes out to tell Pantalone that she will reveal everything if he will not get angry. When Pantalone promises, she tells him of her love for Oratio and her jealousy of Isabella who, she says, also loves Oratio. Pantalone rails at her, and she, reminding him of his promise, goes back in.

FRANCESCHINA

Franceschina arrives. Pantalone questions her about Isabella; she tells him that Isabella loves Oratio and no longer thinks of the Captain, her husband.

ARLECCHINO

At that moment, Arlecchino, hidden, hears the name of the Captain, his master, and seeing them point to the house, wonders about it. Pantalone and Franceschina exit, talking about the situation. Arlecchino says he is going to buy some rose ointment for his master, and he leaves.

THE STRANGER-
CAPTAIN

The Captain, the stranger, enters. He is exhausted by his long ride.

FLAVIO

Then Flavio arrives; thinking the Captain is his friend, he tells him he has not found Pedrolino to talk to him about his plan. The Captain, puzzled because he has never seen Flavio before, says he does not know him, and vexed, he leaves. Flavio follows him in amazement.

CAPT. SPAVENTO

Captain Spavento enters, saying he would like to find Flavio.

FRANCESCHINA

Just then, Franceschina enters, saying, "I will do as much damage as I can to avenge myself for the beating I got," and she mentions Isabella's name. Captain Spavento hears her and asks if she knows a certain captain. She answers no, but that it has been six years since Isabella married him, and she has made him a cuckold in the meantime. When he replies that if a man doesn't know about it, he can't be cuckolded, she says that he doesn't have to know about it to be one. The Captain draws his sword and angrily shouts, "I am the Captain, and I am to be treated with respect." Franceschina runs off.

ARLECCHINO

Arlecchino enters with the rose ointment, saying that this will soothe any sore ass. The Captain listens to him and then asks, "Am I a cuckold?" Arlecchino proves it by saying that he knows that he has a wife, that she lives in that house, and that he therefore must be a cuckold. The Captain strikes him angrily, and Arlecchino runs off, the Captain at his heels. Here the second act ends.

ACT THREE

ORATIO

Oratio enters, miserable because of Flaminia. He calls her.

FLAMINIA

She comes out, calls him a traitor, and refuses to listen to his excuses. Oratio begs her forgiveness.

PANTALONE

At that, Pantalone, who is hidden, stops to listen. Oratio, to pacify Flaminia, says he will speak to her father and ask for her hand, if she will agree. Pacified, Flaminia says she agrees, but she is afraid he is in love with Isabella.

FRANCESCHINA

Thereupon, Franceschina, having heard Flaminia express her fear, comes out and says, "Miss, do not fear—if that were so, he would have to fall out of love with Isabella, because her husband has returned." As Flaminia replies that she is going to marry Oratio now, Pantalone, enraged, comes out and says she cannot marry without his consent. They all plead with him. Finally, Pantalone agrees.

THE STRANGER-CAPTAIN

At that moment, the Captain, the stranger, arrives. Franceschina cries out, "Here is the Captain!" and runs into the house. Oratio greets him, and he returns the greeting. Pantalone does the same, showing that he knows him. The Captain laughs and leaves. Pantalone sends Oratio into the house with Flaminia, and he remains.

CAPT. SPAVENTO

Captain Spavento now enters. Pantalone tells him that he did no good in remaining hidden. Captain Spavento, puzzling over that, asks him who told him of his arrival.

PEDROLINO

Just then, Pedrolino enters, shows him the money he was given, and says that he cannot spend it because he swindled it. Captain Spavento drives him off, and muttering curses, Pedrolino goes into the house. Captain Spavento asks Pantalone about his father-in-law, showing himself to be very displeased with him. Pantalone says he must remove every suspicion from his mind.

ARLECCHINO

Arlecchino now comes out of the inn and tells Captain Spavento that the host does not want to give him any more to eat if he does not give him some honest money. The angry Captain beats him and goes off with Pantalone.

THE STRANGER-CAPTAIN

Then, the other captain enters. Weeping, Arlecchino tells him he had no reason to beat him, and the Captain, thinking he is drunk, calls the innkeeper.

PEDROLINO

Pedrolino comes out and angrily tells him that he will give them nothing more to eat. When the Captain pacifies him by giving him some money, Pedrolino and Arlecchino go into the inn.

DR. GRATIANO

Gratiano arrives. The Captain asks him if he knows anyone in the city, and Gratiano, saying that he knows no one but him, tells him that he wants him to show him his wife. The Captain says he has no wife, calls him a pimp, and leaves. Gratiano says he is telling lies to find out about her.

CAPT. SPAVENTO

At that moment, Captain Spavento arrives, recognizes Gratiano, and takes him aside and asks him whom he was speaking with. Gratiano, thinking he is the same captain, tells him that after being away for six years, it is wrong for him to return to Rome and abuse and dishonor him. Captain Spavento tries to pacify him, but Gratiano turns away in a rage.

PEDROLINO	Just then, Pedrolino comes out and tells Captain Spavento that dinner is ready; he is to come into the inn. The Captain, enraged, draws his sword. Pedrolino runs off, the Captain chasing after him. Gratiano cries, "Look out! Look out!" and goes off.
ISABELLA FRANCESCHINA	Isabella and Franceschina come out; Franceschina tells her mistress that her husband, the Captain, has returned and knows that she is in love with Oratio. She warns her to be careful of him and to accept his return and be satisfied.
THE STRANGER-CAPTAIN	The Captain, the stranger, now enters. Isabella, thinking he is her husband, kneels before him, and begging his forgiveness for loving Oratio, explains that she believed he was dead and so wanted to marry Oratio.
CAPT. SPAVENTO PANTALONE DR. GRATIANO	Thereupon, Captain Spavento enters with Pantalone and Gratiano, and they stop to hear what is going on. The stranger-Captain, saying he wants to share her love, speaks kindly to Isabella. He is about to embrace her, when Captain Spavento draws his sword, and the other captain does the same.
ALL	At that, all come out and step between them. They discover they are brothers who have looked for each other for six years. Oratio marries Flaminia, Captain Spavento goes back to his wife, Isabella; and here the comedy ends.

THE TRAGIC EVENTS *

ARGUMENT

*There lived in Florence two gentlemen called Pantalone and
Gratiano. They were of old and noble families, and bore a long
hatred for each other. Each would try to do the other a bad turn
whenever possible, and so their feud grew. It happened that
Gratiano had a son named Captain Spavento and a daughter
named Isabella. The Captain loved Flaminia, a daughter of his
father's enemy, who, in turn, loved the Captain, and he courted
her in an honorable fashion. Flaminia's brother, Oratio, discovered the Captain walking up and down before his house, and not
knowing the reason, suspected that the Captain was driven by the
same hatred as Gratiano, and that the Captain was looking for an
opportunity to kill Pantalone, Oratio's father. Finally, one day,
Oratio attacked him and left him for dead. Afterward he fled to
Rome where he stayed with a dear friend, a gentleman named
Flavio. Meanwhile, the Captain recovered and persevered in his
love, in spite of what had happened. Oratio had fallen in love
with Isabella, daughter of his enemy, and they exchanged love
letters. Finally, Oratio, driven by his love for Isabella, and violat-
ing his term of banishment from Florence, returned. During that
time, Isabella, unable to bear the suffering of her burning love,
took, with the help of a physician, a potion which would put her
into a death-like sleep; then she planned to steal out of the tomb
and go to find her lover Oratio. Thus, on the same day, it
happened that Oratio returned at the time that Isabella was
believed dead. On his return, he also found his enemy, the
Captain, whom the lovers had believed dead. He was then freed,
as the comedy will show.*

CHARACTERS IN THE PLAY

Pantalone
Pedrolino, his servant

* See Appendix p. 400.

Flaminia, his daughter
Oratio, his son
Franceschina, his servant

Flavio, friend of Oratio

Physician
His servant

Doctor Gratiano
Arlecchino, his servant
Isabella, his daughter
Captain Spavento, his son

Host

Chief of Police
Policemen

Hangman

A Messenger

PROPERTIES

Six lanterns
Trumpet of the Court
Four bucklers
Four short swords
Two headpieces
A hangman's noose
A nightshirt and dagger for Isabella
A sign for the inn

ACT ONE

THE CITY OF
FLORENCE

ORATIO   The disguised Oratio arrives in Florence with Flavio, his friend
FLAVIO   from Rome. He tells Flavio that it has been a month since he
killed, in his city of Florence, a captain, son of a doctor who is an
old enemy of his family and whose daughter he loves very much.
He adds that he has returned to find out if Isabella still loves him,
and Flavio promises to help him in every way possible. They
knock on the door of the inn.

THE HOST	When the host comes out, Oratio asks him if he knows Doctor Gratiano. He says yes and tells him that the Doctor is grieving for the death of his daughter Isabella, who was buried in the tomb a short while ago; and he goes in.
ORATIO	Oratio despairs, and Flavio consoles him; then they go into the inn.
PANTALONE PEDROLINO	Pantalone and Pedrolino enter, armed against Pantalone's old enemy, Gratiano. Pantalone rejoices at the sorrow of the Doctor over the death of his daughter, and gloats that soon he will see the Doctor's son, the Captain, hanged; he can think of nothing but his enemy, Gratiano, and Pedrolino calls him a friend of Death. Pantalone replies that he will send him for Gratiano. Seeing night coming on, they go off up the street.
FLAMINIA FRANCESCHINA	Flaminia enters accompanied by Franceschina and weeping because she has heard that the following morning the Captain is going to be hanged. She begs Franceschina to accompany her to the Chief of Police to find out how things are going. Franceschina says she is going herself, and she sends Flaminia into the house and goes, because it is night.

NIGHT

DR. GRATIANO ARLECCHINO	Gratiano enters with Arlecchino. He is armed because of his feud with Pantalone. He laments with his servant the sudden death of his daughter Flaminia and the sentence which will bring death to his son, the Captain, in the morning. Arlecchino consoles him, vowing that, alone, he will free the Captain from the police, for he feels brave.
PANTALONE	Just then, Pantalone enters with a lighted lantern and sees Gratiano armed. They make threatening motions at each other, call each other villain, and all rush off.
ORATIO FLAVIO	Oratio enters with a lighted lantern, telling Flavio that he is going to the tomb to see Isabella. Flavio tries to talk him out of it, pointing out the danger and asking him to return with him to Rome. Oratio refuses to listen to him and leaves. Flavio follows him.
ISABELLA SERVANT	Isabella enters with the physician's servant and tells him her story of how she pretended to be dead so she could go to find her lover, Oratio, and marry him.
PEDROLINO	At that, Pedrolino comes in with a lantern and walks around Isabella and the servant, looking them over.

ARLECCHINO

Then, Arlecchino enters with a lantern, and he does likewise. He finally asks who they are, and Isabella identifies herself, saying, "I am Isabella." Pedrolino and Arlecchino are frightened and run off. Isabella leaves with the servant, and here the first act ends.

ACT TWO

NIGHT

ORATIO
FLAVIO

Oratio enters, despairing because he did not find Isabella in the tomb. Flavio tries to console him by saying that perhaps it is not true that she is dead, and they knock at the door of the inn to find out if it is true.

THE HOST

The host comes out and again confirms the death of Isabella, saying that he saw her put into the tomb. Despairing, Oratio goes into the house, and the others follow him.

ISABELLA
SERVANT

Isabella enters dressed in man's clothes and accompanied by her servant, who holds a lighted lantern. She is looking for horses to take her and her servant to Rome. They knock at the door of the inn.

THE HOST

The host comes out and promises them horses to take them to Rome, and then, looking closely at her, he gets a good look at her and goes back in, asking them to wait.

ORATIO

Oratio appears, saying that the host told him he saw a stranger who looks like Isabella. He looks closely at the young person; finally, after thinking about it, Isabella reveals herself to be alive. Oratio rejoices, picks her up, and carries her into the house. Marveling at this, the servant follows them.

PANTALONE
PEDROLINO

Pantalone enters, laughing at Pedrolino, who says he saw Isabella. Still laughing, he knocks at his door.

FLAMINIA

Flaminia comes out, and her father tells her that in the morning the Captain is to be hanged, and he will be taken past their house. He goes in with Pedrolino, leaving Flaminia weeping.

FRANCESCHINA

Just then, Franceschina enters with a lantern. She sees Flaminia and confirms what Pantalone said. Flaminia sends her back, ordering her not to return to the house until she has tried to save the Captain from being executed. Flaminia goes back in, and Franceschina exits.

ORATIO
FLAVIO

Oratio enters, telling Flavio he is going to get some horses while Isabella is resting. Flavio says he is going with him, and they discuss the fact that the Captain is still alive, as well as his displeasure at being disgraced.

DR. GRATIANO ARLECCHINO	During the discussion, Gratiano enters with Arlecchino, unseen and without a light. They hear all and quietly go off to the police. Flavio now says he will go to get some post horses, and Oratio calls the host.
THE HOST	The host comes out, and Oratio asks about Isabella. The host replies that he will have nothing to do with spirits.
DR. GRATIANO POLICE ARLECCHINO	At that moment, Gratiano arrives with the police and immediately has them arrest Oratio, and the frightened host goes into the house. Flavio tries to talk them into freeing Oratio, but the police ignore him and lead Oratio away to prison.
ISABELLA	Isabella now enters in a nightshirt with a gown over it. She has heard the news, and she is going to kill herself with a dagger she holds in her hand; she wants to follow Oratio in death. She exits, and Flavio follows her off.
DAY	
FLAMINIA	Flaminia comes out in great agitation, because Franceschina has not returned.
FRANCESCHINA	Franceschina returns with the news that the Captain's sentence could not be stayed, and the procession is coming toward the house. They go into the house.
THE PROVOST POLICE HANGMAN CAPT. SPAVENTO	The Court trumpet sounds off stage, and the Provost Marshall enters, armed with a spear, leading the Captain who, with a noose around his neck, walks toward the scaffold. The Captain requests as a last wish that he be allowed to speak. The Provost Marshall agrees, and the Captain asks forgiveness of those in the house—of Pantalone, his daughter, and everyone involved.
FLAMINIA	Just then, a disheveled Flaminia rushes out and embraces the Captain, saying, "My husband, I will not let you die; you are innocent." Flaminia tells the Provost Marshall, who is amazed at all this, that she will not abandon him, but the Provost Marshall says that he must execute the sentence of the Eight Ministers of Justice, and they continue on. Flaminia and Franceschina follow, weeping, and here the second act ends.

ACT THREE

PANTALONE PEDROLINO	Pantalone and Pedrolino come out of the house. They have heard a great deal of noise in the street, and to their bewilderment, can find neither Flaminia nor Franceschina in the house.

FRANCESCHINA	At that, Franceschina arrives. Alarmed, Pantalone asks her about Flaminia. Franceschina tells him that she went after the executioner, shouting that the Captain is her husband and he is neither thief nor murderer. Pantalone is amazed at this.
A MESSENGER	At that moment, a messenger of the Eight Ministers of Justice arrives to call Pantalone to present himself before them in the case of two very important criminals. Pantalone says he will come. Pedrolino asks him for his wages, and they go off with the messenger to the palace, leaving Franceschina.
FLAVIO ISABELLA	Flavio now enters, consoling Isabella. Seeing Franceschina, Isabella reassures her, but Franceschina tells them of the imprisonment of Oratio and of the situation between the Captain and Flaminia. Isabella is infuriated by the imprisonment of Oratio, and she leaves for the palace with Franceschina.
ARLECCHINO	Arlecchino enters, afraid of being arrested. He sees Flavio and thinks he is a policeman, but they come to an understanding.
DR. GRATIANO	Then, Gratiano enters, saying that Oratio will be hanged first for having violated the sentence of banishment.
ISABELLA	Isabella now arrives, sees her father, and drops to her knees before him. She reveals her love for Oratio and how she feigned death with the help of a physician. Enraged, Gratiano threatens her.
FRANCESCHINA	At that, Franceschina enters with news for Gratiano that the court, on the plea of the gentlemen relatives of Flaminia, has returned to the palace, and Pantalone is happily united with Oratio.
PEDROLINO	At that moment, Pedrolino enters and confirms Franceschina's news. Gratiano marvels at this.
PANTALONE	Pantalone now enters humbly and greets Gratiano who, afraid of some traitorous act, returns the greeting.
CAPT. SPAVENTO	The Captain enters next, drops to his knees before his father, begs forgiveness of Isabella, and pleads that they all make peace before the Magistrate, as he has become Flaminia's husband, and the alliance will be the healing of their feud. Pantalone begs Gratiano to forgive him for the injuries of the past, and as Gratiano weeps for joy, they make peace and forgive all. The Captain marries Flaminia; and Oratio, Isabella. Arlecchino and Pedrolino come to blows over Franceschina, but she tells them that she will pick whomever she pleases. Finally, they cast lots, and Pedrolino wins her; and here the play ends.

THE THREE LOYAL FRIENDS

ARGUMENT

In Rome lived two gentlemen of noble families. One, named Pantalone, was the father of a virtuous young woman named Isabella, and the other, called Cassandro, was the father of a young man named Flavio. These two fathers led happy and contented lives until it happened that Isabella was loved by one Aurelio, who had a sister named Flaminia. Isabella did not return his love, and when he became aware of this, he left Rome in despair, leaving his sister in the charge of a servant. Isabella loved a young nobleman named Oratio, who fell deeply in love with her. It happened then that Flavio, who loved Flaminia, left Rome for Naples to take care of his father's affairs. Here he found Aurelio, who was leading a wretched existence because of Isabella's cruelty. Learning of his friend's difficulties, Flavio offered to give him Isabella to marry if he, Aurelio, would give him his sister Flaminia in marriage. Each pledged himself to the promise, and they returned to Rome. In Rome, Flavio found his dear friend Oratio in love with Isabella. He tried first by deception, and then by way of friendship, to break up their love. After many incidents, they were led to the point of voluntarily killing each other when they were interrupted by Aurelio, who freed them of their debt and made everyone happy.

CHARACTERS IN THE PLAY

Pantalone, a Venetian
Burattino, his servant
Isabella, his daughter
Franceschina, his servant

Cassandro, an old man
Flavio, his son
Pedrolino, his servant

Oratio, a gentleman

Aurelio, a gentleman
Flaminia, his sister
Servant of the house

Captain Spavento
Arlecchino, his servant

PROPERTIES

A postman's costume and a false beard for Burattino
A pouch with 500 scudi
Lanterns and other lights

ACT ONE

ROME

ISABELLA   Isabella enters, lamenting to Franceschina about Oratio's melan-
FRANCESCHINA   choly state, whose cause she does not know. Franceschina tells her
not to worry about it because it is Oratio's nature to be melancholy.

ORATIO   Just then, the melancholy Oratio enters and sees her. He is about
to run off, but Isabella calls him and asks him why he is so
melancholy. Oratio tries to tell her but suddenly breaks into tears
and sobs, and leaves, grief-stricken. Isabella and Franceschina also
begin to weep.

PANTALONE   Pantalone, Isabella's father, enters next, accompanied by his serv-
BURATTINO   ant, Burattino, and seeing them weeping, asks why they are
crying. Isabella tells him she is weary of the world and wants to
become a nun. Pantalone tries to talk her out of it, and after
speaking with him, she says she is resigned to it. Pantalone leaves,
weeping and grief-stricken. Burattino asks Isabella why everyone
is weeping. Laughing, she says she is doing it for her health and
goes into the house with Franceschina. Burattino says he is going
to get to the bottom of the whole business and leaves.

FLAVIO   Flavio and Pedrolino enter. Flavio tells Pedrolino he is going to
PEDROLINO   find a way to get his father to send him to Naples. Pedrolino asks
him why, but Flavio says he can't tell him yet.

FLAMINIA   At that moment, Flaminia appears at her window. She has heard
Flavio say he is going to leave, and grief-stricken, she clenches

her teeth and withdraws, weeping. Then, seeing his father coming, Flavio hides. Pedrolino remains.

CASSANDRO At that, Cassandro, Flavio's father, enters. Pedrolino tells him that Flavio wants to go to Naples to see his friend, a coiner with whom he plans to travel about the world. He adds that Flavio wanted to take him along, but he refused. Cassandro tells him not to say a word about it; he will speak to his son that evening. He goes off alone.

FLAVIO Flavio, having heard all, rushes out of hiding and draws his sword on Pedrolino, who runs off. Flavio chases after him.

CAPT. SPAVENTO The Captain enters with Arlecchino. They have come from Naples to see Flavio, to whom the Captain owes 500 scudi; and after he has paid him, the Captain is going to Milan.
ARLECCHINO

PEDROLINO Then, Pedrolino enters, breathless, having heard it all from a hiding place. He identifies himself, and says he knows the Captain. Then he begins to cry, saying that Flavio, his dear friend, died a few days before and his last words were that his father was to receive any money owed him by the Captain. The Captain is saddened by Flavio's death and says he has the money ready; after he pays it, he is going immediately to Milan. Pedrolino says that Flavio's father has gone to the country and will return the next day. They all go off up the street.

ORATIO Oratio enters with Flavio, who asks him why he is melancholy. Oratio says he himself does not know. Flavio replies that he knows that on his return from Naples, he found himself in love with Isabella, and he suggests that that is why he is melancholy. Oratio agrees, and Flavio says he must stop loving Isabella and promises to give him Flaminia in her place. Oratio thinks this over.
FLAVIO

ISABELLA Thereupon, Isabella appears at her window and shows that she had heard it all.

PEDROLINO Pedrolino and Franceschina come out into the street, listening quietly to all that is said.
FRANCESCHINA

FLAMINIA Now, Flaminia appears at her window.

A SERVANT A servant walks into the street. Isabella tells Oratio to beware; he is not her master, and therefore not able to give her away to his friend. Flavio replies, "Signora, you are wrong." Oratio remains as if spellbound. Flaminia tells Flavio that she is not to be given away by him; if she wanted someone else, she would choose him herself. Isabella tells Oratio that she is not going to give another thought to the whole affair, and she is not going to go through with the bargain he made with Flavio. Oratio, humiliated and crushed, leaves quietly. Flavio calls out after him, "Signor Oratio, remember, you must keep your word." Flaminia says to Flavio, "Ah, traitor, you want to go to Naples to deceive some other woman as you deceived me." Flavio, mockingly, says farewell to the ladies and goes. Angrily, they bid him farewell and one, then the other, goes into the house, followed by the servants; and here the first act ends.

ACT TWO

FLAVIO
PEDROLINO

Flavio hears from Pedrolino that what he told his father was for his benefit and then asks him why he wants to go to Naples. Flavio tells him of his love for Flaminia and that he cannot have her unless her brother, Aurelio, can have Isabella, whom he loves. Then Flavio explains how he is trying to get her by trickery and of the promise he made to Flaminia, knowing that her brother, Aurelio, will not give her away to anyone else because he knows they are in love and has promised to marry her to him. Sighing that it is very complicated, Pedrolino promises to help him and tells him about the arrival of the Captain, his debtor, whom he has led to believe that Flavio is dead, and now he is going to give him the money he owes. They leave to work out a way to get the money.

ISABELLA
BURATTINO

Isabella enters, telling Burattino she is miserable because of what took place between her father and her. When Burattino agrees to help her, she says she wants to speak to Oratio.

ORATIO

Just then, Oratio enters and says, "Here I am, my love." To Isabella's complaints about his refusal to tell her why he is melancholy, Oratio replies that he is afraid to destroy her faith in him. She cannot lose her faith to a traitor, she says, but Oratio pledges his faith, and the happy girl goes into the house. Oratio and Burattino leave.

CAPT. SPAVENTO
ARLECCHINO

The Captain enters next, and he complains to Arlecchino about not having seen Pedrolino so he can pay the 500 scudi and go on to Milan.

FRANCESCHINA

At that moment, Franceschina appears at the window and makes obscene motions. The Captain greets her; she says she will come down into the street, and the Captain has Arlecchino brush him off. Franceschina comes out and learns that he is the Captain who is trying to pay back the money to one Flavio.

FLAMINIA	Just then, Flaminia comes out and hears what he says, and also, that he had promised to go with Flavio to Flanders. The women tell him they would also like to see the world, but seeing Cassandro coming, they go back into the house with promises to return.
PANTALONE CASSANDRO	Pantalone and Cassandro enter, complaining of their troubles— Pantalone, of his daughter who wants to become a nun, and Cassandro, of his son who wants to go to Naples. They finally agree that the two might just as well marry when Isabella has gotten over her desire to be a nun, and Cassandro adds that that would be a better solution.
BURATTINO	At that, Burattino enters and says that Pantalone should be firm and not allow Isabella to become a nun; she should take a husband in obedience to her father's will.
FLAVIO PEDROLINO	Thereupon, Flavio enters, and having heard what the old men want, immediately accepts the offer. Burattino says that first he must speak to Isabella, but Pantalone says he will speak to Isabella and goes off with Burattino as Flavio exits. Pedrolino now tells Cassandro of the arrival of the Captain and of the 500 scudi he is going to give him, explaining that he has told the Captain that Flavio is dead so that he would go to the war in Flanders without him, ignoring the promise he had made in Naples. Cassandro says he did well and praises him.
CAPT. SPAVENTO ARLECCHINO	The Captain arrives. Pedrolino immediately tells Cassandro, "Master, here is the Captain who was a very good friend of your son, Flavio." Then he and Cassandro begin to weep. The Captain gives the pouch with 500 scudi to Cassandro, who invites him into the house. The Captain thanks him, and as Cassandro and Pedrolino leave, he says he would like to take the young woman with him who had spoken with him before.
FRANCESCHINA	Just then, Franceschina enters, and they plan that the Captain will take her away with him, dressed as a man. The Captain and Arlecchino go off.
FLAMINIA	Flaminia, who has heard all, enters now and says that she also wants to go along dressed as a man; she will say she is Franceschina's brother. In that way, she says, she can follow that traitor, Flavio. They agree and go into the house.
PEDROLINO BURATTINO	Pedrolino and Burattino enter. They are planning that Pedrolino will give Burattino 200 scudi to disguise himself as a postman with a false beard and pretend to come from Naples with a letter for Flavio; he is to give the letter to Isabella and say that it is to be passed along via Oratio. Burattino promises to do just as he

says, and Pedrolino starts off to get the postman's costume. Burattino calls out, telling him to meet him in the same place and not to leave until he gets there.

NIGHT

CAPT. SPAVENTO
ARLECCHINO

Since it is dark, the Captain, accompanied by Arlecchino, comes to take Franceschina; they give the signal.

FRANCESCHINA

Franceschina comes out dressed as a man and explains that she is going to take her young brother with her. The Captain agrees, saying he will make him his page. Franceschina calls him.

FLAMINIA

Flaminia comes out, dressed as a man, but Burattino recognizes her. They leave happily. Burattino wonders about it; he withdraws, and here the second act ends.

ACT THREE

PEDROLINO
FLAVIO

Pedrolino enters telling Flavio about the plan with Burattino: Flavio has disguised him, and he is going to have him do a series of things which will get Isabella for Flavio. Flavio is happy. Just then, they see Cassandro coming.

CASSANDRO

Cassandro enters with a lantern. Pedrolino pretends he is out of breath, while Flavio hides before Cassandro can see him. Cassandro says he has been looking for Pedrolino all night.

BURATTINO

Then, Burattino, dressed as a postman, enters and gives a letter to Cassandro, which he reads aloud: a certain person has been arrested as a counterfeiter, and a friend of Flavio writes him that he must leave Rome for Florence or Venice if he also does not want to be arrested. Flavio comes out of hiding. Cassandro, scolding him, starts into the house for the 500 scudi which the Captain was to have given Flavio. He tells Flavio he is to go immediately, and goes in lamenting. The others exit happily.

DAY

AURELIO

Aurelio, Flaminia's brother, enters; he has come from Naples to see the man he has chosen for his sister, his friend Flavio, and to visit his sister. He knocks at the door of the house.

THE SERVANT

Flaminia's servant, who answers the door, does not recognize him; Aurelio asks for a certain Aurelio. The servant replies that nothing has been heard of Aurelio for five years, and he is afraid he is dead. Aurelio asks for Flaminia, his sister. The servant replies that she has gone, dressed as a man, to follow Flavio. Aurelio says nothing, and the servant goes into the house. Aurelio grieves over what has happened between his sister and his friend and exits in despair.

ORATIO
BURATTINO

Oratio enters with Burattino, who tells him what Flavio is going to do about Isabella. Oratio is puzzled about this, and Burattino suggests that Oratio counter Flavio's proposal by telling him he has resolved to give Isabella up on the condition that he yield Flaminia, but Oratio says he does not want to do that. Burattino tells him that Flaminia has gone, and Oratio, happy at this news, says he wants him to provoke Flavio so he will speak up first.

FLAVIO
PEDROLINO

Just then, Flavio enters, sees Oratio, and becomes uneasy. Burattino speaks up, and Oratio says he knows what has been going on and that he is content that Isabella be his. Although Flavio agrees to let things stand, he is suspicious of Oratio.

ISABELLA

At that, Isabella appears at her window, having heard it all. Flavio first wanted Isabella, and Oratio told him he wanted Flaminia, swearing to give him Isabella by trickery. Having ascertained what is going on, Isabella goes back into the house. Flavio says to Oratio, "Oh, Signor, give me my Isabella now, right now!"

FLAMINIA
CAPT. SPAVENTO
ARLECCHINO

Just then, Flaminia enters and exclaims, "Oh, traitor, your Isabella!" With that she draws her sword, and here all draw their weapons, and fighting in complete confusion, they all go off up different streets.

ISABELLA

Isabella, having heard all this from her window, complains about love until she is nearly out of her mind. Finally she goes back into the house.

FLAVIO
ORATIO

Thereupon, Flavio re-enters with Oratio, telling him why he wanted Isabella: he was taking her to give her to Aurelio, his friend, to fulfill a promise made in Naples whereby he would give Isabella in exchange for the friend's sister, Flaminia, with whom he was in love. Because of what he has said, she thinks he is a traitor—he does not love her. She does not know that he has renounced her only to keep his word. Oratio in turn explains that it is Isabella he loves, not Flaminia, and he said what he did because he knew that he could not give Flaminia because she had run away.

ISABELLA

Isabella, hidden, is listening as they go on talking. Oratio goes on to say that he will release Flavio from his word, because he himself has always professed to be honorable and because they have been friends. He is happy, he says, that by his death he will give Isabella to Flavio. At that, Isabella reveals herself, crying out, "My Oratio, your death will be followed by mine!"

CAPT. SPAVENTO At that moment, the Captain enters with Flaminia, who has heard
FLAMINIA everything and now greets her brother, begging his forgiveness and explaining her disguise. Meanwhile, the Captain rejoices that Flavio is not dead as his servant and his father said. Flavio marries Flaminia.

PANTALONE Thereupon, Pantalone and Cassandro arrive. Their sons tell them
CASSANDRO what has happened, and they are happy, but they are even more so when they hear that the story about the counterfeiter was made up.

ARLECCHINO Just then, Arlecchino enters, shielding Franceschina from Pedro-
FRANCESCHINA lino and Burattino, each of whom wants her for himself. All
PEDROLINO come between them and give Franceschina to Pedrolino; and here
BURATTINO the comedy ends.

The Twentieth Day

THE TWO FAITHFUL NOTARIES

ARGUMENT

*In Bologna lived two noble youths who were very good friends;
one was called Oratio and the other, Flavio. Both were in love:
Oratio, with a virtuous young girl named Isabella, daughter of
one Doctor Gratiano, and Flavio, with a beautiful young lady
named Flaminia, daughter of one Pantalone de Bisognosi. The
young men were troubled in their love by one Captain Spavento,
who, traveling with his servant, attempted by any kind of trickery
to take one of the young ladies away from her lover. She eventually became Flavio's wife, and the Captain remained tricked, as
the comedy will show.*

CHARACTERS IN THE PLAY

Pantalone, a Venetian
Flaminia, his daughter
Arlecchino, his servant

Oratio
Flavio, his friend

Doctor Gratiano
Isabella, his daughter
Franceschina, his servant
Pedrolino, his servant

Captain Spavento

PROPERTIES

A great many lanterns
Two suits of clothes and false beards to dress the two notaries

ACT ONE

THE CITY OF
BOLOGNA

NIGHT

ISABELLA
FRANCESCHINA
PEDROLINO

Isabella and Franceschina come out in the dark with Pedrolino, to whom they have given a sleeping potion so that he will not see Isabella's lover, Oratio, come into the house. After sending Franceschina to find Oratio, Isabella goes into the house, and Franceschina goes off, leaving Pedrolino behind.

CAPT. SPAVENTO

Captain Spavento arrives to speak to Flaminia, and Pedrolino starts talking in his sleep.

ISABELLA

Isabella, impatient at Oratio's delay, comes to the window. She sees the Captain, and thinking he is Oratio, comes outside, embraces him, and takes him into the house.

FLAMINIA

Flaminia, at her window, is waiting for Flavio; she hears Pedrolino talking, thinks he is Flavio, and comes outside.

DR. GRATIANO

Just then, Gratiano arrives; Flaminia thinks he is Flavio and embraces him, saying, "My beloved, come into the house so that we can enjoy ourselves," and they go in.

PANTALONE
ARLECCHINO

Pantalone and Arlecchino enter with a lantern; they see Pedrolino and wonder what he is doing. They stop to listen to him talk.

CAPT. SPAVENTO

Just then, the Captain comes flying out of the house.

ISABELLA

Isabella comes after him. She tells her father that the Captain entered the house to seduce and rob her, and he gave Pedrolino such a beating he has killed him. Although the Captain tries to explain himself, they will not listen to him, and they all attack him; he runs away. They all take Pedrolino into the house; then the men come out again and give chase to the Captain.

FLAMINIA

Flaminia, at her window, says that because her father is late, she is going to enjoy her lover in one of the rooms below before he comes. Her lover has vowed to be her husband, she explains, and goes in.

ISABELLA

Isabella, now at her window, laments the delay of Oratio.

FLAVIO

At that, Flavio enters, sees her, and thinking she is Flaminia, speaks amorously to her in a soft voice.

ORATIO | Thereupon, Oratio enters with a lantern and stops to listen. Finally, recognizing Flavio, he draws his sword; Flavio does the same.

FRANCESCHINA
PANTALONE
ARLECCHINO | Franceschina, Pantalone, and Arlecchino enter with lanterns and come between them. Franceschina goes into the house, but Oratio and Flavio fight across the stage and off.

DR. GRATIANO | Suddenly, Gratiano comes flying out of the house.

FLAMINIA | Flaminia comes after him, beating him and calling him traitor for trying to steal her honor. Pantalone attacks him with his weapons; Gratiano drops to his knees, promising to do whatever he wishes, and Pantalone replies that he will have to marry Flaminia. He sends Flaminia into the house and then tells Gratiano that he has much to tell him about the Captain and his own daughter, Isabella. They go into the house. Arlecchino drags Pedrolino into the house, and the first act ends.

ACT TWO

DAY

ISABELLA | Isabella enters, unhappy because of what happened between Oratio and Flavio.

FRANCESCHINA
PANTALONE
DR. GRATIANO
PEDROLINO | Then, Franceschina, Pantalone, Gratiano, and Pedrolino enter. Pantalone tells Gratiano about the beating the Captain gave Pedrolino; Pedrolino interrupts to say that he was not beaten, but that the women of the house gave him something to drink to put him to sleep. Hearing that, the women run into the house, leaving the old men suddenly suspicious, especially because of the fight the night before. They ask Pedrolino to call Isabella. Pedrolino knocks at the door.

FRANCESCHINA | Franceschina comes out weeping and tells them that Isabella has suddenly become dumb. They are amazed at this.

ISABELLA | Isabella now enters, pretending to be dumb. As if possessed, she attacks Pedrolino.

CAPT. SPAVENTO | Just then, the Captain arrives, and she does the same to him. He runs off. Isabella goes into the house with Franceschina, and the old men conclude that the Captain is the cause of Isabella's illness.

CAPT. SPAVENTO | The Captain now returns to explain to Gratiano that his daughter, Isabella, dragged him into the house and he went, believing he was going with Flaminia, who is in love with him.

FLAVIO	At that moment, Flavio enters and tells him he lies in his teeth. They draw their swords and begin to fight. The others come between them, and they go off up the street.
ARLECCHINO	Arlecchino enters now, saying that his mistress weeps all the time because she does not want the Doctor for a husband.
FRANCESCHINA	Thereupon, Franceschina comes out and sees him. They make love. Then they speak of their mistresses—Isabella's love for Oratio, and Flaminia's for Flavio—and how Isabella gave the sleeping potion to Pedrolino.
PEDROLINO	Pedrolino, who has heard all this, enters and says he is going to reveal everything about the love affairs of their daughters to the old men. Franceschina threatens to kill him if he tells them.
ORATIO	Oratio arrives, and Pedrolino immediately runs off. Franceschina tells Oratio that her mistress does nothing but weep because of his fight with Flavio; Oratio tells her Isabella is a traitress and is in love with Flavio. The servants deny it.
ISABELLA	At that, Isabella comes out and tells Oratio that she does not love him. They play a jealous scene. Finally, Oratio says, "Signorina, I know that Flavio is your lover."
FLAMINIA	At that moment, Flaminia comes out, saying that she does not think so because Flavio is in love with her, and she loves him. They make peace.
PEDROLINO	Just then, Pedrolino arrives, saying that he is going to reveal everything to the old men and break up all their plans. They all call him a traitor, and enraged, he calls them names. Oratio draws his sword, and all of them go into the house, shouting "Traitor!" Here the second act ends.

ACT THREE

ORATIO FLAVIO	Oratio and Flavio enter. Oratio makes up with Flavio, who is wretched because Flaminia has taken Gratiano as husband, and promises to help him in every way he can.
PEDROLINO	Just then, Pedrolino arrives, and as they draw their swords to kill him, he kneels and promises to help them in their loves.
FRANCESCHINA	Thereupon, Franceschina comes out and tells them not to trust him.
ISABELLA	Then, Isabella appears at her window and says the same thing.

FLAMINIA	After Isabella, Flaminia appears at her window and repeats the warning a third time. When Pedrolino says he is a good man and wants to help them in spite of the others, they all make up to him. Pedrolino suggests that Flaminia speak up to her father and tell him she doesn't want Gratiano because his breath stinks, and that Isabella should continue to play dumb and act as if possessed. Adding that that they should leave the rest to him, he whispers to the lovers that they are to dress up as notaries. Before they leave, the men bid their women farewell; then Franceschina goes into the house, leaving Pedrolino by himself.
CAPT. SPAVENTO	At that moment, the Captain enters. He is in despair because of Flaminia, and Pedrolino says that he has been looking for the Captain to tell him that Flaminia sends him her love. He assures him that Flaminia does love him and whispers that he is to pretend to be a physician, and when he sees Gratiano, to tell him his breath stinks; when he sees Isabella, who is playing dumb, he is to make certain gestures to cure her. Pedrolino demonstrates how he is to do it, and he promises that Flaminia will not be Gratiano's. The blissful Captain leaves.
ARLECCHINO	Arlecchino enters. He and Pedrolino now agree to work together to help their mistresses, and Pedrolino whispers that when he sees Gratiano, he is to tell him that his breath stinks. Laughing, Arlecchino exits.
DR. GRATIANO	Now Gratiano arrives, and Pedrolino tells him that he believes the Captain is a magician who can tell him what might make Isabella well; Gratiano agrees to do whatever is necessary, and Pedrolino exits.
PANTALONE	Pantalone enters next and tells Gratiano that he will have to marry his daughter; he then comments that Isabella's illness seems to be lasting a long time.
FLAMINIA	Just then, Flaminia comes out, and in an aside tells her father that she does not want Gratiano because his breath stinks; then she goes back into the house.
FRANCESCHINA	Franceschina comes out and says that Isabella still cannot speak; then she tells Gratiano that his breath stinks. Gratiano laughs and sends her back into the house.
ARLECCHINO	Arlecchino comes on to find out about the arrangements for the wedding; he tells Gratiano that his breath stinks, and then goes into the house. Pantalone, to prove to himself that Gratiano's breath stinks, has Gratiano breathe in his face; he says he can smell nothing, but adds that perhaps his own breath stinks also.

CAPT. SPAVENTO	At that, the Captain enters and asks Pantalone for the hand of his daughter; saying that Gratiano's breath stinks terribly, he exits.
PEDROLINO	Now Pedrolino enters and says he has discovered that the Captain really is a magician, and he is going to get him to cure Isabella. When Pantalone asks Pedrolino if the Doctor's breath stinks, Pedrolino says he can't smell it himself, but perhaps he also suffers from the same fault. Pantalone confirms that possibility, saying that he too has the same fault.
FLAVIO	Just then, Flavio, dressed as a notary, comes to prepare the marriage contract, and Pantalone asks him if a woman could marry a man whose breath stinks. Flavio says yes, if the woman is satisfied. Gratiano speaks to the notary, who pretends he cannot stand his stinking breath. Pedrolino tells Pantalone that he must not lose the chance of marrying his daughter to the Doctor, and he will send the notary in the house to examine her and urge her to marry Gratiano. He calls for Arlecchino.
ARLECCHINO	Arlecchino enters and takes Flavio into the house. The old men withdraw.
CAPT. SPAVENTO	The Captain arrives, and Pedrolino stands before him, saying, "Now is the time." With that, he goes into the house.
ISABELLA	Then he returns, leading Isabella, who acts very gay. The Captain pretends to mutter magic words in her ear, and she immediately says, "I am cured by your magic, Signor Captain!" He sends her into the house to rest; then he calls to Pedrolino in an undertone and goes. The old men appear now, saying they have seen it all, and Pedrolino announces that he is going to accuse the Captain of being a witch doctor.
ORATIO	At that moment, Oratio, dressed as a notary, greets the old men, saying he is the Captain's lawyer. Pedrolino urges the old men to send him into the house to examine Isabella in order to work out a better case to punish the Captain. Gratiano sends Oratio into the house.
ARLECCHINO	Almost immediately, Arlecchino enters and says that the notary embraced his mistress as soon as he came in the house. Pedrolino angrily enters the house. Arlecchino continues, telling Gratiano that the notary removed his beard and immediately after embraced his mistress; Gratiano is glad that his marriage has not already taken place.
PANTALONE FLAMINIA ORATIO	Now, Pantalone enters with Oratio, whom he is threatening, but Oratio tells him that Flaminia is his wife and that Pedrolino made the whole thing up. Pantalone, unable to do anything else, says she is his.

FRANCESCHINA   Then, Franceschina comes out to bring the news to Gratiano that the notary has impregnated his daughter; as everyone starts to laugh, Gratiano angrily calls for Isabella.

FLAVIO   Flavio comes out and tells him that Isabella is his wife, and the whole affair was worked out by Pedrolino. Gratiano, seeing that the deed is already done, is content.

CAPT. SPAVENTO
PEDROLINO   At that moment, the Captain comes out and hears from Pedrolino that he must be left without a wife. The Captain draws his sword to kill Pedrolino; all draw their weapons to defend him. Pedrolino then begs the forgiveness of all for having tricked them. They forgive him; and here the comedy ends.

The Twenty-first Day

THE FAKE MAGICIAN

ARGUMENT

In Rome lived two big merchants, one named Pantalone, who had an only child named Flaminia, and the other named Gratiano, who had two children, one named Oratio, and the other, Isabella. The two friends bought attractive places near Rome, where they often went with their families on vacation. It happened that near one of their country places lived a young man of noble, virtuous, and wealthy family, who, as customarily happened, became desirous of Isabella, the daughter of Gratiano, and became fast friends with Oratio, her brother, to whom he revealed his love. He had no other design but to make her his wife, and Oratio promised to do all he could to help him win his sister. He, in turn, revealed that he loved Flaminia, the daughter of Pantalone, a friend of his father. Flavio, Oratio's friend, to please himself and to help his friend, began to entertain the two old fathers and their children in order to bring them together. They persevered, and with time and the help of the servants of both families, the young men won over their loves. As a result of the lovers' enjoyment, the women became pregnant; and, because they were insatiable and too attentive in their love, the old men became suspicious, especially Pantalone, who immediately returned to his native city with his family. It was not long before the women, who were growing big with child, had to carry on a pretense with the help of the servants. One pretended to be sick with dropsy, and the other to be possessed. Flavio, by prearrangement, made out that their illnesses were caused by their stay in the country, and he pretended to be an idiot for a time. Finally, in conspiracy with the servants, one of them pretended to be a magician and shrewdly worked it so that the fathers agreed to marry their daughters to the young men. They revealed all and were pardoned of their sins, and they passed the rest of their lives in great happiness.

149

CHARACTERS IN THE PLAY

Pantalone
Flaminia, his daughter
Pedrolino, his servant

Doctor Gratiano
Isabella, his daughter
Oratio, his son
Arlecchino, his servant
Franceschina, his servant

Flavio, a nobleman

Captain Spavento

A Physician

Policemen

PROPERTIES

Two costumes for ghosts
Many glasses of wine
A cake
Costume for a Magician
A Mercury costume for Franceschina
[Lanterns]
[A ladder]

ACT ONE

CITY OF ROME

PANTALONE   Pantalone enters, and with Pedrolino, his servant, he laments the
PEDROLINO   sickness of Flaminia, his daughter—her belly is growing very
large. Pedrolino blames it on the stay in the country where they
vacationed and says it would be a good idea to find her a husband;
he proposes Oratio. Pantalone, in anger, says he would sooner
see her dead.

FLAVIO   Just then, Flavio appears, possessed; he talks to himself and then
turns to Pantalone, saying, "Your daughter will die"; and acting
in a mad way that scares them, he leaves. Pantalone sends Pedrolino for the physician.

ORATIO ARLECCHINO	Oratio now enters, lamenting with Arlecchino Pantalone's suspicions, which made him leave the villa so quickly that it gave him no chance to talk to him. Arlecchino tells him that when they were at the villa, Flavio had him tell Pantalone that he, Flavio, was possessed, but he still does not know to what purpose.
PEDROLINO	At that moment, Pedrolino returns and says that the physician wants to see Flaminia's urine, adding that the physician is sure to discover that she is pregnant. Oratio, who is doubtful about this, says he wants to talk to her. Pedrolino goes in to get the specimen; the others remain.
FLAMINIA	Flaminia comes out and asks Oratio to help her because she is pregnant; they play a love scene.
ISABELLA DR. GRATIANO	Then, Isabella appears at her window and asks Oratio, her brother, to help her because she also is pregnant and growing very big. Gratiano, from within, calls his daughter and demands to know whom she is talking to. Oratio immediately leaves with Pedrolino, and Isabella comes out to join Arlecchino. Hearing her father coming, she at once begins to sing and dance with Arlecchino.
DR. GRATIANO	Gratiano comes out, and seeing Isabella singing and dancing, thinks she has gone mad. With kind words he sends her into the house; then he calls Franceschina.
FRANCESCHINA	When she comes out, Gratiano takes her with him to go to the riverside to buy some wine, ordering Arlecchino to wash the bottles, and he will send them to the door of the wine cellar. Arlecchino remains.
CAPT. SPAVENTO	At that moment, the Captain enters; he speaks to Arlecchino of his love for Flaminia, and saying he wants to send her a letter, offers him fifty scudi if he will drop it through her window. Together they go off to write the letter.
ORATIO FLAVIO	Oratio and Flavio enter. Flavio tells his friend that he is pretending to Pantalone that he is mad, repeating what he said. Oratio tells him that Pedrolino has found a way they can all get into the houses of their women. Then he tells Flavio that his sister is pregnant by him, and he must do something now that night is coming on.
NIGHT	
ISABELLA	Isabella now appears at her window and plays a love scene with Flavio.

FLAMINIA	Flaminia also appears at her window and speaks with Oratio. She says that her pregnancy is becoming very troublesome: Isabella says the same. Oratio tells the women about Pedrolino's plan and that whatever happens, they are not to be afraid, because they will all be together; the women are happy and go in as the two friends exit.
CAPT. SPAVENTO ARLECCHINO	The Captain enters with a letter for Flaminia. Arlecchino plans to get a ladder, saying he will pretend he is catching birds, and he will drop the letter through the window. The Captain promises him fifty scudi, and Arlecchino goes into the house for a ladder and a lantern. The Captain hides.
PANTALONE	Then, Pantalone enters with a light. He has heard that the physician has ordered some medicine for the morning, and he goes into his house.
ARLECCHINO	Arlecchino comes out with the ladder. The wine has come, he says, and then, stumbling many times, he sets the ladder at Flaminia's window. The Captain makes him hurry. Arlecchino climbs to the top of the ladder.
POLICEMEN	At that moment, policemen with lanterns enter, making a great deal of noise. Arlecchino is frightened, falls off the top of the ladder, and runs off, followed by the Captain. The policemen chase after him, and here the first act ends.

ACT TWO

DAY

PEDROLINO	Pedrolino has heard a lot of noise; he is going for the medicine alone in order to hide the whole business from Pantalone. He goes.
DR. GRATIANO FRANCESCHINA	Gratiano enters with Franceschina. He has slept at his brother's house and tells her he has sent the wine and a cake. He is going now to taste the wine. They knock at the door of the house.
ARLECCHINO	Arlecchino answers, then comes out to welcome his master, telling him the wine has come. Gratiano says he has come to give him money to buy a pound of cheese for breakfast and to taste the wine; he goes into the house with Franceschina, and Arlecchino remains.
PEDROLINO	Pedrolino now enters with the medicine; he makes Arlecchino think it is malmsy. Arlecchino drinks it, suddenly feels nauseated, and goes off as Pedrolino bursts out laughing.

PANTALONE	Just then, Pantalone enters, unhappy about his daughter, and seeing Pedrolino with the bottle of medicine, sends him into the house to give it to Flaminia.
PHYSICIAN	The physician arrives. Pantalone makes overtures to him and begs him to cure his daughter.
PEDROLINO	Just then, Pedrolino comes out, and Pantalone orders him to take the physician to Flaminia so that he can examine her, and he goes. The physician wants Flaminia brought out.
FLAMINIA PEDROLINO	Pedrolino goes into the house, then returns with Flaminia, who finally confesses that she is pregnant by Oratio.
DR. GRATIANO	Thereupon, Gratiano, who has heard all this from a hiding place, comes out. The physician consoles her and sends her into the house; then he goes off with Pedrolino. Gratiano says his son Oratio is a knave, and that is why he wanted to stay at the villa.
ORATIO	Just then, Oratio arrives, and Gratiano begins to joke with him about love, about the villa, and about impregnating women. Oratio suddenly pretends that something has come up and goes.
PANTALONE	Pantalone enters. Gratiano says he has heard about Flaminia's sickness, and he suggests that to cure her she be given as wife to his son Oratio. When Pantalone refuses, Gratiano repeats his "cure," and Pantalone, in anger, goes off to find the physician.
ARLECCHINO	Arlecchino enters with some cheese, which he gives to Gratiano, and he vomits all over it because he drank the medicine. Gratiano says he is going into the house to try the other wine. Arlecchino remains, vomiting.
FRANCESCHINA	At that moment, Franceschina calls him to come open the wine barrel, but he vomits and says he aches all over. Franceschina goes back in.
PEDROLINO	Pedrolino enters and tells him that the physician is a good man. Arlecchino complains about him, vomiting and holding his sides.
DR. GRATIANO	Gratiano, from within the house, calls to Arlecchino and asks him who is with him. He answers that it is Pedrolino, and Gratiano calls him in to have a drink. Pedrolino goes in.
CAPT. SPAVENTO	The Captain arrives, and Arlecchino asks for his fifty scudi for dropping the letter in the window.
DR. GRATIANO	At that, Gratiano comes out, eating, to call Arlecchino. Seeing the Captain, he takes him into the house for breakfast. Arlecchino, still vomiting, follows.

PANTALONE PHYSICIAN	Pantalone and the physician enter. When Pantalone asks for his diagnosis of his daughter's illness, the physician replies that Pantalone ought to marry his daughter to whomever she wishes, that to do otherwise is to suffer, very soon, sorrow and dishonor. "A word to the wise is sufficient," he says, and goes. Pantalone remains, wondering what he meant about honor. He then re-members what Gratiano told him. He hears singing and drink-ing of healths in Gratiano's house and knocks.
DR. GRATIANO CAPT. SPAVENTO PEDROLINO FRANCESCHINA	Gratiano, the Captain, Pedrolino, and Franceschina all come out, still eating and drinking, and drunk as apes. When Pantalone scolds Gratiano, he falls drunk to the ground. After many drunken antics, one after the other falls to the ground in front of the dumbfounded Pantalone.
ARLECCHINO	Then, Arlecchino comes out and carries them, one by one, into the house in many ridiculous ways. Finally, he returns and is about to carry in Pantalone, but he runs off up the street. Arlec-chino goes into the house, and the second act ends.

ACT THREE

ORATIO FLAVIO	Oratio enters, telling Flavio he suspects that his father knows something of his love because of what he had said before.
PEDROLINO	Just then, Pedrolino enters, half asleep from drunkenness; the lovers complain to him because he is taking too long to work things out, but Pedrolino tells them to leave everything to him.
CAPT. SPAVENTO ARLECCHINO	The Captain and Arlecchino enter now, and the Captain tells Arlecchino that he will be paid; then, greeting the lovers and telling them that the Doctor entertained them with the best wine, he leaves. Pedrolino sends Arlecchino into the house to tell the women that soon they will be happy; then he whispers to the lovers, telling them to go to their friend, the costume-maker, and dress as ghosts. They exit.
PANTALONE	Pantalone enters and scolds Pedrolino for being drunk and not attending to the house. Pedrolino blames the Doctor. Then he says he has found someone to cure his daughter.
DR. GRATIANO	Gratiano arrives, and Pedrolino scolds him. Gratiano excuses himself by saying that he is celebrating Shrovetide. Pedrolino tells them again that he has found someone who will cure both daughters. Gratiano pleads for his own daughter, but begins to laugh about Pantalone's, saying that she will never recover if she does not marry his son Oratio. Pedrolino sends them both to the

apothecary's to wait for him, telling them not to say anything about the magician, because he does not want to be recognized. They leave, and Pedrolino remains.

ARLECCHINO Arlecchino arrives, and Pedrolino tells him he wants him to help get their mistresses out of the fix and play a trick on the old men. He sends him off to dress as a magician; when he comes back, he says, he will explain fully what he is to do; but just for now, he can know that when they are near Pantalone, he will pretend to conjure spirits. As Arlecchino goes, Pedrolino knocks at the door of the house to tell the women what is going on.

ISABELLA Isabella and Flaminia both appear at their windows. Pedrolino
FLAMINIA tells the women not to be afraid of anything they see because it will be faked, and all will turn out for the best. As the women rejoice and withdraw, Pedrolino goes to find the young men.

ARLECCHINO Arlecchino now enters with a Mercury's rod, a winged cap, and winged boots. He has worked out the trick, he says, and he calls Franceschina.

FRANCESCHINA Franceschina comes out, takes the things, and whispers to him, pointing to the top of the house. She goes in, and he goes off to get into his own disguise.

PANTALONE The old men enter, and Pantalone tells Gratiano that he is going
DR. GRATIANO to marry his daughter right away in order to cure her; but Gratiano refuses to have her marry Oratio because at the villa she said she despised him. Then Pantalone says that if Gratiano will give him Isabella for wife as he promised, he will agree to give Flaminia to his son Oratio. Gratiano agrees.

PEDROLINO At that, Pedrolino enters, out of breath, saying he has lost sight of the magician.

ARLECCHINO Just then, Arlecchino enters, dressed as a magician, and begins his conjuring tricks. He speaks to the two old men and then, tracing two circles, one on each side of the stage, he puts Pantalone in one and Gratiano in the other. Then he commands them not to move, no matter what they see or hear. Arlecchino then conjures and calls out to the spirits.

ORATIO At his call, Oratio and Flavio enter, dressed as spirits, and go
FLAVIO round and round the circles, frightening the old men. And then, as Pedrolino takes each "spirit" into the house of his mistress, the old men make gestures of amazement, and Arlecchino, looking up into the sky, calls on Mercury, the messenger of the gods, to appear on top of the house.

FRANCESCHINA — Franceschina, dressed as Mercury, appears. The magician asks her the will of the gods concerning the children of the old men. Franceschina says that the gods want Flaminia to marry Oratio, and Isabella, Flavio, and if the fathers do not agree, the spirits are to take them to hell. The old men agree; Franceschina leaves.

ISABELLA — Immediately, Isabella comes out saying, "Dear Father, I am well, and I want no other husband than he who is in the house."

FLAMINIA — Then, Flaminia comes out of the house and says the same. The old men say they do not want to be related to devils. Arlecchino, the magician, says he wants them to know his power; he conjures again.

ORATIO
FLAVIO — Oratio and Flavio appear, each in his own form. Arlecchino marries them; then he removes the old men from the circles. They want to reward him, but he replies that he wants no other reward but Franceschina. They call her.

FRANCESCHINA — Franceschina enters and pretends to be afraid; but then she shows she is happy. Arlecchino commands the old men to forgive all the tricks of a certain Pedrolino. When the old men agree, he pretends to conjure and then removes his false beard from his face to reveal himself.

PEDROLINO — At that moment, Pedrolino enters and confesses to all the tricks done to satisfy the young lovers and to save the honor of their houses; all praise him, and here the comedy ends.

The Twenty-second Day

HE WHO WAS BELIEVED DEAD

ARGUMENT

There lived in Florence a widow who was in love with a noble youth named Oratio. Again and again he was pursued by the widow, but he gave little thought to love. Freely and thoughtlessly he pursued other pleasures. It happened that one day he was invited by letter to visit the widow, who was named Isabella. The young man could not refuse the invitation. He went to her house and laid aside his sword, cape, and hat at her request. Soon she was aroused by him and became so impassioned she begged her lover to marry her. He, refusing, fled from her and her house, leaving behind him his sword, cape and hat. After many trials, and after being taken for dead, he became her husband.

CHARACTERS IN THE PLAY

Pantalone, an old man
Flavio, his son
Pedrolino, his servant

Laura, a widow
Oratio, her son
Flaminia, her daughter

Isabella, a widow

Burattino, servant of Laura

Captain Spavento
Arlecchino, his servant

PROPERTIES

[Money]
[A sword, cape, and hat]

ACT ONE

CITY OF
FLORENCE

ORATIO ISABELLA	Oratio runs out of Isabella's house, where he left sword, cape, and hat, refusing to satisfy her desires. She pleads with him, then threatens him; he keeps demanding his possessions. She says that she will return nothing and she will get even with him. Enraged, she goes into the house, and Oratio remains.
PANTALONE	Just then, Pantalone shouts from within that his chest has been broken into; he comes out, and Oratio runs off up the street. Pantalone looks after him, shouting, "Who goes there?" Then he shouts that he has been robbed.
PEDROLINO	Pedrolino arrives, and Pantalone grabs him, taking out his dagger to find out from him who has broken into his chest. Pedrolino falls to his knees, pleading that he knows nothing.
ISABELLA	Isabella, having heard all this from her window, comes out to tell Pantalone, secretly, that if he will let Pedrolino go, she will reveal the thief. She then tells him that Oratio has stolen everything and that she saw him coming out of Pantalone's house a little while before, boasting he had broken into his chest and robbed him. Pantalone says that he saw him but did not get a good look at him; he thanks her and goes off with Pedrolino, leaving Isabella, who says she wants to see the ruin of Oratio and then exits.
LAURA FLAMINIA	Laura, a widow, enters now, telling her daughter, Flaminia, that she will marry the doctor, and that she must prepare to receive her betrothed. Flaminia says she does not want to marry him; finally she appears to agree, and they call Burattino.
BURATTINO	When Burattino comes out, Laura gives him the list of kinswomen to be invited to the wedding, and they go off together. Flaminia remains, complaining that it is the Captain whom she loves.
CAPT. SPAVENTO	Captain Spavento arrives. Flaminia appeals to him, but he says he does not love her.
FLAVIO	Flavio enters now and sweetly reproaches Flaminia, who says that the Captain was asking after his honor, and she goes in. Flavio reproaches him because Flaminia is the sister of Oratio, his very close friend. Then he exits, leaving the Captain wondering what that meant.

ISABELLA Then Isabella arrives, and seeing the Captain, begins to weep. When he asks her why, she tells him she loves him and that she wants to marry him; but a certain Oratio, Laura's son, forbade her, telling her that if she marries him, he will kill her. The Captain, vexed, promises to kill him and goes. Isabella, happy that she will be avenged, leaves.

ORATIO Oratio now enters, telling Flavio about the trick played on Isa-
FLAVIO bella the widow, and Flavio, in turn, tells him he broke into his father's chest and took 500 scudi.

PEDROLINO Just then, Pedrolino enters and tells them he has heard everything; he threatens to tell Pantalone if they do not give him some money. They calm him, however, and Oratio begs him to get his sword, cape, and hat from Isabella; they are expensive, he says, and promises that another time he will give him something in return. They give him money and leave. Pedrolino marvels at the shrewishness of Isabella toward Oratio.

BURATTINO At that moment, Burattino returns from inviting the women guests to the wedding, and Pedrolino gives him one scudo, telling him to cry and to do just as he tells him. Pedrolino begins to shout, cursing Oratio.

ISABELLA Thereupon, Isabella comes out, and Burattino begins to weep. Pedrolino tells her that Oratio has beaten him and he would fight him, but he has no evidence to prove the beating. If he had something of his to show as proof, it would appear to be true. Isabella says she will give him Oratio's things; she goes in, brings them out, and urges Pedrolino to get Oratio put in prison and punished. She goes in, and laughing, they leave with Oratio's things; and here the first act ends.

ACT TWO

PANTALONE Pantalone enters, telling Laura that her son, Oratio, broke into his
LAURA chest and robbed him of 500 scudi, and they had an argument. Finally, Laura says that she would like to know who the witnesses are.

ISABELLA At that, Isabella comes out and says she is a witness; she has seen him enter and leave Pantalone's house. Laura promises to return the money if the story is true. Pantalone exits. Laura reproaches Isabella for being so shameless, and Isabella abuses her.

BURATTINO Then, Burattino comes out and threatens Isabella.

CAPT. SPAVENTO   The Captain, entering just then, comes between them, shouting at Burattino and Laura. Laura, shouting abuse, goes in, and Burattino stands in the doorway. The Captain, promising Isabella again that Oratio will be killed, says that he has not yet found him. She begs him to do it; the Captain promises he will and goes. Burattino, who says he has heard everything, also goes. Isabella is now alone and moans that Love and Hate are at war in her heart.

FLAVIO   Flavio enters and talks amorously to her. She tells him of Oratio's cruelty and says she hopes soon to hear of his death. Flavio, with fine words, calms her; then he says he tricked her to get Oratio's belongings back, and she shouts and threatens in anger.

CAPT. SPAVENTO   At that, the Captain enters and says, "Signorina Isabella, must I kill this one too?" When Isabella tells him to do as he pleases, the Captain draws his sword; Flavio does the same. The Captain leaves, saying he does not kill in the presence of ladies, for fear they will miscarry. Isabella, outraged, goes into the house.

LAURA   Laura now enters and asks Flavio about her son, Oratio. Flavio says he knows nothing, and that he is his closest friend. Laura shows affection for him, saying that she would willingly take him for her husband, since she has betrothed Flaminia to a doctor who studies in Bologna.

FLAMINIA   Thereupon, Flaminia, having heard everything, tells her mother that she would do better to take the doctor for herself and give her Flavio. Laura, in anger, strikes her and sends her back into the house, and Flavio exits, leaving the furious Laura to herself.

BURATTINO   Just then, Burattino, who has heard all, comes out and tells Laura that she is wrong. She strikes him and goes in. Burattino leaves, weeping.

PEDROLINO   Pedrolino enters, telling Oratio how he got his things back from
ORATIO   Isabella; they laugh.

FLAMINIA   At that, Flaminia appears at her window and tells Oratio that their mother is angry with him because she heard from Pantalone that he broke into his chest and robbed him of his money. When Pedrolino confirms the tale, Oratio laughs. Flaminia then tells Oratio that their mother is in love with Flavio and begs him to do all he can so she does not have to marry the doctor.

LAURA   At that moment, Laura, from within, calls to Flaminia to come away from the window. She withdraws, and the others remain.

FLAVIO   Then, Flavio enters. Oratio tells him what his father said, and he puzzles over it. Oratio asks him what happened, and Flavio tells him everything in detail.

PANTALONE | Pantalone, hidden, hears everything. Now, as Pedrolino complains that his share is small and demands more money, Pantalone, in anger, leaps out, calls them thieves, and draws his dagger. Frightened, they run away up the street.

LAURA | Laura, hearing all the noise, comes to the window. Pantalone begs Laura's pardon, saying that he has discovered the thief, and her son, Oratio, did not rob him; and he leaves.

PEDROLINO | Pedrolino enters, afraid of Pantalone.

BURATTINO | Burattino also enters and tells him that Isabella has given orders to kill Oratio. Pedrolino wonders at that and tells Burattino to go along with him in all he says, because he wants to clear it up. He knocks.

ISABELLA | When Isabella comes out, she learns from Pedrolino that the Captain killed Oratio, but he could have had him jailed. Burattino confirms this and adds that when Oratio was dying, he said; "Isabella mine, I die because of you, and you hate me." Bursting into tears, Isabella cries that she never hated him; she loved him. Then she becomes determined to have the Captain killed, and she goes back in. Pedrolino and Burattino, laughing, say they are going to fight the Captain.

CAPT. SPAVENTO | At that moment, the hidden Captain, who has heard everything, leaps out and draws his sword; they run off, and he chases after them. Here the second act ends.

ACT THREE

CAPT. SPAVENTO | The Captain enters, swearing to avenge himself; he knocks at Isabella's door.

ISABELLA | Isabella comes out and hears from the Captain that he has killed Oratio; she begins to weep and cry aloud.

LAURA | At that, Laura comes out and hears from Isabella that the Captain has killed Oratio, her son; she begins to weep.

FLAMINIA | Then, Flaminia comes out and weeps over the death of her brother; Laura is grief-stricken.

BURATTINO | Burattino arrives, sees Laura grief-stricken, and takes her into the house. The Captain protests his love to Flaminia, who tries to drive him away.

PANTALONE | Thereupon, Pantalone enters and comes between them; the Captain exits, leaving Flaminia to lament the death of her brother.

FLAVIO	Flavio now enters and asks her why she is lamenting; she tells him that the Captain has killed Oratio, and she goes in weeping.
PEDROLINO	Pedrolino now enters and says that the Captain has threatened to kill him. The Captain says he is going to kill him as he did the traitor Oratio. Flavio, seeing that all confirm Oratio's death, believes it himself. Pantalone asks him where the money is that he took from the chest. Weeping, Flavio leaves without answering. Pantalone asks Pedrolino, who likewise leaves weeping, without answering, and the tricked Pantalone exits.
ORATIO	Oratio enters. Having received no news of Flavio, he knocks at the door.
FLAMINIA	Flaminia comes out, and believing him to be the ghost of Oratio, she becomes frightened and runs back into the house.
BURATTINO	Burattino comes out, sees him, and he also runs off. Oratio remains.
ISABELLA	At that, Isabella comes and believes him to be the ghost of Oratio; frightened, she runs back into the house.
LAURA	Then, Laura comes out, becomes frightened, and leaves.
FLAVIO PANTALONE PEDROLINO	Thereupon, Flavio, Pantalone, and Pedrolino, one at a time, come out and then run off in fright.
CAPT. SPAVENTO	The Captain enters. He sees Oratio and draws his weapons; Oratio does the same.
ALL	At the commotion, all come out armed and separate them. Immediately, Isabella tells the Captain, "Ah, traitor, why did you tell me you killed Oratio?" He explains to her that he did it to avenge the wrong done him. He asks Oratio's pardon; Oratio pardons him. At Flavio's begging, Oratio says he will marry Isabella on the condition that Flavio marry his sister, Flaminia. Thus they agree and pledge their vows. Flavio promises to return the 500 scudi he took from his father's chest; and the comedy ends.

The Twenty-third Day

THE POSTMAN

ARGUMENT

*There lived in Venice a merchant named Stefanello Bisognosi
who had a daughter of great beauty and virtue. By letter, he
arranged a marriage in Genoa with a young man of noble family
named Flaminio. It happened that a Venetian gentleman fell in
love with the young lady, and deciding to kidnap her, came to her
father's house. But he was then wounded and left for dead by
Stefanello, who had the help of some ruffians. He fled to Bologna,
and not feeling safe there, went, after some time, to Rome.
Meanwhile, the young man, Flaminio, who was not satisfied with
the marriage arrangement, left his father's house and went to
Bologna under the assumed name of Oratio. Here he met his
betrothed—whom he did not recognize because she lived under
the name of Isabella—and fell deeply in love with her. She had
followed him to Rome under the name of Ortensia. After many
trials, he revealed himself to be Flaminio, and after running
the risk of losing her, he finally married her.*

CHARACTERS IN THE PLAY

Pantalone, then Stefanello
Isabella, his daughter, then Ortensia
Pedrolino and
Burattino, his servants

Doctor Gratiano
Flaminia, his daughter
Franceschina, his servant

Captain Spavento, alone

Oratio, then Flaminio
Flavio, his companion

163

Host

Postman

Servants

PROPERTIES

Sign for the inn
A bat
A chest holding many letters

ACT ONE

THE CITY OF ROME	
A POSTMAN	A postman knocks at Pantalone's door.
PANTALONE	Pantalone appears at the window and peevishly answers, saying he will send for the letters. As Pantalone withdraws, the postman knocks at Gratiano's door.
FRANCESCHINA	Franceschina appears at the window and says, "I'm coming soon."
PEDROLINO	At that, Pedrolino enters and takes the letters for his master, asking if there are any for him.
FRANCESCHINA	Franceschina comes out and takes Gratiano's letters, and the postman leaves. Pedrolino and Franceschina joke and fondle each other. Franceschina then asks him if he has news of Burattino. Pedrolino replies that they have had no news of any of those who left for Bologna. He says he is jealous of Burattino.
FLAVIO ORATIO	Flavio enters, trying to persuade Oratio not to forsake his love for Isabella and leave Rome; Oratio replies that he is forced to leave because he knows that Isabella loves another, explaining that is also why he disobeyed his father and refused to marry the woman offered to him in Venice. He is, therefore, determined to leave for Bologna.
SERVANTS	The servants, who were off to the side, enter the house, and Flavio and Oratio follow as Oratio tells Flavio his story.
ISABELLA	Just then, Isabella enters and says she has heard from Pedrolino that Oratio is in Rome.
FLAMINIA	Flaminia enters to say that Franceschina has told her that Flavio has been seen in the streets of Rome. The two girls see and then

greet each other. Oratio, seeing Isabella, wants to leave; Flavio holds him back. Isabella speaks sweetly to him, but Oratio calls her a traitress. Isabella calls on the others to witness her love, and Flavio and Flaminia vow that it is true. Oratio, out of his senses and impassioned, leaves without a word. Flavio goes after him. Isabella, entering the house, says, "She is cursed who leaves home"; and Flaminia says, "He is cursed who leaves Bologna," and she enters the house.

BURATTINO   Burattino now enters with a felt hat and boots; he comes from Venice and is looking for the Bear Inn to find out where his master has taken a house.

CAPT. SPAVENTO   At that moment, the Captain, who lodges at the inn, enters. They talk, and Burattino says he has one of the Captain's letters. He reads many, among them those of Pantalone, saying, "These are my master's." The Captain notes what he says, takes his own letter, and then calls the host.

THE HOST   The host comes out. The Captain introduces Burattino, and the host takes him into the inn. After the Captain reads his letter in his characteristic manner, he enters the inn.

PANTALONE   Pantalone comes from his house with the letter and knocks at Gratiano's door.

FRANCESCHINA   Franceschina comes out and tells Pantalone that Gratiano is coming. Pantalone jokes with her; she goes in.

DR. GRATIANO   Gratiano enters with his letter in hand; Pantalone announces that he has good news from Venice. When Gratiano asks what it is, he tells his story as given in the Argument, adding that he has sent a servant to Venice to discover the facts, and to confirm his suspicion, he himself is leaving for Bologna. Gratiano now reads his letter, which is all bad news.

PEDROLINO   At that, Pedrolino jokes with him and goes; and here the first act ends.

ACT TWO

CAPT. SPAVENTO   The Captain has gotten Burattino drunk and has taken Pantalone's letters from him, opened them, read them, and found that Pantalone is really called Stefanello, and his daughter, Isabella, is really Ortensia; he sees the names of Pantalone's enemies, and he gives much thought to that.

PEDROLINO

Then, Pedrolino arrives; the Captain questions him and finds that what he read in Pantalone's letters is true. He gives Pedrolino money for helping him in his love for his mistress. Pedrolino tells him not to try to do anything, because she is in love with a Genovese scholar, whom she followed from Bologna to Rome, but he himself will try to help him. Pedrolino leaves, and the Captain remains.

FLAVIO
ORATIO

Thereupon, Flavio enters, asking Oratio why he suspects Isabella's love. When Oratio replies that he is afraid she is in love with the Captain, Flavio pleads with him not to leave Rome until he finds out the truth of the whole business. Oratio promises and goes. Flavio gives a signal under the window.

ISABELLA

Isabella appears at the window and tells Flavio that Flaminia is lovesick.

FLAMINIA

Just then, Flaminia comes out, and Isabella withdraws into the shadows. Flavio asks Flaminia if Isabella loves the Captain.

ISABELLA

At that moment, Isabella, who has heard all from her window, tells Flavio that he has very little faith if he believes that she could stop loving her Oratio for the bragging Captain.

CAPT. SPAVENTO

Just then, the Captain reveals himself, and as the women withdraw, Flavio tells the Captain of Oratio's suspicion. The Captain says to tell Oratio that he loves none of these women, but he is in love with a Venetian gentlewoman. Flavio is satisfied and leaves. The Captain says he has thought about what he must do, and he goes into the inn.

ORATIO
FLAVIO

Oratio now enters and hears from Flavio what has taken place among Flaminia, Isabella, and the Captain. Again, each signals under the window of his love.

ISABELLA

Isabella appears at her window and plays a scene of exchanging sweet talk with Oratio.

FLAMINIA

Flaminia appears at her window and rejoices at their reconciliation. Isabella tells Oratio that she will reveal a secret about her father and herself as a sign of her love.

CAPT. SPAVENTO

Thereupon, the Captain comes out, and after greeting everyone, he says that to make them happy and out of friendship for their fathers, he wants to be a mediator in their loves. Happily, the women hail the Captain and withdraw. The Captain tells Flavio and Oratio that he too is known to have a love in Venice. Oratio promises to help him in his love and pledges his trust, and the Captain reveals the name of his love. Oratio is amazed and starts to tell his story, but at that moment they see the old men coming. The Captain sends the young men off.

PANTALONE
DR. GRATIANO

At that, Pantalone and Gratiano arrive. The Captain asks Gratiano for his daughter's hand in the name of a Genovese gentleman. Pantalone urges him to give her, saying that they can go to Genoa together because he also is going to marry his daughter to a Genovese gentleman. They agree, and Gratiano leaves. The Captain tells Pantalone that he knows he is really Stefanello, and his daughter, really Ortensia. He also tells him that he himself was hired by Pantalone's enemies to kill him, but his love for his daughter has kept him from doing it; and he asks for her hand. When Pantalone promises her to him, the Captain leaves.

BURATTINO

Burattino comes out of the inn, sees Pantalone, his master, and embraces him. Pantalone is happy at the turn of events, and he calls Isabella and Pedrolino.

ISABELLA
PEDROLINO

Isabella enters and kisses Burattino, who says he brings good news; with that they go into the house; and here the second act ends.

ACT THREE

ISABELLA
PEDROLINO

Isabella enters, telling Pedrolino that her father wants to marry her to the Captain and Oratio has accepted Flaminia; but she does not believe him; she sends Pedrolino to find Oratio so she can tell him all. Pedrolino leaves.

FLAMINIA

Now, Flaminia enters, and she tells Isabella that Oratio has asked her father for her hand, and he promised her to him. Isabella laments, calls him traitor, and goes in weeping.

FLAVIO

At that moment Flavio enters and hears all about it from Flaminia.

PEDROLINO

At that, Pedrolino arrives and confirms everything. Flaminia, weeping, goes into the house, and Flavio, feeling miserable, leaves.

CAPT. SPAVENTO
ORATIO

Then the Captain and Oratio enter, and the Captain asks Pedrolino about Pantalone. Pedrolino tries to talk to Oratio, but the Captain keeps interrupting him.

PANTALONE
BURATTINO

Pantalone and Burattino now enter, and seeing the Captain, Pantalone tells him that all he said must be true because he has had letters from Venice which said the same thing. The Captain tells Pantalone he can depend on Oratio's word and then asks

Oratio if he is ready to help him in his love as he promised. Oratio says he is ready. The Captain reveals that Pantalone is Stefanello, and Isabella is his daughter, Ortensia, whom the Captain loves. Therefore, he wants Oratio to make a special plea to her father to give her to him in marriage. Oratio begs Pantalone, who agrees to his request. Pantalone gives her to the Captain, and they go off together. Oratio then laments to Pedrolino over his bad fortune. Pedrolino tells him it is not time to lament because he has taken Flaminia to wife. Oratio says it is not true.

ISABELLA   At that, Isabella comes out and calls him traitor; he denies it.

FLAMINIA   Then, Flaminia enters and agrees with Isabella. He excuses himself by saying that he was betrayed by the Captain and could not take Isabella when she was promised to him in Genoa because he did not deserve her. He reveals himself to be Flaminio de Franchi of Genoa, and Isabella, hearing that name, swoons into the arms of Pedrolino, and he and Flaminia take her into the house. Burattino tells Oratio that, just between them, the Captain has played a trick.

PEDROLINO   Pedrolino returns, and hearing this from Burattino, guesses at the Captain's trick with the letters.

CAPT. SPAVENTO At that moment, the Captain, obviously happy at how everything has turned out, enters, and Pedrolino makes Burattino hide. Then, in a cunning manner, he asks the Captain if he is still lodging at the Bear Inn and if he knows a certain Burattino. When the Captain says he does not know him, Burattino comes out, but the Captain still denies he knows him. They argue, and the servants beat him. He draws his sword.

FLAVIO   Just then, Flavio and Oratio enter fighting.
ORATIO

PANTALONE   Hearing the noise, Pantalone and Gratiano arrive to part them;
DR. GRATIANO   they quiet down. Then Oratio calls the Captain as witness that he did not request Flaminia for wife except as part of a bargain. The Captain says it is so; then Oratio kneels before him, saying that since he takes his wife—without whom he cannot live—then he is to take his life also. The Captain agrees, but first he wants to marry Isabella in his presence, and he tells Pantalone to call her. Pedrolino calls her.

ISABELLA   Isabella comes out. The Captain marries her, saying, "I marry her,
FLAMINIA   and as mine, I return her to you." Oratio thanks him; Flavio then
FRANCESCHINA   marries Flaminia. The Captain reveals the trick of the letters and the simple wit of Burattino. Pedrolino marries Franceschina; and here the comedy ends.

THE FAKE TOFANO

ARGUMENT

There lived in Rome two young men of modest means. One was fatherless, but the other, who was named Flavio, was the son of Doctor Gratiano. They were in love with two comely young ladies, one of whom loved a Captain, who, with the young men, frequently walked the street where the two young ladies lived. Seeing no way of stopping the Captain without provoking him, the young men decided to kill him and throw him into a ditch which flowed into the Tiber. They left him for dead, and after many things happened, he saved himself and married one of the young ladies and became friends with the young men.

CHARACTERS IN THE PLAY

Pantalone, a Venetian
Flaminia, his daughter
Pedrolino, his servant

Doctor Gratiano
Flavio, his son

Oratio, friend of Flavio

Tofano, a Venetian
Isabella, his daughter
Franceschina, his servant

Captain Spavento
Arlecchino, his servant

Merchants

Sailors

PROPERTIES

A dirty and wet shirt for the Captain
Many lanterns
A false beard
A long staff

ACT ONE

THE CITY OF
ROME

ORATIO FLAVIO	Oratio and Flavio enter, laughing at having gotten rid of the Captain, who was their constant, unwelcome companion, and at having thrown him into a ditch.
ISABELLA	Isabella appears at her window and greets Oratio, who tells her what has happened to the Captain. They all begin to laugh.
FLAMINIA	At that, Flaminia, having heard all from her window, scolds Oratio and Isabella. When Flavio tries to pacify her with sweet talk, she, enraged, insults them. They laugh at her, but she goes on scolding them. They reply that she has gone crazy.
PEDROLINO	Then, Pedrolino arrives. Flaminia immediately tells him that she is shouting because of her love, saying that he is a pimp because he would not scold Oratio. They laugh, watching Pedrolino, who leaves in anger and swearing at all of them. They call after him that Flaminia is crazy.
PANTALONE	Pantalone arrives next and asks the reason for all the noise. Isabella immediately goes into the house; Flaminia does the same. Then Pedrolino returns and tells Pantalone that Oratio and Flavio, knowing he was out, tried to force Flaminia, and because she wanted to speak out, they began to call her crazy. Pantalone, enraged, draws his weapon; they draw their swords.
FLAMINIA	At that moment, Flaminia rushes out with a stick to help her father, and they all attack the young lovers.
DR. GRATIANO	Thereupon, Gratiano enters and comes between them. The young men leave, and Flaminia goes into the house. Gratiano calls Pedrolino a pimp—a pimp of his mistress—and saying that Pantalone will soon be disgraced, he leaves. Pantalone turns on Pedrolino with suspicion because of what Gratiano said. Pedrolino protests he is innocent of the charge, and he begins to cry.

ARLECCHINO   Arlecchino now enters, weeping at the death of the Captain, his master. He tells Pedrolino to leave off crying for himself and cry for the death of his master instead, but Pedrolino says to leave him to cry for the loss of his honor. Pantalone hears of the death of the Captain and learns that those who sent him to his death are not yet known.

FLAMINIA   Flaminia, at her window, tells her father that the two murderers are Oratio and Flavio.

ISABELLA   Isabella, now at her window, tells Pantalone not to believe her because she is crazy. Flaminia insists and finally quarrels with him. Pantalone, who is in love with Isabella, threatens his daughter and forces her to go back into the house. Isabella kisses Pantalone, then pretends to go in. Arlecchino, followed by Pantalone, goes off to court to make a complaint against Oratio and Flavio. Pedrolino says he suspects that his mistress is in love with the Captain and vows to find out.

FRANCESCHINA   Just then, Franceschina, Isabella's servant, comes on Isabella's orders to inform the young men what Flaminia said. She speaks to Pedrolino and reveals all concerning the Captain; then she leaves.

FLAMINIA   At that, Flaminia, now at her window, despairs because she believes the Captain is dead. Pedrolino says he is going to play a trick on her, and he begins to cry. When Flaminia asks him why, he says he has just seen a drowned man who looks like the Captain. She moans; Pedrolino shows her a way to avenge herself by pretending to hate the Captain, and in this way make Oratio and Flavio confess the murder. Then, when she makes a complaint against them, he explains, he will support her. She agrees and goes in, weeping. Pedrolino decides to frighten the lovers in order to get their money from them.

FLAVIO   Flavio and Oratio now enter, saying that they have heard all that
ORATIO   Franceschina told Pedrolino, and Pedrolino pretends to be frightened because he saw the Captain drown in the Tiber. He informs them that he knows the Captain was thrown into a ditch the night before. The lovers are frightened by this and know that his mistress will be displeased since she is in love with the Captain. They decide to speak with her. Pedrolino calls her.

FLAMINIA   Flaminia comes out, and praising the lovers, says that she is glad to know they have killed the Captain; she is much obliged to them. Oratio, taken in by her persuasive tone, admits that he did it because he was jealous of the Captain, and she thanks him.

CAPT. SPAVENTO

At that moment, the Captain, dressed in a shirt that is wet and dirty from his climb out of the ditch, reveals himself to all, who, believing him to be a ghost, are frightened and rush off. Here the first act ends.

ACT TWO

ORATIO
FLAVIO

Oratio and Flavio, believing they have seen the ghost of the Captain, show they are still frightened.

FRANCESCHINA
ARLECCHINO

Franceschina and Arlecchino, frightened, come screaming that the ghost of the Captain walks the city. Oratio runs off up the street; Flavio laughs. Arlecchino runs off.

ISABELLA

At that moment, Isabella, attracted by the noise, comes to the window. Frightened, Franceschina runs into the house; Isabella asks Flavio about Oratio. Smiling, he replies that if she comes out, he will tell her. When Isabella comes out, Flavio tells her all. Afterwards, he reveals his love for Flaminia. They speak of the satisfactions of lovers, and Isabella tells him of the favors done for Oratio.

ORATIO

Thereupon, Oratio, having seen and heard all, enters with sword drawn, calling them traitors. Flavio draws his sword, all the while trying, with Isabella, to clear things up, but Oratio does not want to listen to her. Fighting, the two men go up the street, leaving Isabella sorrowful.

PEDROLINO

Just then, Pedrolino enters screaming and saying, "Oh poor fellow! You too are dead because of a woman!" and talking to Isabella, they speak ambiguously. Pedrolino is speaking of the death of the Captain, but Isabella is speaking and believes they are talking of the death of Oratio or of Flavio; they continue to speak ambiguously until she goes into the house weeping and saying she has been the cause of the death of Oratio or Flavio. Pedrolino enters the house believing that they spoke of the Captain, and he had seen his ghost. Now he is convinced that Isabella had him killed.

PANTALONE
DR. GRATIANO

Pantalone now enters asking Gratiano to clear up what he had said. Gratiano tells him he knows Pedrolino is so treacherous that, if he doesn't watch him, he will play the bawd to his daughter.

PEDROLINO

At that, Pedrolino, who was hiding, comes out and calls Gratiano a liar. They come to blows, but Pantalone comes between them and makes peace.

ARLECCHINO	Arlecchino enters, frightened because he again saw the ghost of the Captain, his master. Pedrolino confirms the story of the ghost.
CAPT. SPAVENTO	At that moment, the Captain arrives in new clothes. All are frightened. Pedrolino and Arlecchino run off. The Captain takes Pantalone and Gratiano by the arms and makes them see that he is alive; then he turns to Pantalone and tells him that his daughter, who is in love with Flavio, the son of Gratiano, is a traitress. Pantalone says that can't be so because she has said things which showed she loved him; to clear it up, he calls her.
FLAMINIA	Flaminia comes out and tries to caress the Captain. He reproaches her for what she said to Flavio. She tries to explain, but he scorns her and leaves in a rage, swearing to kill Flavio. Gratiano leaves to warn his son Flavio. Pantalone scolds Flaminia.
PEDROLINO	Pedrolino arrives, and Pantalone asks him to testify to Flaminia's excuse. Planning to trick the Captain, they go to find him, leaving Flaminia happy.
ORATIO	Now, Oratio enters, crying, "Oh woman! Oh, traitorous friend!"
ISABELLA	At that moment, Isabella appears at her window. Although Flaminia sees her, she pretends not to. To make Isabella jealous, Flaminia speaks amorously to Oratio. He, to spite Isabella, responds amorously, blaming Flavio for the Captain's death.
ISABELLA	At that, Isabella, enraged and bitter at what she sees and hears, comes out. Flaminia immediately goes into the house, walking in a most lascivious manner. Oratio tries to leave when he sees Isabella, but she talks so fast that she forces him to listen to her scolding. Then he tries to embrace her, but she rejects him, reproaching him for all he had said to Flaminia. She calls him a traitor and goes back into the house. Oratio is left feeling wretched, and he goes to find Flavio.
PANTALONE CAPT. SPAVENTO PEDROLINO ARLECCHINO	Pantalone, Pedrolino, and Arlecchino enter with the Captain. Having removed all doubts about his daughter from the Captain's mind, Pantalone invites him into the house for a glass of wine.
DR. GRATIANO	Just then, Gratiano enters, and with great humility, begs the Captain not to kill his son Flavio. The Captain, pacified, promises to make peace. Pantalone calls his daughter.
FLAMINIA	Flaminia comes out and greets everyone. With great ceremony they all go into the house for breakfast, and the second act ends.

ACT THREE

NIGHT

ISABELLA   Isabella enters, unhappy because of Oratio.

FRANCESCHINA   Then, Franceschina comes out, and seeing Isabella, reproaches her for her doubts. Isabella says she wants to go find Flavio and marry him to spite Oratio. Franceschina raises many difficulties. Finally, seeing that she is stubborn, she tells Isabella that she has found the answer to her problem: she will dress Isabella up, and she is to do what Franceschina will tell her when she comes into the house. Isabella goes into the house.

ARLECCHINO   At that moment, Arlecchino arrives. Franceschina, pretending she is in love with him, talks sweetly to him and takes him into the house.

ORATIO   Oratio now enters, begging Flavio's pardon and asking him for
FLAVIO   help. Flavio, as a friend, forgives him. Then they hear someone coming and hide.

PANTALONE   Pantalone comes out of the house with his guests, inviting them
CAPT. SPAVENTO   all to have dinner together. Gratiano agrees, and they order
PEDROLINO   Pedrolino to find musicians for dancing at the wedding, and to
DR. GRATIANO   invite Isabella; after that they should know for sure that Tofano is not in the city. They go. Pedrolino remains, saying he is in love with Franceschina; he knocks, hoping to talk to her.

ISABELLA   Isabella comes out and learns of the invitation; she excuses herself from going. Pedrolino tells her that he will make Oratio go also. She does not speak ill of him, but she praises Flavio at the expense of Oratio, who, hidden nearby, hears all. Finally, Isabella says that if Flavio were to go, she would go and take Franceschina with her. Thus they agree, and she goes into the house. Flavio comes forth; he and Pedrolino agree that he is to dress as a musician, and Flavio exits. Oratio, still in hiding, does not show himself.

A SAILOR   A sailor with a lighted lantern now enters, looking for the house of Tofano. When Pedrolino questions him, the sailor says that Tofano has arrived and has stayed to dine with some merchants who accompanied him from Naples; he himself has been sent to give the news to Tofano's daughter, Isabella. When Pedrolino tells him he is his servant and that he will tell the daughter, the sailor leaves. The young men then reveal themselves to Pedrolino, who tells Flavio that in a little while he will return with his musical instrument, and exits. Flavio asks Oratio how he likes the return of Tofano, Isabella's father. Oratio replies that he is desperate and must find him to ask for his daughter's hand. As they go off, Flavio says he has thought of abducting her and giving her to him.

FRANCESCHINA   Franceschina, dressed as Arlecchino and carrying a lighted lantern, looks to see if anyone is around; then she comes out.

ISABELLA   Isabella enters, dressed in the clothes of Tofano, her father.

ORATIO   Oratio, who also arrives just then, sees her, and believing her to be Tofano—she is wearing false hair and a beard like her father's—asks for Isabella's hand. When she answers that she is not going to give her to him, but to Flavio, Oratio says he is going to kill himself. She replies that he can go hang himself and leaves with Franceschina. Oratio is miserable.

PANTALONE   Just then, Pantalone, Tofano, merchants, and others enter and
TOFANO   hear Oratio lamenting, naming Tofano for being thankless and
MERCHANTS   cruel. He says he is going to kill himself. Pantalone, on hearing his voice, recognizes him to be Oratio and presents him to Tofano. Oratio falls to his knees before him, saying, "Signor Tofano, why do you refuse me your daughter? Again, I beg you." Tofano is amazed, for he has never spoken to him before. He gives him hope, saying he is going to accompany the merchants right now, but soon she will be his. Oratio rejoices with Pantalone.

FLAVIO   At that moment, Flavio, dressed as a musician, enters playing an
PEDROLINO   instrument, accompanied by Pedrolino with a lighted lantern. Pantalone sends Flavio into the house and learns from Pedrolino that Isabella will come with Franceschina. Pantalone consoles Oratio.

ISABELLA   Thereupon, Isabella enters, dressed as Tofano. When Oratio asks him about his decision, she tells him curtly that she will not give her to him and goes immediately to avoid being recognized. Oratio, confused, begins to lament; Pantalone is puzzled by it.

TOFANO   Tofano now arrives; he promises to be as good as his word. Then he tells Pedrolino that Isabella has not gone to bed, and he will come to dine at Pantalone's house, where they will be expecting her. As they go into Pantalone's house, Pedrolino knocks at Isabella's door.

ARLECCHINO   Just then, Arlecchino, dressed in Franceschina's clothes and pretending to be a woman, comes out.

ISABELLA	Then, Isabella, dressed as Tofano, arrives, saying, "Here I am, my dear child."
TOFANO	At that moment, Tofano appears at the window and asks Pedrolino if Isabella is coming; Pedrolino wonders about her and runs into the house.
DR. GRATIANO	Gratiano now enters with a lighted lantern, sees Arlecchino, and believes him to be Franceschina; Isabella lets Gratiano see her; he thinks she is Tofano.
FRANCESCHINA	Franceschina arrives, and Gratiano thinks she is Arlecchino.
CAPT. SPAVENTO	The Captain enters, sees Franceschina in Arlecchino's clothes, and calls her Arlecchino. Arlecchino, dressed as Franceschina, answers.
FLAVIO ORATIO FLAMINIA PEDROLINO PANTALONE TOFANO	Then, the rest come out of the house, holding Oratio and Flavio in their midst, and making a great deal of noise. Flaminia complains that she has been robbed by Flavio, and Arlecchino and Franceschina hide.
ISABELLA	At that, Isabella enters, still dressed as Tofano. Together with the Captain and Oratio, all turn on Flavio for trying to rob Flaminia. When she realizes what is happening, she makes them all stop. Then she talks Flavio into yielding her to the Captain. Finally, Isabella kneels before Tofano, her father, and begs his pardon for disguising herself as him. Confessing that she has done all because of Oratio's love, she asks Flavio for husband. Flavio, on his knees, pleads for his friend Oratio, who takes her for wife.
ARLECCHINO FRANCESCHINA	At that moment, Arlecchino and Franceschina arrive; they identify themselves and ask their masters to pardon them. Franceschina becomes Arlecchino's wife; and here the comedy ends.

The Twenty-fifth Day

THE JEALOUSY OF ISABELLA *

ARGUMENT

There lived in Rome a Venetian merchant named Pantalone Bisognosi, a man of leisure, who was given to good food and good company; he had two children, a son named Fabritio and a daughter named Isabella. The son was taken away by Pantalone's brother and was never heard of again. The daughter lived in his house in a manner different from her father's. Meanwhile, as she idled her time away, she became enamored of a very noble and wealthy youth named Oratio, who likewise fell in love with her. They suffered many trials in their love. Finally, her brother Fabritio returned home. Because of their great resemblance, the brother and sister were mistaken for each other; finally he was recognized by his father, and she married her love.

CHARACTERS IN THE PLAY

Pantalone, a Venetian
Isabella, his daughter
Fabritio, his son who resembles Isabella
Pedrolino, his servant

Doctor Gratiano
Flaminia, his daughter
Franceschina, his servant

Oratio and
Flavio, gentlemen and friends

Captain Spavento
Arlecchino, his servant

Burattino, Host

Servants

* See Appendix p. 401.

ACT ONE

ROME	
NIGHT	
ISABELLA	Isabella appears at her window, wondering at the lateness of Oratio, her lover.
PANTALONE DR. GRATIANO BURATTINO	At that moment, Pantalone, accompanied by Gratiano, comes out of Burattino's inn, pleased that he has dined so well. Burattino invites them to come another evening when they can stay longer and enjoy the beautiful courtesans he will bring. They accept the offer and go off to banquet with a friend of theirs. Isabella scolds Burattino for making a whoremonger of her father; he tells her to mind her own business and goes in.
SERVANTS FLAVIO ORATIO FLAMINIA FRANCESCHINA	At that, servants enter with lighted torches, followed by Flavio, Oratio, Flaminia, and Franceschina. Flavio is laughing because Oratio has made Franceschina think that he is in love with her, and now Oratio asks Franceschina to sleep with him. She says she will if her mistress agrees; they all turn and laugh. Flaminia, with much lewd byplay, enters with Franceschina, who also acts lasciviously with Oratio. Oratio signals to Isabella to agree to the request.
ISABELLA	Isabella, who has remained at the window listening to all that took place, says, "He who makes love to the servant deserves to stay in the kitchen, rather than the bedroom." Without waiting to hear his reply, she goes in. The others are astonished.
CAPT. SPAVENTO ARLECCHINO	At that moment, the Captain and Arlecchino enter with lighted lanterns.
ISABELLA	Isabella again comes to the window. She tells them to go to her servant and not to make her wait any longer. The Captain asks Isabella what's going on; she tells him that she has been betrayed and destroyed. The Captain roars. Oratio and Flavio draw their swords on him, and fighting, they go off up the street. Isabella remains at the window.
PEDROLINO	Then, Pedrolino appears at the window with a light.
FRANCESCHINA	Franceschina enters, also carrying a light. Seeing her, Isabella says, "There is that whore who is the cause of everything." Franceschina replies, but Isabella says she does not speak with sluts and withdraws from the window. Franceschina, saying that she knows how it all began, goes in. Pedrolino is still at the window.

ORATIO
: Oratio returns, lamenting over Isabella; he sees Pedrolino, and calls him, asking him to come down with his lantern because he thinks that he is wounded. Pedrolino asks him to wait.

FRANCESCHINA
: Franceschina, near Isabella's window, whispers amorously to Oratio, pretending to be Isabella.

ISABELLA
: Isabella appears at her window and listens.

PEDROLINO
: Pedrolino comes out with a lantern. Isabella says, "Ah, traitor, I have caught you again making love with that whore." Franceschina, laughing, withdraws. Oratio tries to explain, but Isabella refuses to listen to him and closes the window in his face. Oratio remains lamenting with Pedrolino.

PANTALONE
DR. GRATIANO
: Thereupon, Pantalone and Gratiano enter with a lantern, both drunk. Oratio leaves. Pedrolino scolds Pantalone for his evil life, saying that one night he will find his daughter pregnant. Pantalone, laughing, goes into the house, and Gratiano tells Pedrolino to knock at his door. Pedrolino knocks.

FLAMINIA
: Flaminia comes out and scolds her father for his drunkenness. Gratiano embraces her and takes her into the house. Pedrolino remains, laughing.

CAPT. SPAVENTO
ARLECCHINO
: Now the Captain, accompanied by Arlecchino, enters, roaring with anger and ordering Pedrolino to call Isabella; he is going to tell her that, for love of her, he has killed all her lovers. Pedrolino laughs.

FLAVIO
: Flavio, who has heard the Captain's boasting, tells him he lies in his teeth; and he draws his sword. The Captain and Arlecchino flee, Flavio after them. Laughing, Pedrolino goes back into the house; and here the first act ends.

ACT TWO

DAY

ORATIO
: Oratio says he has not been to bed all night for thinking of the great wrong Isabella has done him.

PANTALONE
PEDROLINO
: Pantalone enters and learns from Pedrolino that Isabella is in love with Oratio. Shouting, Pantalone says, "It is impossible that Isabella, my daughter, is in love with Oratio."

FRANCESCHINA
: At that moment, Franceschina comes out and tells Pantalone that it is true; many times she has heard them talking amorously together.

FLAVIO

Flavio enters and scolds Franceschina, having heard all she said. Franceschina, enraged, says that he will be sorry and goes into the house. Pantalone tells Flavio not to pay any attention to the words of a servant and leaves with Pedrolino.

ISABELLA

Isabella appears at her window and indicates that she has heard all; she thanks Flavio for what he did, saying she did not want to answer that slut Franceschina.

FLAMINIA

Flaminia now appears at her window and tells Isabella that she should not speak so abusively of her servant. When both Isabella and Flavio beg her pardon, Flaminia says to Flavio that now she knows how little he loves her, and feeling scorned, she goes into the house. Flavio feels bad, and Isabella consoles him, saying that that traitor Oratio is the cause of all this trouble; then she goes into the house.

ORATIO

Oratio, having heard all that Isabella has said, is unhappy. Flavio now consoles him.

PEDROLINO

Pedrolino, out of breath, comes looking for Oratio; when he sees him, he tells him that Pantalone has said that although Isabella is in love with him, it has done him no good. He thinks one thing and does another, and he is negotiating to marry her to someone else. Oratio is unhappy, so all go to try to work out a solution.

CAPT. SPAVENTO
ARLECCHINO

The Captain and Arlecchino come swaggering in, bragging about the fight the night before.

FABRITIO

Fabritio, Isabella's brother, now enters; he has come from Sicily to find his father. Since he looks just like her, the Captain and Arlecchino think he is Isabella. The Captain makes an amorous appeal to him. Fabritio, angered, draws his sword. The Captain says he does not fight with women and leaves; Arlecchino does the same and leaves. Fabritio knocks at the door of the inn, hoping to rent a room from Burattino.

BURATTINO

Burattino comes out, welcomes him, and then asks where he comes from and who he is. Fabritio tells him his story and then goes in. Burattino says that he must be Isabella, daughter of Pantalone, whose wicked life is causing his children's ruin. He leaves to find Oratio.

ISABELLA

Isabella enters, dressed as a man, having found the occasion to get the clothes in a performance of a play given by the servants. She wants to find out if Oratio is unfaithful, but seeing her father coming, she leaves.

PANTALONE PEDROLINO	Pantalone enters, asking Pedrolino what he has been doing with Oratio and Flavio. When Pedrolino gives an excuse, Pantalone says he is going to marry Isabella to Gratiano. Pedrolino reproaches him, but Pantalone says he wants to do things his own way; he knocks at the door.
DR. GRATIANO	Gratiano enters, and Pantalone tells him of his offer to Isabella: he is to give all of his inheritance to her if Fabritio, his son, born at the same time as Isabella, does not return. Fabritio, he explains, was taken away by Pantalone's brother, and they have had no news since. Gratiano agrees.
BURATTINO	Then, Burattino, who has heard that Gratiano is to be the groom, comes out, laughs at him, and goes back into the house. Pantalone insists all the while that Gratiano has taken Isabella's hand.
BURATTINO	At that, Burattino returns and says, laughing, that in the inn is a youth who says he wants to talk to a Venetian. Pantalone tells him to bring him out and sends Pedrolino to call Isabella. Pedrolino goes in and returns to say that Isabella is not in the house. Pantalone is worried.
BURATTINO FABRITIO	Burattino comes out with Fabritio, the young man, to talk to Pantalone; Pantalone and Gratiano both think he is Isabella and scold him. They try to grab him, and Fabritio shouts for help.
ORATIO	At that moment, Oratio arrives. Fabritio says, "Sir, free me from the hands of these men." When Oratio draws his sword and chases them off, Fabritio thanks him. Oratio, thinking he is Isabella, begs his pardon for the involuntary offense he gave. Fabritio laughs and says he knows of none and goes into the inn. Oratio, unhappy, leaves; and the second act ends.

ACT THREE

CAPT. SPAVENTO ISABELLA	The Captain enters, complaining to Isabella of the affront done to him. Isabella replies that she had never seen him before she had appeared in these clothes. The Captain asks her to tell him her story. She tells him that she has dressed in a man's clothes to prove to Oratio that he is a traitor; she asks him to help her prove his faithlessness, promising to be his wife. The Captain agrees, and she leaves to go back home.
FLAVIO	Flavio arrives. Seeing him, the Captain says that all is peaceful; then he says they must, between them, call a truce for a few days until they can work out their differences. He asks Flavio about his

friend Oratio, and Flavio replies that he does not know where he is, and the Captain goes off in a huff. Flavio decides that he made a mistake in telling Oratio that Isabella is dressed in man's clothes.

ARLECCHINO

Arlecchino now arrives and arrogantly asks Flavio about his master. Flavio, furious at his bad manners, beats him.

FRANCESCHINA

Just then, Franceschina enters and scolds Flavio for beating Arlecchino. Flavio, angered, is about to beat her too, but Arlecchino picks her up and carries her off.

PANTALONE

Pantalone enters, despairing because of his daughter. He sees Flavio and complains to him about Oratio having helped his daughter. Flavio makes excuses for Oratio and begs him to pardon Isabella.

ISABELLA

At that, Isabella arrives. Pantalone, on seeing her, is angered and demands she tell him why she is wearing those clothes. She heatedly tells him that for a time she was in love with Oratio, but because he wronged her, she put on those clothes in order to pick a fight with him; with that she exits, and Pantalone, weeping, begs Flavio to follow her and talk her out of her plan. Flavio goes.

FABRITIO

Fabritio comes out of the inn. Pantalone does not see him come out, but finally catches sight of him and thinks he is Isabella. Again, he begins to beg her not to fight; Fabritio laughs, saying he does not know him.

PEDROLINO

Pedrolino now enters, and thinking he is Isabella, reproaches Fabritio. He tells him that she should respect her father. Fabritio makes fun of him.

FLAMINIA

Flaminia enters and tells Fabritio—she too is deceived—that she has reason to be angry with her; she does not like to see her dressed in man's clothes, as she is a woman; and if she does not want to go into her father's house, she can go into her own house with her. When Fabritio asks if it is all right with the old man, Pantalone says that it is, and as Fabritio and Flaminia embrace and go into the house, Pantalone and Pedrolino leave to find Oratio so they can come to some agreement.

BURATTINO

Burattino enters and says he has heard everything, and it will be a fine thing when she finds out he is a man.

FRANCESCHINA
ARLECCHINO

Just then, Franceschina and Arlecchino enter, arguing because Arlecchino has enjoyed Franceschina, and he will give her only one lira. They ask Burattino to be the judge, but he says that he will have to see the merchandise before he can tell the price.

CAPT. SPAVENTO
ORATIO
FLAVIO

At that moment, the Captain, Oratio, and Flavio enter. The Captain tells Oratio of Isabella's faithlessness, and Oratio is enraged. Flavio comes between them, promising all will be worked out. Then Franceschina goes into the house; Arlecchino leaves; Burattino goes into the inn. The Captain stays, insisting they cannot agree.

FRANCESCHINA

At that, Franceschina comes out, saying that Isabella has become a man.

PANTALONE
DR. GRATIANO

Then, Pantalone and Gratiano arrive. When Franceschina tells Gratiano that she found a young man embracing his daughter, Flaminia, Pantalone reassures Gratiano that it is only his daughter, Isabella, in man's clothes. Gratiano goes into the house to see. Pantalone begs Oratio to make peace with Isabella, promising to give her to him as wife. Again the Captain says that is not possible.

FABRITIO
DR. GRATIANO

Just then, Fabritio and Gratiano come out of the house, both shouting at the same time. Fabritio finally explains that he is a man, the son of Pantalone de Bisognosi; he was taken off as a small child by his uncle, who is dead. He has come to see if his father is still alive. Pantalone greets him with great joy, and the Captain says he is going to find Isabella. Fabritio goes to take the hand of his wife, and Pantalone again begs Oratio to make peace with Isabella.

PEDROLINO

Pedrolino now arrives, saying that the Captain is bringing Isabella and is determined to fight Oratio. Pantalone despairs.

CAPT. SPAVENTO
ISABELLA

Thereupon, the Captain immediately arrives with Isabella and draws his sword on Oratio, calling him traitor. Oratio drops to his knees, saying he has done no wrong. When Isabella reminds him of the amorous words he said to Franceschina, he replies that he was only joking with the servant. Franceschina confesses that she imitated the voice of Isabella at the window for spite. Flavio and everyone beg Isabella to forgive Oratio. She accepts the story, forgives him, and takes him for husband. The Captain roars, saying that Isabella, by her own word, is his. Oratio draws his sword, replying that he who would take Isabella, must first take his life; the Captain is pacified. Oratio marries Isabella, and Arlecchino marries Franceschina for having enjoyed her, saying that all must go to visit Fabritio, Isabella's brother, who has returned to his country. They all go into Gratiano's house to celebrate the weddings; and here the comedy ends.

The Twenty-sixth Day

THE ALEXANDRIAN CARPETS *

ARGUMENT

There lived in Bologna two students, young gentlemen of Rome of good family and noble fathers, one named Oratio, the son of Pantalone Bisognosi, and the other named Flavio, the son of Doctor Gratiano. It happened that while at school in Bologna, the young men fell in love with two young ladies of noble families. The young ladies returned their love, and during their honorable courting, the young men were called back to their native land by their parents. When the young men left, the young ladies, after a long wait, decided, each without telling the other, to leave her country and her parents and go to Rome where they met. After many trials they were reunited with their lovers, and to the satisfaction of all were married by their parents.

CHARACTERS IN THE PLAY

Pantalone, a Venetian
Oratio, his son
Pedrolino, his servant
Olivetta, his servant

Doctor Gratiano
Flavio, his son

Claudio Francese
Franceschina, his servant

Fabritio, that is, Isabella in man's clothes
Arlecchino, her servant
A footman of Isabella's father

Flaminia, dressed as a gypsy

Policemen, who talk

* See Appendix p. 401.

184

PROPERTIES

A chest with a large cover
Two Alexandrian carpets
A Turkish merchant's costume
A slave's costume for Pantalone
A large traveling bag
A written letter for Claudio
Another letter
A courier's costume

ACT ONE

THE CITY OF ROME	
PANTALONE ORATIO	Pantalone enters, reproaching his son for chasing women, gambling, and leading a life of vice after he returned from school at Bologna. Oratio makes excuses.
FLAVIO	At that, Flavio enters, greets Oratio, and hears him say that Pantalone is wrong about him. They go off together, leaving Pantalone complaining of the bad habits that Oratio has taken up.
DR. GRATIANO	Then, Gratiano, father of Flavio, enters and Pantalone tells him that his son Flavio is corrupting his Oratio. Gratiano laughs at this, saying that youth must follow its own way, and Flavio is not corrupting his son. Pantalone wants to know who is corrupting him then.
PEDROLINO	At that moment, Pedrolino arrives and listens to the argument. Gratiano, pointing at Pedrolino, tells Pantalone that Pedrolino is the one who is corrupting Oratio, and Flavio also. Pantalone believes him and says that he is also stealing things in the house. Pedrolino defends himself by telling Pantalone that Oratio took away the two Alexandrian carpets. Pantalone despairs, and with Gratiano goes to the Jewish merchants to see if the carpets have been sold. Pedrolino has told Pantalone what he did so that he himself could give the carpets to Oratio.
CLAUDIO FRANCESE	Claudio Francese enters, reading a letter in which a merchant in Lione informs him that one of his correspondents has rescued his brother, named Giachetto, and soon he will be in

Rome. The merchant is sending him with a Levantine who has ransomed him for 300 scudi. Pedrolino notes the sense of the letter, then approaches Claudio and talks about Pantalone, who, because he is penniless, will have to sell the two Alexandrian carpets. He urges Claudio to buy them, and he goes into the house for them. Claudio will give fifty gold crowns for them and hold half the money, promising on his honor not to say anything to Pantalone and pay the rest sometime later in the day. Claudio has Pedrolino call his servant, Franceschina.

FRANCESCHINA　　Franceschina comes out and jokes with Pedrolino, who takes the carpets and carries them into the house. Claudio leaves. Pedrolino comes back out and goes off to find Oratio and give him the money.

ISABELLA　　Isabella enters, dressed in man's clothes. She has left Bologna and
ARLECCHINO　　come to Rome because of her love for Flavio. She is traveling with Arlecchino, who carries a bag. She speaks of finding an inn.

ORATIO　　At that moment, Oratio enters, complaining about his father and saying he wants to leave Rome because he is so unhappy. Isabella shows that she recognizes Oratio from Bologna, but she says nothing about it. Then, speaking to him, she tells him she is on her way to Naples. Oratio asks her to stay in Rome for two days longer, offering to accompany her to Naples. Isabella accepts his offer. Oratio then invites her to stay in his house and not bother looking for an inn. He calls Olivetta.

OLIVETTA　　Olivetta, Oratio's servant, comes out to receive them into the house. Oratio tells her Isabella is called Fabritio, and they go into the house with all the ceremony of masters and servants.

FLAMINIA　　Flaminia, who has also come from Bologna, enters, dressed as a gypsy. She is in love with Oratio, but she does not mention his name. She praises the city, speaks of the power of Love, and of the ingratitude of her lover, still not naming him.

PEDROLINO　　Just then, Pedrolino enters. He has been unable to find Oratio. Flaminia hides.

ORATIO　　At that moment, Oratio arrives and hears from Pedrolino about the trick of the carpets and of the twenty-five gold crowns received. Oratio then tells Pedrolino about the strangers who come from far away, sends him to buy some food to honor the occasion, and goes into the house, leaving Pedrolino.

FLAMINIA　　Flaminia then enters, approaches Pedrolino, and calls him by name. She reads his palm, tells him he is a thief, and speaks of the carpets he stole from the house. Pedrolino is amazed.

FRANCESCHINA	At that, Franceschina comes out, and Pedrolino asks her to go to the nearby inn and buy some food, gives her the money, and tells her there is a lot to buy. Franceschina goes off to buy the food, leaving Pedrolino talking to the gypsy, who tells him that he has been traveling about the world and to Bologna.
FLAVIO	Then, Flavio enters and asks about Oratio. Pedrolino tells him he is in the house with a stranger. Flavio looks at the gypsy many times, then goes into the house. Pedrolino asks the gypsy to tell his master his fortune too.
FRANCESCHINA	Thereupon, Franceschina enters with a chest full of food. Pedrolino has her take it into Pantalone's house and sends the gypsy with her to tell the fortunes of the people in the house. Pedrolino, being alone, hears the voice of Pantalone, and goes into the house.
PANTALONE	Pantalone arrives, desperate because he has not heard anything about the missing carpets.
FLAVIO	At that, Flavio comes out of Pantalone's house, bows without speaking, and goes into his father's house immediately.
ISABELLA	Isabella comes out of Pantalone's house, also bows without speaking, and goes into Gratiano's house. Puzzled, Pantalone also bows without saying a word.
PEDROLINO	Immediately, Pedrolino comes out, bows, and goes off up the street.
FRANCESCHINA	Now, Franceschina, who comes out with the chest on her head, bows and goes into Gratiano's house.
FLAMINIA	Immediately, Flaminia comes out, bows, as did Franceschina, and enters after her.
ORATIO	Following Flaminia, Oratio comes out, bows, and goes into Gratiano's house.
ARLECCHINO	Thereupon, Arlecchino comes out, bows, and enters Gratiano's house. Pantalone, seeing that no one says a word, leaves without saying a word to anyone and goes off up the street, bowing to everyone. And here the first act ends.

ACT TWO

PANTALONE PEDROLINO	Pantalone enters, complaining to Pedrolino because he saw so many people coming out of his house. Pedrolino tells him that the young man is the son of Claudio, who has come from France

and who, because he wants to make his home far from his father, needs to buy some furniture. For that purpose, Oratio brought him into the house to sell him some of his things; and if Pantalone had not come when he did, Oratio would have sold him everything. When they heard Pantalone coming, they immediately left the house, afraid and silent. The other people had come into the house because they were curious to see the furniture. Enraged, Pantalone goes to find Claudio. Pedrolino remains alone, laughing.

ORATIO DR. GRATIANO	Just then, Oratio enters, begging Gratiano to rent him a room for three or four days. Meanwhile, Pedrolino goes into the house. Gratiano promises to help Oratio even if Pantalone holds it against him. They hear noise in Gratiano's house.
FLAMINIA PEDROLINO	At that moment, Flaminia comes running out of the house, chased by Pedrolino, who, she cries, is trying to rape her, and calling him traitor, she runs off. Pedrolino, calling her thief, chases after her. Oratio and Gratiano laugh.
ISABELLA FLAVIO	Isabella then comes out with Flavio, who learns that Gratiano has kindly offered him a room for a few days. She thanks him, and Gratiano and Flavio exit, leaving Oratio and Isabella.
PEDROLINO	Then, Pedrolino returns, in despair at having lost the gypsy, with whom he has fallen in love. Oratio consoles him, then reproaches him for the wrong he does to Franceschina and to Olivetta, who love him. Pedrolino says he is not sure of any one of them.
FRANCESCHINA	Thereupon, Franceschina, who has heard every word, comes behind him and grabs him by the throat as if to strangle him. Pedrolino cries out. Oratio separates them and makes peace. On his knees, Pedrolino begs Franceschina's pardon, and she then goes into the house. Pedrolino calls Arlecchino.
ARLECCHINO	Arlecchino comes out. Pedrolino sends him into Pantalone's house to fetch Isabella's traveling bag. Isabella asks Oratio if Flavio is about to fall in love. Oratio says he believes not, but that in Bologna, where they went to school together, he said that he was courting a young lady of noble family, more to pass the time than for any other reason. Isabella asks Oratio if he loved any lady. Oratio says yes, that he still loves her.
PEDROLINO ARLECCHINO	At that, Arlecchino returns with the traveling bag, and Pedrolino sends him into Gratiano's house. Isabella excuses herself to go take a rest in Gratiano's house and goes in. Oratio then tells Pedrolino that any way he can he must get some money because he is going to Naples with the stranger. Pedrolino says that, short

of selling his own father, he doesn't know where he is going to get any money. They hear Pantalone coming, and they leave.

PANTALONE Pantalone enters, desperate, because he has not found Claudio.

CLAUDIO Just then, Claudio arrives and greets Pantalone, who immediately calls him a villain. Claudio thinks he is angry because of the carpets; he talks to Pantalone in metaphor, saying that the fear of bankruptcy forces Pantalone to speak recklessly. Pantalone tells him that his son has come from France and wants to buy the furniture right out of his house. Claudio replies that he has no children, and he bought only the two Alexandrian carpets but will not say from whom. Enraged, Pantalone draws his dagger on Claudio, who runs off, and Pantalone chases him, shouting, "Stop, thief! Stop, thief!"

PEDROLINO Pedrolino enters, looking for Pantalone.

PANTALONE At that moment, Pantalone returns and says that Claudio saved himself by running into a shop. Pedrolino asks him what happened, and Pantalone tells him everything. Pedrolino then tells him that Claudio is a fraud; everything he accepted from Oratio in the house should be his, and Pantalone confirms this. Pedrolino next tells him that Claudio is waiting for his brother, a slave, ransomed from the Turks by a merchant. This Pedrolino learned by listening when Claudio read his letter. But since, after so many years, Claudio could not recognize his brother, Pedrolino urges Pantalone to pretend to be the brother. Then he could go into Claudio's house and recover all the things stolen from him. Pantalone agrees to this stratagem and goes into the house to disguise himself.

ISABELLA Isabella enters, speaking of the pain it gives her to see how Flavio has forgotten her.

FLAMINIA Then, Flaminia enters alone, and not seeing Isabella, rails against Oratio and against herself, naming Isabella, who hears her and goes over to identify her as her neighbor in Bologna. When Isabella approaches, Flaminia tries to tell her fortune. Isabella lets her, then speaks directly to her, calling her Flaminia. Finally they reveal themselves to each other, and speaking of their loves, promise to help each other.

FRANCESCHINA Franceschina then comes out. She is jealous of the gypsy over Pedrolino. She shouts at Flaminia, telling her to get out or else she will beat her. The women scream back at her. Furious, she calls them both sluts.

ARLECCHINO At that moment, Arlecchino arrives and tries to restrain Isabella, his mistress. Franceschina jumps on him as if to strangle him.

DR. GRATIANO | Thereupon, Gratiano comes out and, separating them, sends Franceschina into the house. Then, fondling the gypsy, he takes her into the house with Isabella.

PEDROLINO
PANTALONE | Pedrolino comes out dressed as a Levantine, accompanied by Pantalone dressed as a slave. They do a scene, playing at talking Turkish. Then they knock at Claudio's door.

FRANCESCHINA | Franceschina comes out and says that Claudio is not home, but he will return. She goes back in, and they remain, waiting.

CLAUDIO | Just then, Claudio arrives. Pedrolino tells him he is the merchant who ransomed his brother Giachetto. Claudio, rejoicing, embraces his brother and pays the three hundred gold crowns to the merchant. Then, happy, he takes his brother into the house. Laughing, Pedrolino leaves; and the second act ends.

ACT THREE

PEDROLINO | Pedrolino enters, laughing at the trick he played on Claudio. He starts thinking of ways to get Pantalone out of the house.

ARLECCHINO | At that moment, Arlecchino arrives. Pedrolino sends him into the house to get Pantalone's clothes, promising to help him in his love for the gypsy. Arlecchino returns, puts the clothes in a corner, and calls Claudio; then he goes back into Pantalone's house.

CLAUDIO | Claudio comes out, and Pedrolino tells him that if he will give him Franceschina, he will reveal a piece of treachery that was done him. Claudio promises. Pedrolino reveals that the slave is not his brother but Pantalone, who disguised himself in order to be able to kill him in his own house at night. Claudio is enraged. Pedrolino tells him to go right away to the magistrate and have Pantalone arrested. Claudio goes off, leaving Pedrolino.

PANTALONE | Then, Pantalone comes out with the carpets which he found in Claudio's house. Pedrolino, pretending to be breathless, tells him that a thief, sent by his son to rob for him, is in Pantalone's house and he, Pedrolino, has locked him in. Pantalone puts his clothes on, gives the carpets to Pedrolino, and goes off to see the magistrate. Pedrolino remains.

ORATIO | At that, Oratio arrives, and Pedrolino tells what he has done. Oratio makes him turn over the three hundred gold crowns, and they agree to find horses and leave together for Naples. Oratio goes off. Pedrolino puts the carpets in the house and returns.

POLICEMEN	At that moment, policemen arrive, sent by Pantalone to arrest the thief in his house. Pedrolino lets them into the house and then hides.
ARLECCHINO POLICEMEN	Arlecchino is led out by the police, who think he is the thief. He complains and finally breaks away from them; with a great deal of noise, the policemen chase off after him while Pedrolino laughs.
DR. GRATIANO	Gratiano comes out to ask what the noise is all about. Pedrolino tells him that Pantalone caught his son and Oratio in the act of robbing his house. Gratiano, enraged, goes to get the police. Pedrolino laughs.
ISABELLA FLAMINIA	Isabella then enters with Flaminia, telling her how they can reveal themselves to their lovers. Not seeing Pedrolino, they call each other by name. Pedrolino, hiding, recognizes them as the women who knew the young men in Bologna; then he shows himself and they, finding they are discovered, drop to their knees before him and say that without his help they will not be able to enjoy their lovers, and if not, they would wish to die. Pedrolino drops to his knees between the two women, and weeping, kisses now one, then the other. Finally he promises to help them and sends them into Gratiano's house to dress in women's clothes. They go in, while Pedrolino begins to work out various devices.
ORATIO	At that moment, Oratio enters and tells Pedrolino that he has found horses, and everything is ready to go. Weeping, Pedrolino tells him he has heard from a woman who has come from Bologna that Flaminia, whom he loved so much, is dead, and in dying she uttered his name many times. Oratio weeps with grief. Pedrolino says he may talk to the woman and calls her.
FLAMINIA	Flaminia comes out in her own clothes. Oratio recognizes her and rushes to embrace her. She tells him all she did for love of him, and Oratio promises to marry her. Flaminia then reveals that Fabritio is Isabella, who is in love with Flavio, and begs him to do all he can to make Flavio marry Isabella. Oratio marvels at this and promises to do all he can.
FLAVIO	Just then, Flavio arrives. Oratio introduces him to Flaminia, and Flavio embraces her as a friend. She tells him that Isabella loves him and begs him to go to Bologna. Flavio replies that he cannot go now for love of his father. Pedrolino says that a messenger has come to speak to them. He calls.
ISABELLA	Isabella comes out in woman's clothes. Flavio, seeing her, is dumbfounded. Finally he rushes to embrace her, and promises to marry her.

PANTALONE
DR. GRATIANO

Then, Pantalone enters with Gratiano, arguing with him over having his son arrested.

CLAUDIO
POLICEMEN

At that moment, Claudio enters and has Pantalone arrested. Distressed by that, Pedrolino drops to his knees and begs Pantalone's pardon for all the tricks he played: first the selling of the carpets; then the selling of Pantalone as a slave; for giving money to his son to go to Naples; for having had Arlecchino arrested; and for selling the gypsy. Then he tells them he is the one who gave wives to Flavio and to Oratio, and he shows them their wives. The old men say that they are not pleased.

ARLECCHINO

Arlecchino then enters, rejoicing because the footman has come to talk to Pantalone and Gratiano.

THE FOOTMAN

The footman of Isabella's father enters, sees her, and greets her. He presents letters which say that the fathers of the young men are advised that their daughters have followed their lovers, and if they agree, the marriage of the young people should follow to confirm their friendship. All rejoice. Pedrolino marries Franceschina, and here the comedy ends.

The Twenty-seventh Day

THE FAITHLESS ONE *

ARGUMENT

There lived in Venice one Stefanello Bottarga, a very rich merchant, who, because of his great wealth, was much envied and hated. It happened that once as he left for Padua, he was attacked by his enemies and left for dead. Then one of his faithful servants learned that his master's chief steward had done it; and afraid that the same might happen to him, the servant left Venice with Stefanello's daughter and much of his wealth. Stefanello did not die, but returned, his old self, with his son. After many years, at Mantua he came upon the place where, through many strange events, he found his servant, his daughter, and his riches, and at the same time made peace with his enemies. Afterwards, he found a wife for his son and returned to his native Venice, where he lived happily the rest of his life.

CHARACTERS IN THE PLAY

Pantalone, then finally, Stefanello Bottarga
Oratio, his son
Burattino, his servant

Flavio, a gentleman
Pedrolino, his friend
Flaminia, believed to be his daughter

Isabella, dressed in man's clothes, daughter of Cassandro
    Aretusi Bolognese, who does not appear

A Courier

Franceschina, hostess

[Captain Spavento]

[Arlecchino]

[Gratiano]

* See Appendix p. 404.

193

ACT ONE

THE CITY OF
MANTUA

PANTALONE

Pantalone comes down the street reading a letter from Cassandro Aretusi Bolognese, in which he learns of the confirmation of the match between his son Oratio and Cassandro's daughter Isabella, and that he is to send his son immediately to Bologna to be married. He knocks at the door of the house.

BURATTINO

Burattino appears at the window, half asleep. Pantalone asks him if Oratio is at home. Burattino says he does not know, and he goes to look in his room. Pantalone begins to read the letter again and sees that it was written on the twentieth, and it has now been ten days since it was written. He perceives that there is no response from his son and that Burattino does not return. He complains that he has always had bad luck with his children and his servants, and he goes into the house.

ISABELLA
A SERVANT

Isabella enters dressed in man's clothes. She had fled from Bologna to avoid marrying Oratio and to follow Flavio, her lover, who was to wait for her in Ferrara; she enters, lamenting to her servant that she did not find Flavio in Ferrara. The servant tells her that they left Bologna much later than he, and Flavio had reason to come to Mantua. She knows that Flavio has an uncle in Mantua who could give them some information. At that moment they hide.

PANTALONE
ORATIO
BURATTINO

Pantalone enters, reproaching Oratio for sleeping too late. Then he reads him the letter from Cassandro Aretusi, which Isabella and her servant overhear, acknowledging Oratio would be her husband. Oratio listens to the letter and rejoices, saying he wants to go immediately to his dear wife. Isabella thinks up a tale and tells her servant to follow what she says. Then she greets Pantalone, asking him about an inn. Pantalone points to it, then hears that she comes from Bologna. He asks her if she knows Cassandro Aretusi. She says yes, that he has made a match between Oratio, the son of Pantalone, and his daughter, Isabella, but the poor girl died a sudden death. Hearing this, Oratio falls half dead with grief into the arms of Isabella. Grieving, Pantalone has the servants carry him into the house. Then he asks the youth how long ago Isabella died, and she says it is six days. Pantalone says it is possible because the letter was written ten days ago.

SERVANT	At that, the servant returns and consoles Pantalone. Isabella is amazed by Oratio's grief.
BURATTINO	Burattino then enters, telling them that Oratio has regained consciousness, but wishes to die with his wife. Burattino offers the hospitality of the house to the youth. She thanks him, and Pantalone enters the house with Burattino. The servant asks Isabella why she said what she did to stop Oratio's departure and tells her she doesn't realize what a bad thing she has done. They knock at the door of the inn.
FRANCESCHINA	Franceschina, the hostess, comes out. Seeing the youth, she fondles him and takes him and the servant inside to give him a room.
FLAVIO PEDROLINO	Flavio enters, telling Pedrolino that he did not find Isabella in Ferrara as they had agreed; she has come to Mantua. Pedrolino says he is unhappy about leaving Flaminia, his daughter, at home as they must remain out of Bologna for some time. Flavio replies that, since he must find Isabella, Pedrolino should return to Bologna while he leaves for Milan.
PANTALONE	At that moment, Pantalone enters, saying he wants to find someone from Bologna. Flavio tells him that he comes from Bologna, and that he also knows Cassandro, and it has been ten days since he left the city. Then Pantalone begins to weep, saying he weeps for the death of Isabella, his daughter-in-law and daughter of Cassandro, who died six days ago. At this news, Flavio leaves, grief-stricken. Pedrolino, who has been watching Pantalone closely, shows that he knows him and leaves. Pantalone goes off up the street.
CAPT. SPAVENTO ARLECCHINO	Captain Spavento and Arlecchino enter, having come from Rome on their way to Milan. The Captain praises the city of Mantua and says he is going to stay four or five days. They knock at the door of the inn.
FRANCESCHINA	Franceschina comes out to receive them, saying that they are welcome, and they enter.
BURATTINO	Burattino comes out, saying that Oratio does nothing but weep; he marvels that one could fall so much in love by letter.
ISABELLA	At that, Isabella comes out and listens to Burattino, who, seeing her, tells her all the compassionate words which Oratio spoke on the death of his betrothed Isabella. She leaves, weeping outright, to the astonishment of Burattino.
PANTALONE	Then, Pantalone arrives. Burattino tells him to go into the house to console Oratio. Weeping, Pantalone sends Burattino into the house and remains, still weeping.

GRATIANO	Thereupon, Gratiano comes out and asks Pantalone why he is weeping. Pantalone tells him and asks his advice about it. Gratiano gives him contradictory advice, without coming to any useful conclusion. Irritated, Pantalone tells him to go chase himself, and Gratiano leaves. Pantalone, weeping, goes into the house to console Oratio; and here the first act ends.

ACT TWO

FLAMINIA	Flaminia, dressed as a pilgrim, arrives from Bologna, having followed Flavio, whom she loves. She expresses her fear of Pedrolino, her father, and speaks of the force and power of Love.
BURATTINO	At that moment, Burattino arrives. She asks him if he knows one Rudolfo Belmonte, uncle of a scholar named Flavio, who studied in Bologna. Burattino says he does not know him. He fondles her and tries to kiss her, but she calls him a villain.
PANTALONE	At that, Pantalone arrives, scolds Burattino, and sends him into the house. Flaminia thanks him and asks for a place in Mantua where she can rest for a day without fearing for her honor. Pantalone promises to give her a room and calls Burattino.
BURATTINO	Burattino comes out to take Flaminia into Pantalone's house. They go in, leaving Pantalone, who says he feels great compassion for this young lady who reminds him of his own little girl, lost when he had to leave Venice because of his enemies. He then goes into the house.
GRATIANO ARLECCHINO	Gratiano enters with Arlecchino to go to see the marvels of Mantua and the beauty of its women. Together, they go off up the street.
FLAVIO PEDROLINO	Flavio and Pedrolino enter, grieving over Pantalone's news of Isabella's death. They count the days since they left and find that it is possible that she is dead. They feel wretched. Pedrolino despairs at having left his daughter Flaminia in the care of a servant, revealing that she is in love with him. Hearing that, Flavio tells him if it is true that Isabella is dead, he will take Pedrolino's daughter for wife. Pedrolino tells him that when he decides to give her in marriage, he will reveal something very important. Then he tells Flavio that Pantalone looks like his old master, and perhaps he is in great danger.
ORATIO	At that moment, Oratio comes out of the house, pensive and melancholy. He greets the strangers, asking them where they come from. Flavio says from Bologna. Oratio begins to weep.

Flavio learns that he weeps for the death of Isabella, daughter of Cassandro Aretusi. Flavio also begins to weep and so leaves. Oratio asks Pedrolino why the gentleman was weeping. He replies that Flavio weeps every time he sees someone else weeping.

PANTALONE At that, Pantalone comes out with a letter to be sent to Bologna. Pedrolino tells him that in an hour he is leaving for Bologna, that he can trust him with it, and Pantalone gives him the letter. Then Pedrolino asks the old man his name, his last name, his country, and about his children. Pantalone, suspecting him of being an enemy, gives an excuse for not answering, and Pedrolino leaves. Then Pantalone regrets having given him the letter, consoles Oratio, and goes. Oratio complains about love and about the death of his betrothed.

ISABELLA Then, Isabella comes out and listens to him. Oratio recognizes her as the one who gave him the news of the death of his betrothed. He greets her and asks if she knew Isabella and how beautiful she was. She then begins to tell him that she herself resembles her; they are the same age and alike in many ways. Then she says to him, "Sir, you see these hands; notice that they are the very same hands." Oratio kisses them. Then Oratio says, "Your hair is just like Isabella's," and praises her hair. She suggests that her eyes and her mouth are the same. Then Oratio embraces and kisses her and says, "Why can I not thus kiss my dear wife?"

BURATTINO At that, Isabella weeps, and Burattino arrives, and reproaches Oratio for kissing a beardless youth.

PEDROLINO Then, Pedrolino enters and recognizes Isabella.

FLAVIO Flavio arrives, and he also recognizes her. Suspicious of Flavio, Isabella immediately hides her face behind her riding cloak and leaves to avoid being recognized. Flavio and Pedrolino follow her.

FLAMINIA Thereupon, Flaminia, who has stood behind the door and has recognized her father Pedrolino, comes out. She also has recognized Isabella. She takes Oratio by the hand and leads him into the house. Burattino is astonished at her actions and goes into the house.

CAPT. SPAVENTO The Captain enters, praising Mantua. Then he tells Arlecchino he
ARLECCHINO is leaving for Milan the following day. Afraid of losing his love, Arlecchino says he has fallen in love with the hostess and that he would like to take her along. The Captain tells him to call Franceschina, and Arlecchino calls her.

FRANCESCHINA | Franceschina comes out. The Captain tells her of Arlecchino's love, but adds that if she must love, she must love the master, not the servant, and all go into the house, including the jealous Arlecchino.

PEDROLINO | Pedrolino enters, saying he is almost certain that the old Venetian is his old master, and Isabella has run away. He decides to open the letter which Pantalone gave him. He opens it and reads the signature which says Stefanello Bottarga. Having confirmed his suspicion, he begins to think of what to do.

BURATTINO | At that, Burattino comes out, says he is in love with the pilgrim, and utters his own name. Pedrolino, hearing the name of Burattino, recognizes him, approaches him, and pretends to be a magician. He calls him by name and asks after one Pedrolino. He goes through many motions and gestures so that Burattino takes him without question for a magician.

PANTALONE | Pantalone arrives, sees the stranger, and asks him why he has not left with the letter. Pedrolino says he has sent it with one of his spirit servants. Pantalone marvels at this. Burattino tells him that Pedrolino is a magician. Pedrolino then calls Pantalone Stefanello Bottarga and tells him that his daughter is not dead and that, likewise, Isabella is not dead. Pantalone embraces the magician and begs him to come into the house to console Oratio. Here the second act ends.

ACT THREE

ORATIO | Oratio comes out, rejoicing at what the man he thinks is a magician has told him. He was told he must try to find the youth who gave the news of Isabella and bring him to the house. He calls his father.

PANTALONE
PEDROLINO | Pantalone and Pedrolino come out, and at the urging of the magician, Pantalone leaves with Oratio to find the youth and bring him to the house. Pedrolino is unhappy about seeing Flaminia in Pantalone's house.

BURATTINO | At that, Burattino comes out and begs the magician to help him in his love for the pilgrim. Pedrolino promises his help, and they go into the house.

ISABELLA | Isabella arrives, saying she thinks it has been a long time since she saw Flavio and Pedrolino. She speaks of the old man and of her new love, the love of Oratio which surpasses that of Flavio.

FLAVIO

At that moment, Flavio, who has heard all, enters and reveals himself. He calls her a faithless woman and reproaches her for her faithlessness. She is overcome with grief and leaves without a word. Flavio, grief-stricken, remains.

PEDROLINO
BURATTINO

At that, Pedrolino comes out, telling Burattino, "My daughter belongs to Flavio, and Isabella to Oratio." Immediately, Flavio draws his sword. Pedrolino runs off, Flavio after him. Burattino laughs; he says he is not afraid of any of Pedrolino's devils because he ran away from a mere man.

PEDROLINO

Suddenly, Pedrolino returns, out of breath. He tells Burattino that that was the great devil himself, who is angry at Burattino because he wants to enjoy the pilgrim; but if he wants her, he must remain mute for three days. If he speaks during that time, he will be possessed by a demon. Burattino agrees and walks a short distance without speaking, making signs with his hands to the magician. Pedrolino goes off to find Pantalone, leaving Burattino.

FLAVIO

Then, Flavio enters and asks for Pedrolino. Burattino, believing him to be a devil, shows by gesture that he is afraid and does not speak. Angered, Flavio beats him.

ARLECCHINO

At that, Arlecchino enters and reproaches Flavio for hitting the poor man. Flavio draws his sword on him.

CAPT. SPAVENTO

Thereupon, the Captain arrives and draws his sword on Flavio to defend Arlecchino, who runs off. Flavio chases Arlecchino, and the Captain chases Flavio. Burattino remains, making mute, fearful gestures.

FLAVIO

Flavio returns, and Burattino again makes signs and does not speak.

FLAMINIA

At that, Flaminia, having heard Flavio from her window, comes out and kneels before him and speaks of her love for him and all that she has done for him, but Flavio is suspicious.

THE SERVANT

Just then, Isabella's servant arrives. Weeping, he tells Flavio that if he wants to see his wife alive, he is to come with him. Flavio immediately says, "Isabella mine, because of you, I want to die." Then he leaves, followed by the servant. Flaminia goes after him, saying, "You will die for Isabella, and I will die for you!" Burattino, with gestures, says they are all devils.

PANTALONE

At that, Pantalone enters and asks for the magician. Burattino makes gestures but does not speak. Angered, Pantalone beats him. Burattino, weeping, tells him that the great devil has sent the pilgrim and the magician, and if he talks, he will be possessed. He begins to think he is being possessed and runs off, leaving Pantalone.

PEDROLINO Then, Pedrolino enters, intending, for the sake of everyone, to reveal all. He sees Pantalone and kneels before him, calling him Stefanello Bottarga and his old master. He reveals himself to be Pedrolino, Pantalone's old servant and valet; he recalls Pantalone's old enemies of Venice and explains that when he had heard of Pantalone's death, he was afraid for his own life and fled with Hortensia, Pantalone's little girl. He took with him jewels and money and raised her as his own child, maintaining her honor. Pantalone, nearly weeping for joy, raises him and asks for his daughter.

ORATIO
FLAVIO
CAPT. SPAVENTO
SERVANT
At that moment, Oratio and Flavio enter fighting, and the Captain and Isabella's servant try to separate them. Finally, in his defense, Flavio calls on Isabella's servant to testify that Isabella is in love with him, that she begged him to take her away so that she would not have to marry Oratio, and that they agreed to meet in Ferrara where he was to wait for her; but for some unknown reason, she came to Mantua. Finally he is urged by the Captain and by Pantalone and everyone to await Isabella's choice. They send the servant to call her. Pedrolino, meanwhile, reveals to Flavio that Flaminia, believed to be his daughter, is really Hortensia, the daughter of Pantalone, whose real name is Stefanello Bottarga. All say it is true.

ISABELLA
SERVANT
FLAMINIA
At that, Isabella arrives with Flaminia and the servant. Then she kneels before Flavio, saying that she has fallen completely in love with Oratio but knows she is doing a great wrong, and he will be free of her, that, in effect, he will see her die. After Isabella speaks, Flaminia kneels and says to Flavio that the life and death of three people are in his hands. If he takes her to wife, she and Isabella and Oratio will all live, but on the other hand, if he will not, they all three will die. Flavio stops to think about it. Soon, Pantalone, the Captain, and all the others around beg Flavio to grant Flaminia's request, which is just and reasonable. Flavio is pacified. He raises Isabella, and as his own, gives her to Oratio, and he marries Flaminia. Then all rejoice, saying the father of Isabella would be told all that happened to his daughter.

BURATTINO At that moment, Burattino arrives, saying he is possessed. He acts as if possessed by a demon. Pedrolino tells him it was only a joke. Burattino replies, joke or no joke, he feels a ravenously hungry demon on his back. Pantalone persuades him it was indeed a joke; and here the comedy ends.

FLAVIO THE FAKE MAGICIAN *

ARGUMENT

In Pesaro lived a young man of modest means who loved a young woman, the daughter of one Pantalone, a rich merchant, a man more clever than wise. Through his cleverness, he became skillful in his cunning. The young man, named Flavio, was told that it was impossible to marry the young woman because she was an only daughter, and because of her wealth, she was courted by many. For all that, by his own will and luck, and by pretending to be a magician and working various tricks, he won the young lady for his wife with the thanks of her father and of all his relatives.

CHARACTERS IN THE PLAY

Pantalone, a Venetian
Flaminia, his daughter
Pedrolino, his servant

Doctor Gratiano
Isabella, his daughter

Burattino
Franceschina, his wife

Oratio and
Cinthio, friends

Flavio, alone

Captain Spavento
Arlecchino, his servant

Policemen, who talk

* See Appendix p. 404.

PROPERTIES

A beard like Pantalone's
A nightshirt
Red breeches and shoes like Pantalone's
A dress like Franceschina's
A porter's costume
A bat
A magician's costume

ACT ONE

THE CITY OF
PESARO

PANTALONE DR. GRATIANO	Pantalone and Gratiano enter, speaking of the beauty and grace of Franceschina, wife of Burattino. They discover that they are rivals; they then call each other names and come to blows.
PEDROLINO	At that, Pedrolino enters and separates them. He is told the reason for their quarrel, and he becomes enraged because he too is in love with Franceschina. Then all three start fighting.
CAPT. SPAVENTO ARLECCHINO	At that moment, the Captain enters with drawn sword. He and Arlecchino pretend to have been fighting and make a great deal of frightening noise. All three rivals for Franceschina run off.
FLAMINIA	Flaminia then appears at her window. She is in love with the Captain. She greets him and entreats him. The Captain says he does not love her and looks at her contemptuously.
ISABELLA	Thereupon, Isabella appears at her window, hoping to make Flaminia jealous and to have some fun with the Captain. She greets him, and they speak together amorously.
ORATIO	While the Captain is rejoicing over the love of Isabella, Oratio, who loves Isabella, arrives. Seeing the Captain speaking with her, he beats the Captain, who runs off. Arlecchino also runs off, and Oratio chases after them. Isabella, laughing, says, "Blessed are these hands." Flaminia replies, "Your tongue is tiresome," and they begin to quarrel.
FRANCESCHINA	At that, Franceschina arrives. She tries to stop the quarrel, taking Isabella's side. Flaminia calls her a slut. Franceschina says she lies.

BURATTINO
Burattino, husband of Franceschina, comes out and sends her into the house. Then he tries to settle the quarrel, also taking Isabella's side. Flaminia calls him a cuckold, saying, "Your own father sleeps with your wife," and she goes in. Isabella withdraws, leaving Burattino weeping over his lost honor.

PEDROLINO
Then, Pedrolino arrives and hears from Burattino what Flaminia said to him. He says he is going to speak with Doctor Gratiano about his honor. Pedrolino tells him that Gratiano is in love with her. Burattino, in despair, curses the hour he took a wife and goes Pedrolino complains about Flaminia's revealing that Pantalone loves Franceschina.

CINTHIO
Then, Cinthio, who loves Isabella, enters and asks Pedrolino to help him. Pedrolino promises to do all he can but on the condition that he help Pedrolino in his love for Franceschina. Cinthio promises. Pedrolino knocks.

ARLECCHINO
Arlecchino, in disguise, enters and hides in order to hear everything.

ISABELLA
Isabella appears at her window to watch.

FLAMINIA
At that, Flaminia appears at her window to watch.

FRANCESCHINA
Then, Franceschina comes out. Cinthio, with smooth talk, speaks of Pedrolino's love for her and urges her to take him.

PANTALONE
Pantalone then enters and hides so he can hear what is going on.

BURATTINO
At that, Burattino arrives and also hides to listen, but he does not realize that Cinthio is speaking for Pedrolino. Franceschina, after listening to Cinthio, puts her hand in her purse and gives him some money, saying, "I am glad to see that you have been to a pimp's school." Cinthio is about to answer, when they all begin calling him, "Pimp, pimp, pay off the pimp!" Finally he is enraged and leaves; each goes into his house, and the first act ends.

ACT TWO

PANTALONE
PEDROLINO
Pantalone and Pedrolino enter. Pantalone is enraged at Flaminia's telling Burattino that he enjoyed his wife and asks Pedrolino if he is in love with her. Lying, Pedrolino says no, but says he is wooing her for Gratiano. Then he scolds Pantalone for being in love with Franceschina. Pantalone starts to go into his house in anger; Pedrolino, seeing Burattino coming, raises his voice.

BURATTINO	Burattino arrives in time to hear Pedrolino shout, "I want to remind you that it is a terrible thing to dishonor that poor man Burattino." Hearing that, Burattino tells Pedrolino he is a good man. Humiliated, Pantalone beats Pedrolino, but Burattino separates them.
FRANCESCHINA	At that, Franceschina, hearing the commotion, comes out and scolds Pantalone, taking Pedrolino's side. Enraged, Pantalone calls her a slut and goes off up the street. Franceschina, weeping, comes into Pedrolino's arms; then, regaining her composure, she sends Burattino off to bring charges against Pantalone. Burattino, leaving his wife in the hands of his fellow countryman, goes off. Franceschina, embracing Pedrolino, tells him she aches to be a mother. Pedrolino says he will be the father, and they go in to enjoy themselves.
CINTHIO ORATIO	Cinthio enters with Oratio, laughing at the trick Franceschina played on him and about the pimp routine. Then he and Oratio begin talking of their loves. They discover they are rivals for the love of Isabella and agree to talk to her about it. They knock.
ISABELLA	Isabella comes out and hears of their love for her. Then she asks what part of her has made them fall in love. Oratio says he has fallen in love with her beautiful body, praising the beauty of each part of her. Cinthio says he has fallen in love with her soul and speaks of the beauty of it, saying that it has filled him with a burning passion for her. After listening to each tell what part of her has made him fall in love, Isabella answers that Cinthio enjoys the beauty of her soul, and she leaves that with him; that Oratio, her betrothed, will enjoy the love of her body, and she goes in. Cinthio is grief-stricken. Oratio tells him to be patient and leaves.
FLAVIO	Flavio, Cinthio's very dear friend, enters and consoles him. He promises to do all he can to help as he also is in love. He sends Cinthio into his house. Then he discourses on his love for Flaminia and on her cruelty.
CAPT. SPAVENTO ARLECCHINO	At that moment, the Captain, armed from head to toe and angered at the beating he received from Oratio, enters. Flavio hears what happened and promises to arrange matters so that Oratio does not marry Isabella. Then they go off.
DR. GRATIANO BURATTINO	Gratiano enters, scolding Burattino because he wanted to bring charges against Pantalone. Burattino says he doesn't know whom to trust and that he is being betrayed by somebody. Hearing that, Gratiano replies that Pedrolino has cuckolded him. Burattino says

he is not telling the truth, that Pedrolino is his faithful friend. They hear talking in Burattino's house and go near to listen.

FRANCESCHINA
PEDROLINO

Franceschina and Pedrolino are inside talking amorously together. Franceschina asks Pedrolino would he marry her if her husband were to die. Pedrolino replies yes and says other pleasant things to her. Burattino wants to shout at them, but Gratiano keeps him from shouting and urges him to bring charges against Pedrolino. They leave together to go to the court to have Pedrolino arrested.

FRANCESCHINA
PEDROLINO

Franceschina and Pedrolino come out laughing at the trick they played on Burattino. They pet each other affectionately; then Franceschina goes into the house, and Pedrolino remains.

FLAMINIA

At that, Flaminia appears at her window. She has heard all and says she is going to tell her father Pantalone. Pedrolino asks for her help, promising to help her get the Captain, whom she loves, if she can get her father to pardon him.

PANTALONE

Suddenly, Pantalone enters, enraged at Franceschina. He hears the name of the Captain and wants to know what's going on about the Captain. Shrewdly, Flaminia tells her father that the Captain, who is in love with her, has beaten Pedrolino because he refused to play the pimp for him, and because she called him a villain, and weeping, she goes back in. Pantalone rails against the Captain, calling his name and telling Pedrolino that if he wants to remain with him, he must do two things: one is to beat the Captain, and the other is to get Franceschina for him.

FLAVIO
CAPT. SPAVENTO
ARLECCHINO

At that moment, Flavio enters dressed as a magician. He instructs the Captain and Arlecchino to hide; then he approaches Pantalone and reveals his profession, saying he can help him avenge himself on his enemy, the Captain, and then get Franceschina for him to enjoy. He tells him to go dress himself as a porter and orders him to bring along a bat. Pantalone, overjoyed, goes off. Pedrolino begs the magician not to allow Pantalone to enjoy Franceschina. The magician calls her.

FRANCESCHINA

Franceschina comes out and learns from the magician that he can arrange for her to enjoy her lover, Pedrolino, without her husband suspecting. She thanks him, whereupon the magician orders Pedrolino to dress as a woman and she, in a quarter of an hour, is to appear, but until then she is not to speak.

BURATTINO

At that, Burattino returns, having brought charges against Pedrolino. Immediately, Flavio draws a circle with his wand, then embraces Burattino, kisses him, and leaves without saying a word.

Pedrolino does the same and leaves. Arlecchino kisses Franceschina and leaves. Franceschina embraces and kisses her husband. They go into the house, and here the second act ends.

ACT THREE

ISABELLA Isabella enters, discourses on love, and wonders why she has not seen Oratio.

FLAVIO Flavio enters, still dressed as a magician. He tells Isabella he is a magician who left his remote homeland to help her, making her understand that he is a kinsman of Oratio. He has come only to bring happiness to them and to make her father agree to their marriage. All this he will do in half an hour. Isabella thanks him and leaves, happy.

BURATTINO Burattino comes out and tells Flavio that his wife does not talk. The magician tells him that he has been betrayed by his wife, and he will help him avenge himself. Burattino begs him to do so, and Flavio sends Burattino off to find some cheese powder and goldsmiths.

FRANCESCHINA Franceschina comes out of the house and says not a word, but the magician makes her go back in.

ORATIO At that moment, Oratio arrives. Flavio tells him he is a magician, kinsman of Isabella, come from his unknown land to preside over the disorder Oratio brought about when he left the homeland of his parents to pursue his love and that, by his magic, he will make her Oratio's wife. Oratio rejoices. Then the magician explains that he has transformed her into the likeness of a neighbor of Oratio's, so that she is not recognized by her other relatives; and he will show Oratio how to change her back to her own likeness, if he promises to marry her. Oratio promises. The magician then orders him to close his eyes and to kiss her as soon as she comes into his house. Then Flavio hides Oratio and calls out Franceschina, telling her not to talk or she will die on the spot. He gives her to Oratio, who thinks that she is Isabella thus transformed. Flavio takes Oratio's cape and hat, and then Oratio goes into his house, taking Franceschina with him, leaving Flavio outside.

FLAMINIA Just then, Flaminia appears at her window, lamenting because she has not seen Pedrolino acting as go-between in her love for the Captain. Flavio talks to her, telling her he is a magician and kinsman of the Captain. He has talked to Pedrolino and has transformed the Captain into the image of her father so that he will not be recognized, and in a quarter of an hour, he will have him come to her. Flaminia thanks him and goes back in, happy. Flavio remains.

CINTHIO   Cinthio arrives, and Flavio immediately puts Oratio's cape and hat on him and has Cinthio knock on Isabella's door.

ISABELLA   Isabella comes out and leads Cinthio into the house, thinking it is Oratio.

BURATTINO   Burattino enters and tells Flavio he can't find the powder. The magician sends him for the police so that he can have taken to prison whoever makes him a cuckold, planning, meanwhile, to send them into Oratio's house. Burattino happily goes off, leaving Flavio.

DR. GRATIANO   Gratiano arrives, complaining because Franceschina was handed over to a rascal like Pedrolino. Flavio notes all he says, then speaks to him, saying he is a magician and wants to help him enjoy Franceschina. He orders Gratiano to go dress up as a soldier like Captain Spavento. Gratiano, happy, goes off to disguise himself. Flavio explains he did that to keep him from going into his house.

PANTALONE   At that moment, Pantalone enters dressed as a porter and carrying a bat. He gives the bat to the magician, who pretends to conjure with it, telling Pantalone of its powers. He makes him believe that when he beats a man with it, immediately he will be changed into a woman; when he beats a woman, immediately she will be changed into a man. So as long as he holds it, no one can attack him. Pantalone, happy, goes off to try it and to find the Captain. Flavio says he is going to dress up to look like Pantalone and goes off.

ORATIO   Oratio appears at the window to find the magician because the woman does not change her appearance when he kisses her with his eyes closed.

PEDROLINO   At that, Pedrolino appears, dressed as a woman and in clothes like Franceschina's. He stands before Oratio's door. When Oratio sees him, he believes he is the woman who was in the house with him and calls to her, telling her not to leave.

PANTALONE   At that moment, Pantalone arrives and, seeing the woman, he tries out the bat and hits him.

ORATIO   At the instant he hits him, Oratio arrives and separates them, but Pantalone hits Pedrolino again. Pedrolino finally reveals himself to be a man. Pantalone laughs, thinking that that proves the power of the enchanted bat. Then he is about to hit Oratio, saying he is going to change him into a woman, but Oratio says he does not want to be changed. Pedrolino runs off.

FRANCESCHINA   Just then, Franceschina comes out of Oratio's house. Pantalone hits her. Oratio recognizes her as the woman who was in the house; he embraces her and again takes her into the house. Pantalone praises the magician for his great power.

FLAVIO   At that, Flavio enters, dressed like Pantalone, wearing a beard like his. Pantalone sees him and asks him who he is. Flavio says he is the soul of Pantalone looking for the body of Pantalone, who had left it as the result of an old vendetta over love. Pantalone asks where he is going. Flavio says he is going to be a companion to Flaminia, his daughter. Pantalone again praises the magician, and he hides to see what his daughter will do. Flavio knocks.

FLAMINIA   Flaminia comes out, and seeing him, thinks he is her love thus transformed and takes him into the house. Pantalone laughs at his daughter's simpleness.

DR. GRATIANO   At that moment, Gratiano enters dressed like the Captain. Pantalone, thinking it is the Captain, beats him.

BURATTINO
POLICEMEN   Immediately, Burattino arrives with the police. Seeing Pantalone beating the Captain, the police arrest him. Gratiano runs off. Burattino sends some of the police into Oratio's house. They go in and return with Franceschina and Oratio.

FRANCESCHINA
ORATIO   Franceschina tells them she was in the house by the power of the magician who put her there. The policemen recognize Pantalone and are told by him that the magician had him put on that costume.

PEDROLINO   Then, out comes Pedrolino, who says, "He made me dress in woman's clothes so that you would beat me."

ISABELLA
CINTHIO   At that moment, Isabella comes out, arguing with Cinthio. They discover they were tricked by the magician, who, Isabella says, told her he would give her to Oratio.

DR. GRATIANO   Then, Gratiano enters and says that the magician made him take a beating. Pantalone asks his pardon, saying he believed he was hitting the Captain.

FLAMINIA   At that, Flaminia comes out of the house screaming that the spirit of her father had violated her. All are astonished at this. Pantalone declares he is going to kill that spirit. Meekly, he calls to him.

FLAVIO

Flavio comes out and reveals himself, saying he did all that he did only to get Flaminia, whom he loves. He begs the forgiveness of everyone; all then praise him for his cleverness. Pantalone gives him Flaminia as wife, and Cinthio marries Isabella.

CAPT. SPAVENTO
ARLECCHINO

Thereupon, the Captain enters and draws his sword on Oratio, who tells him he wants to die anyway because he has lost Isabella, but Flavio makes peace with the Captain and reconciles Burattino and Pedrolino. Pedrolino tells Burattino that he and Franceschina knew he was listening at the door, and what they said was only meant to be a trick on him. Burattino believes him, takes Franceschina for a good and beautiful wife; and here the play ends.

THE FAITHFUL FRIEND *

ARGUMENT

There lived in Naples two noble young gentlemen, one called Oratio and the other Flavio; both were in love with a very lovely young lady named Isabella, daughter of one Pantalone de Bisognosi, a Venetian, first citizen of the city of Naples. Oratio was, in turn, loved by the young lady, but meanwhile, he did not know of his friend's love. It happened that, counting on his faithful friend, he abducted the young lady and hid her in Flavio's house, where lived Flavio's sister, Flaminia, who was much in love with Oratio. Disguised as Isabella, she ran away. Meanwhile, Isabella remained in the possession of Flavio, who kept her for his friend Oratio; finally, after many adventures, the young men were left content and happy with their ladies and with their families.

CHARACTERS IN THE PLAY

Pantalone, a Venetian
Isabella, his daughter
Pedrolino and
Arlecchino, servants

Doctor Gratiano
Flaminia and
Flavio, his children

Oratio, a lone gentleman

Captain Spavento

Musicians, his friends

Captain of the police guard
Policemen, who speak

* See Appendix p. 404.

Police Corporal, who speaks

Franceschina, a neighbor

PROPERTIES

Many lanterns
Blood and paste to fake a wound
A seat made of a large block of wood
Many strips of linen and bandage material to dress a wound
A lantern for the guards

ACT ONE

THE CITY OF
NAPLES

NIGHT

PANTALONE
ARLECCHINO

Pantalone enters with a lighted lantern, saying he has been told by the regent and the captain of the guard that his daughter Isabella has run away. He suspects Pedrolino, whom he does not trust; then Arlecchino says that he suspects Oratio has run off with her. They hear someone coming and go into the house, whereupon Arlecchino immediately appears at the window to listen.

ORATIO
PEDROLINO

At that, Oratio and Pedrolino enter, looking for Pantalone to find out if he knows anything about the disappearance of his daughter; Oratio tells Pedrolino that he has abducted Isabella and hidden her in the home of Flavio, his very best friend. Arlecchino immediately goes in. Pedrolino warns Oratio not to trust his friend, for he is a young man, and tells him that, furthermore, Flaminia, Flavio's sister, is in love with him. Oratio, walking up and down, finally makes Pedrolino hide, then signals to Isabella to come out to talk with him.

ISABELLA

Isabella timidly comes out, saying to Oratio that Flavio, his friend, has not yet returned home.

FLAMINIA

At that moment, Flaminia appears at her window and overhears them. Isabella immediately asks Oratio if he has ever loved another woman. Oratio says definitely not. She pleads with him to take her away from the house as soon as possible. Oratio promises to do so and sends her back into the house, saying, "Go in, for in this house lives all the happiness and goodness I possess in the world." She goes in. Hearing Pantalone coming, Oratio and Pedrolino go off.

PANTALONE
ARLECCHINO

Pantalone and Arlecchino enter. Arlecchino is telling Pantalone what Oratio has said, and that he has placed her in the house of his friend Flavio. He says nothing of Pedrolino, for he did not recognize him; they see Gratiano coming with a lighted lantern.

DR. GRATIANO

At that, Gratiano enters with his lighted lantern; he is coming to the house for dinner. Pantalone approaches him and invites him to his house for dinner. Gratiano answers that he has nothing for him; then he pretends that he has lost a note and goes off looking for it. Pantalone becomes very suspicious. Arlecchino offers to go into the house because of Olivetta, the servant, who is in love with him. He has entered many times before with a ladder. They agree and go in to settle things.

PEDROLINO

Pedrolino enters; hidden, he has heard everything, and planning to tell Oratio, he goes off.

FLAMINIA

Flaminia appears at her window, wondering why neither her father nor her brother come home; then she speaks openly of her love for Oratio.

ISABELLA

At that moment, Isabella, who lives on the ground floor, hears Flaminia speaking; she calls to her to come down into the street. They talk: Flaminia tells Isabella that Oratio has deceived her, having brought her here for her brother Flavio, and Oratio is in love with her, recalling the words Oratio spoke at the door of the house. Believing what Flaminia tells her, Isabella laments Oratio's betrayal, and speaking of her honor, she goes in weeping. Flaminia says she thinks her desperation will drive her away, but if not, then she begs Love to bring it about that Oratio does not become Isabella's lover, but hers, and she goes in.

CAPT. SPAVENTO
MUSICIANS

Captain Spavento enters with musicians to serenade Isabella, whose father had promised her to him in marriage.

DR. GRATIANO

Then, Gratiano arrives for dinner. The Captain invites him to go to dinner with him instead, but Gratiano says he is fasting and enters the house. The Captain begins the morning serenade.

ARLECCHINO

Arlecchino comes out, recognizes the Captain, and asks him whom he is serenading. The Captain tells him Isabella, his betrothed. Arlecchino tells him that Isabella has run away. The Captain roars, and Arlecchino flees into the house.

PEDROLINO

Pedrolino, hearing the commotion, comes out, pretends to have a gun hidden, and makes motions as if to shoot the Captain, who runs off with the musicians. Pedrolino laughs.

PANTALONE	At that, Pantalone enters with a lighted lantern to see who is there. Pedrolino hides.
ARLECCHINO	Then, Arlecchino enters with a ladder. The light in Pantalone's lantern blows out, and there is much stumbling around in the dark. Arlecchino finally places the ladder at Gratiano's window and climbs up.
PEDROLINO	At that, Pedrolino, changing his voice, starts to beat Pantalone. Arlecchino, frightened, falls from the ladder and runs off. Laughing, Pedrolino leaves, and thus the first act ends.

ACT TWO

NIGHT

FLAVIO PEDROLINO	Flavio tells Pedrolino that he does not go home to wait on Isabella, whom he loves very much, for he does not want to wrong his friend, Oratio. Pedrolino tries to dissuade him from his love; but Flavio says he can't help himself, and sighing, he leaves. Pedrolino wonders about this.
ORATIO	Oratio arrives and learns from Pedrolino that he must take Isabella out of the house at the first opportunity. He asks why, but Pedrolino refuses to tell him, and recalling the time when Spaniards were feared in Naples, sends him to get some Spanish clothes for Isabella to disguise herself in and so leave the house. Oratio goes and leaves the lantern.
ISABELLA	At that moment, Isabella, in desperation, comes out of Flavio's house to run away. Pedrolino talks with her, and she tells him that Flaminia said Oratio had betrayed her. Pedrolino laughs, assuring her of Oratio's faithfulness, explaining that he has gone for a disguise so he can take her away with him. She is to go inside and wait for him on the first floor; happy and reassured, Isabella goes into the house. Pedrolino leaves.
FLAMINIA	Flaminia, at the window, shows that she has heard all. She withdraws, saying that it has not happened yet.
CAPT. SPAVENTO	The Captain, desperate, knocks on Pantalone's door to find out more about what Arlecchino told him.
ARLECCHINO	At that, Arlecchino, at the window, half asleep, speaks to the Captain, always repeating what he says in reverse. The Captain, in a very loud voice, asks if Pantalone is at home.
PANTALONE	Pantalone, inside the house, orders Arlecchino to say no. The Captain, enraged, roars.

FLAVIO

Thereupon, Flavio arrives and draws his sword; the Captain flees. Flavio remains.

ISABELLA

Isabella, hearing the noise, comes out, recognizes Flavio, and asks him why he does not come home where everyone is waiting for him; he says he did not return home because he loves a certain lady who is cruel. Isabella asks who his lady is. Flavio says he cannot tell her because of his respect for the lady; he suggests that in order not to wrong both the lady and his friend, he will go away. He urges Isabella to remain in the house.

PEDROLINO

Pedrolino recognizes her and calls her name in a loud voice.

CAPT. SPAVENTO

At that moment, the Captain enters without a lantern, hears Isabella, and talks in a whisper, disguising his voice. Pedrolino thinks it is Oratio disguised as a Spaniard; giving the signal, he calls him, then tells Isabella that she is to go with Oratio, who has returned disguised as a Spaniard to take her away with him. The Captain takes her in his arms and carries her off, Pedrolino following after.

FLAMINIA

Flaminia appears at the window, says she has heard everything, and laments that she has not been able to bring off her own deception. Flavio hates everyone and pities his sister and himself.

PEDROLINO

At that, Pedrolino, out of breath, enters, and weeping, tells Flavio that Isabella is in the hands of the Captain, whom he thought to be Oratio. Flavio goes to rescue her, followed by Pedrolino. Flaminia is happy at this turn of events and says she will go into the room where Isabella left her hat and cape.

ORATIO

Oratio then enters disguised, and remarking that it is nearly dawn, gives the signal for taking Isabella away.

FLAMINIA

At that moment, Flaminia, in Isabella's hat and cape, comes out of the house. Oratio thinks she is Isabella and takes her by the hand.

THE CAPTAIN
OF THE GUARD
POLICEMEN

Accompanied by policemen, the captain of the guard enters with lanterns and seizes Oratio. The captain has been informed by Pantalone that she, Flaminia, is Isabella. He sends her off with his corporal to be put in the custody of his wife and children. Then he turns to Oratio and tells him he does not want to send him to prison. On pain of death, he must leave the city and be gone by the following morning. He exits, leaving Oratio lamenting and complaining against Love and his desperate fortune. He draws his sword to kill himself.

FLAVIO

Then, Flavio arrives and grabs his arm. He consoles him, saying that he has rescued Isabella from the Captain and has put her in Franceschina's house. Oratio is so overjoyed he cannot speak and goes off. Flavio, in despair, says he wants Oratio to know some day that he is his faithful and true friend. Then he leaves.

DAWN

PANTALONE
ARLECCHINO

Pantalone and Arlecchino enter. Pantalone sends Arlecchino to the captain of the guard to find out if he has news of his daughter and to tell him of his suspicions concerning Oratio and Gratiano. Arlecchino goes.

DR. GRATIANO

Gratiano arrives, and Pantalone questions him about the people in his house. Gratiano is suspicious and will tell him nothing. Pantalone, enraged, rails at him, accusing him of being an accomplice of his son Flavio in helping his daughter Isabella run away. Gratiano says he lies in his teeth. They draw their swords, and fighting, go off up the street.
Thus the second act ends.

ACT THREE

DAY

ORATIO
FRANCESCHINA
PEDROLINO

Oratio, Franceschina, and Pedrolino enter. Franceschina is telling Oratio that Flavio took Isabella to her house. She says there is not a man in the world who loves her as much as he does; but because of his loyalty to Oratio, he would rather die a thousand deaths than do him wrong, that he wept and left the house. Then she, weeping, left to find Oratio and tell him of Flavio's great love. Oratio asks her to go after Flavio, and she goes. Oratio recalls the words of Pedrolino: that it would be risky to trust her to Flavio, and Flaminia is in love with him. Pedrolino confirms the truth of this.

ARLECCHINO

At that, Arlecchino arrives. Pedrolino tries to chase him, but Arlecchino will not be chased, telling him and Oratio that Pantalone has found a policeman who informed him that his daughter is held prisoner in the room of the wife of the captain of the guard, that Pantalone gave the captain a drink and ordered him to arrest Flavio for wounding the Captain, and Pedrolino for holding his arms so he could stab him. Oratio, frightened, runs off, followed by Pedrolino. Arlecchino remains.

DR. GRATIANO

Then, Gratiano arrives, having heard that Flaminia, his daughter, is held prisoner by order of Pantalone.

PANTALONE   At that moment, Pantalone arrives, saying he wishes his daughter would die in prison. Gratiano complains to Pantalone that his daughter Flaminia has been locked up; Pantalone says it's his daughter Isabella, not Flaminia. Gratiano goes into the house to look, then returns to say that Flaminia is not at home. They argue again. Arlecchino separates them; then he asks Pantalone if he has seen Isabella in prison. Pantalone answers no, but that one of the watch told him so. Arlecchino suggests that they clear up the whole business by going to see the captain of the guard. They go off, Gratiano saying he suspects Arlecchino.

FLAVIO   Thereupon, Flavio enters. He has learned that his sister Flaminia is in prison, that she was found with Oratio, who wishes to free her to let her die at home. Flavio wonders about this and complains of Oratio.

ISABELLA   Just then, Isabella enters. After she had been all around the city, she decided to return to her father. Flavio asks her if Oratio came to her at Franceschina's house. She replies that she disdains to remain in the house of such a woman; she left to return to her father's. Flavio tells her that Oratio has sent his sister Flaminia away, and that, although he is in love with her, he has always honored friendship above Love.

ARLECCHINO   Arlecchino, up the street, overhears this; Isabella sympathizes with Flavio and complains of Oratio's neglect.

THE CORPORAL   At that, the corporal enters and orders the arrest of Flavio for fighting with the Captain; he is about to take Isabella to prison, but Flavio resists him, and the corporal, overcome by anger, draws his sword.

PEDROLINO   With the help of Arlecchino and Pedrolino, who suddenly enter, Flavio fights the corporal and is wounded in the head; after much spilt blood, the corporal runs off. Weeping, Isabella binds Flavio's head wound, and Pedrolino tells them to take Flavio into Pantalone's house; all go. Pedrolino remains to go to find a surgeon.

CAPT. SPAVENTO   At that, the Captain enters in armor and walking on crutches. Pedrolino tells him that Flavio is looking for him with twenty-five men in order to kill him, but that it would be better if they made peace. Pedrolino offers him terms, to which the Captain agrees.

PANTALONE   Just then, Pantalone enters and says all is cleared up and that Gratiano is right; Flaminia is the one in prison, not Isabella. He sees Pedrolino and is about to leap on him, but holds back when he sees the Captain, who is his enemy. Pantalone calls for a chair for the Captain.

ARLECCHINO   Arlecchino brings in a chair. Pantalone tells the Captain to sit, informing him that he is a surgeon and wants to see if the wound is mortal; Pantalone removes the bandages and finds no wound. Arlecchino beats the Captain with a stick, and he runs away. Pedrolino scolds Pantalone for wanting to marry Isabella to the Captain. Pantalone says he did it to join the Spaniards, remembering the force of the Spaniards when they were in Naples; then he laments about Oratio and Isabella. Pedrolino and Arlecchino tell him that she is in the house, and Pantalone believes them.

DR. GRATIANO   At that, Gratiano enters with his daughter, whom he has freed, FLAMINIA   and before Pantalone, he begins to roar and orders Flaminia to relate what happened; Flaminia says she will tell but that she wants to appeal to Pantalone to pardon his daughter Isabella. Pantalone promises. Flaminia reveals that she is in love with Oratio, who loves Isabella; that Isabella was taken off by Oratio and placed in Gratiano's house to be taken away later; that she thought she was going off with Oratio when she was taken by the captain of the guard. She asks Pantalone to tell Isabella and Oratio that she is going into a convent; before she goes, she wants to see her brother Flavio. Pedrolino tells her he is in the house. Pedrolino and Arlecchino go into the house with her.

ORATIO   At that moment, Oratio arrives and remains hidden to listen.

ISABELLA   Then, Isabella, with the help of Pedrolino and Arlecchino, brings FLAVIO   out the wounded Flavio, his head bandaged. Flavio begs Panta-PEDROLINO   lone's pardon for being in his house. Then he reveals his great ARLECCHINO   love for Isabella and relates what she did for him. Falling to his knees, he begs Pantalone to give Isabella to Oratio, his best friend, because he intends to live in solitude as Flaminia plans to do. They ask for his fatherly benediction. All weep.

ORATIO   At that Oratio, moved by the words of Flavio, and as a final gesture to show his friendship and his love, gives Isabella to Flavio, and he takes Flaminia, with the consent of the fathers, who praise the generosity of Oratio and promise to come to an agreement with the Captain. All are happy and go into Pantalone's house to celebrate the nuptials; and the comedy ends.

The Thirtieth Day

THE DISGUISED SERVANTS *

ARGUMENT

*There lived in Genoa a rich and honored man named Leone
Adorni, who lived very happily because of his wealth and also
because of his pleasure in his two children, left for him to raise
after the death of his wife; one was a boy named Cinthio and the
other a girl named Isabella. It happened, at the time, that Isabella
fell in love with a noble young stranger, who, traveling, spent the
night at her father's house while on his way back to his city of
Florence to take care of his affairs. Isabella, unable to endure
being away from her lover, resolved to tell her brother, Cinthio,
who, moved more by curiosity than good judgment, suggested to
his sister that she dress as a man, and together they would go to
Florence. Thus they left and arrived in Florence and decided on
the following course: Isabella would pose as a servant in the
house of her lover, and Cinthio would become a servant in the
house of another. It came to pass that the sister of her lover
believed Isabella to be a man and became enamoured of her, and
Cinthio fell in love with the sister and finally won her. When it
became known, they were brought together by her father, and
each was given his love.*

CHARACTERS IN THE PLAY

Pantalone, a Venetian
Oratio and
Flaminia, his children
Fabritio, servant, then Isabella
Pedrolino, a servant

Doctor Gratiano
Cinthio, a servant, brother of Isabella
Hortensia, a slave, then sister of Flavio

* See Appendix p. 405.

Flavio, alone, friend of Oratio

Leone Adorni, Genovese, father of Isabella and Cinthio

Servants who speak

A servant of Pantalone, who speaks

Captain Spavento
Arlecchino, his servant

PROPERTIES

A silver basin
A silver pot
Traveling clothes, that is, felt hat, boots, and spurs

ACT ONE

THE CITY OF
FLORENCE

PANTALONE   Pantalone berates Pedrolino for having brought him Fabritio, a
PEDROLINO   servant in his house, who has now impregnated his daughter
             Flaminia; Pedrolino consoles him with the fact that Fabritio is
             the son of a very rich merchant. Pantalone says nevertheless he is
             a servant and that he will send him back to his father at once, and
             he would like to poison all his servants; then he complains of the
             wicked life of his son, Oratio. Pedrolino says that as he has found
             a husband for his daughter, Pantalone should find a wife for
             Oratio. Pantalone, grumbling, goes off; Pedrolino stays.

DR. GRATIANO   Gratiano enters, shouting at Oratio for having found him flirting
             with his slave in his house; Oratio begs his pardon. Pedrolino
             comes between them and sides with Gratiano. Oratio, enraged,
             draws his sword.

PANTALONE   At that moment, Pantalone arrives and takes part in the quarrel;
             Oratio, seeing his father, immediately runs away. Pantalone asks
             Pedrolino what it is all about. Pedrolino tells him that Gratiano
             was going to kill his son Oratio. Furious, Pantalone draws his
             dagger on Gratiano.

POLICEMEN   Just then, policemen enter, see Pantalone, draw their weapons,
             and take him prisoner. Pedrolino tells the policemen that Panta-
             lone wanted to take a slave from Gratiano by force and then
             wanted to kill him. Pantalone is unable to defend himself and is
             taken away. Pedrolino immediately tells Gratiano that he de-

fended him in order to gain time so Oratio could rifle Pantalone's house, make peace with Gratiano by paying him for the slave girl, and have enough time in the house with her. Gratiano agrees this is a good plan, and in gay spirits, they go to find Oratio.

FABRITIO
FLAMINIA

Fabritio enters, consoling Flaminia with the hope of a quick return of the servant sent to his father in Genoa; he reprimands her for her jealousy and sends her into the house. Alone, Fabritio regrets revealing her love to her brother Cinthio and laments the cruelty of Oratio. She says she is determined to get her brother's permission to reveal her identity to Oratio.

CINTHIO

At that, Cinthio, Fabritio's brother, arrives. Fabritio tells him that Flaminia, whom he seduced during the night, is pregnant. She led Flaminia to believe she was lying with Fabritio to help Cinthio out, but now she wants to reveal herself as Isabella to Oratio in order to end his desire to seduce Gratiano's slave. Cinthio, who must await the return of the servant with a reply from Genoa, tries to console her.

DR. GRATIANO

Gratiano enters, scolding his servant Cinthio for being out of the house. Cinthio tells him that he was ordering Fabritio to tell Oratio, his master, not to come into the house any more to talk to the slave or Cinthio would crack his skull; he pretends to draw his sword in anger. Gratiano restrains Cinthio and takes him into the house; Fabritio remains, laughing.

ORATIO
FLAVIO

Oratio enters, telling Flavio that he does not love the slave girl, knowing that Flavio loves her, and as they are friends, he, Oratio, would never wrong him; Flavio thanks him, offers to help him in any way he can, and leaves. Oratio regrets doing any wrong to Flavio and feels good about having told him he will not wrong him. Fabritio reprimands Oratio for loving the slave girl, whom he does not recognize, and for offending his friend, but Oratio replies that he can't help himself.

PEDROLINO

At that, Pedrolino arrives and reprimands Fabritio for talking to Oratio, knowing this is an imposition on his master. Then he tells Fabritio that he is to give him a silver basin and a silver pot because the master wants Pedrolino to act as his pimp. Fabritio gives him the keys so he can get the things, and Pedrolino goes into the house. Fabritio turns to Oratio to again reproach him for the love he has for the slave. Oratio laughs and looks closely at Fabritio.

PEDROLINO

At that moment, Pedrolino returns with the silver basin and silver pot; then he sends Fabritio to the post to pick up letters for his master. Fabritio goes. Oratio tells Pedrolino that if Fabritio

were a woman, he thinks she would be in love with him. Pedrolino laughs, saying, "Then you do not yet know which Fabritio
is?" Changing the subject, he tells Oratio of Pantalone's imprisonment and gives him the silver, which he is to give as pledge to
Gratiano for his slave; they call him.

DR. GRATIANO

Gratiano appears at the window and answers gravely; then,
seeing the silver, he comes out and caresses Oratio and Pedrolino.
He calls Cinthio.

CINTHIO

Cinthio comes out to take the silver, and together they do honor
to Oratio and Pedrolino. Between them, they go through great
ceremony and words of praise; then all go into Gratiano's house;
and here the first act ends.

ACT TWO

PANTALONE
FABRITIO

Pantalone learns that Pedrolino, on his part, has taken the silver
basin and the silver pot to act as pimp and that he said nothing of
Pantalone's imprisonment. Pantalone, enraged, drives Fabritio
away. Fabritio, intimidated, leaves.

PEDROLINO

At that moment, Pedrolino arrives. Pantalone threatens him;
Pedrolino confesses that he was uncertain about making the
police take him prisoner, and he made him give him the silver to
buy the slave whom Oratio loved, finally, so that he would not
have to marry her; he says that he has already spoken to someone
who would buy her immediately from Pantalone, promising to
give him silver for all those days spent in prison and to buy the
slave also so that Oratio cannot have her. Pantalone is pacified,
speaks ill of Oratio, and says he has done wrong in driving
Fabritio away, recognizing in him something noble; Pedrolino
confirms this. Pantalone sends him to find out if there are any
letters from Genoa. Pedrolino goes and Pantalone enters the
house.

ORATIO
DR. GRATIANO

Oratio enters telling Gratiano he wants to have dinner with him
that evening. Gratiano consents and calls his servant Cinthio.

CINTHIO

Cinthio comes out. Gratiano sends him with Oratio to bring the
food into the house, and he entreats Oratio, at the first chance, to
send Cinthio with the money to pay off the sum of 300 scudi.
They agree, and Gratiano goes into the house.

FABRITIO

Fabritio, having observed the entire thing, reprimands Oratio for
loving a slave girl, who is in love with, and pregnant by, a captain
whom she looks for from time to time, and adds that he has said

the same to the slave girl; then Fabritio tells Oratio of a most beautiful lady, who is much in love with him, a lady that Fabritio's brother knows very well. They go to find Cinthio and discover who the lady is.

FLAVIO

Flavio appears from his hiding place, having heard everything; he says he feels very bad about Oratio's offense and betrayal of him, but he cheers himself up with the thought that Oratio's love will not be returned.

HORTENSIA

At that moment, Hortensia, the slave, appears at the window. Flavio reveals his love, but Hortensia says she cannot return his love as she loves another. Flavio asks who her lover is.

DR. GRATIANO

Just then, Gratiano calls from within, then comes to the window and shouts at Flavio, who leaves; Gratiano withdraws.

CAPT. SPAVENTO
ARLECCHINO

The Captain enters with Arlecchino. He has returned from Naples, where he has been for about eight months; he has come to find Gratiano, with whom he left a slave and all he had. Arlecchino asks him where he found the slave. The Captain says that he rescued a small girl in Trapani, Sicily, from a galley ship which had been boarded by rescuing pirates about eight years ago. Arlecchino begins to weep, saying that just so many years before he, with his master and a small child, had been captured by Turks, but he does not remember the name of the Captain who took them from there and says that he would like to find Gratiano, the old steward of the house.

PEDROLINO

At that, Pedrolino, who has heard all from a hiding place, enters and is asked by the Captain if he knows Gratiano; Pedrolino answers yes, that he is dead, and his possessions are in the hands of the court as the result of his will; also, he says, Gratiano had impregnated the slave girl and Pantalone, his master, out of charity, took her into his home until she gives birth. The Captain says he is the one who made her pregnant some eight months ago; then he asks which is the gentleman's house. Pedrolino shows him Gratiano's house but says there is no one at home and to return in an hour, when he can speak with someone. Captain Spavento goes off with Arlecchino; Pedrolino says that if Oratio does not work fast, he will lose the slave girl, and, having noted the words of the Captain, that is, that he had impregnated the slave girl, he has now thought of a plan to regain the silver.

ORATIO
FABRITIO

At that moment, Oratio enters with Fabritio, who is telling him that the lady who loves him is a foreigner. Pedrolino interrupts Fabritio's speech and says the slave girl loves a captain. He confirms it by saying that he himself spoke to the Captain a short time before. The men hear Pantalone coming and go off. Fabritio hides.

PANTALONE
FLAMINIA

Pantalone enters, asking Flaminia why she is getting fat; she gives him many excuses. Pantalone, however, blames Fabritio. Flaminia pretends innocence. Pantalone, enraged, says he knows all, and threatening her, leaves. She remains, weeping.

FABRITIO

Fabritio comes out of hiding to talk with her and console her.

PEDROLINO

At that, Pedrolino arrives, which ends their conversation. Pedrolino tells them he knows something and has known it for more than a month now. Fabritio asks him what he knows. Pedrolino hints that Fabritio has impregnated Flaminia. Fabritio, smiling, says that Pantalone in this affair knows nothing, but says nothing further. Pedrolino says that Pantalone has been waiting a month for a letter from Genoa informing him who Fabritio and Cinthio, his brother, are. Then he promises to help them; he sends Flaminia into the house and instructs Fabritio to tell Gratiano that Oratio has gone to the Shop of the Three Kings, where he is having clothes made for himself and the slave girl; then he withdraws as Fabritio knocks at the door.

DR. GRATIANO

Gratiano comes out, and Fabritio gives him the message. At once they go to the merchant's shop. Pedrolino returns immediately and calls the slave girl.

HORTENSIA

Hortensia comes out and is told that the Captain, who has arrived, has been robbed in the streets of Naples and is ashamed to go about poorly dressed; therefore, she must send him money or something with which to buy some clothes. Hortensia does not know what to give him. Pedrolino suggests she give him the silver basin and silver pot. She goes in to get them, brings them out, and gives them to Pedrolino; then, in gay spirits, she goes back in. Pedrolino remains.

PANTALONE

Pantalone arrives, sees the silver, and praises Pedrolino for being a good man; Pedrolino tells him the slave girl gave them to him and that a captain will pay very well for them. Pantalone sends Pedrolino into the house with the silver.

CAPT. SPAVENTO
ARLECCHINO

At that moment, the Captain comes to hear news of the slave girl. He sees Pantalone and asks him if he is Pantalone. Pantalone says yes. The Captain insinuates that he has his woman in the house. Pantalone, thinking that this is the captain mentioned by Pedrolino, answers yes, but that he cannot let him have her until night.

FLAMINIA

Just then, Flaminia, within the house, cries out in labor pains. Pantalone becomes desperate. The Captain demands to know who cried out. Pantalone says it is just a woman of his household. The Captain thinks it is his slave girl and tells Pantalone that he has impregnated the woman who is screaming. Pantalone says no, Fabritio did it. The Captain insists it was he and tries to get into the house. Pantalone attempts to stop him. The Captain draws his sword; Pantalone does the same, and making a terrible racket, they go up the street fighting; and here the second act ends.

ACT THREE

CINTHIO

Cinthio enters, having sent the food for the evening dinner, and having done a good turn for his sister.

FABRITIO

At that moment, Fabritio arrives and tells her brother that Pedrolino knows everything, but that neither he nor Pantalone knows their secret, that is, that Cinthio comes every night through the window and lies with Flaminia, who thinks she lies with Fabritio.

PEDROLINO

Just then, Pedrolino, having heard everything, reveals himself and threatens them. Fabritio and Cinthio fall to their knees before Pedrolino and tell their story as it appears in the Argument. They explain that they pretended to be servants, and Flaminia fell in love with Fabritio, thinking her to be a man, and how, because of their trickery, Flaminia was made pregnant by Cinthio, and neither Pantalone nor Pedrolino knew about this. Pedrolino tells them that Flaminia has just given birth to a male child; he sends Cinthio off to dress as a woman and then to return immediately. He orders Fabritio to go to Flaminia and reveal the deception. Pedrolino remains.

PANTALONE

At that, Pantalone enters and learns immediately from Pedrolino that Flaminia has given birth to a male child. Pantalone begins to weep; Pedrolino consoles him by telling him it is not the first time that such a thing has happened; then he tells him that the slave girl would make a good nurse for Flaminia and the baby, and he is not to doubt that Oratio no longer loves her, having heard that she has been made pregnant by the Captain. Pedrolino promises, further, that Oratio will marry a lady of quality.

CINTHIO

Thereupon, Cinthio, dressed in the clothes of Isabella, enters. Pedrolino tells Pantalone that this is the slave girl, and he will take her into Flaminia's room. Pantalone himself takes her into the house. Pedrolino laughs, then withdraws.

CAPT. SPAVENTO

Then, the Captain enters and walks up and down in front of Pantalone's house.

DR. GRATIANO	Gratiano arrives next, happy after having been to the draper's to have the clothes made; the Captain sees him, and having heard that he is dead, thinks it is Gratiano's ghost; he is frightened. Gratiano assures him that he is not dead, but the Captain flees; Gratiano follows. Pedrolino remains, laughing.
ORATIO	At that moment, Oratio enters, a changed man because of what Pedrolino and Fabritio said; Pedrolino tells him that Fabritio has something very important to say to him and has been waiting for him. Pedrolino goes into the house to call him, while Oratio waits, wondering about the lady Fabritio told him about.
FABRITIO	Fabritio comes out, and after acting very timid, reveals herself to be Isabella, daughter of Leone Adorni of Genoa. Oratio, entirely happy, embraces her.
PEDROLINO	Then, Pedrolino enters and tells the rest of the story of Cinthio and Flaminia; he sends them into the house to see her brother's wife and the baby boy, but cautions them that they must then withdraw to a ground floor room for love of the old man. Pedrolino remains.
CAPT. SPAVENTO	The Captain enters, frightened, still believing that Gratiano is a ghost.
DR. GRATIANO	At that moment, Gratiano arrives. Pedrolino begs the Captain's pardon for telling him Gratiano was dead and for playing a trick on him. The Captain approaches Gratiano politely, and then they call Hortensia.
HORTENSIA	Hortensia, the slave girl, enters, and seeing the Captain, embraces him lovingly. Arlecchino keeps looking at the slave girl and she at him; finally they recognize each other and weep over the death of their father. The Captain consoles her, and they enter happily into Gratiano's house. Pedrolino remains.
PANTALONE	Just then, Pantalone arrives. Pedrolino informs him that he has found a wife for Oratio, and the wife is Fabritio; Pantalone says he does not understand.
THE MESSENGER	At that, the messenger from Genoa enters, sees Pantalone, and with great rejoicing, tells him to come with him to the post to meet someone who has come with him, because he has some very good news. Happily, they go off.
FLAVIO	Flavio enters, speaking of the infamy of his false friend, and saying that he is so disgusted with Oratio that he would like to leave and return to Rome, having lost rapport with Oratio, for love of whom he had come from Rome.

DR. GRATIANO
ARLECCHINO

At that moment, Gratiano enters, gives money to Arlecchino to buy food for dinner, and learns from him that Hortensia gave birth to a little girl, and she was the daughter of one Eugenio Alidori; Flavio, hearing his father's name, speaks to Arlecchino and recognizes him. He reveals himself to be Hortensia's brother and goes into the house to see his sister.

PANTALONE
LEONE ADORNI
SERVANTS
PEDROLINO

Pantalone, Leone Adorni, servants, and Pedrolino all enter, happy at the arrival of Leone Adorni, father of Isabella and Cinthio. Pedrolino goes into the house to tell the news; they remain talking together.

CINTHIO
ISABELLA

At that, Cinthio and Isabella come out, fall to their knees, and beg forgiveness of their father and of Pantalone. The old men pardon them for all their errors and arrange it so that Oratio marries Isabella and Cinthio, Flaminia.

FLAVIO
DR. GRATIANO
HORTENSIA
CAPT. SPAVENTO
ARLECCHINO

At that moment, the others enter and rejoice with Oratio; then Flavio informs everyone that Hortensia, his sister, is the wife of the Captain.

PEDROLINO

Just then, Pedrolino enters with the baby in swaddling clothes; everyone kisses the baby; and the play ends.

THE PEDANT*

ARGUMENT

There lived in the city of Venice a very rich merchant named Pantalone de Bisognosi who had for a wife a very beautiful young lady named Isabella. By her he had a son named Oratio, who, as was the custom of the time, was tutored by one M. Cataldo, a pedant. Because the said Pantalone was a man who loved wine and women, it happened that more and more he quarreled with his wife, and many times the wife was consoled by the pedant. It happened that one day—after the usual quarrel—the pedant decided to try the wife of Pantalone and awaited the opportunity of more discord and another quarrel between husband and wife to reveal his love for her, pleading with most affectionate words for the return of his love. The lady, who much esteemed her honor, after promising him satisfaction, revealed all to her husband, who worked out a very neat plot and punishment as an example to all other pedants, as will become known in the story.

CHARACTERS IN THE PLAY

Pantalone, a Venetian
Isabella, his wife
Oratio, his son
Pedrolino, his servant
[Facchino, the porter]

Doctor Gratiano
Flaminia, his daughter
Fabritio, his son, a beardless youth
Burattino, his servant

Cataldo, tutor of Oratio

* See Appendix p. 405.

Captain Spavento, a stranger
Arlecchino, his servant

PROPERTIES

A large copper tub
Three long knives
Three butcher's aprons
A nightshirt for Cataldo
A long cord
A stick

ACT ONE

VENICE

PANTALONE ORATIO	Pantalone is scolded by his son Oratio for being a glutton and whoremaster and for leading his mother, Isabella, a terrible life. Pantalone replies he will live according to his own wishes.
CATALDO	At that, Cataldo, the pedant and Oratio's tutor, arrives and comes between them with peaceful words; he leads Pantalone away. Oratio says that his father does not know the wicked nature of the pedant, and they go well together.
ISABELLA PEDROLINO FACCHINO	Just then, Isabella enters, beating Pedrolino and the porter, whom she found in the cellar stealing a barrel of wine. The porter flees; Oratio reprimands his mother. Isabella replies that he is a wretch like his father, and she will avenge herself, and she goes into the house. Oratio leaves sorrowfully, and Pedrolino goes off to find Pantalone.
CAPT. SPAVENTO ARLECCHINO	The Captain enters; having come from Naples on his way to Milan, he says he likes Venice and sings its praises.
ISABELLA	At that, Isabella appears at the window, sees the Captain, and drops her handkerchief. The Captain picks it up. Isabella comes out, and the Captain wants to return her handkerchief, but she refuses to take it. The Captain then gives her a ring which she accepts. The Captain asks if she is married. Isabella, sighing, says yes, as Pedrolino arrives. She sees him and goes in.
PEDROLINO	Pedrolino approaches, but, while still hidden, he heard her sighs and saw the Captain give her the ring; now he jokes with the Captain, telling him that the lady with whom he was talking is his wife. The Captain, offering him much money, asks him to find

some beautiful girl to sleep with him. Pedrolino says that he will act as go-between between him and his wife. The Captain, satisfied, leaves with Arlecchino. Pedrolino declares he will tell Pantalone everything to avenge the beating he got from Isabella.

ISABELLA   At that moment, Isabella appears at the window, having heard everything; she mocks Pedrolino by calling him husband. She comes out mimicking him; then, angrily, she calls him villain and tells him she will expose all his knavery to Pantalone. She goes back in, and Pedrolino goes off in despair.

ORATIO   Oratio enters, unhappy because of his father and Flaminia, whom he loves.

FLAMINIA   At that, Flaminia appears at her window and talks with Oratio; they play a love scene. Flaminia then tells him that Fabritio, her brother, wants a favor of him, and she will send him out. She goes into the house, and Oratio waits.

FABRITIO   Then, Fabritio enters and asks Oratio if he would do anything to have his tutor given to him for his education. Oratio agrees, but first Fabritio will have to give him Flaminia, his sister, for wife. Fabritio says, "When you make me a scholar of your master, then I will give you my sister for wife." Immediately his father arrives.

DR. GRATIANO   Gratiano at once says, "You will not be a scholar of his tutor, nor will that one have my daughter for wife."

PEDROLINO   Pedrolino enters and declares Fabritio will be a scholar of the pedant, and Oratio will have Gratiano's daughter for wife. Gratiano, laughing, says he will give it to him; Pedrolino replies, "I shall be the one who gives." Gratiano sends Fabritio into the house; then, still laughing at Pedrolino, he leaves. Pedrolino tells Oratio to leave the matter to him, adding that there are many things he wants to say to his mother.

ISABELLA   At that, Isabella appears at her window. She has heard everything; she comes out with a stick and beats Pedrolino hard. Then she turns on Oratio, who, without attempting to defend himself, runs off. Isabella, still threatening Pedrolino, goes into the house. He remains, weeping.

ARLECCHINO   Just then, Arlecchino enters with a dish of macaroni to give to Pedrolino from the Captain. He gives it to Pedrolino, who, weeping, takes it, saying he is weeping because of something that happened to his wife, and thus weeping, he begins to eat. Arlecchino also begins to cry and to eat.

BURATTINO   At that, Burattino enters, sees them eating macaroni and weeping, and he also begins to weep and to eat until all the macaroni is eaten. Pedrolino, still crying, tells Arlecchino to kiss the Captain's hand for him and goes. Burattino says the same, also crying, and goes. Arlecchino, crying and licking the platter, goes; and thus the first act ends.

ACT TWO

PANTALONE
PEDROLINO

Pantalone enters and learns from Pedrolino that his wife gave a handkerchief to a strange captain, that in return she received a ring as a gift, and that she beat him. Pantalone wonders about it, having never known his wife to be unfaithful.

DR. GRATIANO

At that moment, Gratiano arrives, saying to Pantalone that his servant is trying to marry off the children of others in his own way and urges Pantalone to attend to his own household, reprimanding him for the life he leads, especially as he is an old man.

ARLECCHINO

Then, Arlecchino enters and asks Pedrolino how his wife is, calling him Sir Sensual. Pedrolino tells Pantalone that this fellow is crazy; he drives him off.

CATALDO

Cataldo, the pedant, arrives; he is greeted by all. Pantalone tells him all that occurred between his wife and the Captain, saying that Pedrolino had reported everything.

FABRITIO

At that, Fabritio enters, greets the pedant, to the disgust of his father, who considers the pedant a knave. As the pedant observes that Gratiano knows him for what he is to spite him, he makes much of Fabritio and gives him a book of verse pedantically written by Fidentio, master of all pedants. Pantalone asks Cataldo's advice about what he has told him. The pedant says that Pedrolino is not to repeat what he has said, and Pantalone is to leave his wife to him; he will get the truth from her. Pantalone agrees.

ORATIO

Oratio then arrives and greets his master. The pedant reprimands him for not attending to his studies and to his duties in the house; he reprimands Pantalone for not maintaining discipline; then he consoles them and sends them all off. Alone, he speaks of his life and his vices. Under the pretense of moral sentiments, he says, he hides all his wickedness; he knocks on Isabella's door.

ISABELLA

Isabella comes out; she greets the pedant who, complaining and pretending, reports to her the gossip her husband told him about the ring she received from the Captain. Isabella confesses having done wrong and blames her husband, who chases other women. The pedant tells her that if she wishes to satisfy her desires, she does not have to go to a stranger, but to a person in the household, one known; and with much smooth talk he offers to satisfy her himself, promising to make peace between her and her husband. Isabella, in gay spirits, goes in to placate her husband. The pedant, seeing that Isabella will be content without another, is happy and leaves.

PEDROLINO   Pedrolino, hidden, has heard everything and says the pedant is a rascal and that his mistress is of a mind to go along with him.

FLAMINIA   At that, Flaminia appears at the window to ask Pedrolino about Oratio.

CAPT. SPAVENTO   The Captain enters, sees Flaminia, and asks Pedrolino about the young lady. Pedrolino tells him she is the daughter of the husband of the house and that he will speak to her on the Captain's behalf. He plans to entertain the people in the house and thus give the Captain an opportunity to talk to her. Pedrolino goes inside; then appearing behind Flaminia's window and disguising his voice, he tells the Captain to come dressed as a porter within half an hour, that Flaminia will let him into the house without the others suspecting. The Captain goes, and Pedrolino withdraws.

ORATIO   Oratio, who has heard all, is unhappy.

PEDROLINO   At that moment, Pedrolino comes out of the house and consoles Oratio by telling him it is a trick. He promises that Flaminia will be his, but they must watch out for the pedant; he takes him off to tell him what to do.

PANTALONE   Pantalone enters. He is waiting for the pedant's reply concerning
DR. GRATIANO   the business between Isabella and the Captain. Gratiano speaks ill of the pedant, whom he considers a knave and an adulterer, but Pantalone defends him. Gratiano knocks at the door of his house.

FABRITIO   Fabritio comes out. Gratiano asks him if he has seen the pedant. Fabritio says no.

CATALDO   At that, Cataldo, the pedant, arrives; all greet him. He tells Pantalone that his wife is the most faithful and honorable woman living, and he would like to make permanent peace between them. Pantalone agrees. Cataldo then calls Isabella.

ISABELLA   Isabella comes out, and at the pleading and persuasion of the pedant, is reconciled to her husband; finally the good pedant declares expansively that peace be with all and kisses everyone, Isabella last; then he leaves. Fabritio does the same and leaves; Gratiano does the same and leaves. Isabella embraces her husband, saying, "Peace be with us," and they go into the house, happy. Here the second act ends.

ACT THREE

ORATIO PEDROLINO	Oratio enters, enraged at the pedant and Isabella because of what Pedrolino has told him and swears that he cannot believe such wickedness.
FLAMINIA	At that, Flaminia comes out, and they play a flirtatious scene. Pedrolino decides that the Captain must be beaten.
CAPT. SPAVENTO	Just then, the Captain arrives, dressed as a porter. They torment him; then Flaminia plays up to him as if to take him into the house. Then she beats him. The Captain runs off; then Oratio and Flaminia hold hands as a pledge of marriage.
BURATTINO	At that, Burattino arrives, saying he wishes no one harm; they soothe him, and he goes into the house with Flaminia. Oratio leaves to find his father. Pedrolino remains, still enraged at the pedant.
PANTALONE ISABELLA	At that moment, Pantalone enters with Isabella, speaking well of the pedant, who has made peace between them; Isabella, smiling, tells her husband all that has occurred between her and the pedant and that he gave her to understand he would take care of all her wanton desires. Pantalone is thunderstruck, having always taken him for a good man. He asks his wife to prove that he is a rascal. Isabella says she will prove it; she will tell him that the following night her husband will not sleep at home because he must go out of town on important business. Pantalone agrees to her plan; she goes in, and he remains.
DR. GRATIANO	Then, Gratiano, who has heard all, greets Pantalone and tells him he dreamed that the pedant cuckolded him.
PEDROLINO	At that, Pedrolino arrives. Pantalone calls him a gossip and a liar. Pedrolino says that what he told him is true, as he will soon find out. Gratiano insists he always took the pedant for a rascal.
CATALDO	At that moment, Cataldo arrives, speaking fine words and flattering everyone. Pantalone tells him he must go away for three or four days, and that night he will be out of the city. The pedant assures Pantalone that under his watchfulness and loyalty all will be well, that he knows how to care for the family and to keep the peace of his lord; then, with much ceremony, he leaves. Pantalone remarks that he finds it hard to believe that the pedant is a rascal

as they say. He leaves Pedrolino on guard, then goes off with Gratiano to the Rialto. Pedrolino hides.

CATALDO

At that, Cataldo, the pedant, returns. Pedrolino moves farther off; the pedant joyfully says that the opportunity to enjoy Isabella at her convenience has come, and he has recognized in her the desire to find pleasure with him; he knocks on her door.

ISABELLA

Isabella comes out, sees Cataldo all worked up, and asks him the cause of his sickness. The good pedant tells her that he is dying for love of her, and if she does not return his love, he will die, all the more since her husband has gone out of the city that night. Isabella, to trap him, tells him to go into her room, to undress, and to get up on the bed; that she, meantime, will visit Flaminia to make certain she will not disturb them, as she usually comes to visit when Isabella's husband is out of the city at night. The pedant happily goes in to undress. Pedrolino comes out of hiding; Isabella sends him to tell her husband and her son, and to bring their friends and relations; then she goes to lock the pedant in the room.

ARLECCHINO

Arlecchino enters and says he cannot find his master. He speaks to Pedrolino, and they recognize each other as fellow countrymen; they recall their many relations and embrace.

ORATIO

At that, Oratio enters and learns from Pedrolino that Arlecchino is his relative and the pedant is in the house locked in the bedroom.

FLAMINIA

Flaminia comes out, and Oratio marries her then and there before the two servants.

BURATTINO

At that moment, Burattino comes out. Pedrolino summons Arlecchino and Burattino, telling them that he needs their help to carry out justice.

PANTALONE
DR. GRATIANO

Just then, Pantalone and Gratiano enter, hear of the nuptials between Oratio and Flaminia, and are content. Pedrolino tells Pantalone that the pedant is trapped.

ISABELLA

At that, Isabella comes out, laughing about the pedant, who is locked in the bedroom and waiting; she wonders how they are going to punish him. After many suggestions, they decide to castrate him; the men all go into the room, while the women wait.

FABRITIO

Fabritio arrives, and Flaminia tells him that he will soon see his master, his new master, nicely altered.

ORATIO
PANTALONE

Soon they hear a cry and all the men come out, leading Cataldo, the pedant, in a nightshirt, tied with a strong rope; he screams

DR. GRATIANO PEDROLINO ARLECCHINO BURATTINO CATALDO	and pleads with them. Pedrolino, Arlecchino, and Burattino go back into the house. The pedant falls to his knees, begging forgiveness and confessing his knavery, declaring Isabella to be a faithful and honorable young lady.
PEDROLINO ARLECCHINO BURATTINO	At that moment, Pedrolino, Arlecchino, and Burattino enter dressed in butchers' aprons and hog gelders' aprons, holding long knives and a large copper tub.
CAPT. SPAVENTO	Suddenly, the Captain bursts in on this spectacle. The pedant pleads with him. The Captain says he has no authority, but hearing that they intend to castrate him, he urges them to give him smaller punishment, such as a whipping, or else drive him out of the city. They agree, and with three sticks, they beat him thoroughly; then, shouting and cursing, they drive him away as a disgraceful example to all other pedant rogues and rascals like himself. Then they happily discuss marriage preparations for Flaminia, not forgetting to invite the Captain; and the comedy ends.

THE TWO DISGUISED GYPSIES *

ARGUMENT

*There was in Rome a merchant named Pantalone de Bisognosi, a
Venetian, who by marriage had two children, one named Oratio
and the other Isabella. She was much loved by a young man
named Flavio, son of a Bolognese doctor named Gratiano; she in
turn loved him very much. It came about that Flavio was sent by
his father on an important mission to Leone of France, and while
on the sea, he was captured and enslaved by pirates. This news
reached Isabella, who loved him so much that, with a servant, she
went traveling through various parts of the world looking for
him. She took jewels and money from her father, and when her
money was spent, to save her honor and life, she went about
disguised as a gypsy; they traveled about for a long time, and
after much searching, they returned again to Rome. There she
was recognized by her father, and after some time she found her
lover and her brother, who, because of her disappearance, had
gone mad; she finally married her lover as she had desired.*

CHARACTERS IN THE PLAY

Pantalone, a Venetian merchant
Oratio, his son
Franceschina, his servant

Doctor Gratiano
Flaminia and
Flavio, his children

Isabella, a Gypsy, then the daughter of Pantalone
Pedrolino, servant, as gypsy

Captain Spavento
Arlecchino, his servant

* See Appendix p. 406.

PROPERTIES

Three women's dresses
Gypsy clothes for Pedrolino
Many lighted lanterns
Clothes for a madman

ACT ONE

FLAVIO
CAPT. SPAVENTO

Flavio enters, telling the Captain what has happened since his father Gratiano sent him to France when, during the sea voyage, he was enslaved by Turks. He says two years have passed since he was rescued from a Maltese galley and that on his return to his country, he has not found his love or his servant, to whom he confided all his secrets, and he has not been happy from that time to this; the Captain consoles him with friendly words, and they go off together.

FLAMINIA
FRANCESCHINA

Flaminia, daughter of Gratiano, enters, telling Franceschina of her love for Oratio, son of Pantalone, who has gone mad. Franceschina weeps at the memory of her husband Pedrolino and of Isabella, her mistress lost for ten years. Flaminia asks her to help Oratio and goes into the house. Franceschina, believing her husband to be dead, says she is in love with a captain.

CAPT. SPAVENTO

At that moment, the Captain enters, swaggering in front of Franceschina, who reveals her love. The Captain scoffs at her. Franceschina goads him on, saying that he must take her by force; they struggle.

PANTALONE
DR. GRATIANO

Pantalone and Gratiano arrive during the struggle and ask what is going on. Franceschina swears that the Captain has been trying to rape her. They fight and chase the Captain away; then Pantalone, her master, sends Franceschina into the house. Pantalone learns from Gratiano the melancholy of his son Flavio, who has returned home; Pantalone tells of the loss of his daughter, of his servant, and of the madness of his son who remains at home, adding that he thinks Oratio has become mad over the loss of his sister. They console each other.

FRANCESCHINA

At that, Franceschina comes out, shouting that Oratio is having fits of madness. The old men leave sorrowfully. Franceschina remains, speaking of the cruelty of the Captain.

PEDROLINO
ISABELLA

Just then, Pedrolino and Isabella enter, dressed as gypsies. They beg alms of Franceschina; she asks them to tell her fortune; she wants to know if her husband is dead or alive. Pedrolino tells her he is dead, and she is saddened.

FLAMINIA

At that, Flaminia comes out and also wants to have her fortune told, asking if Oratio, her lover, will become sane again.

PANTALONE
DR. GRATIANO

But then, Pantalone and Gratiano arrive; Flaminia goes into the house; Franceschina does the same. The gypsies remain, and the old men give them alms. Gratiano then goes off. Pantalone questions the gypsies about various things, and in order to learn certain facts, he invites them to stay in his house; they enter with great ceremony.

ARLECCHINO

Arlecchino, servant of the Captain, comes looking for him.

PEDROLINO

Pedrolino comes rushing out, chased by the madman.

ORATIO

Oratio, dressed as a madman, stands between them, doing and saying many mad things; then he beats Pedrolino and Arlecchino. Arlecchino runs off up the street, and Pedrolino dodges into the house. Oratio follows him; and here the first act ends.

ACT TWO

FLAVIO

Flavio enters, saying that he has dreamed a dream which made him very happy and walks on, having spoken his own name.

PEDROLINO

At that, Pedrolino, who has overheard him, follows and asks Flavio for alms. Flavio drives him away. Pedrolino then plays the fortune teller, calling Flavio by name. Flavio, astonished at that, asks about Isabella. Pedrolino tells him she is dead. Flavio, in despair, wants to kill himself. Pedrolino restrains him, promising to let him see her body. Thus they agree. Flavio goes and Pedrolino remains.

ISABELLA
PANTALONE

Isabella comes out, chased by Pantalone, who wants to seduce her. Pedrolino steps between them, reprimanding Pantalone and saying that it is no wonder his children run away and go mad; all this comes about because of his sins. Pantalone is amazed by this and is humbled. Pedrolino pretends to leave with the gypsy girl. Pantalone pleads with him to remain in the house; then he asks about his daughter Isabella. Pedrolino tells him she is alive. Pantalone rejoices and calls his servant out of the house.

FRANCESCHINA

Franceschina comes out and is ordered by Pantalone to give the keys to all Isabella's chests to the gypsy girl and to honor her as her mistress. Pedrolino, in return, tells Pantalone that no day will pass that he will not receive some good news. Pantalone promises that if his daughter is found, he will marry the gypsy; he goes off happy. The gypsy girl goes into the house. Franceschina asks Pedrolino for help in her love for the Captain. He promises this and sends her into the house. Pedrolino thinks about the situation and finally decides to dress the gypsy girl as Isabella in her own clothes to carry out a scheme he has in mind and then goes into the house.

CAPT. SPAVENTO | The Captain enters, asking Gratiano for his daughter, Flaminia, in marriage. Gratiano replies that he wants to find out how his daughter feels about it and calls her out.
DR. GRATIANO
BURATTINO

FLAMINIA | Flaminia comes out, and learning of the intention of the Captain and her father, declares boldly that she does not want to marry him and goes back into the house. The Captain swaggers off with Arlecchino; Gratiano leaves.

FRANCESCHINA | Franceschina and Pedrolino run out of the house, chased by the madman.
PEDROLINO

ORATIO | Oratio, the madman, comes out and plays a ridiculous scene with them; then he grabs Franceschina and carries her off up the street. Pedrolino cries out.

FLAMINIA | At that, Flaminia comes out and pleads with the gypsy to help her. He promises that that night she will enjoy Oratio; he will give her the signal. Flaminia, happy, goes into the house. Pedrolino remains.

CAPT. SPAVENTO | At that moment, the Captain enters, sees him, and is told to return in about half an hour because he is going to put him to bed with Flaminia. The Captain rejoices and goes.

FLAVIO | Then, Flavio enters, looking for Pedrolino, who sees him and immediately puts a cloak over his head, ordering him to stand still; then Pedrolino goes into the house and brings out a beautiful chair.

ISABELLA | Then, he goes into the house again, and brings out Isabella. She is placed in the chair, dressed as she had been, and closes her eyes as if she were dead; then Pedrolino removes the cloak from Flavio's head and withdraws. Flavio sees Isabella, recognizes her, and thinks she is dead. He moans and laments, praising every part of her beautiful body; overcome by grief and passion, he falls as if dead to the ground. Isabella opens her eyes, and thinking he is really dead, laments over the body of her lover; then, seeing him move a little, she goes into the house before he recovers. Flavio, rising from his fainting spell and not seeing her there, becomes frightened and runs off.

PEDROLINO   Pedrolino, who has seen all while hiding, goes up the street laughing; and here the second act ends.

ACT THREE

FLAVIO   Flavio, still frightened, creeps around Isabella's house.

PEDROLINO   At that moment, Pedrolino arrives. Flavio greets him, asking him to show him again the body of Isabella. Pedrolino makes the excuse that he can't; Flavio pleads with him. Pedrolino tells him he does not want to. Flavio threatens to kill himself. Finally Pedrolino agrees to allow him to see her if he will agree to kill himself over her body; he promises to bury them together. He says Flavio is to return in half an hour. Flavio leaves and Pedrolino remains.

DR. GRATIANO   Gratiano enters and learns from Pedrolino that Franceschina is in love with him; Pedrolino gives him a message to come dressed as a woman. Gratiano rejoices and goes off. Pedrolino remains, saying he wants to confuse everybody.

CAPT. SPAVENTO   At that, the Captain arrives. Pedrolino suggests that the Captain
ARLECCHINO   give a good word to Franceschina. The Captain says he'll do it. Pedrolino calls her.

FRANCESCHINA   Franceschina comes out, and the Captain gives her the good word, telling her he will come dressed as a woman late at night, and she is to leave the door open. He then goes.

ISABELLA   Then, Isabella enters and tells Pedrolino she will die from the long delay; he tells her to be patient for a little while longer, because they are near the end of their troubles, and they go into the house.

PANTALONE   Pantalone and Gratiano enter, saying that everyone will be made
DR. GRATIANO   happy. They speak ambiguously.

ORATIO   At that, Oratio enters and plays a mad scene with them.

ISABELLA   Isabella comes out and sends Oratio into the house. Gratiano
PEDROLINO   turns to Pantalone and says to him, "Signor father, the gypsy wants to find your daughter, and I want to make your son Oratio well; but I want you to promise to do me two favors." Pantalone promises to be faithful and Gratiano goes in. Pantalone remains with Pedrolino, who promises to bring the gypsy girl to his bed

at night, but says he is to marry her as he promised. Pantalone goes into the house. Pedrolino remains.

NIGHT

FLAVIO

Flavio enters, finds Pedrolino, and tells him he has come again, as they agreed, to see the corpse of Isabella. Pedrolino tells him to wait in the shadows, and he goes in to get Isabella.

ISABELLA
PEDROLINO

Isabella, her eyes closed, comes out, led by Pedrolino. She remains standing in the middle of the stage. Then he reveals her to Flavio, who says he will kill himself. Pedrolino says when it is time for him to die he will tell him. He pretends to make a circle around Isabella with a wand, then pretends to draw diabolical signs and makes her move one hand, then the other; then he opens one eye, then the other; then he makes her walk, sing, dance, laugh, and do other actions of a live person. Finally, Isabella reveals herself to be alive and embraces Flavio; Flavio embraces her. Pedrolino sends them into the house to make Oratio well; he says when he gives the signal, Flavio is to bring Oratio out into the street. Pedrolino remains.

CAPT. SPAVENTO
ARLECCHINO

The Captain enters dressed as a woman. Pedrolino recognizes him and sends Arlecchino to dress as a woman; Arlecchino goes.

DR. GRATIANO

At that, Gratiano enters dressed as a woman. Pedrolino signals the Captain, who goes with Gratiano into Gratiano's house.

FLAMINIA

Then, Flaminia comes out and asks Pedrolino for her reward. Pedrolino promises she will have her lover soon.

FLAVIO
ORATIO

Pedrolino signals to Flavio, who brings Oratio out asleep.

FLAMINIA

At that moment, Flaminia comes out again. Pedrolino signals Oratio, and Flaminia takes him into the house. Pedrolino remains.

ARLECCHINO

At that, Arlecchino returns dressed as a woman. Pedrolino puts him in Pantalone's house, telling him there is a fine wench waiting for him. Arlecchino goes in. Pedrolino takes off his clothes on stage and says he is going to sleep with Franceschina and goes in.

CAPT. SPAVENTO

The Captain comes out running.

DR. GRATIANO

Gratiano chases after him with a lantern; both have been tricked by the gypsy.

ARLECCHINO

At that moment, Arlecchino comes out running.

PANTALONE

Pantalone chases after him with a lantern; both have been tricked by the gypsy.

FLAVIO ISABELLA	Then, Flavio and Isabella come out, saying the gypsy has brought them together.
ORATIO FLAMINIA	Oratio and Flaminia come out, saying that the gypsy has cured Oratio.
FRANCESCHINA PEDROLINO	Franceschina comes out, shouting that the spirit of her dead husband is trying to impregnate her. All are afraid of Pedrolino. On her knees, Isabella demands her two favors of Pantalone: one, that Oratio be married to Flaminia, and the other, that Isabella, his daughter, be married to Flavio. Pantalone says he does not know where she is. Isabella reveals herself to her father. Pedrolino reveals himself. Overjoyed, Pantalone gladly grants both favors; all are happy, and the comedy ends.

THE FOUR FAKE SPIRITS

ARGUMENT

There lived in the university town of Perugia two merchants of great wealth, who, with their families, lived in peace and contentment—one was named Pantalone de Bisognosi and the other, Cassandro Aretusi; Cassandro had to leave the city on business and left his daughter, Isabella, with Pantalone, his friend, until his return. Pantalone had a son named Oratio who was with her morning and evening and fell passionately in love with her, but he could not make her his wife. After many difficulties, and with the help of a shrewd and cunning servant, in spite of her father, he won her, and they lived happily.

CHARACTERS IN THE PLAY

Pantalone, a merchant
Isabella, left by her father, Cassandro
Oratio, son of Pantalone
Pedrolino, his servant
Franceschina, his servant

Doctor Gratiano
Flaminia, his daughter
Nespola, his servant

Flavio, a lone gentleman

Captain Spavento
Arlecchino, his servant

Nicoletto, a rogue

PROPERTIES

A spiritualist costume

ACT ONE

THE CITY OF
PERUGIA

CAPT. SPAVENTO
ARLECCHINO

Captain Spavento enters, telling of his love for Isabella, daughter of Cassandro Aretusi, left in the custody of Pantalone de Bisognosi. Arlecchino tells him he hasn't got a chance because Oratio, Pantalone's son, is in love with her, and Pedrolino, his servant, is his confidant; the Captain threatens great destruction.

PANTALONE

At that moment, Pantalone enters and hears from the Captain that he wants to marry Isabella more than anything in his life. Pantalone says he can't marry her without her father's consent. The Captain roars and threatens Pantalone.

PEDROLINO

Pedrolino enters because of the noise made by the roaring Captain, who tells him he is Oratio's pimp and lives on young lovers, and roaring, he leaves with Arlecchino. Pantalone questions Pedrolino about Oratio's love. Pedrolino says he knows nothing and that it cannot be; they call Isabella.

ISABELLA

Isabella comes out, and Pantalone tells her that he wants to give her a husband, and by her choice, he would give her Oratio, his son; he has observed their goings on at the table—over their glasses and by the touching of the feet. Pedrolino signals to Isabella many times. Isabella, not knowing what to say, says that Pedrolino is enamored of her and he always pinches her and squeezes her hand. Pantalone, enraged, says he will drive him from the house without more ado; at last Pedrolino reveals that Isabella is in love with Oratio.

FRANCESCHINA

Then immediately, Franceschina comes out of the house and says that Pedrolino lies, but it is true that he is in love with Isabella; they start hitting each other; Pantalone comes between them. The women go into the house, and Pantalone drives Pedrolino away and then goes in. Pedrolino, in despair, leaves.

ORATIO
FLAVIO

Oratio enters, telling Flavio, his friend, of his love for Isabella and of his suspicion that the Captain, who is a very good friend of Cassandro, her father, wants to marry her. His father, Pantalone, will not agree to his love; he asks Flavio to help him by requesting Isabella in marriage of Pantalone, who is to agree to write her father in France and thus start the long negotiations. Flavio promises to do it and asks Oratio to help him in his love for Flaminia, daughter of Gratiano. Oratio asks him if she likes him. Flavio tells him he believes she loves him.

FLAMINIA — At that moment, Flaminia enters and tells Flavio that he may be sure of her love, and she can prove it.

NESPOLA — Nespola enters and confirms the love of her mistress for Flavio; they play a love scene until Oratio sees Gratiano coming.

DR. GRATIANO — Gratiano enters, and Oratio immediately turns on Flavio, shouting that, plead as he might, his father will not give her to him as wife. Flavio wonders at his words, and seeing Gratiano, quietly withdraws. Gratiano thanks Oratio and sends the women into the house. Afterwards, Oratio reveals to Gratiano that Flavio is in love with Flaminia, whom he too loves, and he never revealed his love to Flavio, nor anyone else; but now, seeing that Flavio is seeking to marry her, he desires her also and asks to marry her. Gratiano agrees to give her to Oratio, and they leave together. Flavio has heard everything and calls Oratio a traitor.

PEDROLINO — At that moment, Pedrolino enters and calls him a liar. Flavio draws his sword.

PANTALONE — Pantalone enters and comes between them; he hears from Flavio that he has been quarreling with Pedrolino for being Oratio's pimp for Isabella, with whom he himself is in love, and he asks for her in marriage so that Oratio cannot have her. Pantalone drives off Pedrolino, who runs off; then he agrees to Flavio's proposal and calls Franceschina.

FRANCESCHINA — Franceschina comes out and hears from Pantalone that Isabella is to marry Flavio. Franceschina reprimands him, telling him he must wait for her father's approval. Pantalone says he will act on his own; he has her call Isabella.

ISABELLA — Isabella comes out and learns that Flavio is to be her husband; she refuses without the consent of her father Cassandro. Pantalone says he has the permission of her father to marry her to whomever he wishes and makes her take Flavio's hand.

ARLECCHINO — At that, Arlecchino arrives, saying that the marriage is illegal because Isabella is betrothed to his master. Pantalone laughs and goes into the house with the women. Arlecchino argues with Flavio, saying that he will never have Isabella. Flavio becomes enraged, draws his sword on Arlecchino, who flees, chased by Flavio; and the first act ends.

ACT TWO

PANTALONE
FRANCESCHINA — Pantalone sends his servant Franceschina to call Nicoletto, his henchman, to frighten the Captain. She goes, leaving Pantalone.

CAPT. SPAVENTO ARLECCHINO	The Captain enters, happy because he has received a letter from Cassandro, the father of Isabella, who consents to her being his wife. He shows the letter to Pantalone, which he reads aloud, but first he gives him a letter from Cassandro which came in his mail. Pantalone reads the letter and finds that she is not to marry the Captain. The Captain roars, curses Cassandro, threatens to kill Pantalone, and says he will take her and others and rushes off with Arlecchino. Pantalone laments having Isabella in his household.
DR. GRATIANO	At that moment, Gratiano enters, happy about the wedding of his daughter Flaminia. He tells Pantalone that his son will be the husband of his daughter. Pantalone rejoices.
PEDROLINO	Then, Pedrolino, who has heard everything, enters and approaches Pantalone, who, straightened out about Oratio's love, takes him back into his household and has him call Isabella.
ISABELLA	Isabella comes out and is given orders to make preparations in the house for her wedding with Flavio and Oratio's with Flaminia, daughter of Gratiano; they all leave. Isabella complains about Oratio's betrayal.
FRANCESCHINA	At that, Franceschina enters, saying that the henchman is coming right away. She sees Isabella weeping and asks her why she weeps. Isabella tells her everything. Franceschina consoles her, telling her she believes it is a conspiracy between Oratio and Flavio, as she knows how much Oratio loves her.
FLAMINIA NESPOLA	Just then, Flaminia comes out; they greet each other and begin talking. Flaminia says she is unhappy because Oratio is to be her husband. Franceschina asks her why. She answers that she is in love with Flavio. Franceschina says she must forget him because he is to marry Isabella. Isabella confirms this. Flaminia then says, "Flavio is to be your husband?" She makes a deep curtsy; then she goes to her door, repeats her words, makes another deep curtsy, and goes in. Nespola copies Flaminia's actions and also goes in. Isabella weeps over the loss of Oratio.
ORATIO	At that moment, Oratio arrives. Isabella continues to weep, calling him traitor, and infuriated, she goes into the house without listening to what he has to say. Oratio, confused, asks Franceschina what it is all about. Franceschina tells him all that happened and about the arrangements for the marriages—that is, Oratio is to marry Flaminia and Flavio, Isabella. Hearing someone call her, Franceschina goes into the house. Oratio remains lamenting.

DR. GRATIANO	At that, Gratiano enters and tells Oratio that his father is looking for him. Oratio, for no apparent reason, gives a terrible shriek.
PEDROLINO	Then, Pedrolino arrives and says to Oratio, "I have found you, Signor Husband." Oratio, angered, draws his sword; Pedrolino flees, and all run off.
PANTALONE NICOLETTO	Pantalone orders Nicoletto, his henchman, to beat up the Captain. Nicoletto agrees to do it, commenting on the Captain's swaggering, and goes.
ARLECCHINO	Arlecchino enters, saying he has heard the order and will go to warn the Captain. Pantalone remains, looking for Oratio.
PEDROLINO	At that moment, Pedrolino enters, frightened, and gives the news to Pantalone that Oratio is possessed by an evil spirit (is out of his wits) and has probably killed Gratiano; they hear noises of fighting.
ORATIO FLAVIO	Suddenly, Oratio and Flavio enter fighting.
FRANCESCHINA	Franceschina, at the window, also sees the young men fighting; they go on fighting up the street; all follow, and the second act ends.

ACT THREE

ISABELLA FRANCESCHINA	Isabella is in despair over the fight between Oratio and Flavio.
ORATIO	Just then, Oratio, out of breath, arrives, and seeing Isabella, pleads with her to listen to him. She agrees, and Oratio tells her all that happened between himself and Flavio, and Gratiano and himself, and that he made up the proposal to ask Flaminia for wife so they could have control of the situation and make an exchange for the one each wants.
FLAVIO	At that, Flavio arrives, and having heard everything, asks Oratio to listen to what he has to say; then he tells him that he was suspicious because of what Oratio said to Gratiano against him. They make peace between them and call Flaminia.
FLAMINIA	Flaminia comes out and is immediately informed about everything, and each promises to marry the woman he loves, that is, Oratio will marry Isabella and Flavio, Flaminia; they appeal to Pedrolino, who says he has thought of a plan. Pantalone believes Oratio is possessed; so Pedrolino tells Isabella that when he gives

the signal, she must pretend that she too is possessed; he sends the women into the house to await his signal, then instructs Flavio to dress as a magician and take Oratio with him, again pretending to be possessed. They go, leaving Pedrolino.

CAPT. SPAVENTO
ARLECCHINO

The Captain enters and learns from his servant, Arlecchino, that Nicoletto, Pantalone's henchman, is going to kill him and he is a terrible rogue. Pedrolino immediately approaches them, seemingly all out of breath; he tells the Captain he has been hunting for him. Pedrolino urges him to change his costume and to remain disguised for three or four days. The Captain, frightened, agrees with this suggestion and changes clothes with Pedrolino, that is, hat and cape. Then the Captain goes. Arlecchino speaks with Pedrolino, and they agree to help the Captain in his difficulties; they leave.

PANTALONE

Pantalone enters in despair about Oratio.

DR. GRATIANO

At that, Gratiano enters and tells Pantalone that Oratio, his son, is truly possessed. Pantalone is grief-stricken.

ARLECCHINO

Just then, Arlecchino, by Pedrolino's instructions, enters, frightened, saying that Oratio has alarmed the whole town because he is possessed.

PEDROLINO

At that, Pedrolino enters, frightened, and confirms that Oratio is possessed. Pantalone despairs.

FLAVIO

Flavio enters, dressed as a magician; he pretends to have seen Oratio and offers to cure him if he is found immediately. In haste, Pantalone sends Pedrolino and Arlecchino to fetch him. Flavio remarks to Gratiano that anyone who has children these days lives in great peril. Gratiano agrees and appeals to him for help.

PEDROLINO
ARLECCHINO
ORATIO

At that moment, Pedrolino and Arlecchino enter leading Oratio, bound, raving in different tongues, and acting as one possessed, crying out that he is a stubborn spirit. Flavio declares that those spirits which possess him are spirits of lechery and they must be brought within the presence of women to drive them out. Pantalone calls Isabella; Gratiano calls Flaminia and the servants.

ISABELLA
FRANCESCHINA
FLAMINIA
NESPOLA

Isabella, Franceschina, Flaminia, and Nespola come out and stand watching. Flavio begins conjuring over Oratio, who cries out that he is a lustful spirit and will not leave Oratio's body until his body is joined with the body of Isabella. Pedrolino signals to Isabella, and she immediately begins to pretend to be possessed. Flavio conjures over her, and she cries out that she is a lustful spirit and will not leave the body until her body is joined with that of Oratio. Pantalone pleads with the magician to free their bodies of the spirits; he must do whatever he can. Flavio cures them by marrying them. Immediately Flaminia also pretends to be possessed; Flavio conjures over her; her spirit shouts that she will not leave until she has Flavio. Gratiano appeals to Flavio and agrees to do anything. Pedrolino pretends to be possessed, saying he wants Franceschina; they give her to him.

NICOLETTO   Nicoletto, the henchman, comes on looking for the Captain to kill him. Pantalone orders Nicoletto not to kill him since he has pardoned the Captain. Nicoletto, suddenly enraged, shouts that he will kill everybody, but the magician threatens that if he does not be quiet, he will become possessed; the henchman calms down.

CAPT. SPAVENTO   At that moment, the Captain, who has heard everything, appeals to the magician, who reassures him. Worried, Gratiano points out to the magician that all that is missing is Flavio. The magician says that he will make him appear very soon; he conjures, then reveals himself saying, "Flavio, whom you seek, is here." All laugh at the joke played on Pantalone and Gratiano; and the play ends.

The Thirty-fourth Day

THE FAKE BLIND MAN

ARGUMENT

*There lived in Rome a Venetian merchant named Pantalone de
Bisognosi who sent his son, Oratio, to Naples on business. The
son was seized by the Turks, enslaved, taken to Algeria, and given
to the viceroy, who was ruler and governor. It happened then that
Oratio found among the slaves a young Roman. They became
such good friends that they were of one mind and feeling. Oratio
waited from day to day to be rescued. He was ransomed and
finally the time for his departure came, but he made it clear that
he did not want to leave Algeria if his friend Flavio did not go
with him. This understanding came to the attention of the viceroy, who, seeing such a strong friendship, promised to return
Flavio also and freed both together. The two young men went to
Marseilles and from there to Leone of France; there Oratio found
a French merchant, who, by order of his father, was to be paid to
take him to Italy and thence to Rome. Oratio and Flavio were
received in the house of the merchant and were well treated. The
merchant had a beautiful daughter named Isabella, with whom
Oratio fell in love at first sight. He confided his love to his friend
Flavio and sought his help. Flavio promised to talk to her, and
while waiting the opportunity, he remembered that he too had
fallen in love with her and when they had eloped and were
captured and made slaves, she was freed because of a treaty between Turkey and France. Whereupon, made bold and sure of not
being recognized by her he loved, because he has grown a beard,
he returned to talk with her, and while he spoke for his friend,
Isabella recognized him, and overcome by joy, she embraced him
and held him fast in her arms. While he was in her embrace,
Oratio chanced upon them and saw them; stricken with contempt
and unable to act otherwise, he declared that Flavio, as penance
for his transgression, was to wander about for three years with his
eyes closed, living only on alms. Flavio accepted this punishment
and went off on his travels. Isabella learned of this hard sentence
imposed by Oratio; she urged Oratio, on the strength of his love,*

to find Flavio, pardon him, free him from his sentence, and bring him to her. Oratio left to do Isabella's bidding. He looked all over the city of Rome and, after many trials, freed his friend, found his love, and all ended happily.

CHARACTERS IN THE PLAY

Pantalone, a Venetian
Flaminia, his daughter
Oratio, his son
Pedrolino, his servant
Franceschina, his servant

Doctor Gratiano
Cinthio, his son

Isabella, daughter of the merchant from Leone
Claudio, her tutor
Ricciolina, his servant
Arlecchino, his servant

Flavio, a Roman gentleman
Burattino, his companion

PROPERTIES

Two capes and two caps for the traveling women
A three-legged stool for the blind man
Dirty clothes for the blind man
Bread and wine for alms
Another costume like Pantalone's

ACT ONE

ROME

DR. GRATIANO ISABELLA CLAUDIO ARLECCHINO RICCIOLINA	Gratiano enters with Isabella, who received his name from her father, his correspondent and friend, who confided to him that she has come to Rome for her devotion. He promises to help in any way he can and puts his household, with all of his servants, at her disposal. Isabella accepts all with gracious thanks. Gratiano calls his son.
CINTHIO	Cinthio comes out, and on his father's orders, greets Isabella with an affectionate embrace, and taking her by the hand, leads her into the house with all the others. Gratiano remains.

PANTALONE   Pantalone enters and tells Gratiano that he wants to talk to his son Cinthio. Gratiano excuses himself by saying that he must entertain some guests who have come from France and goes in. Pantalone knocks at Gratiano's door.

CINTHIO   Cinthio comes out. Pantalone begs him to try to persuade his son and Cinthio's friend, Oratio, not to go back to France. He says he does not know why he wants to return, but that since his rescue from the Turks, he has not been himself. Saying he will do what he can, Cinthio leaves to prepare for the arrival of guests. Pantalone then knocks at the door of his own house.

FLAMINIA   Flaminia appears at her window, weeping. Pantalone thinks she weeps because Oratio wants to leave.

PEDROLINO   At that, Pedrolino comes out to tell Pantalone that Flaminia is not weeping because her brother wants to leave, but because he scolded her after being told that she is in love with Pedrolino. Flaminia says he is not speaking the truth.

FRANCESCHINA   At that, Franceschina comes out and informs Pantalone that Pedrolino is the one who was discovered to be in love with Flaminia. Pedrolino says she lies.

FLAMINIA   At that moment, Flaminia comes out and confirms what Franceschina said; both women attack Pedrolino. Pantalone separates them, and Pedrolino, defending himself against the women, lifts Pantalone onto his back and carries him off. Dumbfounded, the women stare after them and then go into the house.

FLAVIO
BURATTINO   Flavio, in tatters and disguised as a blind beggar, enters with Burattino, his guide, who believes he is really blind. They stop at every door, begging alms.

FRANCESCHINA   Just then, Franceschina comes out and gives them bread and wine for alms. She shows she likes Burattino, who makes lewd gestures. Telling them to come often for alms, she goes back in. They go off singing.

CINTHIO
ORATIO   Cinthio and Oratio enter. Oratio explains why he wants to return to France, telling his story as it appears in the Argument and saying he has not been able to find his friend. Because of his love for a woman, he wants to return to Leone, and weeping, he collapses in Cinthio's arms. Cinthio calls for help.

FRANCESCHINA   Franceschina comes out, sees Oratio unconscious, and calls his sister.

FLAMINIA   Flaminia comes out and weeps over her brother.

PEDROLINO   Pedrolino arrives and weeps for his master. Oratio regains consciousness, and turning to face all of them, says, "Oh, weep for my misery, for I am near death." All weep.

PANTALONE   At that moment, Pantalone arrives and asks Oratio the reason for all the weeping. He gestures his inability to speak and leaves without saying a word. Pantalone asks all of them, one by one, the reason they weep, and each, one by one, does the same as Oratio did and then goes in. Cinthio leaves last, and Pantalone, also weeping, goes into the house; and the first act ends.

ACT TWO

PANTALONE   Pantalone enters, unhappy because of Oratio's melancholy and
PEDROLINO   because he does not know the cause. He orders Pedrolino to knock at the door of Gratiano's house because he wants to speak again to Cinthio.

CLAUDIO   Claudio, the tutor, appears at the window and talks to them. They play a ridiculous scene in French. Finally Claudio says that there is no one in the house but the mistress, and he goes back in. Puzzled, Pantalone asks Pedrolino to knock again.

ISABELLA   At that, Isabella appears at her window and tells Pantalone that Gratiano and his son are not at home, but to leave his name so she can tell Gratiano when he returns home. Pantalone gives his name and surname. Isabella says she knew in France a certain Oratio Bisognosi. Pantalone says that is his son, and almost weeping, tells her that Oratio has been melancholy ever since he was rescued by the Turks. Isabella asks how long it has been since he returned to Rome, and Pantalone answers that it has been only a short time. Pedrolino takes close note of what Isabella has said.

ARLECCHINO   Just then, Arlecchino comes out and goes through an elaborate ceremony with Pantalone and Pedrolino. Isabella asks Pantalone to show her servant the mail box. Arlecchino starts off, followed by Pantalone, who says he will go with him to show him the box, and they go. Pedrolino says he suspects that Oratio's illness is connected with the guest, she having asked after Oratio, and in a most piteous tone.

CINTHIO   At that moment, Cinthio comes out and inquires about Oratio. Pedrolino asks that he tell him the reason for Oratio's melancholy, if he knows. Cinthio answers immediately that Oratio loves a woman in Leone, France, but now his father is waiting for him at the bank, and Pedrolino is to tell Oratio to come to him at once, and he goes. Pedrolino says he must find out if the guest is from Leone.

BURATTINO   Just then, Burattino enters, guiding Flavio. They go asking alms
FLAVIO   at Pantalone's house.

FRANCESCHINA   Franceschina comes to the window, and seeing Burattino, is filled with joy and tells him to wait. Then she comes out with bread and wine and other things, which she gives to Burattino, fondling and caressing him. Pedrolino, hiding, stays to listen.

FLAMINIA   Flaminia also comes out and talks to the blind man. She asks him how long he has been blind and from what country he comes. Flavio says it was a short time ago that he went blind, and he comes from Rome. Franceschina takes Burattino into the house to give him some beer and to give Flaminia a chance to speak to the blind man. Flaminia learns from the blind man that he has hope of becoming well again, that with the kisses of a young woman he will regain his sight. Flaminia at once kisses him on the eyes.

PEDROLINO   Pedrolino, still hiding, remains to watch; he is in love with Franceschina and is jealous at her having taken Burattino into the house.

FRANCESCHINA   At that moment, Franceschina comes back out to bring beer to the blind man; Flaminia gives him the beer herself. Flavio says he accepts all in charity, and she again kisses him. Enraged, Pedrolino reveals himself and reprimands everyone. They turn on him, the blind man with a club. Pedrolino flees, the women go into the house, and the beggars go off.

ORATIO   Oratio enters, looking for Pedrolino.

PEDROLINO   At that moment, Pedrolino returns in a fury. When Oratio asks him the cause, Pedrolino replies that he has been taunted by the blind man. Then he demands to know the cause of Oratio's melancholy, but to Oratio's amazement, and before he can answer, Pedrolino tells him that he fell in love in Leone, France, and his love is in Rome and in the house of Cinthio, his friend. Suddenly Oratio is happy, and he asks Pedrolino to knock at the door of Cinthio's house.

RICCIOLINA   Ricciolina appears at the window and learns that they want to talk to her mistress. She tells them that she will soon come out and withdraws.

ISABELLA   At that, Isabella comes out; Oratio recognizes her and rushes up to embrace her, but she drives him off, calling him a faithless wretch, and then tells him that until he finds Flavio, he will not hear a good word from her and she came from France just for that reason; then turning on her heel, she goes into the house. Oratio is again in despair. Pedrolino tries to console him, but Oratio, beside himself, runs off, followed by Pedrolino.

BURATTINO

Burattino, at Flavio's word, gets a stool and Flavio sits down while Burattino leaves him alone and goes to beg alms. Finding himself alone, Flavio laments the fortunes of Love and the cruelty of his friend.

ISABELLA

At that, Isabella appears at the window, hears the blind man talking to himself, and at his voice and words, recognizes him as Flavio. She comes out into the street, and after listening to him, laments the turn of events. Flavio recognizes her by the sound of her voice. She reveals herself to him, begging him to open his eyes. Flavio refuses because he does not want to offend his friend Oratio. She asks him again, kissing him to make him open his eyes, but he faithfully keeps them closed.

BURATTINO

At that moment, Burattino, hidden, has heard that his companion is not blind. He calls him a traitor, saying that he would like to kill him. Since he has lost his job as guide, he will now become a guide on his own. Isabella beseeches Flavio not to leave until she returns. Flavio promises.

ARLECCHINO

At that, Arlecchino returns, and Isabella, angered, takes him into the house.

PANTALONE

Pantalone enters to talk to Gratiano, but hearing the blind man lamenting his love, he stops to listen.

PEDROLINO

Pedrolino enters, and seeing Pantalone observing the blind man, laughs.

FRANCESCHINA

At that moment, Franceschina comes out because she has heard the blind man, and being afraid that Pedrolino will inform Pantalone what happened between Flaminia and the blind man, she begins to shout loudly so Flaminia will hear, "Signor, hurry, your daughter is dying." Pantalone and Pedrolino rush into the house. Flavio says that that was the voice of the servant who gave him alms.

ISABELLA

At that, Isabella comes out, says she will give Arlecchino to Flavio as a guide, and goes back into the house; she returns dressed as Arlecchino, and starts leading him off.

BURATTINO

Just then, Burattino arrives and again curses the blind man, calling Arlecchino a knave who still plays the pimp because he guides the blind man. Thus all leave; and the second act ends.

ACT THREE

PANTALONE PEDROLINO	Pantalone asks Pedrolino how things are going between Flaminia and the blind man, remarking that they are in love. Pedrolino tells him to speak to Franceschina because she knows all that's going on; he calls her.
FRANCESCHINA	Franceschina comes out; threatened by Pantalone, she confesses that Flaminia is in love with the blind man, and she saw them kiss many times. Pantalone sends her into the house; then he laments the bad fortune he has had with his children.
ORATIO	At that moment, Oratio enters, resolved to go round the world to find Flavio. Pantalone, hearing his resolve, despairs. Oratio tells his father that it would satisfy his desire if he had for wife the guest who is staying in Gratiano's house; then he would not leave. Pantalone rejoices.
DR. GRATIANO CINTHIO	Just then, Gratiano and Cinthio arrive, and Pantalone asks Gratiano to give to his son Oratio as wife the guest who is staying at his house. Cinthio urges his father Gratiano to give her to Oratio, for Gratiano had planned to give her to Cinthio, because of the great friendship he had with her father in France. However, he is now satisfied to give her to Oratio; they call Isabella.
ARLECCHINO	Arlecchino enters in Isabella's clothes. Gratiano is puzzled by this disguise, until Arlecchino tells him that Isabella has gone off with Flavio. Oratio, enraged, threatens Arlecchino, who flees quickly; Oratio rushes after him like a madman, and all follow.
FLAMINIA FRANCESCHINA	Flaminia enters and accuses Franceschina of revealing to her father her love for the blind man. Franceschina begs forgiveness and tries vainly to talk her out of her love. Flaminia insists she is going to ask her father to give him to her for husband.
BURATTINO	At that moment, Burattino arrives. Flaminia asks about the blind man, whereupon Burattino reveals that he is not blind, he faked blindness for love of a woman, and he is a gentleman. Flaminia, hearing this, loves him all the more. Franceschina says she must think of a way to find him, and they go into the house, taking Burattino with them.
ISABELLA FLAVIO	Isabella enters in Arlecchino's clothes, leading Flavio, who tries to persuade her to return to Gratiano's house and dress herself as a woman and take Oratio for husband. She says she does not love him; Flavio insists she does and that it is for her honor and her father's happiness.

PEDROLINO
At that moment, Pedrolino enters weeping, believing that in desperation Oratio has drowned himself in the Tiber; he cries that the blind man is the cause of all the evil, and seeing him, tries to beat him. Isabella fends him off, and Pedrolino runs away. Flavio again asks Isabella to marry Oratio; finally she says she wants to go on guiding him in her own clothes, that it is three years since she made her love known to Oratio, and it is all over.

FLAMINIA
FRANCESCHINA
Just then, Flaminia enters dressed as Pantalone, her father, with Franceschina dressed as Burattino. Flaminia, seeing the blind man, runs to embrace him, but Isabella comes between them. Flaminia, thinking she is a man, reveals that she is Flaminia, Pantalone's daughter, and in love with the blind man whom she wants to marry, or she will die. Isabella, recognizing her as Oratio's sister, becomes confused, and seeing Oratio coming, they withdraw.

ORATIO
At that moment, Oratio enters, weeping over the cruelty of Isabella and the ingratitude of Flavio; he plans to kill himself, saying these last words: "Isabella, why did you call me a faithless wretch? I call on heaven to testify and show that I absolved Flavio of the oath which I made him take to remain three years with his eyes closed, praying that these, my last words, reach the ears of Flavio; and immediately thereafter I wish to die."

FLAVIO
Suddenly, Flavio enters, reveals himself, opens his eyes, and takes Oratio's hand. Then he kneels before Isabella and pleads with her to become Oratio's wife. Isabella refuses. Flaminia, on her knees, pleads with Isabella not to refuse to marry Oratio, her brother. Isabella, after turning it over in her mind, turns to Flavio and tells him that since he has shown such greatness of soul as to give to others all that he loves in the world, she wants to show that she can do as much in giving what she loves—as much as she loves Flavio, she takes him by the hand and gives him to Flaminia, suggesting that as Flavio gave her to Oratio, so she gives Flaminia, his sister, to Flavio, his dear friend. Oratio and Flavio agree to Isabella's proposal; they pledge their loyalty and embrace, saying that they will settle with their fathers.

PANTALONE
DR. GRATIANO
CINTHIO
PEDROLINO
At that moment, Pantalone, Gratiano, Cinthio, and Pedrolino arrive and from the lovers learn briefly what has occurred among them. They agree to everything and rejoice.

FRANCESCHINA
ARLECCHINO
Franceschina enters dressed in Burattino's clothes with Arlecchino dressed in Isabella's clothes; each laughs at the exchange of dress.

CLAUDIO Then, Claudio enters, and Isabella tells him of their happiness; he
RICCIOLINA rejoices.

BURATTINO Burattino enters dressed as Franceschina. Everyone laughs. They
are all very content. Oratio and Flavio are to send the ransom to
the Pasha of Algeria who let Flavio go on the promise of Oratio,
and to write to Leone, France, to the father of Isabella and inform
him of the marriage of his daughter. They then have three
weddings: Oratio marries Isabella; Flavio marries Flaminia; Pedrolino marries Franceschina; and the comedy ends.

The Thirty-fifth Day

FLAVIO'S DISGRACE

ARGUMENT

There lived in Rome a very beautiful widow named Isabella, who was descended from a very honorable family, and after she became a widow, she was pursued by many cavaliers. It came to pass that she fell in love with a young nobleman named Flavio, the only son of a Venetian gentleman called Pantalone de Bisognosi. It happened then that by the action of one of her servants, she became angry with her lover, who, feeling much scorned, turned all his love to another woman, to whom he became very attentive. By a neat trick, Isabella finally gets him for her husband.

CHARACTERS IN THE PLAY

Pantalone, a noble Venetian
Flavio, his son
Pedrolino, his servant

Isabella, a gentle widow
Franceschina, her servant

Oratio, a gentleman
Flaminia, his sister
Burattino, his servant

Captain Spavento
Arlecchino, his servant

PROPERTIES

A soldier's helmet
Sword and buckler for Burattino
A bucket with water

258

A urinal with white wine in it
A club
A lady's cloak for Pedrolino

ACT ONE

THE CITY OF
ROME

PANTALONE
FLAVIO

Pantalone enters, beating his son Flavio because he found him trying to break open his money chest. Flavio denies it. Pantalone beats him, saying he is no son of his and refuses him his hat and cape. Flavio tries to tear them out of his hands. Pantalone cries for help.

PEDROLINO

At that, Pedrolino enters with the bar of a door and comes between them.

BURATTINO

Burattino does the same. Flavio withdraws near the house of Isabella, the widow.

FRANCESCHINA

At that moment, Franceschina, Isabella's servant, comes to the window and throws a pan of dishwater on Flavio's head. All then go into the house, while Flavio goes off in despair.

CAPT. SPAVENTO
ARLECCHINO

Captain Spavento enters swaggering. He speaks of his love for the widow, Isabella, and of his jealousy of Flavio. He says he wants to speak of his love with Oratio, Flaminia's brother; he orders Arlecchino to knock on her door.

BURATTINO

Burattino comes to the window. To frustrate the Captain, he pretends he does not understand him; the Captain roars, threatens to kill him, and leaves.

ISABELLA
FRANCESCHINA

Isabella enters beating Franceschina for soaking Flavio; Franceschina begs her pardon; then she tells Isabella that Flavio is a traitor, that he is deceiving her and loves Flaminia; she offers to prove it. Isabella, turning on her heel, goes into the house. Franceschina has thought up a shrewd idea to prove that Flavio loves Flaminia; she knocks on Flaminia's door.

FLAMINIA

Flaminia comes out and learns from Franceschina that Flavio is in love with her, that he wants to talk to her, and he wants to come in disguise so as not to make the neighbors suspicious; between them they think of ways to work it out. Franceschina says they can borrow some of Oratio's clothes so that Flavio can come disguised in them. Flaminia sends Burattino into the house for Flavio's clothes.

PEDROLINO   Pedrolino, hidden, has heard everything.

BURATTINO   At that moment, Burattino brings out the clothes. Franceschina takes them, saying to Flaminia that later Flavio will come to her. Flaminia, rejoicing, goes into the house. Burattino asks Franceschina for a kiss; she gives him one, to the terrible rage of Pedrolino. After she goes into the house, Pedrolino says he is going to play a trick on Franceschina.

ORATIO   Just then, Oratio arrives and from Pedrolino learns that Franceschina has been in his house, stolen a suit of clothes, and made his sister believe that Flavio is in love with her. Oratio says it is important that Flavio love his sister, because then he will cease to suspect that Flavio loves Isabella, as he himself loves her with all his soul. He tells Pedrolino to knock on her door to clear the matter up.

ISABELLA   At that moment, Isabella appears at her window and is greeted by Oratio. Pedrolino tells Isabella that she should love Oratio, not Flavio, who loves Flaminia and is going to marry her. Oratio will be faithful. Isabella asserts that she does not believe Flavio would ever marry Flaminia.

CAPT. SPAVENTO   At that, the Captain, who has heard all, tells Isabella that he
ARLECCHINO   believes what Pedrolino says because that is the way he wants it! No one else but he can pretend to the love of Isabella. Oratio tells the Captain he is unworthy of Isabella; they exchange sharp words, then draw their swords.

ISABELLA   Isabella, to keep them from fighting, speaks sweetly to them. She says if they love her, they will part on friendly terms; because of this, they shake hands with each other, kiss Isabella's hands, and bow reverently to her. Isabella, returning their greeting, goes into the house laughing; everyone leaves; and the first act ends.

ACT TWO

FLAVIO   Flavio enters, dressed in Oratio's clothes; Franceschina urges him
FRANCESCHINA   to go thank Flaminia for the clothes. Flavio agrees, saying he will go right now. Franceschina immediately goes into the house to tell Isabella as Flavio knocks on Flaminia's door.

FLAMINIA   Flaminia comes out and recognizes him. They exchange pleasant words.

ISABELLA   At that moment, Isabella comes out, and by Franceschina's doing, thinks that Flavio is talking to Flaminia because he is in love with her; she climbs out through the window, jumps on Flavio, and begins to hit him without giving him a chance to speak; alarmed, Flavio runs off, and the women start fighting over him.

ORATIO

Just then, Oratio arrives, comes between them, sends his sister into the house, and reprimands Isabella, who angrily speaks ill of Flaminia and goes into her house. Oratio accuses Franceschina of being a thief. Franceschina replies that she is not. Oratio insists that she is.

PEDROLINO

At that moment, Pedrolino arrives and immediately says he can prove she is a thief. They begin to argue then to fight.

CAPT. SPAVENTO
ARLECCHINO

The Captain enters and comes between them. Franceschina thanks him, and infuriated, goes into the house. Oratio tells the Captain that he wants to fight him. The Captain asks Oratio if he is a gentleman and a cavalier. When Oratio answers yes, the Captain says he must show his credentials; then they will fight. He leaves, with Oratio following him. Pedrolino challenges Arlecchino, who gives the same response as the Captain did, and then he goes. Pedrolino remains, saying he is going to fix Flavio, and knocks at the door.

FLAMINIA

Flaminia comes out, still fearful because of the brawl she had with Isabella. She learns from Pedrolino that Flavio has promised Isabella he would make Oratio, her brother, beat her. Flaminia is enraged at Flavio; Pedrolino urges her to have Flavio beaten and to hire a ruffian to do it for her. She agrees and goes into the house. Pedrolino says he knows that Pantalone is in love with Flaminia, and he plans to play a trick on him.

PANTALONE

At that moment, Pantalone, enraged at his son Flavio, enters. Pedrolino persuades him to do a service for Flaminia, his inamorata, and takes him into the house to dress him in his son's clothes.

FLAVIO
BURATTINO

Then, Flavio enters and learns from Burattino what took place between Flaminia and Franceschina, who made Flaminia believe that he was in love with her, and with that end in mind, she had stolen one of his suits. Flavio puzzles over this and says he is going to straighten out Flaminia because Franceschina's treachery has made Isabella angry with him. Burattino enters the house, leaving Flavio.

CAPT. SPAVENTO

At that moment, the Captain enters, and with great courtesy, he asks Flavio whom he loves; Flavio replies that he loves Isabella. The Captain says he must forget about her, but Flavio declares that it is impossible and becomes very voluble.

ISABELLA	Isabella appears at the window and greets the Captain familiarly to make Flavio jealous. The Captain haughtily tells Flavio that he can do nothing else but forget about her; he swaggers, defies everyone, and leaves. Flavio, humbly, tries to speak to Isabella, but she shuts the window in his face. Flavio laments his bad fortune.
FLAMINIA	At that, Flaminia, provoked by Burattino, comes out and asks Flavio what he wishes to say. Flavio says that Franceschina has betrayed her and him, because it is not true that he is in love with her, that he loves someone else. Flaminia, enraged, calls him a wretch.
PANTALONE PEDROLINO	Just then, Pantalone, dressed in the short coat of a ruffian, enters with Pedrolino. Pedrolino, disguised, tells Flaminia that Pantalone is a ruffian. Flaminia calls to him and asks that he beat up Flavio; she points him out and goes into the house. Flavio stands apart, very unhappy. Pantalone looks him over carefully to see if Flavio recognizes him.
ISABELLA	Isabella, who has remained at the window, calls Franceschina to come see what is going on in the street.
FRANCESCHINA	Franceschina comes to the window to look. Pantalone and Flavio recognize each other. Flavio reprimands his father; arguing and shouting, they come beneath Isabella's window. At that moment, Franceschina empties a chamber pot on them, and off they run. Here the second act ends.

ACT THREE

ORATIO CAPT. SPAVENTO	Oratio and the Captain enter, fighting.
ARLECCHINO	Then Arlecchino comes between them with the bar of a door.
FRANCESCHINA	At that moment, Franceschina comes out and learns that they are fighting over Isabella; she tells them to forget about her because she is in love with Flavio.
PEDROLINO	Pedrolino then arrives and confirms what Franceschina has told them.
ISABELLA	Just then, Isabella comes out and tells them the same thing; she suggests that Oratio take to wife a beautiful and gracious nun from the convent, and the Captain take Flaminia, Oratio's sister, for she herself is determined to marry none other than Flavio. They all agree, and with Oratio's consent, they call Flaminia.

FLAMINIA | Flaminia comes out and is reconciled with Isabella. She learns of her brother's determination to carry out Isabella's suggestion, and she agrees to everything. Franceschina begs pardon for taking the suit and for all the trouble she caused; she says she did it because Isabella had beaten her. Then Oratio and the Captain leave. Isabella says she doubts that Flavio loves her now.

BURATTINO | Burattino, who has learned all that took place, says he can prove that Flavio still loves Isabella. Pedrolino promises to remove all the bad feeling from the whole business. He sends all the women into Flaminia's house; then he tells Franceschina to remain at the window. When she sees Flavio, she is to call him for Flaminia; then he tells Burattino he also is to call him immediately for Flaminia; they agree and go inside. Pedrolino remains.

FLAVIO | Flavio then enters, sees that he is driven away and hated by Isabella, and decides to give himself over to Flaminia's love.

PEDROLINO | At that moment, Pedrolino approaches him, pretending to be out of breath, and tells Flavio that he has been looking for him for Isabella. Flavio rejoices.

FRANCESCHINA | Then, Franceschina calls Flavio for Flaminia. Pedrolino wrangles and quarrels with her. Flavio intervenes.

BURATTINO | At that moment, Burattino also calls Flavio for Flaminia, who is in the house weeping because she wants no other husband than Flavio. Flavio is happy and says he wants Flaminia; he will leave Isabella to the Captain, whom she loves. Pedrolino urges Flavio to take Flaminia out of her brother's house and sends him to find a room. Flavio goes, taking Burattino with him. Pedrolino remains.

ISABELLA | Then, Isabella enters, complaining about Flavio because of what Franceschina has told her. But Pedrolino consoles her, saying that he is going to play a trick on Flavio; he leaves Franceschina on guard to make sure no one goes into Flaminia's house, and he goes in with Isabella. Franceschina remains; then she begins to cry.

PANTALONE | Pantalone arrives and asks Franceschina where Pedrolino is. She tells him that the poor man is dead, that Flaminia has killed him. Pantalone weeps and leaves to make certain of it. Franceschina laughs.

CAPT. SPAVENTO ORATIO ARLECCHINO | At that, the Captain, Oratio, and Arlecchino arrive and ask after Flavio. Franceschina tells them to hide and they will have a big laugh. They hide.

BURATTINO | At that moment, Burattino enters and tells Franceschina that Flavio has found a room for Flaminia.

FLAVIO   Just then, Flavio arrives to take Flaminia away. Moved and overwrought, he stands under Isabella's window and says, "Oh, Isabella, because of your cruelty I take Flaminia away with me."

ISABELLA   At that moment, Isabella enters, dressed in Pedrolino's clothes, and tells Flavio that soon Flaminia will come, and he will enjoy her despite Isabella. Flavio begs Pedrolino not to speak ill of Isabella; in spite of her cruelty, she is a fine woman.

PEDROLINO   At that, Pedrolino, dressed in Flaminia's clothes, enters, and Flavio rushes up to kiss her. Pedrolino reveals himself.

FRANCESCHINA   Then, Franceschina declares they are tricked; Isabella silences her and reveals herself. Flavio gladly accepts her, having been tricked, and pledges his faithfulness to Isabella; he tells her he has always loved her.

PANTALONE   At that moment, Pantalone arrives, hears about the arrangements, agrees, then sees Pedrolino dressed as a woman and Isabella dressed as Pedrolino; he begins to laugh.

CAPT. SPAVENTO   At that, the Captain, Oratio, and Arlecchino come out of hiding,
ORATIO   and among them they conclude the nuptials: Flavio marries
ARLECCHINO   Isabella; the Captain, Flaminia; Oratio, Aurelia, sister of Isabella; and Pedrolino, Franceschina; and the play ends.

The Thirty-sixth Day

ISABELLA, THE ASTROLOGER *

ARGUMENT

*There ruled in Naples as Deputy Regent a noble gentleman
named Lucio Cortesi, a Spaniard, who had a most noble daughter
named Isabella. She was loved by a gentleman named Oratio
Gentili. It happened that when her brother Flavio was informed
of Oratio's courting his sister, he was overcome by his great
Spanish sense of honor and determined to attack Oratio at night
and kill him. At the same time, Oratio had conceived the same
plan for Flavio. One night they met and fought. As a result of the
fight, Flavio was left wounded and dying and was thrown into the
sea; but he saved himself, and for shame, went wandering
through the world for a long time. Oratio was arrested and
condemned to death; while he waited execution, Isabella, the
regent's daughter, who loved him, planned to save him with the
help of the prison guard by ordering that a frigate be prepared on
which she would elope with him. The unhappy lover was taken
away and waited on the frigate for Isabella and the guard to join
him. When a sudden storm came up, he was blown out to sea,
captured by pirates, and taken to Algiers as a slave. When this
news was brought to Isabella, in desperation she took a ship that
was sailing for Alexandria, Egypt; she posed as the servant of a
great Arabian astrologer and philosopher who lived there and
who was much inclined toward speculation. He worked out some
principles which, in a short time, became part of astrological
truth. Flavio, meanwhile, finding himself thrown into the sea by
his enemy Oratio, grabbed onto a piece of wood floating on the
water and was found by pirates and enslaved. He too was taken to
Alexandria and sold by the pirates to a very rich merchant. Flavio
liked the daughter of the Arabian astrologer, who lived in a villa
near that of his master, and such was his secret love affair with
her that she became pregnant. It happened that the merchant had
to leave at once on an Alexandrian vessel going to Naples on
business, and he took Flavio with him. Flavio was not able to say*

* See Appendix p. 406.

good-bye to the young Turkish girl. Seeing herself abandoned and betrayed, the girl spoke to Isabella, who was her friend, and learned from her that because of the death of her master in Italy, Isabella would like to go with her. She pleaded with the Turkish girl to take her, and they agreed to leave and thus came to Italy. After being in Naples for some time, Isabella practiced and perfected the art of astrology. Landing in Naples at about the same time, Oratio, while with his master, was taken by a galley of Naples and robbed as they sailed upon the sea; for fear of the law, he pretended to be a Turk who did not wish to be freed. Finally, after many turns of events in the story, they arrived at a happy and blissful ending.

CHARACTERS IN THE PLAY

The Deputy Regent
Flaminia, his daughter
Pedrolino, a servant among many others

Gratiano, a medical doctor (The part of Gratiano can be played by Pantalone.)
Cinthio, his son

Turkish merchant of Alexandria
Memmy, his slave, then Flavio, son of the Regent

Isabella, an astrologer, then daughter of the Regent, under the name Haussa Turca
Rabbya Turca, with a veil, her companion

Aguzzino, of the Naples galley
Amett, slave, finally Oratio
Eight Turkish slaves
Captain of the galley

Arlecchino, a pimp

Policemen

PROPERTIES

Slave dress and iron chains
Eight barrels of water
A beautiful chair for the Regent
A beautiful palace in the prospect of the scene
    and a chair at one side

ACT ONE

NAPLES

AGUZZINO SLAVES AMETT, A SLAVE	Aguzzino comes with galley slaves to get fresh water at the well of the palace of the Regent. He sends the slaves into the palace for the water and remains with Amett, seated on two barrels. Aguzzino asks the slave why he feels bad and sighs every time that they come to the palace to get water. Amett tells him that in Algiers, he had a friend named Oratio, who became a slave because of an unhappy love affair; this friend had recounted many times the story of his misfortune; Amett repeats it all as it is set down in the Argument. He sighs as if pitying his friend. Aguzzino recalls the incident, which occurred many years before. Amett then tells him that the said Oratio is dead. Aguzzino says it would be a good thing to tell the news to the father of the man who was killed by Oratio, because they would then have something to drink.
THE SLAVES	The slaves then return with barrels full of water, and all are escorted by Aguzzino off toward the galley.
THE ALEXANDRIAN MERCHANT MEMMY, HIS SLAVE TURKISH SERVANTS	The Alexandrian merchant enters and informs his slave, Memmy, that he will leave for Alexandria in two days, and now that they have gathered draperies of silk and gold, he wants to travel on the ship, which is ready to sail, but first he will make a list of trinkets to take from Naples to Alexandria; and he goes with his servants. Memmy remains alone and says this is his native land, but he does not want to reveal himself to his countrymen because he must return to Alexandria where he has left his loved one, who is Turkish.
PEDROLINO	At that moment, Pedrolino, steward of the Regent, enters with servants carrying goods; he sends them into the palace. Then he is questioned by the slave and asked if the father of one Flavio, called Lucio Cortesi, the Regent, is still alive and if his sister named Isabella is still alive. Pedrolino wonders at him and says that they are alive but that the sister has fled from Naples; no news has been heard of her. The slave says he knew Flavio in Alexandria, and he is alive.
THE MERCHANT SERVANTS	Then, the merchant arrives, and seeing Pedrolino talking with his slave, inquires what he does for a living. Pedrolino says he's a pimp. The merchant then asks him to find a beautiful Spanish courtesan, and Pedrolino promises him one. The merchant leaves

with Memmy and the servants. Pedrolino wonders if he should tell the Regent about Flavio.

ARLECCHINO

At that, Arlecchino, a street pimp, enters. Pedrolino asks him for a courtesan for the merchant. Arlecchino reads the names of a great many courtesans of many nationalities from a long list and says that much later he will have a very beautiful one for him, but he will have to get a license from the Regent to go out at night without a light. Thus they are agreed. Pedrolino goes into the palace; Arlecchino sings the praises of the pimp's trade and leaves.

ISABELLA
RABBYA

Isabella, dressed as a Syrian, plays the astrologer with Rabbya Turca, her companion and child of the astrologer. She tells Rabbya she still remembers her father, one of the best astrologers among the Arabs, from whom she learned the art of astrology, and how near the time of his death he made an astronomical sign, saying that he saw by that sign that she would return to her native land, and meanwhile, she was to be happy and content, for it would come to pass one day. She tells again the story of her misfortune as it is set down in the Argument and finally adds that he said, just as she will some day be happy, it is for the best that he not tell her whose child she was. Rabbya says that she will know one day.

ARLECCHINO

Just then, Arlecchino enters, looking for new material for his business; he sees the women and tries to lead them to his whorehouse. They tell him they are not that sort; Isabella informs him she is an astrologer, and looking into his palm and into his face, she tells him he is a pimp and the galley and the gallows threaten him. Arlecchino tries to take them to his place by force.

THE REGENT
SERVANTS

At that moment, the Regent comes from his palace and roars at Arlecchino, who, frightened, runs off. Then he turns to the women and asks them what it was that made Isabella an astrologer and brought her to Syria. Jesting, the Regent asks her what is an astrologer. Isabella gives him an account of the art of astronomy, subdivided into many other arts. The Regent is amazed, all the more so as she calls him by name, telling him that she knows all his affairs better than he; then the women go off. The Regent is struck dumb; then he orders all his servants that while they remain in the vicinity, they are to be on the lookout for any criminal acts and for those two women, for he would have them taken into the house where he could question them further. They all go off.

GRATIANO CINTHIO	Gratiano enters and learns from Cinthio, his son, that he loves Flaminia, daughter of the Regent, and he wants to marry her. Gratiano reprimands him and asks him if he wants to end as Oratio ended after all these years. Cinthio replies that Flaminia loves him. Gratiano refuses to agree and leaves. Cinthio remains despairing, afraid because of what his father said to him.
PEDROLINO	At that moment, Pedrolino enters, and Cinthio confides his love to him; Pedrolino consoles him by telling him that he will give him good advice but wants to tell him in front of Flaminia; he goes into the palace to tell her to come to the window, then returns.
FLAMINIA	At that, Flaminia comes to the window; while Pedrolino stands watch, she talks to Cinthio; they play an amorous scene. Then Pedrolino speaks to Cinthio, telling him that he must go to the Regent and say to him: "Sir, if I were to bring news to your Excellency that Flavio, your son, were alive, would you in gratitude grant me your daughter Flaminia in marriage?" If the Regent says yes, he is then to tell him right out that Flavio is alive. Flaminia, believing Flavio to be dead, feels that she has been tricked and goes in weeping. Cinthio accuses Pedrolino of tricking him, since it is impossible that Flavio is still alive, and he goes off in anger. Pedrolino follows him to straighten things out; and the first act ends.

ACT TWO

THE REGENT SERVANTS	The Regent returns from his trip through the neighborhood to return to the palace; he asks his servants if they found the astrologer; they say no.
AGUZZINO AMETT	At that moment, Aguzzino enters, greets the Regent, and gives the news that Oratio, who killed his son Flavio, died in Algiers, a slave in chains. Amett confirms that Oratio died at his side. The Regent says they are to return after dinner, when he will give them refreshment, and he enters the palace. Amett, sighing, promises Aguzzino that he will get him more to drink, and they go off.
GRATIANO CINTHIO	Gratiano enters and learns from Cinthio what Pedrolino has told the Regent. Gratiano says that he does not believe it and suggests that Pedrolino is a go-between in his love for Flaminia, and that she trusts no one but him.
PEDROLINO	Just then, Pedrolino enters, looking for the astrologer. He sees Gratiano, to whom he says that Flaminia, his mistress, is in love with his son Cinthio and will marry no one else. He asks Cinthio

if he has spoken to the Regent yet and told him what he had said to tell him; Cinthio says no. Pedrolino again urges him to do it; finally Cinthio goes into the palace to inform the Regent. Gratiano leaves; Pedrolino exclaims, "Where the devil is the astrologer?"

ISABELLA

Isabella enters and immediately says, "I am here." Pedrolino tells her that the Regent, her master, wants to speak to her again and would like to know from her if a certain Oratio is alive or not, having heard from one Aguzzino and a slave of his that he died in Algiers. Isabella says that right now she cannot come, but in an hour she will go to see the Regent and will tell him everything. Pedrolino gives her two gold crowns and asks her to tell him if Flavio, the son of the Regent, is alive or dead, because a certain merchant from Alexandria has said that Flavio is alive; she is amazed at this news and promises Pedrolino she will tell him the truth. Pedrolino goes; Isabella, left alone, laments her fortune because the truths of the astrologer seem to her dubious, and she has learned from the stars always that Oratio is her love. She decides to talk to Aguzzino, with the slave and with the Alexandrian merchant, to find out the truth about what Pedrolino has said, and she goes.

THE MERCHANT
MEMMY, HIS
SLAVE
SERVANTS

The merchant enters, asking his slave the reason for his moodiness and for his not eating; Memmy says he does not feel well.

RABBYA TURCA

At that, Rabbya enters with her child in her arms. The merchant, seeing her dressed in Turkish clothes, asks her where she comes from. She says she is a native of Alexandria and daughter of an Arabian astrologer and Muhammadan named Amoratt and that her father, while he lived, had a villa just outside the city. The slave observes her closely and suddenly falls as if dead to the ground. The merchant is amazed at this and has his men carry him to the ship; he goes along with them. Rabbya, having recognized her lover, laments his betrayal.

ISABELLA

At that moment, Isabella enters and learns from Rabbya that she has seen the traitor who is the cause of her misfortune and who stole her honor—the father of her child. Isabella beseeches her to tell her more of the history of her misfortune. Rabbya says there is yet time and goes to repose herself. Isabella marvels at the great steadfastness of Rabbya, suffering in silence. Then, turning to her own particular story, she says she recognized in Amett the face of Oratio. Oratio then is alive, and Flavio also is alive, but his life is in great danger.

AGUZZINO
AMETT

At that, Aguzzino enters with Amett, his slave, to go to the Regent for some assistance. Isabella immediately hides; Aguzzino tells Amett there is plenty of time, and he is going into the house of Arlecchino, the pimp, to entertain himself; Amett is to wait for him outside the door.

ARLECCHINO

Arlecchino comes out to take Aguzzino into the house, and Amett remains at the door to wait for him.

ISABELLA

At that moment, Isabella comes forward, and seeing the slave, asks where he comes from. Amett says he comes from Algeria. She asks him if he has recognized a Neopolitan slave in that city. He answers that he knew a certain Oratio from Naples who died in his arms. Isabella wonders if it were he who gave that news to the Regent, and Amett says yes. She declares that he lies. She knows through the art of astrology that Oratio lives, and she accuses Amett of telling the Regent otherwise only for gain; she threatens him, and the slave finally says, "All right, since you know so much, tell me if my Isabella is dead or alive?" She replies that she is dead. The slave makes her repeat it many times. Finally, overcome by grief, he cries, "I am alive? Do I breathe? Am I Oratio? Then I will kill him." He rushes about shouting; Isabella watches him closely.

THE REGENT
SERVANTS
CINTHIO

At that moment, the Regent arrives. Oratio immediately falls to his knees and reveals who he is; his own name he concealed under the name of Amett; the Turks, taken from a galley of Naples, having said that Isabella is dead, make him also want to end his life. The Regent marvels at the constancy of Oratio and has him taken to prison. The Regent remains with Cinthio, speaking of what has happened.

SERVANTS
POLICEMEN

Then, servants enter with policemen and tell the Regent that Oratio made all who heard his story weep.

AGUZZINO
ARLECCHINO

Then, servants enter with policemen and tell the Regent that Aguzzino taken to prison. Arlecchino tries to prevent them, so the police also take Arlecchino to prison, and the second act ends.

ACT THREE

ISABELLA

Isabella enters, lamenting that she did not reveal herself to her lover; her faith still intact and pure, she has suffered to see him taken to prison. She must either find a way to free him or die with him.

RABBYA TURCA

At that moment, Rabbya Turca enters with her baby. She is transformed after having seen her lover, the slave Memmy; she sees Isabella, who asks her again to tell her the name of the man who stole her honor; she says she does not know his Christian name, explaining briefly that this slave was the slave of an Alexandrian merchant who had a villa near that of her father, that he often said he would marry her and make her a Christian, and after he went to Alexandria with his master, she did not see him again or know where he had gone. Isabella consoles her again, telling her that she has seen by way of her art that Rabbya will soon be happy.

MEMMY

Just then, Memmy, the merchant's slave, comes looking for the astrologer because she was the companion of Rabbya Turca, his inamorata; Rabbya recognizes him, calls him traitor, and reproaches him for leaving her after all their promises of love. Memmy falls to his knees and begs her forgiveness, telling her that his master took him across the sea, and that he did not have a chance to see her. She does not accept his excuses; Memmy then appeals to the astrologer, her companion, saying that Naples is his native city, and in order to return to Alexandria to see his love, he did not reveal himself to his father, who is the ruler of the city. Isabella, assured that he is her brother Flavio, pleads with the Turk to resolve their differences. The Turkish girl agrees. Isabella brings them together and kisses their baby; then she asks him to agree to pardon two people who had injured him. Memmy agrees, whereupon Isabella commands him to pardon Oratio, who now is in danger of losing his life. The slave seems doubtful that he can save Oratio, but at the urging of his Rabbya, he agrees, takes up his child in his arms, and they all go off in gay spirits.

GRATIANO
CINTHIO

Gratiano enters, learns from Cinthio, his son, that Oratio, who killed Flavio, son of the Regent, is in prison on pain of death, and the following morning they will execute him after being tried. Cinthio says further that the Regent had promised Flaminia he would bring news that Flavio is alive.

PEDROLINO

Then, Pedrolino enters, desperate because he has not seen the merchant or the slave from Alexandria, much less the astrologer; he fears that Oratio will die.

ISABELLA

At that moment, Isabella arrives. Pedrolino immediately falls to his knees and begs that she, with her art, free Oratio from the sentence of death, and also to tell him whether Flavio is alive or dead. She consoles him by telling him all; she affirms that Flavio is alive and says she wants to talk to the Regent. Cinthio, happy to hear this news, tells Isabella that the Regent is close by, holding public audience.

THE REGENT
CAPTAIN OF
GALLEY
SERVANTS

At that, the Regent enters with the captain of the galley. The Regent asks him what he wants, and he replies that he wants Aguzzino and his slave Amett who are locked up, that His Excellency has no jurisdiction over the men of his galley and the galley of the King of Spain. The Regent reveals that Amett is not Turkish, but is a certain Oratio who killed his son, Flavio, that Oratio is living under a Turkish name so as to remain incognito; however, he agrees to return Aguzzino to him. The captain is satisfied with this.

ISABELLA

At that moment, Isabella comes before the Regent. She states that she appears before him to bring him happiness and consolation, although when they first met, everything indicated just the opposite. The Regent receives her joyfully. Isabella requests that the Regent have Oratio, the one who killed his son, brought before him. The Regent orders Oratio to appear, sending Pedrolino with the servants for him. While they go for Oratio, Isabella gives a moral discourse, telling them that all their seeming troubles which come from heaven are, in reality, for the greatest happiness of men.

THE MERCHANT
MEMMY, SLAVE
SERVANTS

Then, the merchant enters, having been informed of everything by Flavio, the merchant's slave. Memmy kneels before the Regent, saying that when His Excellency has finished with the business at hand, he wishes to speak to him about a most important matter.

RABBYA

At that, Rabbya enters with her child in her arms, bows before the Regent, saying that she appears before him in the name of justice.

SERVANTS
PEDROLINO
ORATIO
POLICEMEN

At that moment, servants bring Oratio, in chains, before the Regent, whom Oratio begs to put him to death in the name of justice. The Regent declares he does not want to wait until the following morning but wants him to die that very day. Quickly, Isabella informs the Regent that she can prove that Oratio cannot be put to death because he made a pact with his enemy; whereupon she shows the pact written in Flavio's hand. The Regent marvels at this and demands to know where Flavio is. The merchant then presents Memmy, saying, "Signor, here is your son, Flavio." The Regent receives him with great joy. Isabella presents his little grandchild and his daughter-in-law, saying briefly that they are his, and he is obliged to make them Christians and make Flavio her husband. The Regent rejoices even more. Pedrolino then calls Flaminia.

FLAMINIA   Flaminia comes out of the palace, kisses her brother, her sister-in-law, and the child. This done, Isabella has the Regent give Flaminia to Cinthio, as he promised. Immediately after, she turns to Flavio and says to him, "Now it is up to you to do a second favor, to pardon a second person, and furthermore, to beg pardon of his father." Flavio does so immediately. Then Isabella, on her knees, reveals herself, telling what happened and what was said (concluding all that is set down in the Argument), and finally she begs for the life of Oratio or the death of them both. The Regent, weeping, raises her to her feet, kisses her, and pardons Oratio, who, reconciled with Flavio, begs his forgiveness. He is granted it and also given Isabella, Flavio's sister, for wife, who is all the more dear when she is found to be so virtuous and learned in the art of astrology. The Regent promises the merchant a ransom for Flavio, but the merchant says he wants nothing. He only asks Flavio to make a beautiful gift to bring to the Pasha of Alexandria and to free Aguzzino and Arlecchino.

AGUZZINO   Aguzzino and Arlecchino are brought on and freed. Gratefully,
ARLECCHINO   they thank the Regent; and the comedy of *Isabella, the Astrologer,* ends.

The Thirty-seventh Day

THE HUNT

ARGUMENT

There lived in the city of Perugia four fathers with families. The first was called Pantalone de Bisognosi, the second was Gratiano Forbisone, the third, Burattino Canaglia, and the fourth, Claudione Francese, by which they were known to everyone. Pantalone had a daughter named Isabella; Burattino, a daughter named Flaminia; Gratiano, a son named Flavio; Claudione, son known to everyone as Oratio. It happened that the young men fell in love with the young women, and against the will of their fathers (who wanted to marry the young ladies to other young men), they were, as doctors, guided to the houses of the daughters, to whom they were finally married to the satisfaction of their fathers.

CHARACTERS IN THE PLAY

Pantalone, Venetian
Isabella, his daughter
Pedrolino, his servant

Burattino, a merchant
Flaminia, his daughter
Franceschina, his servant

Doctor Gratiano
Flavio, his son
Arlecchino, his servant

Claudione Francese, a merchant
Oratio, his son

Captain Spavento

PROPERTIES

Hunters' clothes for the four fathers
Ridiculous hunter's clothes for Arlecchino

Three hunting horns
Four hunting dogs
A live cock
A live monkey
A live cat
Long hunter's poles
Rabbits and other animals killed in the hunt
A club

ACT ONE

PERUGIA

DAWN

PANTALONE — Pantalone appears at the window and blows a horn to call the hunters to the hunt.

DR. GRATIANO — Immediately, Gratiano appears at his window and sounds his horn in response.

CLAUDIONE — At once, Claudione appears at his window and sounds his horn.

BURATTINO — Then, Burattino appears at his window, sounds his horn, and says all is ready; the others repeat that all is ready and thus retire one by one, in order, Pantalone being the last to withdraw.

ISABELLA — Isabella then appears at her window and invokes the sun to bring light to the world so that she might see her lover Oratio.

FLAMINIA — At that, Flaminia appears at her window at the other side of the stage and reproves Aurora for not leaving the arms of her old lover Tithonus, saying, "Ah, you hussy, aren't you ashamed to torment me so? Why don't you come?" Isabella, thinking that Flaminia is speaking to her, withdraws, and Flaminia still scolds Aurora.

PEDROLINO — At that moment, Pedrolino, at the window opposite Flaminia's, says, "Oh, you sluggard, I am going to tell everything to Signor Burattino." Flaminia thinks he is speaking to her; she withdraws. Pedrolino continues talking to Franceschina, saying that she had promised the night before to awaken him early in order to meet him as they had planned before the masters went off to the hunt.

FRANCESCHINA — Franceschina begs forgiveness, saying that she had to tend to her master; Pedrolino comes out, and they kiss and go off to enjoy each other.

ARLECCHINO — Arlecchino enters, dressed as a hunter, with a dog on a leash; he enters sounding his horn and making a great deal of noise.

DR. GRATIANO	At that, Gratiano enters, dressed as a hunter, with a live cock ready for sport.
CLAUDIONE	Then, Claudione enters, dressed as a hunter, with a cat on a leash.
BURATTINO	Next, Burattino enters, dressed as a hunter, with a monkey on a leash; they all hear noise in Pantalone's house.
PANTALONE PEDROLINO FRANCESCHINA	At that moment, Pantalone, angry, comes out beating Pedrolino and Franceschina, whom he found together in the barn. Pedrolino denies it. Burattino asks his servant what she was doing. Franceschina says that Flaminia sent her to ask Isabella if she would stay with her in the house until the hunters returned, but Pantalone tried to steal her honor. Pedrolino confirms this. Everyone scoffs at Pantalone. Pedrolino and Franceschina leave; all the others go off to begin the hunt, sounding their horns.
ISABELLA	Isabella comes out, still discoursing on what she spoke at her window and wondering why Oratio is taking so long to appear.
ORATIO	At that, Oratio appears at the door, still dressing, having been awakened by the noise of the hunters; he greets Isabella; they play a love scene and start to go into the house to enjoy each other.
CAPT. SPAVENTO	Just then, Captain Spavento arrives, and begins to talk boldly to Isabella, not seeing Oratio.
PEDROLINO	At that moment, Pedrolino enters with a bag and swaggers up to the Captain. The Captain tries to snatch it from him, but Pedrolino hits him with it. The Captain then draws his sword, and Oratio draws his sword to defend Pedrolino.
FRANCESCHINA	At that, Franceschina comes out because of the noise, punches the Captain in the face, and goes back in the house. Isabella goes into her house; Pedrolino runs off up the street, the Captain after him with Oratio following; and the first act ends.

ACT TWO

PEDROLINO	Pedrolino enters, frightened by the Captain and determined to play a trick on him.
ISABELLA	At that, Isabella comes out lamenting her bad fortune; she appeals to Pedrolino for help, and he promises to bring Oratio to her.

FLAMINIA   At that moment, Flaminia sends Franceschina to find Flavio. Seeing Isabella, she greets her and begs her pardon for what she said at the window, explaining that she was accusing Aurora, replying to what Pedrolino said to her at the window. Pedrolino explains that he was scolding Franceschina for being late in coming to him as she promised. They laugh at their being deceived by his words and appeal to Pedrolino for help.

ORATIO   At that, Oratio arrives at that side of the stage where Flaminia is, and not seeing Isabella, he greets Flaminia and kisses her hand in a very courteous manner. Isabella angrily watches all this.

FLAVIO   At that, Flavio enters where he cannot see Flaminia; he bows to Isabella, but she says, "God give you much joy, Signor Oratio." Oratio turns, and seeing her, rushes up to her to kiss her hand. She slaps him and goes into the house. Flavio sees Flaminia; he does as Oratio did with Isabella; she slaps him and goes into the house.

FRANCESCHINA   Then, Franceschina arrives; she sees Flavio. The lovers complain about the way their women treated them, not understanding the reason for their action. Pedrolino declares that Isabella is in the wrong.

ISABELLA   At that moment, Isabella comes out to tell Pedrolino that he lies; she beats him. Franceschina says she is doing wrong to hit for no reason; Isabella threatens to hit Franceschina too, but she runs off. Flavio tries to excuse Oratio. Isabella says she is going to hit him with a club; Flavio says he will kiss her hand and goes. Oratio tries to speak to her, but she will not listen and goes into the house. Oratio, despairing, goes to find Flavio.

PEDROLINO   Pedrolino says this is his day of disgrace, but he wants nothing more than to revenge himself on the Captain.

FRANCESCHINA   At that, Franceschina arrives; they agree to play a trick on the Captain, and go off together, Franceschina to give Flaminia's letter to Flavio, which she had forgotten to give him. They exit.

ISABELLA   Isabella then appears at her window and complains that Oratio is in love with Flaminia.

FLAMINIA   At that, Flaminia appears at her window and tells Isabella she is wrong; they agree between them.

CAPT. SPAVENTO   Then the Captain arrives, saying he is going to kill Pedrolino and those who side with him. The women remain to listen.

PEDROLINO   At that, Pedrolino arrives, dressed as a porter with a patch over his eye, begging alms of the Captain, who roars at him. Pedrolino fixes him with a stare. The Captain asks him why he is staring at him in that way. Pedrolino, pretending to be a physiognomist and astrologer, tells him if he does not stop carrying weapons for three days, he is in danger of being run through. The Captain, frightened, gives him alms and goes. Pedrolino discovers himself to the women. He tells them that when he finds the Captain without his arms, he will beat him. Laughing, the women withdraw.

ORATIO   At that moment, Oratio enters, complaining about Isabella.

FLAVIO   Then, Flavio arrives, reading Flaminia's letter in which she asks him to come see her while her father is out hunting.

PEDROLINO   Thereupon, Pedrolino, breathless, enters to tell the lovers that the old fathers are returning from the hunt; they ask him to help them, and he promises to bring them to the women they love.

ISABELLA   At that, Isabella appears at the window and informs Pedrolino that he promises too much.

FLAMINIA   Flaminia also appears at her window and says the same thing; finally they agree to Pedrolino's plan and put themselves in the hands of Pedrolino and Franceschina.

FRANCESCHINA   At that, Franceschina arrives, saying that the Captain is coming without his sword. Pedrolino makes everybody but Franceschina withdraw.

CAPT. SPAVENTO   Then, the Captain arrives without his sword. Pedrolino and Franceschina kid him about his being without his sword. The Captain, afraid, says that he does not want to be run through. Pedrolino scoffs at him; finally Franceschina, with some well-chosen words, jumps on his back and rides him like a horse. Pedrolino, with a stick, beats him over the backside. Franceschina, having forced him to the ground, bows reverently to him, saying, "God give you joy, Signor Captain," and goes into the house; Pedrolino does the same and leaves. Then the others come out of hiding. Flavio does the same and leaves. Oratio does the same and leaves; Isabella the same; Flaminia the same. Finally the Captain bows reverently to the audience, saying, "God give you joy, gentlemen," and leaves; and the second act ends.

ACT THREE

PANTALONE   Pantalone, Gratiano, Burattino, Claudione, and Arlecchino return
DR. GRATIANO   from the hunt with much wild game; they rejoice, sounding their
BURATTINO   horns and each, making lewd gestures, enters his house. Panta-
CLAUDIONE   lone, alone outside, knocks several times at his door.
ARLECCHINO

PEDROLINO	Pedrolino comes out and tells Pantalone not to make any noise because Isabella is not well and is going to bed.
ISABELLA	At that, Isabella comes out, pretending to have a fever; Pantalone and Pedrolino send her into the house of Burattino to stay with Flaminia because they are accustomed to staying together; she agrees to go. They call.
FRANCESCHINA	Franceschina enters weeping, saying Flaminia has a fever.
BURATTINO	At that, Burattino comes out, says his daughter is sick, and they all go in to see her.
CAPT. SPAVENTO	The Captain enters, saying he is resolved to suffer many indignities in order to escape the evils of the gallows.
ARLECCHINO	At that, Arlecchino enters, and seeing him without his sword, creeps up behind him and suddenly blows the horn in his ear. The Captain, frightened of being run through, runs off. Arlecchino chases him, blowing his horn.
ORATIO FLAVIO	Oratio and Flavio enter, looking for Pedrolino so that he can take care of their affairs.
PEDROLINO	At that moment, Pedrolino arrives, weeping, and tells the lovers that Isabella and Flaminia are ill with high fevers. The young men are filled with despair.
ISABELLA	Then, Isabella comes out, says it is not true, and they are to do whatever they are told to do. Arlecchino withdraws. Pedrolino sends Oratio and Flavio to disguise themselves as doctors; rejoicing, they go off.
ARLECCHINO	At that, Arlecchino enters, says that he has heard everything, and he is going to play a fine trick on them all and leaves. Pedrolino remains.
PANTALONE	Pantalone enters and urges Pedrolino to go for the two doctors as they decided earlier in the house; Pedrolino goes. Pantalone remains.
DR. GRATIANO	Gratiano hears of the illness of their daughters, of many secret horse remedies and of much other nonsense, and they leave.
PEDROLINO	Pedrolino enters, saying the doctors are late in coming.
ORATIO FLAVIO	At that moment, Oratio and Flavio enter, dressed as doctors. Pedrolino knocks at the women's door and arranges it so that each receives her lover. Pedrolino waits.
ARLECCHINO	Arlecchino, dressed as a doctor, enters Flaminia's house. Pedrolino thinks he is the doctor sent by Burattino.

CLAUDIONE	At that, Claudione, father of Oratio, enters. Pedrolino then relates to him all that he has arranged with the young men dressed as doctors, who are now enjoying their women. Then he begs to be forgiven by Pantalone, his master.
DR. GRATIANO	Just then, Gratiano enters and Claudione tells him what has occurred with Oratio and Flavio; Gratiano promises to make Pantalone forgive Pedrolino.
PANTALONE BURATTINO	At that moment, Pantalone enters and learns from Pedrolino that the doctors are in the house; then, turning to Burattino, he says that Burattino will have to pay the two doctors who are in his house, whereupon Pantalone and Burattino go into their own houses. The others remain with Pedrolino; they hear noises.
PANTALONE ORATIO ISABELLA	Thereupon, Pantalone comes out with one of the doctors, demanding that the doctor let him see his face. Oratio shakes his head; Claudione, his father, reveals him to be his son. He then pacifies Pantalone, who agrees that Isabella is to be his wife, but he wants to send Pedrolino to the galley and whip Franceschina. Pedrolino flees.
BURATTINO	At that, Burattino comes out and begs everyone to make less noise so that in peace the doctor can probe his daughter Flaminia; all laugh.
FLAVIO FLAMINIA	Burattino, enraged, goes into the house, then returns with Flavio, who refuses to show his face. Gratiano reveals him to be his son Flavio, who takes Flaminia for wife, and knowing all to be the work of Pedrolino, he agrees with Pantalone to send him to the galley [jail]. Burattino goes back into the house; the others hear more noise.
BURATTINO ARLECCHINO FRANCESCHINA	Next, Burattino leads the doctor out, having found him atop Franceschina; they reveal Arlecchino and give Franceschina to him as wife. All plead for Pedrolino and get him pardoned.
PEDROLINO	Pedrolino enters and falls to his knees; he says he was wrong to do what he did and admits his error. However, he is resolved to forgive everyone and everything. Everyone laughs.
CAPT. SPAVENTO	At that moment, the Captain suddenly arrives. Pedrolino tells him to put his sword on because the lying astrologer only played a joke on him; and the comedy ends.

THE MADNESS OF ISABELLA

ARGUMENT

Oratio, a Genoese gentleman, loved a gentlewoman of that city. Living many miles from the city, she told her lover that he would have to move to where she lived. The lover, who wanted only to be near her, took an armed ship to make the journey and on his way was ambushed by some Turkish vessels. He was enslaved and taken to Algeria. This event became known to all of Genoa, and the unfortunate woman retired to a convent, where she said she would live the rest of her life.

It happened that Oratio was then sold to a great captain who had married a Turkish girl from the Seraglio. She was a most graceful and beautiful creature, and when she laid eyes on the slave, she fell in love with him. They met quite often and exchanged words of love. They decided that she was to become a Christian, and he would take her to his native country and marry her. They also decided to take her two-year-old child with them. Thus they planned their escape and, with other Christian slaves, they were to board an armed boat which would take them off secretly. Meanwhile, it happened that the Captain, the husband of the Turkish girl, while at his villa a short distance away, sent word to his wife to come to him immediately. Taking advantage of this opportunity, and without the other Turks suspecting, they left and were soon sailing on the high seas bound for Majorca. When the Captain heard of the flight of the armed vessel, he took a galley and pursued the fugitive ship. After some time, he overtook and came alongside the vessel carrying the Christians. Seeing no possible escape, his wife forced a Turk to dress in Oratio's clothes and he, at the sight of her husband pursuing her, was forced to jump into the sea, while Oratio hid in the hold of the ship; then in a high voice, he called to the Captain to save him. Unable to defend itself, the armed vessel was taken. The Captain boarded the vessel and learned how the slave Oratio tried to run off with her while she, with the help of her Turks, seized him and threw him into the sea. The husband believed the

282

*made-up story of his wife, and immediately took her child in his
arms. Then he turned to one of the armed men and told him he
wanted him to shoot at that traitor in the sea who was trying to
save himself. Just then she turned to her husband (who did not
expect the shot) and shot him, killing at the same time her
husband and child. On hearing all the commotion, Oratio (according to the plan) immediately came up out of the hold. He
again became master of the vessel, boldly opposing the Captain's
galley and put it to flight. Then they continued their voyage and
arrived at Majorca where, with great solemnity, the Turkish girl
was made a Christian. In a short time they went from there to
Genoa, where they lived happily for a while, but misery befell the
Turkish girl, who became known as Isabella. After many misfortunes whereby she became mad, her beloved husband was restored
to her, and they were made happy again.*

CHARACTERS IN THE PLAY

Pantalone, a Venetian
Oratio, his son
Isabella, taken as wife
Franceschina, her servant
Burattino, her servant

Doctor Gratiano

Flaminia, a gentlewoman
Ricciolina, her servant

Flavio, a gentleman
Pedrolino, his servant

Host

Captain Spavento
Arlecchino, his servant

PROPERTIES

A large traveling bag
Clothes for the madwoman
Specially-made little divers vessels
A vessel of beautiful glass
A bladder of blood

ACT ONE

GENOA

FLAVIO
PEDROLINO

Flavio enters and grieves with his servant Pedrolino that Flaminia, after she left the convent, has not been as cheerful as she was when she was within the walls; however, he is not surprised that she is worse, and here he relates the story about Flaminia and the Turkish girl made Christian in Majorca as it is set down in the Argument, telling Pedrolino that he does not believe Oratio married the Turkish girl, but he will find out from a servant, his countryman, who went to Genoa from Majorca. Flavio tells him to come on, and they go off up the street.

ORATIO
ISABELLA
FRANCESCHINA
BURATTINO

Oratio, Isabella, Franceschina, and Burattino come from a park where they have been passing the time. Isabella asks Oratio why he has been so melancholy after having arrived at his native land. Oratio replies that it is his nature. She begs him to marry her as he had promised in Algeria; Oratio assures her that in a short time he will make good his promise; then he sends Isabella, Franceschina, and Burattino into the house. Burattino goes in muttering that Oratio is probably tired of Isabella. Oratio remains, sighing for love.

FLAMINIA

At that moment, Flaminia appears at her window and greets Oratio, saying, "Have you sent your wife for a walk?" Oratio immediately replies, "I have sent my death for a walk and not my wife!" Flaminia says that if he has not married her, he should do so as an obligation to her honor; Oratio looks at her, and nearly weeping, he leaves without saying a word. Flaminia says she understands those words and those sighs, that Oratio remembers still his love for her and, happy, she goes in.

CAPT. SPAVENTO
ARLECCHINO

Captain Spavento enters. He comes from the island of Majorca, where he was serving his king, on his way to Milan, and he wants to remain a few days in Genoa to see if he can find out anything about the Turkish girl who was made a Christian in Majorca. Arlecchino remembers the gentleman who baptized her; the Captain says his name is Oratio Bisognosi. They finally find the inn they have been looking for and call for the host.

THE HOST

The host comes out to receive Arlecchino with his things. The Captain says he wants to walk as far as the square, but that he will return at the hour for dinner.

RICCIOLINA

At that moment, Ricciolina, Flaminia's servant, comes from the villa; the Captain flirts with her.

PEDROLINO	Pedrolino arrives and, jealous, argues with the Captain. Ricciolina goes into the house. The Captain roars at Pedrolino, and still roaring, he stands under Isabella's window.
BURATTINO	Just then, Burattino from the window, throws a caldron of warm water on him. The Captain, soaked, goes into the inn and Pedrolino withdraws.
PANTALONE	At that, Pantalone enters, worried because his son Oratio is not marrying Isabella as he promised he would in Algeria; he knocks on the door.
BURATTINO	Burattino comes out, and Pantalone asks him if he knows why Oratio doesn't marry Isabella. Burattino says he does not know.
PEDROLINO	At that, Pedrolino comes out of hiding; he tells Pantalone that if he can keep a secret, he will tell him the reason. Pantalone promises, and Pedrolino explains that before Oratio was made a slave he loved Flaminia, and she loved him and loves him still. Because of her return from the convent Oratio will not marry Isabella. He finishes by saying he would tell them more, but being afraid, he must remain silent.
FLAVIO	Then, Flavio arrives. Immediately Pedrolino accosts him; Pantalone hails Flavio, and with great ceremony, leaves. Pedrolino informs Flavio that Pantalone does want Oratio to marry Isabella so he will not be living in sin. Flavio rejoices at this news.
FLAMINIA	At that moment, Flaminia appears at her window. Flavio hails her and complains of the little he has seen of her since she came out of the convent. Flaminia, with fair speech, makes excuses; Pedrolino taunts her with the saying that the old love drives out the new. Flaminia pretends not to understand him; she calls him an impudent rascal and withdraws. Flavio laments to Pedrolino that she has touched him to the quick.
FRANCESCHINA	Franceschina, in the doorway, hears Pedrolino tell Flavio that Flaminia is loved by Oratio and he, by her, and Oratio will not marry the Turkish girl made Christian, because he is in love with Flaminia. This makes Flavio angry with Pedrolino, and he leaves. Seeing Franceschina, Pedrolino hails her. Franceschina asks him whom he was talking to. Pedrolino answers that he is her master's rival, in love with Flaminia, who lives in that house. He points it out to her, saying again that Oratio is also in love with her. Franceschina goes into the house, and Pedrolino goes to find Oratio.
PANTALONE ORATIO	Pantalone enters, asking his son Oratio why he does not marry Isabella as he promised. Oratio tells him it is because he is in love

with Flaminia, that he was before he was made a slave, and that is the reason he can't. Pantalone says he owes nothing to Flaminia, but that he should certainly attend to his obligation to Isabella in spite of his reasons, which he already knew very well, because they were told to him by a porter.

PEDROLINO

At that moment, Pedrolino arrives; Pantalone says, "This is the porter." Oratio asks Pedrolino who told him that he is in love with Flaminia. Pedrolino answers that all Genoa knows it; then he reprimands Oratio for not marrying Isabella and for not obeying his father. Oratio is angered.

FLAVIO

At that, Flavio enters and inquires what business Oratio has with his servant. When Oratio does not answer, Pedrolino roars at him; Pantalone tries to make peace between them, but Flavio turns away in anger.

ISABELLA

Isabella, at the window, has overheard. Flavio sees her, turns to Oratio, and tells him he must marry Isabella because for him she became a Christian, and he must be faithful to his promise instead of trying to marry Flaminia. "This," says Flavio, "would be a great wrong," and he adds that Oratio is not acting like a gentleman. Oratio draws his sword; Flavio draws his. They fight and thus go off up the street, Pantalone and Pedrolino going after them. Isabella, weeping, withdraws; and the first act ends.

ACT TWO

ISABELLA
FRANCESCHINA

Isabella points out Flaminia's house to Franceschina and then sends her to find out what happened to Oratio. Remaining alone, she says she knows of Oratio's betrayal, but because of her love for him, she is content to die quickly, for she sees that she disgusts him.

FLAMINIA

At that, Flaminia appears at the window. Isabella sees her and hails her, saying that since they live near one another, they should become friends. Flaminia thanks her, and for a time they speak pleasantly.

BURATTINO

Then, Burattino enters, out of breath from the fight between Oratio and Flavio. Flaminia asks him if Oratio has been hurt. Burattino answers that he does not know. Isabella asks Flaminia if she would feel bad if Oratio were hurt. Flaminia answers, "It would hurt me more than it would hurt you, signora."

CAPT. SPAVENTO

At that moment, the Captain enters and sees Isabella, recognizes her as the one who had been made a Christian in Majorca, and greets her. She answers his greeting; then she turns to Flaminia and says, "Signora, I will not be here much longer. I am leaving, and I hope it consoles you." She goes in with Burattino. The Captain greets Flaminia, who asks him where he knew that woman (Isabella). The Captain says he knew her in Majorca where she was made a Christian.

ARLECCHINO

At that, Arlecchino enters with a brush and brushes down his master. The Captain plays the gallant with Flaminia.

RICCIOLINA

Just then, Ricciolina comes out, sees the Captain, and recognizes him to be the one who flirted with her. She turns on Flaminia and orders her to leave her lover alone. Arlecchino hails her.

ORATIO

At that, Oratio enters, and seeing the Captain talking to Flaminia, begins to leave in anger; Flaminia begs him not to go in anger at her because the Captain is his wife's friend. Oratio, at these words, draws his sword. The Captain flees, with Oratio chasing him. Arlecchino follows them, and the women go back into the house.

ISABELLA
BURATTINO

Isabella and Burattino enter, seeking news of the fight.

PANTALONE
FLAVIO
PEDROLINO

At that moment, Pantalone comes on, exhorting Flavio to make peace with Oratio. Flavio declares he will not make peace with Oratio until he marries Isabella as he is obliged to do, and he wants Oratio to know that he is a big traitor. Isabella, holding a knife aloft, rushes up to him, exclaiming that he lies, and stabs him. Flavio falls to the ground, bleeding.

ORATIO

Just then, Oratio arrives. Isabella embraces him and tells him she has avenged him. Oratio takes her into the house. Frightened, Pantalone and Burattino also go in. Pedrolino weeps over his wounded master and calls Flaminia from the house.

FLAMINIA
RICCIOLINA

Flaminia rushes out and bends over Flavio, weeping. Flavio is still bleeding and cannot rise. He tells Flaminia that by her cruelty, he loses his life and his honor, killed by the hand of a woman. Flaminia, stung by his words, tries to console him, repenting what she has done to him.

DR. GRATIANO

Then, Gratiano, physician and surgeon, enters. Flaminia pleads with him to take care of Flavio's wounds. Gratiano, Ricciolina, and Flaminia carry Flavio into Flaminia's house to care for him.

ISABELLA
ORATIO

Isabella then asks Oratio to free her if he loves Flaminia, but reminds him that when he was first made a slave, he promised to marry her, and if he does still truly love her, Isabella, she will try to make him very happy. Oratio denies loving Flaminia, saying he loves no one else but her, and he caresses her more than usual and seems so affectionate that he sends her into the house consoled. Then he remains alone, saying that in his breast, love, obligation, and loyalty are at war. Then, seeing someone approaching, he leaves.

GRATIANO
FLAMINIA

Gratiano enters, telling Flaminia that she must keep the wounded man in good spirits, for then there is hope of making him well; meanwhile, he will go for some medication. Flaminia wonders to herself how she could have done such a great wrong to Flavio and decides that she will avenge him, if not against Isabella, then against Oratio.

ORATIO

At that moment, Oratio arrives and greets her. She ironically asks him when he is going to marry that warrior of his, for she understands Isabella gave Flavio a good stabbing. Oratio is struck dumb.

ISABELLA

Isabella, at the window, hears all. Then she comes to the door and listens to what Oratio says to Flaminia. He declares he will never marry Isabella as he promised when he was first a slave. Then he will be free to marry Flaminia, and whenever she is ready to be his, he will get rid of Isabella by deceit, and, if necessary, by poisoning her. Flaminia is happy at his confirmation of faith, and embracing him, she leads him into the house. Isabella is struck dumb; then bursting out in a bitter volley of words against Oratio, against Love, against Fortune, and against herself, she finally falls into a mad frenzy.

RICCIOLINA

At that moment, Ricciolina comes out shouting, "Oh, the poor young man," that this was murder! She tells Isabella that Oratio has been killed. Isabella, who is mad with only intervals of clarity, has her repeat over and over that Oratio is dead. Finally, saying that her soul demands the soul of the traitor, she goes completely mad, tears her clothes from her body, and as if pushed by some force, goes running up the street. Ricciolina, frightened, rushes into the house; and the second act ends.

ACT THREE

ORATIO
FLAMINIA

Oratio quarrels with Flaminia, protesting that with false intent she had taken him into the house, then assaulted him with a weapon to try to kill him. Furious, Flaminia swears she is sorry she was not able to kill him since he is the worst of traitors, and she sees that she was blind to believe a single word he spoke.

RICCIOLINA   At that moment, Ricciolino comes out shouting that Flavio is tearing the bandages from his wounds. Flaminia immediately rushes into the house with Ricciolina. Oratio says he has been in great danger, that if Flavio could have helped Flaminia, he would now be dead. Also, he perceives the great wrong he has committed in thinking only of abandoning Isabella.

PANTALONE   At that, Pantalone arrives and asks about Isabella, saying that she is not at home.

DR. GRATIANO   Then, Gratiano enters, carrying many crucibles with which to treat Flavio; he tells Pantalone that he just exerted himself greatly in order to save himself from a madwoman, the Turkish girl whom Oratio, his son, took with him from Algeria. Pantalone is amazed to hear this, and Oratio is dumbfounded. Gratiano goes on into Flaminia's house. Oratio goes off to find Isabella, leaving Pantalone, who sadly calls to someone in the house.

BURATTINO   Burattino comes out. Pantalone asks him how long Isabella has been gone from the house. Burattino says he doesn't know.

DR. GRATIANO
RICCIOLINA   At that, Gratiano comes out, telling the servant that they must apply medication as he ordered. Ricciolina promises she will not forget and goes back in. Pantalone appeals to the doctor for a report on Isabella. Gratiano says that they must treat her while her illness is beginning, because then he can cure her with his marvelous secrets. Pantalone calls.

FRANCESCHINA   Franceschina comes out. Pantalone instructs her to go find Isabella, and with the help of Burattino and others, to seize and bind her and bring her to the house. Then he accompanies Gratiano up the street. Franceschina and Burattino remain.

ISABELLA   At that moment, Isabella enters, dressed as a madwoman. She stands between Burattino and Franceschina, declaring she wants to say something of great importance. They stop to listen, and she begins to speak: "I remember the year I could not remember that a harpsichord sat beside a Spanish Pavane dancing with a gagliarda of Santin of Parma, after which the lasagne, the macaroni, and the polenta dressed in brown, but they could not stand one another because the stolen cat was the friend of the beautiful girl from Algeria. Even so, it pleased the caliph of Egypt to decide that the following morning both were to be put in the stocks." She raves on, saying similar mad things; they try to grab her, but she runs off up the street, and they chase after her.

PEDROLINO   Pedrolino enters on his way to get Flavio's relatives to come and take him from Flaminia's house. Pedrolino admires Gratiano, who, he feels, is a great doctor with many secrets.

PANTALONE	At that moment, Pantalone enters, despairing because he has not found Isabella. Pedrolino says to himself that he is going to play a trick on Pantalone; he tells him that Flavio died of his wound inflicted by Isabella and that she, together with Oratio, is condemned to die. Pantalone is filled with despair. Pedrolino, pretending to weep, goes off, leaving a mournful Pantalone.
ORATIO	Then, Oratio enters, desperate because he cannot find Isabella. Pantalone tells him that she has gone mad because she saw him go into Flaminia's house and saw them embrace, but, worse still, Flavio is dead and the police are going to arrest him and Isabella. At this news, Oratio loses all hope.
FRANCESCHINA	At that moment, Franceschina enters shouting, "Run! Run! if you want to see the madwoman!" and she leads them off up the street.
CAPT. SPAVENTO ARLECCHINO	The Captain enters, declaring he is going to kill Oratio before he continues on to Milan.
ISABELLA	At that, Isabella enters, dressed as a madwoman, and tells the Captain she knows him, that she saw him among the forty-eight celestial figures when the dog star danced with the moon dressed in green, and other nonsensical things. Then with her stick she beats the Captain and Arlecchino, who run away with Isabella chasing after them.
PANTALONE	Pantalone enters forlorn and afraid that in his desperation, Oratio will kill himself.
DR. GRATIANO	At that moment, Gratiano enters with a vial. He explains that it is a secret compound made with Hellebore with which he is going to cure Isabella immediately. He has tried it many times in the hospitals for the insane in Milan.
ISABELLA	Just then, Isabella arrives very quietly and comes between Pantalone and Gratiano; she whispers to them to remain quiet and not make any noise because Jove is going to sneeze, and Saturn is going to let go a powerful fart. Then, babbling other such nonsense, she asks them if they have seen Oratio alone against all Tuscany.
ORATIO	At that moment, Oratio arrives, saying, "I am here, my soul." And she responds, "The second life of Aristotle is the spirit which was released from a bottle of muscatel in a mountain flask, and for that reason, a whaling ship was seen doing service for the island of English where the people could not piss." She improvises other such nonsense.

PEDROLINO
BURATTINO
FRANCESCHINA
CAPT. SPAVENTO

Just then, Pedrolino, Burattino, Franceschina, and the Captain enter, all shouting, grab the madwoman, and overcoming her, they hold and bind her. Gratiano immediately takes his secret compound which heals all the senses and makes her drink the liquid from the vial. Little by little, she recovers and regains her senses; then, seeing Oratio, she recalls in a few phrases how much she has done for him, lamenting that he betrayed her and abandoned her for another woman. Oratio confesses his wrong and his failure; he begs her forgiveness, saying that he wants to marry her as soon as possible. Isabella, now entirely happy, says she will forget all that happened in the past and accepts him gladly. Pantalone rejoices.

FLAVIO
FLAMINIA
RICCIOLINA

At that moment, Flavio enters with his arm around Flaminia's neck. He sees Isabella, who humbly begs his forgiveness, telling him that Oratio has pledged his faith in marriage. Flavio rejoices and forgives her. Thus Oratio marries Isabella; Flavio, Flaminia; Pedrolino, Franceschina; and Burattino, Ricciolina; and the comedy of *The Madness of Isabella* ends.

The Thirty-ninth Day

THE PICTURE

ARGUMENT

A company of actors was performing in Parma, and the principal actress, as was the custom, was visited by one of the most noble cavaliers of the town. She took from around his neck a very beautiful locket of gold which hung from a chain. In it was the picture of a beautiful married lady who had given it to the cavalier, whose name was Oratio. While they conversed, the actress, who was called Victoria, deftly removed the picture from the locket. She returned the locket and chain to the cavalier, and at the end of the visit they parted, she to her room and he to his home. It happened that not many days later, the husband of the aforementioned lady came to visit the actress. Not knowing the gentleman, she showed him the picture of his own wife. He was dumbfounded and demanded to know the name of the person who gave the picture to her. The actress told him. The husband, whose name was Pantalone, pretended not to know the lady, and taking his leave, returned home in a rage, determined to kill his adulterous wife. At home, his wife made up a convincing story and placated him. Meanwhile she enjoyed her lover, and the husband himself, by a strange occurrence, led the lover to his own door.

CHARACTERS IN THE PLAY

Pantalone, a Venetian
Isabella, his wife
Pedrolino, servant of the house

Doctor Gratiano
Flaminia, his wife

Oratio, gentleman of Parma
Flavio, his friend

Captain Spavento

Arlecchino, his servant

Victoria, an actress
Piombino, an actor

A Cardsharp

Various men with many arms

Lesbino, a page, then Silvia Milanese

PROPERTIES

Playing cards
Four lanterns
Two clubs
Many standby arms
A small picture of a woman

ACT ONE

THE CITY OF
PARMA

ISABELLA   Isabella speaks of the uproar between her husband and herself
PEDROLINO   because he saw her picture in the possession of an actress to
              whom it was given by Oratio; and, afraid that Oratio has lost his
              love for her, she sends Pedrolino to get the said picture from
              Oratio. Pedrolino says she is not to blame and consoles her. She
              goes into the house, and Pedrolino goes to find Oratio, comment-
              ing that Oratio does wrong to betray a lady who, for his sake,
              risks the honor of herself and her husband. He goes.

CAPT. SPAVENTO   Captain Spavento enters, telling his servant Arlecchino that he
ARLECCHINO   will be going more and more to the theatre if Signora Victoria,
                 his love, is playing; he does not want to leave Parma for Naples
                 until he has enjoyed her favor. Arlecchino remarks that he is
                 wasting his time, for such women are not to be obtained as easily
                 as men believe.

LESBINO   At that moment, Lesbino, the page, that is, Silvia Milanese, the
              Captain's inamorata, sees him, and with the permission of Arlec-
              chino, is to accompany them as page. The Captain tells Arlec-
              chino to talk to Piombino, interpreter for Signora Victoria, and
              he leaves with the page. Arlecchino remains.

FLAMINIA   Then, Flaminia appears at her window and calls to Arlecchino, whom she doesn't know, asking him to do her a favor by taking a letter to a gentleman named Flavio, whose practice it is to walk in the piazza where the gentlemen gather. Arlecchino takes the letter and promises to deliver it. Flaminia gives him a couple of gold coins and withdraws. Arlecchino stands staring up at Flaminia's window.

DR. GRATIANO   At that moment, Gratiano, Flaminia's husband, enters, and seeing him staring up at her window and seeing the letter, becomes suspicious and asks him what he is looking for and from whom is the letter. Arlecchino says it was given to him by one Flavio to give to a woman. Gratiano takes it from him, beats him, and calls him a pimp.

PANTALONE   Just then, Pantalone comes between them. Arlecchino, about to leave, looks at the old men and says, "Do what you can, because you are a cuckold," and he goes off. Puzzled, the old men look at each other, saying, "I don't know if he is talking to me or to you." Finally they discuss their suspicion of their wives—Gratiano about Flavio, and Pantalone about Oratio—on account of a certain picture.

FLAVIO   At that moment, Flavio arrives. Gratiano immediately and accusingly gives him the letter and scolds him. Flavio receives it humbly, and the old men go. Flavio opens the letter and discovers it is from Flaminia, who hotly demands that he go no more to the theatre; he gives in to her request and makes a signal toward Flaminia's window.

FLAMINIA   Flaminia, understanding the sign, comes to the window, sees him, and they argue.

ISABELLA   At that, Isabella appears at her window and remains to hear how Flavio makes excuses to Flaminia; then she advises Flaminia not to trust the traitor, that she is right in her suspicions. Both women withdraw without saying any more. Flavio is dumbfounded and then sighs, "Oh, poor Flavio."

ARLECCHINO   At that, Arlecchino, hearing him say Flavio, asks him if he is Flavio, the lover of Flaminia. When Flavio answers yes, Arlecchino declares he is going to pass on to him the beating he got on his account, but as he raises his stick to beat him, Flavio draws his sword. Arlecchino flees, with Flavio chasing him.

ORATIO
PEDROLINO   Oratio then enters and says he cannot return the picture that Isabella wants because it is at the goldsmith's, who is repairing the locket. Pedrolino smiles slyly. Then he asks how long it has

been since Oratio's been to the play, asking him about all there is to be seen and finally about Signora Victoria. Oratio becomes suspicious.

ISABELLA   At that moment, Isabella comes out on a pretext and demands her picture. Oratio makes excuses. She calls him a traitor and tells him she knows very well that he loves the actress to whom he gave the picture; she reproaches him for all she has done for him and says that for that reason and because of the picture, her husband wanted to kill her. Enraged, she calls Pedrolino and goes into the house without listening to what Oratio has to say. Pedrolino turns to Oratio, accusing him of wronging his master, and goes in. Oratio laments to himself the arrival of that company of actors, saying only evil things of them; finally he speaks ill of Victoria, who has brought him only danger and unhappiness.

CAPT. SPAVENTO   At that moment, the Captain enters, and hearing him speak ill
ARLECCHINO   of the actors and of Victoria, defends them, saying that the theatre is a noble entertainer, and Signora Victoria is an honored lady; Oratio, enraged, declares he lies. They draw their swords; then the Captain asks Oratio if he wants to die with him; Oratio says yes. The Captain then replies that he is going to write down their agreement, including the pardon for whatever the outcome, because if it happens that he kills Oratio, he does not want to be tried for it in court. Furthermore, he is going to write it so that whoever kills the other will not be molested by the law, and he strides off. Arlecchino remarks that the Captain wants to get out of a great deal, and he follows him off. Oratio also follows; and the first act ends.

ACT TWO

VICTORIA   Victoria, the actress, richly dressed in gold chains, bracelets,
PIOMBINO   pearls, diamonds, and ruby rings, accompanied by Piombino, enters and praises the city of Parma, the Duke, and the court, and speaks of the infinite courtesy they receive from the gentlemen of Parma.

PEDROLINO   At that, Pedrolino comes from the house and hails them. She asks after Pantalone, his master. Pedrolino says he is not at home, exhorting her to love him for being a man of merit.

ISABELLA   Just then, Isabella appears at her window and remains to watch. Pedrolino, seeing her, continues to praise Pantalone's experience and again recommends him to her. Victoria asks where Gratiano's house is. Pedrolino points it out and praises him also as a man of deserving wealth, generous and liberal with the women.

PANTALONE　At that moment, Pantalone arrives, and seeing Isabella at the window, restrains himself from greeting Victoria, who, on leaving, asks Pedrolino to say hello to Pantalone for her, and she goes. Isabella withdraws from the window. Pedrolino says in an aside he will play the go-between for the actress with Pantalone, making him believe that she is in love with him. Worried, Pantalone speaks of his suspicion of his wife because of the picture. Pedrolino pacifies him by saying that there are many people who carry pictures from this person to that, asking for nothing more than to have a picture of a beautiful woman. Pantalone, relieved of his suspicion, says he wants to send a gift to the actress Signora Victoria, and they go off together.

ORATIO　Oratio enters and laments with Flavio Isabella's picture falling
FLAVIO　into the hands of the actress Victoria, as it is set down in the Argument. Flavio promises to speak to Isabella for him; Oratio offers to speak to Flaminia for him.

ARLECCHINO　At that, Arlecchino enters with a letter. Seeing Oratio, he tells him it is the agreement and the pardon which the Captain sends to him. Oratio, enraged, hits him and sends him off. Flavio knocks at Isabella's door.

ISABELLA　Isabella comes out, and Flavio begs her to listen to what Oratio has to say for himself. She finally agrees to listen.

ARLECCHINO　As Oratio begins to speak to her, Arlecchino arrives and immediately tells Oratio that if he does not leave off loving the actress Victoria, the Captain will kill him without more ado, and he exits. Isabella at once calls Oratio a traitor, saying he cannot deny that he is in love with that traveling whore, and enraged, she goes into the house without listening to what he has to say. Oratio, desperate, says he is going to kill the Captain and then himself; Flavio tries to console him.

PEDROLINO　Then, Pedrolino arrives and from Oratio learns all that has occurred with Isabella; Oratio appeals to Pedrolino for help. Pedrolino says to leave everything to him; he will work it all out. He knocks.

ISABELLA　Isabella comes out. Pedrolino begs her to be reconciled with Oratio. She acts coy. Pedrolino says that everyone must stay where he is for his own good; then he knocks at Flaminia's door.

FLAMINIA　Flaminia comes out, and she also acts coy. Pedrolino tells the young men to speak their piece. Oratio speaks at great length, placates Isabella, and they make up. Flavio does the same with Flaminia, and they too make up. Pedrolino informs them all that the two old husbands are in love with the actress, and this will give the lovers a chance to enjoy themselves. Isabella says that she will not make up with Oratio until he gets the picture back from the actress, but she does not want him to go back to her to get it. Pedrolino sympathizes with Isabella's feeling and says he will visit the actress and get it. Isabella goes into the house. The young lovers leave. Flaminia asks Pedrolino to help her out. Then she sees Gratiano coming.

DR. GRATIANO   Gratiano arrives, and Pedrolino immediately begins arguing with Flaminia, saying, "I know if your husband goes to the theatre or where he goes." Flaminia understands what Pedrolino is doing. She pretends to be jealous of her husband, and calling him a knave, goes into the house. Gratiano, who has stopped to listen, approaches Pedrolino, who tells him that the actress Victoria has been at his house and asked after him, and for that reason his wife scolded him. He says that the actress is in love with him.

PIOMBINO   At that moment, Piombino arrives and greets Gratiano in the name of Signora Victoria, for whom he wants to borrow a silver basin and a pot for a play which is to be presented. Gratiano says he will send them by Pedrolino. Piombino tells Gratiano then that Signora Victoria is in love with him, and because of him alone, she despises other gentlemen who court her in her house and in the theatre. Gratiano rejoices heartily, and, promising Piombino a fine gift, goes into the house. Pedrolino and Piombino agree to get as much money as they can from the old men and divide it between them. Then they go off.

CAPT. SPAVENTO   The Captain enters and says he can't stand still until the time
LESBINO   comes for the play because of the great love he has for the actress Victoria. Lesbino tries to persuade him to leave that love, saying that it is not good for his honor or his reputation to love a traveling actress whose profession takes her all over the country. Then she asks if he had ever been in love before. The Captain says yes, that in Milan he loved a very beautiful young woman whom he could not hope for because her father wanted to marry her to someone else.

ARLECCHINO   At that moment, Arlecchino enters and tells the Captain that Signora Victoria is in a goldsmith's shop; if he wants to see her, he is to go with him. Happy, the Captain confides to Lesbino that he could tell him many things about that woman in Milan, but that a new love calls him elsewhere, and he goes. Lesbino asks Arlecchino if he would be offended by one who took the life of his master. Arlecchino, enraged, says he would kill him without more ado. Lesbino tells him the whole story of his love for Silvia, who has sent him to kill the Captain, adding that if he is as faithful a servant of the Captain as he says he is, he would rightly kill him because he has come to kill his master. Shocked, Arlecchino declares he does not want to kill him, but he wants to prevent Lesbino from killing the Captain; then, excited, he gives a loud cry.

ISABELLA   At that moment, Isabella appears at her window.

FLAMINIA   Flaminia appears at her window. They hear Arlecchino call Lesbino villain and beat him; then Arlecchino leaves. Lesbino weeps over his bad fortune. She reveals that she is a woman who loves the Captain very much, but he does not love her. Instead, he has a new love, the actress, whom she wishes to kill with her sword.

ARLECCHINO   At that moment, Arlecchino returns and sneaks up behind Lesbino to kill him. The women rush out and stop him, drive him away, disarm Silvia, and take her into Flaminia's house. Here the second act ends.

ACT THREE

VICTORIA
PIOMBINO   Victoria and Piombino enter speaking; they say they have been to dinner at the house of a gentleman who loves Victoria and have been given fine gifts, mentioning particular gifts given to players in most of the principal cities of Italy in which she too was favored by many presents, and finally, how she tricks and laughs at those lovers who give her nothing. Piombino urges her to love no one, but to attend to the business of acquiring some wealth for her old age.

PEDROLINO   At that moment, Pedrolino arrives. Victoria and Piombino fondle him, saying that they want to make him an actor. Pedrolino protests he doesn't have the talent.

PANTALONE   At that, Pantalone arrives. Victoria thanks him for the beautiful present and says that night she will see him at the theatre before the play begins, because she wants to give him something that will be very dear to him. Pantalone promises to come and withdraws.

FLAVIO   At that moment, Flavio greets Victoria and she, Flavio. He is nervous and would like to leave before Flaminia sees them, but Victoria holds him back with amorous speech.

FLAMINIA	Then, Flaminia, who from her window has seen Flavio talking to the actress, comes out enraged, and gives Flavio a slap, then runs back into the house. Flavio, putting his hand to his cheek, leaves without saying another word. Victoria laughs.
PANTALONE	At that, Pantalone returns, scolds Flaminia for her shameless behavior, and brags that he has a modest and well-behaved wife; then he sees Victoria, and again they speak words of courtesy.
ISABELLA	Isabella then comes out and scolds her husband because he plays the lecher with all women, sometimes staying five or six months without sleeping with his wife, adding that, furthermore, with all his defects, he doesn't deserve to mount her. Embarrassed, Pantalone runs off. Isabella then turns on Victoria and snaps that if she were on the same level with an actress, she would give her a piece of her mind and then goes back into the house. Victoria laughs, saying that when the company of players comes to town, married women many times are left with their tongues hanging.
PEDROLINO	At that, Pedrolino, who has heard everything, laughs.
DR. GRATIANO	At that moment, Gratiano arrives. Pedrolino says to Victoria, "Look, here is the other pigeon to be plucked." Victoria complains to Gratiano that she does not see him and she despises all her other lovers for him alone; she pretends to weep. Piombino tells Gratiano that Pantalone has sent as a gift a pearl necklace, but in order not to wrong him, she would not accept it, saying that Signor Gratiano would buy a more beautiful, a more valuable one. Gratiano, happy, promises to do great things for Victoria, and Piombino reminds him of the basin and vessel of silver for the play which is to be played that night. Gratiano says that he will send them later with Pedrolino, and with lewd talk, he takes leave of Victoria, taking Pedrolino away with him. Victoria and Piombino laugh at his simple wit.
ORATIO	At that, Oratio enters, greets Victoria, and asks for his picture. She laughs at him, saying she has no idea what he is talking about and leaves. Oratio remains, bemoaning the situation.
ISABELLA	Then, Isabella, who from her window saw him talking to Victoria, scolds him again. Oratio vainly makes excuses.
ARLECCHINO	At that moment, Arlecchino enters and tells Oratio that Isabella has shown a passion for him, but now she is in love with his master's page, and between her and Flaminia they are going to sleep with him. Isabella confirms this to make him sorry; then she calls Flaminia, telling her to bring her new lover to the window.

FLAMINIA LESBINO	Flaminia, understanding Isabella's desire to make Oratio suffer, calls Lesbino to the window, who says, "You command me, Signora." Oratio, seeing him, is enraged; he quarrels with Isabella and Flaminia.
PANTALONE	At that, Pantalone arrives. [Oratio and Arlecchino leave.] He asks the cause of all the noise. Isabella tells him that Oratio wanted to remove the page by force. Pantalone is enraged at the young man, asking what did he intend? Isabella explains that the page is a young woman named Silvia Milanese who is in love with a Captain; she disguised herself in order to follow him, and she found him here in Parma in love with an actress and that, perhaps, this same actress is Pantalone's goddess. Pantalone is humiliated. Isabella explains that the poor girl, in desperation, wanted to kill herself, so she and Flaminia took her in; now as a favor, they want Pantalone to find the Captain, who always goes to the theatre. To see Silvia and the Captain brought peacefully together, Pantalone agrees to go that night to the play, saying he will do this favor gladly. Meanwhile, he says, Isabella must take charge of the young woman; the women withdraw from their windows. Pantalone remarks that this is a fine opportunity for him to go to the play without his wife's suspecting him, and he goes off.
PEDROLINO	Then, Pedrolino enters, saying he has had the silver basin and vessel all along because he wanted to give them to the actress himself to coax her to stay.
ISABELLA	At that moment, Isabella comes out and relates to Pedrolino what happened with Oratio; then she tells him Lesbino is really Silvia, who loves the Captain. She begs Pedrolino to work matters out so that Silvia will marry the Captain. Pedrolino has Isabella call her.
FLAMINIA LESBINO	Flaminia and Lesbino come out; Flaminia laments the slap she gave to Flavio on account of the actress, but Pedrolino comforts her, saying he will remedy everything.
ARLECCHINO	Then, Arlecchino arrives. Pedrolino is friendly to him and reveals Silvia, who is in love with his master. Arlecchino greets her, and they all agree to trick the Captain in order to make Silvia happy.
ORATIO	At that moment, Oratio enters, and seeing Lesbino, his successor, draws his sword, intending to kill him. The women laugh, then mock him for drawing his weapon on a woman. When Oratio learns about Silvia, he is pacified and begs their pardon.
FLAVIO	Flavio then enters and complains to Flaminia about the slap she gave him. Pedrolino tries to bring them together by saying that they can enjoy themselves in bed that night until the play is over,

that it will go on until six that night, and they can do what other women do while their silly husbands enjoy themselves at the play; he sends them all into Isabella's house. He instructs Isabella to put Lesbino, undressed, in the room on the ground floor. Agreed, all go into the house. Pedrolino and Arlecchino remain.

CAPT. SPAVENTO   At that moment, the Captain arrives. Arlecchino withdraws. Pedrolino steps forward and tells the Captain he has the opportunity to enjoy the actress Victoria, saying she has been in Pantalone's house since four, without his wife's knowing anything about it; Pedrolino takes him by the hand and leads him into the house, leaving Arlecchino.

PEDROLINO   Pedrolino returns, saying he has accommodated the Captain according to his need. He warns Arlecchino that they must be on the lookout for the arrival of the old men, and they sit down on the ground.

A CARDSHARP   At that moment, a cardsharp enters with a lantern and sees the two servants; he begins to weep, pretending to have lost a great deal of money at cards and to have been left with only ten gold pieces. The servants invite him to play, and he sits down with them. The cardsharp wins the money and clothes of Pedrolino and Arlecchino, leaving them in their underwear, and goes happily off. The servants bemoan their bad luck, and then hear a great deal of noise coming from the theatre.

PANTALONE
DR. GRATIANO
PIOMBINO
VICTORIA   At that moment, Pantalone, Gratiano, and Piombino run on, fleeing from a great fight in the theatre and between them holding Victoria, who appeals for help, she being the cause of the quarrel.

GENTLEMEN
GALLANTS   At that, gentlemen and gallants rush on with their swords drawn, looking for Victoria. They see her between Pantalone and Gratiano and beat them with the flat side of their swords, then they take Victoria away from them and lead her off. Piombino, in desperation, follows them off. Pantalone and Gratiano are surprised to see the servants in their underwear. They all agree that plays are good pastimes and good entertainment, but they breed much scandal; they knock at Pantalone's door to tell the women that they have not found the Captain in order to tell him about Lesbino, that is, Silvia Milanese, who is in love with him.

ISABELLA
FLAMINIA   Isabella and Flaminia enter, inquiring if the play is over. Pantalone explains that a fight disrupted it and so they did not see the Captain. Isabella answers that the Captain is in the house with Silvia because Pedrolino tricked him into believing that the actress was there waiting for Pantalone. And because she and

Flaminia were afraid that the Captain, seeing himself tricked, would make trouble, they asked Signor Oratio and Signor Flavio to stay in the house with them a while to play cards. Pantalone assures her that she acted wisely; then they hear arguing within.

CAPT. SPAVENTO
ORATIO
FLAVIO

At that moment, the Captain, from within, cries that he was betrayed. Oratio and Flavio try to quiet him; but he refuses to be pacified, and all come out. Pantalone and Gratiano also plead with him; finally the Captain is placated, saying that Silvia is the daughter of a rich Milanese merchant and he loved her, but the actress had bewitched him into forgetting about her; he is content to marry her. Isabella and Flaminia urge their husbands to leave off going to the theatre and to attend to their households and to their wives; the men say they will do that. They call Silvia.

LESBINO

Lesbino, that is, Silvia, comes out to be married to the Captain. Pantalone and Gratiano want to give a banquet in Pantalone's house to celebrate; thus they go in to supper; and the comedy ends.

The Fortieth Day

THE JUST PUNISHMENT *

ARGUMENT

There was in Rome a gentleman who had fallen in love with a young woman named Flaminia, a Venetian. He made a request to her uncle, who was her guardian, to marry her. With the permission of her father and her brother, who lived in Venice, he agreed, to the great joy of the young woman, who loved the young man very much. There was at the same time in Rome one Oratio Cortesi, a gentleman of Rimini, who courted a gentlewoman named Isabella, a widow. However, he became inflamed with love for Flaminia. There was also a young scholar, called Flaminio, who was enamored of Isabella. He lived under the name of Cinthio and acted as servant to Oratio, whom he befriended. Oratio was a close companion of Flaminia's uncle, and they were often seen together. For this reason Flavio became so jealous that, overcome by his jealous passion, he was forced to leave Rome and went off to the war in Hungary. When the young woman heard of this, she resolved and swore not to marry any other man, holding all the more to her vow when she received official notice of his death in the war, for which reason Flaminia's uncle nearly passed away. (This news was a device of Flavio's.) Oratio immediately pursued Flaminia, and by working many tricks, came close to marrying her. But Flavio, who was believed dead, arrived in time. Oratio was punished for his errant ways by the sentence of Isabella, although he escaped death. Then Flaminia married Flavio; and Isabella, the disguised lover; and they lived happily ever after.

CHARACTERS IN THE PLAY

Pantalone, a Venetian
Flaminia, his daughter
Pedrolino, his servant

* See Appendix p. 407.

Isabella, gentlewoman and the widow
Franceschina, her servant

Oratio, a gentleman
Cinthio, his servant, then Flaminio, gentleman

Captain Spavento
Flavio, his friend, dressed as a slave
Arlecchino, his servant

Customs porters

PROPERTIES

Clothes for a slave
Two trunks
A dagger
Four lanterns

ACT ONE

ROME

ISABELLA
FLAMINIA
FRANCESCHINA

Isabella enters and learns from Flaminia as they come out of her house that she does not love Oratio, as Isabella has been given to understand, but loves Flavio, her betrothed, believed dead; for that reason Isabella need not fear Flaminia is her rival. Isabella says that she also made a vow after the death of her husband, a vow to love no other but Oratio, who had already promised to marry her; but after he heard of Flavio's death, he became very cold and restrained about the whole affair. Flaminia again reassures her and goes into the house, leaving Isabella and Franceschina.

FLAVIO

At that moment, Flavio enters as a slave with chains around his legs and asks them for the house of Flaminia, a Venetian noblewoman. The women point it out to him, then ask him who he is. Flavio answers that he is the slave of a captain who comes from the war in Hungary, a very good friend of a certain Flavio of Rome, who died in his arms and left everything he had to Flaminia. Isabella and Franceschina go into the house, while Flavio remains, discoursing on the evil that jealousy causes.

PANTALONE
PEDROLINO

At that, Pantalone and Pedrolino enter, having come to Rome from Venice; they ask the slave for the Inn of the Bear and ask whose slave he is. Flavio replies he belongs to a captain who has returned from the Hungarian war. Pantalone asks him if he knew his son-in-law named Flavio, a Roman who went off to the war eight years ago and was killed, for whose death a brother of his in Rome is grieving. That brother was the guardian of Flaminia, his daughter, while he was away. The slave begins to weep, and without speaking, shows his sorrow. Pantalone is amazed at this weeping and says that it would be well to find the captain from whom he might learn news about Flavio, his son-in-law.

ORATIO

At that moment, Oratio arrives, meets Pantalone, and after talking to him, finds he is the brother of Tosano Bisognosi, who says that he was a very good friend of his brother. Pantalone embraces him and asks for the house of Flaminia, his daughter. Oratio inquires if he ever received his letters and that of his daughter which asked if he would consent that Flaminia become his wife. Pantalone says no, but he is content that she be his wife. Oratio informs Pantalone that she is in the convent waiting for his consent. Oratio invites him into his house, saying meanwhile he will send word to Flaminia of her father's arrival. Pantalone accepts this courtesy, and they go into Oratio's house.

FRANCESCHINA

Franceschina comes out and goes to Flaminia to hear what news the slave brings.

CINTHIO

At that, Cinthio, servant of Oratio, enters and sees Franceschina, with whom he is in love; they talk and kiss. Then she tells Cinthio that she comes from Flaminia, to whom she went to learn of any news of Flavio, who was Flaminia's husband, killed in Hungary.

PEDROLINO

Then, Pedrolino comes out and starts off to get his master's things from the customs. Cinthio wants to know why he is coming from his master's house. Pedrolino explains there are newly arrived guests from Venice. Curious, Cinthio goes in to find out. Pedrolino asks Franceschina whose servant she is. She replies that she serves a widow named Isabella. Pedrolino says that he too is going to serve a widow who is in a convent, but she would soon be coming out to be married. Franceschina, as an excuse to ask him many questions, goes with him to show him the way to customs; they leave.

ORATIO
CINTHIO

Oratio enters, telling Cinthio that he signaled to him so that Flaminia's old father would not see him. He tells him all he told Pantalone and says he wants him to pretend to be a porter of the monks bringing a letter to the old man from Flaminia, saying that he cannot talk to his daughter without permission and license of the Superior, and she cannot come to the house. To rebuke him, Cinthio recalls to him Isabella's love, but Oratio laughs and goes in. Cinthio explains that he has been in love with Isabella for these many years, that he is a gentleman and lives in servitude only for love of her; but now he is going to tell her of the betrayal which Oratio has planned. He knocks.

ISABELLA

Isabella comes out and immediately asks about her Oratio. Cinthio replies that he is no longer hers, for he is about to marry another, not naming the woman. Isabella declares it is certain that Flaminia will not marry him and accuses him of carrying evil tales against Oratio, his master. Cinthio suggests that all he says and does comes from his feeling for her and for a gentleman who these many years has been in love with her; for his love, this gentleman remains the servant of his greatest enemy. She insists she will marry no one but Oratio Cortesi.

PEDROLINO

At that moment, Pedrolino enters, and hearing those words, says, "Signora, I must inform you that Oratio Cortesi is marrying the daughter of my master, she who is in the convent," and he goes into the house with the porters. Isabella is astonished at these words. Cinthio affirms that all Pedrolino said is true.

FRANCESCHINA

At that, Franceschina enters, bringing news to Isabella that Flaminia's father has come, and that Oratio will marry her; he is even now at the convent. Isabella becomes furious. Cinthio tries to console her, but she begs him to leave her alone, and he humbly leaves. Isabella complains of love, of the betrayal of Oratio, and goes into the house.

CAPT. SPAVENTO
FLAVIO
ARLECCHINO

The Captain, Flavio, and Arlecchino enter, Flavio beseeching them to keep his secret until Flaminia begins to suspect. Flavio makes Arlecchino knock; then he withdraws.

FLAMINIA

Flaminia comes out and learns from the Captain that he was the best friend of her dead husband, who died beside him and who, before he died, gave him something in a little chest and a letter written with his own dagger, requesting the Captain to present it to Flaminia in his name; the Captain then gives her everything. Flaminia recognizes Flavio's things and reads the letter aloud, which says that he was jealous of Oratio. Flaminia weeps, and weeping, says that her husband lived in great error, thanks the Captain, and goes into the house. Flavio, weeping, embraces the Captain, who, consoling him, goes off with him. Arlecchino notes where Flaminia went in and then leaves; and the first act ends.

ACT TWO

ORATIO   Oratio enters, very happy because he hopes to make Flaminia his wife. He is looking for Cinthio to give him the fake letter.

CINTHIO   At that, Cinthio enters, much disturbed on Isabella's account. He takes the letter with instructions to tell Pantalone he is a porter from the convent. Cinthio says he will not fail. Then he relates how he had been in the house of a gentleman, his former master, whom he found near death because he heard that Oratio was to marry Isabella, with whom he was very much in love. Oratio pretends to be sad over the gentleman's fate and offers, when he learns the gentleman's name, to renounce Isabella by his own action in order to save this man's life. Cinthio gives his name, Flaminio Adorni, a Genoese; thus agreed, Oratio leaves to write a letter to Isabella. Cinthio begs Love to favor him in this undertaking.

FRANCESCHINA   At that moment, Franceschina comes out and again reminds Cinthio of his love. Cinthio speaks sweet words to her, commanding her to tell her mistress that he will come to see her and give her good news. Franceschina, happy, goes into the house. Cinthio remains.

ORATIO   Then, Oratio returns with the letter written in his own hand, renouncing Isabella in favor of Flaminio Adorni. He gives it to Cinthio, and they speak of the honor of a gentleman in keeping his word. Cinthio leaves. Oratio says he wants to talk to Flaminia. He knocks.

FLAMINIA   Flaminia comes out, and seeing him, is disturbed. Oratio tells her he has received a letter from her father, who has agreed to their marriage. Flaminia, angered, says she will never be his wife and that he should give his attention to Isabella; then she repeats that she will never be his wife, and will never change her mind, especially since she has discovered that her dead husband went to Hungary only because of his suspicion of Oratio. Oratio stubbornly answers he will have no other wife but her. Flaminia, losing her temper, begins shouting at him.

ARLECCHINO   At that, Arlecchino enters, recognizes her, and hearing their argument, orders Oratio, "Leave that woman alone. She is married." Then Arlecchino threatens him. Flaminia goes into the house. Oratio hits Arlecchino, who, still threatening him, leaves. Oratio remains.

PEDROLINO Then, Pedrolino enters and says he is looking for that servant. Oratio sees him and orders him to call Pantalone. Pedrolino goes into the house for him and soon returns with Pantalone.

PANTALONE Pantalone insists he wants to talk with his daughter. Oratio says
PEDROLINO there is plenty of time and that he will find someone who will swear that he, Pantalone, is her father, it being a long time since he has seen her.

CINTHIO At that, Cinthio enters, disguised as a porter from the convent. Oratio points out to him that Pantalone is the father of the Signorina Flaminia who is in the convent. Cinthio tells Panatalone he has a letter from his daughter saying that her father should immediately go to prepare the marriage ceremony and asking permission of the Superior to leave the convent so that she can please both her father and Oratio, her husband. Pantalone says to tell his daughter that all will be done and to greet her in his name. Then he goes off with Oratio. Pedrolino looks closely at Cinthio. He recognizes him, and as Cinthio leaves, Pedrolino says he knows the porter is a fake. Pedrolino remains.

FRANCESCHINA Just then, Franceschina comes out because her mistress is desperate and has sent her to find Cinthio. Pedrolino invites her to the nuptials of the daughter of his master. At that moment they hear the noise of people approaching, and they go off together.

CAPT. SPAVENTO The Captain enters with Flavio and Arlecchino, who repeats all
FLAVIO that happened between Oratio and Flaminia. Flavio asks the
ARLECCHINO Captain to go to Flaminia and ask her if she would like to send anything to Hungary, and to leave it to him to avenge himself on his enemy. Then he withdraws. Arlecchino knocks.

FLAMINIA Flaminia comes out and greets the Captain, who tells her that he is returning to Hungary and would like to know if there is anything she cares to send. Flaminia says she would like to kill Oratio herself and then go with the Captain to Hungary to die and be buried near her dead husband. She requests that he let Arlecchino stay near the house so she could send him to report what has taken place. The Captain leaves with Flavio. Arlecchino hides to act as spy, and Flaminia remains.

ISABELLA At that moment, Isabella arrives, sees Flaminia, and is amazed because she was told that Flaminia was in a convent, and with the consent of her father, she would marry Oratio. Flaminia replies that Oratio is a traitor who would soon pay the price for his betrayal.

FRANCESCHINA At that, Franceschina arrives, giving the news to Isabella that Oratio is coming with Flaminia's father, that they have worked out the deed for the dowry, and she will be his wife. Flaminia says Franceschina is mad, because her father is in Venice; then she goes into the house. Isabella and Franceschina remain. Isabella is beside herself.

PANTALONE
ORATIO
PEDROLINO

Just then, Pantalone enters, rejoicing with Oratio after having signed the contract, saying that today he would see his daughter, and she would be the wife of Oratio. Oratio, seeing Isabella, takes Pantalone aside and tells him not to pay any attention to what that woman says, because she is crazy. Isabella, enraged at hearing him say that, calls him a traitor who betrays at the same time Flaminia, her father, and her honor, and still raging on, she reveals to Pantalone that his daughter Flaminia is not in a convent and Oratio has been trying to marry his daughter after he learned of the death of Flavio, but he was first her lover. She sends for Flaminia. Franceschina knocks on her door.

FLAMINIA

Flaminia comes out. Isabella tells her that this is her father come from Venice. Flaminia embraces her father and takes him into the house. Pedrolino lifts Franceschina and carries her into the house. Isabella then turns on Oratio, calling him many names. He tries to calm her.

CINTHIO

At that moment, Cinthio arrives and stops to listen. Oratio so handles her and speaks to her that Isabella is calmed down and waits to be led into the house. Cinthio then reveals himself, reminding Oratio of the promise he made. Oratio ignores him. Cinthio calls him a traitor and draws his sword. Oratio draws his own on Cinthio, and fighting, they go off up the street; and the second act ends.

ACT THREE

FLAMINIA
PANTALONE

Flaminia asks her father only to pretend to return to Venice and instead to withdraw for a few days until she avenges her dead husband on Oratio, he being the cause of it all; but before she finds him, he is to be told that she wants to speak to him and will pretend to agree to do as he wants. Pantalone agrees with her plan.

PEDROLINO

At that moment, Pedrolino enters and begs pardon for having carried Franceschina into the house. He requests that she be taken as a servant, for she is ashamed to return to her mistress' house. They call her.

FRANCESCHINA

Franceschina, feeling ashamed, enters and learns from Flaminia that she is to go to Isabella and ask her permission to give her

Pedrolino as husband. Pantalone goes with Pedrolino to find Oratio; Flaminia goes into the house.

ISABELLA   At that, Isabella enters, grieving because of the fight between Oratio and Cinthio. She asks Franceschina to go find out what has happened. Franceschina goes. Isabella remains, marveling at the ardor of Cinthio.

CINTHIO   At that moment, Cinthio arrives. Isabella scolds him. Cinthio says he did everything for love of her and because of Oratio's betrayal. With few words, he shows her the written renunciation made of her to Flaminio Adorni, a Genoese gentleman. She reads the letter in great anger, then asks who is Flaminio; Cinthio, kneeling, reveals himself to be Flaminio, and that for many months he lived in servitude, unknown to anyone. Isabella raises him up, then asks him to give her some time to think about the whole matter. Cinthio leaves and she, infuriated, enters the house.

ORATIO   Oratio enters, filled with despair at what has happened.

PANTALONE   Then, Pantalone enters, and Oratio, on his knees, begs pardon of
PEDROLINO   Pantalone for all his deception, and attributing all he did to the great love he has for Flaminia, his daughter, begs him to give her to him for wife. Pantalone raises him up, saying he is content. He will talk to his daughter and make her agree. He will, that very night, go to talk to her. He orders Pedrolino to stay with Oratio and goes. Pedrolino knocks on the door.

FLAMINIA   Flaminia comes out and is told by Pedrolino that by the command of her father, she is to agree to marry Oratio; then Pedrolino leaves. Oratio begs Flaminia to marry him and tells her she is to dismiss from her mind any thought that he ever loved Isabella.

ISABELLA   At that moment, Isabella, at her window, hears everything. Flaminia, playing along with him, says she wants to be his, especially since they have the consent of her father. Oratio begs of her the favor to return to see her that night. She agrees, and Oratio pledges that the following morning he will marry her in a solemn ceremony. He goes, and then Flaminia calls on the soul of her dead husband to come to her aid. Isabella, desperate, withdraws. Flaminia remains.

CAPT. SPAVENTO   At that moment, the Captain, Flavio, and Arlecchino come to
FLAVIO   learn what has happened. Flaminia tells them the time has come
ARLECCHINO   to make known her innocence to her dead husband and that she will, by her own hand, kill Oratio, then go with the Captain to Hungary to die beside her husband's grave. She asks the Captain to leave Arlecchino. The Captain says he will leave a more suitable person and gives her the slave.

FRANCESCHINA	As she is about to enter the house with the slave, Franceschina arrives. Flaminia leads her into the house with the slave. The Captain and Arlecchino stand guard.
NIGHT	
ISABELLA	Isabella comes out dressed as a man. She is determined to kill Oratio when he goes to Flaminia.
CINTHIO	At that moment, Cinthio, with a lantern, recognizes her. He urges her to avoid the danger she risks in committing murder.
ORATIO FRANCESCHINA	Just then, Oratio comes to see Flaminia. He knocks on her door. At that, Franceschina, at the window, tells him that Flaminia awaits him in her bed. Oratio is amazed to see Franceschina in that house. Suddenly Isabella attacks Oratio with drawn sword. Oratio flees into Flaminia's house to save himself. Isabella bewails that her attack was not successful.
PANTALONE PEDROLINO	Then, Pantalone enters with a lantern to see what Flaminia has done. Isabella, on seeing him, abuses him, saying that his daughter is nothing but a treacherous woman. They hear noise in Flaminia's house.
ORATIO FLAMINIA FLAVIO	At that moment, Oratio comes running out of the house, followed by Flaminia, who is trying to kill him. Flavio flings himself on Oratio, and holding him, exclaims that revenge belongs to no one but him, for he is Flavio, the Roman, husband of Flaminia.
CAPT. SPAVENTO ARLECCHINO	At that moment, the Captain enters with a lantern and parts them. Flaminia embraces her husband Flavio, then begs him to let her avenge herself on Oratio. He refuses. Oratio, on his knees, begs for his life. Isabella begs Flavio to give Oratio to her, as she was the most offended of all. Flaminia also begs her husband Flavio to give him to Isabella. All beg for Oratio's life, all except Cinthio. Finally, Flavio gives him to Isabella, who makes Oratio confess all his betrayals and then shows him the letter of renunciation which he made of her to Flaminio Adorni, a Genoese. Oratio confesses his betrayals. Finally, Isabella forces him to swear to accept whatever punishment is imposed on him. Oratio swears. She immediately sentences him to leave his present way of living at once and to go off to live in solitude, he being unworthy to live among men. She says then that she will do what he, in trickery, had promised—that is, that she will marry Cinthio, who is really Flaminio Adorni, Genoese; and she takes him as husband. Oratio is mute as stone. At last he says he will go to carry out his punishment and leaves. And thus Flavio marries Flaminia; Cinthio, Isabella; and Pedrolino, Franceschina; and the comedy ends.

Seventeenth-century engraving of Pantalone by Jacques Callot.

Late seventeenth-century engraving of Arleccino. This engraving is probably a portrait of Evaristo Gherardi, the celebrated Commedia dell'Arte actor who played in repertory in France from 1689 to 1697.

THE MAD PRINCESS

A Tragedy

ARGUMENT

The Prince of Morocco, in love with the Princess of Portugal, went to the court of the King, her father, and after confessing his love for her, eloped with her. Going by sea, they passed the Strait of Gibraltar and arrived at the kingdom of Fessa. Here they stayed the night, feeling safe, and were welcomed by the Princess of Fessa, in the name of the King, her father, and invited to enter the city and stay at the King's palace. Immediately on seeing the beauty of the Princess of Fessa, the Prince of Morocco fell in love with her, and desiring to marry her, slipped away from the Princess of Portugal, hid with one of her servants, and fled before day. But he was overtaken by the Prince of Portugal, was killed, and his severed head was presented to the Princess by her brother, the Prince of Portugal, his enemy. After grieving for a long time over the head of her lover, the Princess went mad and drowned herself in the sea. The Prince was killed by the father of the Prince of Morocco, and the King was cruelly murdered by the people. The King of Fessa gave to his only daughter and heir to the throne as a gift a noble youth for page, who was handsome, gracious, and well-mannered. They were often together, and time and again she heard her father say that if he were a woman, he would fall in love with the page. She was of such a passionate nature that, listening to these words, she fell passionately in love with the page, and such was her love that they made love more and more often. When the King learned of this love, he had the page killed, his heart torn from his breast and sent to the Princess. She wept bitterly, placed the heart in a cup of poison, drank the liquid, and thus killed herself. Whereupon the King, in despair and overwhelmed by other misfortunes, and supplanted by one of his dearest friends, killed himself by his own hand.

CHARACTERS IN THE PLAY

Mohamet, King of Fessa
Fatima, his daughter the Princess

Pelindo, Fatima's page
Burattino, clown
Many pages
Counselor
Captain and soldiers

Tarfe, Prince of Morocco
Alvira, Princess of Portugal
Selino, attendant of the Prince
Pedrolino, his servant

Belardo, Prince of Portugal

Many sailors
Soldiers

Divers Messengers

Giaffer, General of the King of Morocco

Many Moorish soldiers

PROPERTIES

A very beautiful ship
Two boats
A tent
Four beautiful traveling bags
Four lighted torches
Four basins of silver
Many flasks of wine
A covered golden goblet
A vase with water
Divers standing arms
A head like that of the Prince of Morocco
A fake moon which sets
Tribunal of the King of Fessa

The play can be done on land and on water, and in the middle of
the scene is the door to the fortress of Fessa.

ACT ONE

FESSA

TWILIGHT

SQUIRE   A boat arrives in which are two sailors, one a squire of the Prince
SAILORS   of Morocco, who comes to set up a tent in which to house the
              Princess of Portugal.

A SHORE GUARD	At that, a shore guard enters and asks who they are. The squire informs him. The guard then gives them permission to land and says he will inform the King. The squire and the sailor come ashore and set up the tent.
MOHAMET, KING OF FESSA FATIMA, HIS DAUGHTER PELINDO, PAGE COURT	Then, Mohamet, King of Fessa, appears on the wall; he learns from the squire that the Prince of Morocco is approaching and has with him the Princess of Portugal, his bride, taken along with his consent. The King orders his daughter and the page to go forth and welcome the Prince and the Princess to his kingdom. All go except those who are pitching the tent. Then they hear a trumpet sound and drums as the ship of the Prince of Morocco arrives.
TARFE, PRINCE OF MOROCCO ALVIRA NURSE SERVANTS	The ship docks from which debark Tarfe, Prince of Morocco, with Alvira, Princess of Portugal, and her nurse. They find the tent set up. The Princess expresses the fear that her brother will follow her, but the Prince says he expects the King, his father, will come to meet him to honor them. Then the gates of the city are opened.
PAGES FATIMA PELINDO COURT	Pages with lighted torches enter, followed by Fatima with all the court in train. She welcomes the Princess, who courteously thanks Fatima for the welcome. Then and there the Prince of Morocco falls in love with the Princess of Fessa, who returns to the city, leaving the others to enter the royal tent.
PEDROLINO SLAVES	Pedrolino, Tarfe's servant, debarks from the ship with many slaves, carrying the goods of the Prince, his lord. They also enter the tent, leaving someone on guard with a light.
THE GUARD	The guard, by order of the King, illuminates the entire wall for the honor of the Princess.
BURATTINO PAGES	At that, Burattino, the King's jester, leads many pages with lighted torches and silver basins filled with gifts to be given to the royal guests. They come playing and singing Moorish songs and dances.
PEDROLINO	Pedrolino receives all, and again dancing and playing, they all enter the tent.
FATIMA PELINDO	Fatima, on the wall, talks amorously with Pelindo, each expressing great love for the other.
WAITINGMEN	Waitingmen arrive, and by order of the King, lead Fatima off to sleep. Pelindo, having with him his musical instrument, sings love songs while he is on the wall.

TARFE SELINO	At that, Tarfe, Prince of Morocco, enters with Selino, his valet. He stops to listen to the singing, which pleases him, saying he would like to know who that is. He has Burattino, the King's jester, called.
BURATTINO	Burattino enters and tells Tarfe that the singer is the page of Fatima, given to her by the King, her father, two years before, and he is beautiful and virtuous. Tarfe sends him back into the tent; then he reveals to Selino his love for Fatima, the Princess of Fessa, and declares he is resolved to abandon the Princess of Portugal, and before the dawn comes—when they are to embark— he will run off in the hope of winning Fatima for his wife from her father, the King. So saying, he goes in. Selino laments this betrayal which Tarfe plans; he calls a sailor.
THE SAILOR	The sailor comes and is sent by Selino to the captain of the ship to tell him that at the rise of the moon he is to come with the ship to take the Prince. The sailor goes. Selino remains.
BURATTINO PAGES	At that, Burattino and pages come out of the tent, playing and singing and dancing. Burattino says the Prince has given him nothing and that he has an ugly face. They call at the gate.
A GUARD	A guard opens the gate and all go in, playing and dancing a Moorish dance, and the first act ends.

ACT TWO

NIGHT	
THE CAPTAIN	The moon appears, all stained with blood. At that moment, the ship arrives. Upon it the captain is still. Then, an armed boat appears.
CAVALIER SOLDIERS	Aboard it a cavalier stands armed. He challenges the ship, demanding to know whose it is; the captain tells him. Immediately the cavalier, very angry, jumps out, draws his sword, and a furious battle then starts between those from the boat and those from the ship.
TARFE SELINO	Tarfe enters in his nightshirt with Selino, who brings his apparel, but first the ship withdraws and the others, fighting, go off the stage, leaving the empty boat, into which Tarfe and Selino enter. Selino rows; Tarfe expresses some pity for the Princess of Portugal, as does Selino. Still rowing, they go off.
ALVIRA	Alvira enters in her nightshirt, frightened because of the flight of Tarfe. She bewails Tarfe's betrayal and begins to weep.

PEDROLINO

Then, Pedrolino, who has witnessed the betrayal of the Prince, arrives. At that moment, the moon sets.

KING MOHAMET
FATIMA
PELINDO
PAGES

King Mohamet, with a lighted lamp, then comes to visit Tarfe, having heard he is going to leave on the second watch. He sees Alvira weeping and asks her why. Overcome by grief, she swoons into the arms of the King. The King has her taken to the city with his daughter and the pages, and remaining alone, says that compassion for Alvira has kindled something in his breast, and he has suddenly fallen in love with her. He goes back into the city with his servant.

PELINDO
BURATTINO

Pelindo, on the wall, speaks of the betrayal of Tarfe; Burattino remarks that others who are covetous have also the look of traitors.

FATIMA

Then, Fatima enters, saying she has left Alvira on the bed to rest. She talks to Pelindo of the betrayal of Alvira. Pelindo says he will never commit such a betrayal. Fatima takes Pelindo aside and tells him she will go alone to their trysting place and wait for him as they have done other times. She goes; Pelindo remains with Burattino; then they hear the sound of trumpets and drums, and another ship arrives in port.

BELARDO
SOLDIERS

Belardo, Prince of Portugal, all bloody, disembarks with his soldiers. Burattino asks them who they are; they tell him and march off to tell the King. The others remain; one soldier holds the head of Tarfe, Prince of Morocco, in his hand.

DAY

MOHAMET

At that, Mohamet, the King, comes out of the city; he sees the Prince covered with blood and asks the reason. The Prince tells him that he was informed of the flight of his sister Alvira with Tarfe, that he followed him, and at daybreak seized Tarfe's ship but did not find him aboard; then, seeing a small boat with only two men in it, he overtook it. In it he found Tarfe and killed him; now he has only to find his sister Alvira. The King asks him as a favor—having first embraced him—to pardon his sister, who has been betrayed, and he orders the Princess called in the company of his daughter.

FATIMA
ALVIRA

Fatima and Alvira arrive; Alvira, on her knees, begs pardon of her brother, telling him how she was betrayed. Belardo pardons her at the urging of the King; then he presents her with the head of his enemy. She receives it, begging her brother to leave her alone for a while to vent her feeling upon the dead traitor. He agrees, leaves some guards, and then he goes into the city with the

King. Alvira expresses her grief for the death of her lover, and speaking many strange, wild words, she becomes frantic, mad, and delirious, tearing her hair and ripping her clothes. She turns to run out of the city toward the sea. The guards go in to tell Belardo.

A SQUIRE
THE GUARD

At that moment, a boat arrives with a squire in it. Then the guard enters and asks who he is; the squire says he is one of the King of Morocco's men. With his ships and other vessels he has come to meet Tarfe, his son, who has run off with Alvira, Princess of Portugal.

MOHAMET
BELARDO
COURT

At that, Mohamet appears on the wall and learns all; Belardo begs as a favor from the King, all his wooden warships to fight the King of Morocco and kill him. The King consents, and they go to prepare to fight.

THE GUARD

The guard enters and orders the squire to push off in his boat; he threatens him and calls him villain. The squire departs, saying that soon his own King of Morocco will come to punish them all; then they hear noises of soldiers inside the city, preparing to fight on the ship along with the sailors; then all quiet down.

MOHAMET
COUNSELOR
PAGES

At that moment, Mohamet, the King, enters and tells his counselor that he wants to give his daughter Fatima to Belardo, and he would take for wife Alvira, Belardo's sister. The counselor says they must wait to see the outcome of the battle.

PEDROLINO

At that, Pedrolino enters, weeping because he has seen the Princess Alvira go mad, running toward the sea. The King is astonished.

BURATTINO

Then, Burattino, who has made all withdraw to one side, enters and tells the King that Pelindo and Fatima, his daughter, are sleeping together. The King, angry, leaves with all his train. Pedrolino asks Burattino what he has told the King.

ALVIRA

At that moment, Alvira, mad, enters, doing and saying many mad things and all the time joking about the head of Tarfe and of his betrayal. She says to them, "I am not surprised that the water from the river is sweet and the sea is salt, because the salad is always together with its philosophical oil and with your Strait of Gibraltar or, as you will, Zibilterra, either one or the other name it comes to be called, even as you wish to your fatal destiny; that poor Ursa Major ties his boots with a pinching lace and goes to dig oysters and large muscles in the Gulf of Duckweed near Syria. A thing is or it isn't. If you wish it, so it is, and it is an evil year when God grants it to you; and in your basket you will find an evil Easter; and in your accustomed manner you will reap evil always, for all from above is purposeful." Pedrolino and Burattino laugh and improvise other nonsense in imitation of what she has said. Then she begins to beat them, so they run off along the seashore, and she follows. Here the second act ends.

ACT THREE

MOHAMET
COUNSELOR
PELINDO
COURT

Mohamet, the King, has Pelindo led in, manacled; Pelindo accuses himself of the wrong committed in order to save Fatima. The King gives the secret order of what is to be done to Pelindo and has him taken away; he orders his daughter to be brought to him.

FATIMA

Fatima appears intrepid before him, without kneeling; she says it is true that Pelindo is her lover, and it is his fault, for he always praised the beauty of the page, saying that if he were a woman he would love none other but Pelindo; she says these words he uttered kindled her love for Pelindo and now he can do what he wishes with her and Pelindo. The King, in anger, has her taken away. Then he remains with his counselor.

A MESSENGER

At that moment, a messenger enters and tells of the death of Belardo, Prince of Portugal, by the hand of the King of Morocco, along with the great slaughter of his men, and now he comes in anger to destroy Mohamet's kingdom. Then they see the mad Alvira upon a rock at the sea's edge; they stare at her in awe.

ALVIRA

Suddenly, Alvira appears on a very high rock. After shouting a great deal of mad nonsense, she at last says: "Oh, what a magnificent mirror appears before my eyes. In this mirror I see the sun all aflame, ready to roast on the spit over a fire of ice that traitor, the Prince of Morocco, for stealing a hen from a cock at the inn of the Moor. Ah, oh me, you too will arrive, taken by the old thief and to beat him well about the face, place you on the salt and feed him to a crew of Astomites. Up, up, cavalier of honor. It is from here one leaps the perilous river. This is the road to Mount Flagon. This is the true way of the menstrual flows and the dungheap. This is the famous chariot of Fusina, and this is the true caldron of the macaroni in which are to be found the breeches and gowns of the wisest philosophers. Farewell, farewell, all, farewell." Having said this, she jumps into the sea, drowns, and is soon no more. The King is deeply grieved by the death of Alvira.

A MESSENGER	At that moment, a messenger brings a covered goblet made of gold to the King, who commands that it be given to his daughter Fatima. Then, in despair, he leaves to die. All follow him out. The messenger remains.
FATIMA WAITING MAIDS	Then, Fatima enters with her waiting maids, all dressed in black. The messenger, weeping, tells of the death of Pelindo, whose heart was torn from his breast. He tells how Pelindo kissed him, saying that he kissed his Fatima, and that she was for all time engraved on his heart. Then he died. Fatima takes the gift of her father, the King, sees the heart of Pelindo, kisses it, weeps over it, and then, taking from her bosom a little vial full of a deadly poison, bathes the heart in it and then drinks the poison. Thus intrepid to the last, she dies with her two maids. The sound of distant trumpets is heard.
PEDROLINO BURATTINO THE CAPTAIN SOLDIERS	At that moment, Pedrolino, Burattino, the captain, and soldiers appear on the wall, looking off toward the oncoming armada of the King of Morocco, who has destroyed the ships of Belardo, and of King Mohamet of the Kingdom of Fessa.
A MESSENGER	Suddenly, a messenger enters, weeping. He tells of the death of King Mohamet. He says the King had returned to his room with his captain and ordered him to kill him, or he would kill the captain, and that in this sad business of life and death, the captain was forced, by his own love of life, to kill his lord with one thrust of his sword. He tells also of Fatima and of her dying of poison which had bathed the heart of Pelindo, her beloved page. Then they hear again the sound of arms, of trumpets, and drums.
A MESSENGER	At that moment, a messenger arrives who gives news of the death of the King of Morocco, killed by the guard of King Mohamet, King of Fessa. Trumpets again sound.
GENERAL GIAFFER MOORS	The General of the King of Morocco, known as Giaffer, enters the city by the back gate, then comes out the front gate, displaying the standard of victory over the throne of Fessa.
THE CITIZENS PEDROLINO BURATTINO	The citizens of Fessa enter, kneel, and offer themselves up as prisoners. Pedrolino and Burattino enter, do the same, and speak of all the kings being killed. Then all go into the city to take out the treasures of the dead king and of the city. Trumpets sound in rejoicing, and the tragedy of *The Mad Princess* ends.

The Forty-second Day

THE COMICAL, PASTORAL, AND TRAGICAL EVENTS

A Mixed Opera

ARGUMENT

Pantalone Bisognosi, a Venetian, and Gratiano Forbicioni, a Bolognese, were, as small children, taken to Greece by their fathers. After their fathers died, they married women of Sparta, which was ruled by King Oreste. The two old men each had a child—one a daughter named Flaminia, and the other, a son named Oratio. The children fell in love with each other. It came about that Pantalone, father of Flaminia, promised his daughter to a captain of King Oreste who, at that time, had to go to Bizantium by command of the King. No sooner had he gone and become established in the court there than Gratiano demanded that Pantalone give his daughter to his son, Oratio, who had long been friends with her. The captain returned from the city of Bizantium and demanded the promised daughter from the father. She, finding the whole affair very involved, managed, through the help of a cunning servant and the intervention of amorous encounters, to marry Oratio.

Meanwhile Pantalone and Gratiano had acquired, among the many valuable gifts from the ruler of the city not far away, two porters, one named Pedrolino, and the other Burattino, their old servants. Pedrolino had a daughter named Fillide, who, in order to follow her exiled lover, pretended to be dead and, with the help of her herdsman, pursued her lover in the disguise of a shepherd and found him. Shortly after, it happened that Sireno, her shepherd lover and son of Burattino, was called back to the home of his beloved, who, before he left, promised his dear Fillide that he would inform her father what had come to pass and from him obtain a pardon to return and take her for wife. Sireno returned home, and immediately on laying eyes on the beautiful Amarillis, fell in love with her. The nymph loved a shepherd named Tirsi who loved Fillide. Seeing that her lover did not return to her, Fillide, afraid of what might have happened, returned to her paternal home in the disguise of a shepherd. Finding Sireno making love to Amarillis and feeling scorned, she

321

wounded him with an arrow, and after many events, Fillide, with the good wishes of her father, became the wife of Tirsi, and Sireno married Amarillis.

While Pedrolino, Burattino, Pantalone, and Gratiano rejoiced in the marriage of their children, they heard of the sudden arrival of the army of King Oronte of Athens, who had camped near the city of Sparta. He received as an ambassadorial sign, the head of Bramante, King of Mycena, who had stayed within the city to appease some old enemies. Having seen the treachery of Oreste committed on the person of King Bramante, Oronte made every effort to enter the city. Meanwhile, because of Oreste's love for Althea, the beloved of his brother Alidoro, the death of all the principal persons of the royal family followed and finally the death of Oronte.

CHARACTERS IN THE MIXED WORK

Pantalone, a Venetian
Flaminia, his daughter
Pedrolino, porter of the villa, father of Fillide, the nymph

Gratiano, a doctor, a Bolognese
Oratio, his son
Burattino, his servant and porter of the villa, father
   of the shepherd Sireno
Franceschina, his servant

Flavio, Spartan gentleman

Isabella, Spartan widow

Captain of King Oreste
Arlecchino, his servant

Fillide, daughter of Pedrolino, a nymph called Coridone

Sireno, shepherd son of Burattino

Two Satyrs
Amarillis, a nymph
Tirsi, a lone shepherd
Lisetta, a shepherdess

Cavicchio and
Caccialboncio, peasants

Shepherd Tubicina

Priest of the temple

Many shepherds
Arlecchino, servant of Sireno
Mezettino, a peasant

Oreste, King of Sparta
Alidoro, his beardless brother
Valet of Alidoro

Althea, daughter of the dead Bramante, King of Mycena
Nurse of Althea

Two messengers

Oronte, King of Athens

Two Captains
Armed cavaliers
Many soldiers

ACT ONE

SPARTA

PANTALONE GRATIANO	Pantalone and Gratiano enter and speak of their affairs, their wealth, their children, their foremen who are taking care of their possessions, and of their being loved by their king, Oreste. Gratiano asks for the hand of Pantalone's daughter Flaminia for his son Oratio. Pantalone says that he has promised her to a captain of the King, but if he does not return he will give her to his son.
PEDROLINO	At that, Pedrolino, Pantalone's porter, enters with a chest full of goods.
BURATTINO	Burattino, Gratiano's porter, enters with a similar chest; they greet their masters. Pantalone asks Pedrolino if he has had news of his daughter, who has run away from the villa. Pedrolino, weeping, says no. Burattino tells Gratiano that his son, who was sent into exile by the court, has returned home; then each enters his house with his servant.
ORATIO FLAVIO	Oratio comes from Isabella's house, troubled because she has called him a traitor and afraid that Flaminia will trick him into marrying her. Flavio is about to take him back into the house.
ISABELLA	At that moment, Isabella, the widow, appears at her window. She tells Flavio to let the traitor Oratio go, and Isabella and Oratio argue, showing one and then the other to be jealous. Flavio tries all the time to reconcile them, but to no avail.

FRANCESCHINA — Then, Franceschina arrives. Isabella asks her if she had been told that Oratio would take a wife. Franceschina replies yes. Oratio, enraged, turns on her. She flees, Oratio after her. Flavio follows him off, and Isabella withdraws.

PANTALONE
PEDROLINO — Pantalone comes out of the house telling Pedrolino that he has betrothed Flaminia to the Captain, but as he has not returned, he will give her to Gratiano's son, Oratio. Pedrolino says that he has done right; he has met his obligation.

FRANCESCHINA — At that, Franceschina, frightened, enters and stands off on the side to hear.

GRATIANO
BURATTINO — Just then, Gratiano enters and tells Pantalone he wishes to have the wedding that very night and has already invited all his relatives. Now he must go find his son Oratio. Pantalone is satisfied with the arrangements; however, he is bothered by a dream that he had, that the Captain had returned and made a great roaring. Gratiano assures Pantalone he is no longer obliged to honor his promise and that he would back him up in court.

THE CAPTAIN — At that very moment, the Captain arrives and greets Pantalone, calling him father-in-law. Gratiano immediately contradicts him and announces that Flaminia is betrothed to his son Oratio. The Captain ignores Gratiano and informs Pantalone that he wants Flaminia as he promised. Pantalone is alarmed and feels himself caught.

FLAMINIA — Flaminia, at the window, has heard everything; she speaks freely to the Captain, declaring that she does not want to be his wife. Gratiano begins to make fun of the Captain, who draws his sword and forces everyone to flee, chasing after them; only Pedrolino and Franceschina remain. She asks Pedrolino to arrange matters so that Flaminia marries the Captain, and Oratio could have Isabella, since he is in love with her. She further explains that when she told Isabella that Gratiano said Oratio will be Flaminia's husband, Isabella wanted to kill her. Pedrolino, having thought about what Franceschina, his beloved, has said, decides that he will find Oratio and tell him straight out that Flaminia will not be his wife, neither his nor the Captain's; content, Franceschina goes, leaving Pedrolino.

ISABELLA — At that moment, Isabella, at her window, asks Pedrolino when his mistress is to be married. Pedrolino, to provoke her, answers that he left Pantalone and Oratio a short time before, going to make out the marriage contract and buy jewels for the bride. She, sighing and weeping, retires. Pedrolino laughs.

ORATIO — At that, Oratio enters, worried and unhappy about Isabella. Pedrolino, to make him jealous, hints that he knows why Oratio is so sad and finally says it is because Flavio is to marry Isabella and he is to marry Flaminia, it being thus arranged by Gratiano, his father; then he goes, leaving Oratio feeling miserable.

THE CAPTAIN — Then, the Captain enters and announces that he is resolved to leave Flaminia. Oratio replies that if the Captain would take her, he would leave her for him. The Captain, thinking that Oratio has been intimidated for fear of him, begins to shout and threaten outrageously. Oratio, suddenly enraged, draws his sword; the Captain flees. Oratio remains.

ISABELLA — At that moment, Isabella comes out and calls him villain and coward for renouncing his Flaminia to the Captain. Oratio answers in anger, and they refuse to listen to each other; each calls the other traitor. Infuriated, Isabella goes into the house, and Oratio turns away to weep.

FLAVIO — Just then, Flavio greets him. Oratio at once accuses him of betraying the best friend he had in the world; then bursting into a rage, he draws his sword on Flavio.

FLAMINIA — At that, Flaminia comes out, grabs Flavio by the arm, and hurriedly takes him into the house. Oratio remains, bewailing his fate, and overcome by an extreme grief, falls to the ground as if dead.

FRANCESCHINA — Then, Franceschina, his servant, enters and weeps over him.

PANTALONE
GRATIANO
PEDROLINO
BURATTINO — Pantalone, Gratiano, Pedrolino, and Burattino also enter and are astonished to see Oratio in this state. Franceschina says that Oratio died of sorrow at not being able to have Isabella, whom he loves. Oratio begins to revive, and Pedrolino falls to his knees.

ISABELLA — At that moment, Isabella, at her window, overhears Pedrolino, on his knees, tell Oratio that he has been the cause of his misfortune; he begs forgiveness, explaining that what he said to Isabella he said to provoke her. Isabella rejoices at hearing this, as does Oratio, who begs his father to give him Isabella. Gratiano, with the consent of Pantalone, says he will give Flaminia to the Captain.

THE CAPTAIN — At that moment, the Captain arrives. Pantalone says he will be as good as his word and give him Flaminia to marry as he promised; he knocks on the door of the house.

FLAMINIA — Flaminia, when told that the Captain is to be her husband, says straight out that she does not want him because she has taken another husband. Angered, the Captain demands, "Who is this other husband?"

FLAVIO   Flavio enters and arrogantly declares, "It is I." The Captain at once backs down, saying he does not want to disappoint his lady, and thus Oratio marries Isabella.

ISABELLA   Isabella comes out and takes Oratio for husband; Flavio marries Flaminia; and Pedrolino, a widower, marries Franceschina. Each goes in with his spouse. Burattino and Pedrolino are given permission by their masters to return to the villa, and they go; thus ends the first act of the opera and finishes the comedy.

ACT TWO

ARCADIA,
SPARTA

SIRENO   Sireno, wounded in the flank, is being carried in by two satyrs.
SATYRS   He relates the story: While he was talking with Amarillis, a strange young shepherd, in hiding, shot an arrow into his flank and afterwards fled quickly away. This caused him to immediately fall in love with Amarillis. The satyrs console him, saying they know of a cure and of other soothing herbs to make him well, and they take him off to their dwelling.

AMARILLIS   Amarillis enters with Lisetta, a shepherdess, saying that Coridone
LISETTA   has wounded Sireno. Lisetta asks her if she loves Sireno; Amarillis answers no. Lisetta then reveals that she herself is in love with Sireno and believes that Amarillis loves Tirsi, and Coridone is in love with her; Lisetta speaks ill of the beardless boy.

ARLECCHINO   Arlecchino and Mezettino, peasants, enter and hail the women in
MEZETTINO   a ridiculous manner; each offers to be their servant, to serve the nymphs. Amarillis asks Arlecchino about Sireno, and Lisetta asks Mezettino about Tirsi.

CAVICCHIO   At that moment, Cavicchio, country servant of Amarillis's father, brings food to the reapers. He laughs at the two peasants who love the nymphs; they quarrel and fight. The nymphs, however, separate them and restore peace. Lisetta takes some ricotta, saying she wants them to eat together as a sign of love, and they must eat it according to her orders. Lisetta puts them back to back and ties their hands together. Then she puts the dish of ricotta on the ground, and they [the nymphs] leave, saying to Cavicchio that when they have eaten, give them something to drink, and they go. When one bends over to eat the ricotta, he lifts his companion behind him, on his back; they do this alternately many times. Finally Arlecchino picks up the dish and walks off, eating the ricotta, with Mezettino tied on his back; Cavicchio follows, laughing.

CORIDONE   Coridone, who is Fillide dressed as a shepherd, enters and relates the story of her misfortune as it is set down in the Argument; then she says that since she has wounded Sireno and found him to be in love with Amarillis, she is resolved to end her life in the sepulchre where she will pretend to be dead. Seeing someone coming, she goes in.

TIRSI   Then, Tirsi, a shepherd in love with Fillide, enters. He spends more and more of his time weeping on her sepulchre and now returns again to weep on it; he begins to lie down on the sepulchre, saying that he will end his life on this, her sepulchre. He begs sleep to bring him his love in a dream, and so falls asleep.

BURATTINO   Burattino enters, telling Pedrolino that he has been told that a
PEDROLINO   shepherd boy had wounded his son Sireno with an arrow, and when he finds out who he is, he is going to kill him and all his kin. Pedrolino promises to help him; they go off to visit the shepherd.

FILLIDE   Fillide, having heard the lament of Tirsi, feels compassion for the shepherd. In his dream he sings madrigals to the beauty of Fillide.

AMARILLIS   At that moment, Amarillis enters, sad because she has not found Tirsi. Fillide immediately hides. Amarillis sees the sleeping Tirsi and begins to praise all of his person, part by part.

A SATYR   As she is about to kiss him, a satyr capers on and carries her off, saying that the other is not her shepherd. She cries out for help as he carries her off up the path. Tirsi awakes, and Fillide appears on the sepulchre. Tirsi sees her, but she immediately hides, leaving him shocked and frightened.

ARLECCHINO   At that moment, Arlecchino enters to talk to Tirsi. Mezettino, his
MEZETTINO   servant, also wants a word with him; however, Tirsi, staring into space, departs without answering a word. Mezettino follows him. Arlecchino remains, and chancing to look at the sepulchre, sees Fillide's head.

CORIDONE   Coridone, that is, Fillide, has raised her head to see if anyone is there. Arlecchino, thinking her to be a spirit, backs off in terror. She again hides in the sepulchre, and Arlecchino runs off.

CACCIALBONCIO PEDROLINO	Caccialboncio then enters, telling Pedrolino that his master dreamed that Fillide, his daughter, came back to life. Pedrolino weeps again over her death, and seeing her tomb, weeps over it. Caccialboncio consoles him.
THE SHEPHERD TUBICINA	At that, the shepherd Tubicina rings the bell and calls all the shepherds in his domain to the temple. All go. Caccialboncio, the peasant, remains.
CORIDONE	Then, Coridone, that is, Fillide, rises from the sepulchre. She tells her herdsman, Caccialboncio, who has been her constant friend and companion, that although she wounded Sireno for betraying her, she has gained the love of Tirsi, whose constancy in loving her she has recognized. They hear someone coming and hide in the sepulchre.
SIRENO AMARILLIS SATYRS	At that moment, Sireno enters, telling Amarillis that he does not want her against her will, but if she does not love him, he is determined to die by the wound he received on her account, reminding her that he betrayed the most faithful nymph in all Arcadia for love of her. Only she can save him. As she falls into deep thought, they hear music.
SHEPHERDS SHEPHERDESSES PEDROLINO BURATTINO ARLECCHINO MEZETTINO PRIEST TIRSI	Shepherds enter playing various instruments, followed by many shepherds and others, two by two, with many things to eat and to drink to honor their dead. Tirsi, kneeling, prays for the repose of Fillide's soul and gives to the nymphs a vial filled with his tears.
CACCIALBONCIO	At that moment, Caccialboncio appears, to the astonishment of all, out of the sepulchre. He tells the priest that if Pedrolino will pardon his master, he will give him the best of news. Pedrolino promises. Caccialboncio then calls Fillide.
CORIDONE	Coridone, that is, Fillide, comes out of the tomb, her hair falling loosely. All are frightened, but she reassures all of them, then asks her father's pardon and reveals to the priest that in order to follow Sireno, she pretended to be dead and made them entomb her. With the help of Caccialboncio, she dressed as a shepherd and events followed, as given in the Argument. She concludes by saying she is to be given to the faithful Tirsi; thus they give him to her for husband, and Sireno takes Amarillis for wife. They pardon Caccialboncio, and all return to the temple; and here the second act of the play ends and is the end of the pastoral.

ACT THREE

SPARTA

PEDROLINO BURATTINO	Pedrolino and Burattino enter. They have come to the city to tell their masters that they have found their children and have taken them home. They marvel at seeing the great host of armed men near their city of Sparta.
PANTALONE GRATIANO	At that moment, Pantalone and Gratiano enter and learn the good news concerning their children from their porters, which makes them rejoice. Then they hear of the camped army. Pantalone says that he understands from a spy that King Oreste is coming forth, and the foreign army is that of Oronte, King of Athens. However, he does not know why Oronte has come, and they go to the palace to find out. Trumpets sound.
ORONTE ARMED CAVALIERS PAGES	Just then, Oronte, King of Athens, enters, wondering about the ambassadors to be sent him by Oreste, King of Sparta. He says he has heard that Bramante, King of Mycena, with his daughter Althea, had, the night before, entered the city of Sparta, having come by sea with a great armada. He judges that Bramante has come seeking Oreste's protection. He orders that the camp keep moving up.
A SOLDIER	At that, a soldier brings news of the arrival of the ambassadors. Oronte tells them to approach. The soldier goes. Trumpets sound the arrival of the ambassadors.
PANTALONE GRATIANO SERVANTS	At that moment, Pantalone enters, nobly dressed as an ambassador. He shows his credentials, then presents to Oronte the head of King Bramante in a silver dish with a red cover. Oronte is shocked; then he reads a letter which says that Oreste, to revenge the death of his father, had King Bramante killed, and because of his desire to remain on friendly terms and maintain peace in his kingdom, he sends him the head of their mutual enemy. Oronte, showing compassion for the suffering of King Bramante, drives the ambassadors off, then scornfully gives the order that the camp is to be brought closer to the city. Then he goes off, carrying the head of Bramante, followed by all the others.
ORESTE ALTHEA NURSE COURT	Trumpets sound, then Oreste arrives; he tells Althea he has had her father, King Bramante, killed to avenge the death of his own father, who was killed by Bramante's command. Althea replies that her father had him killed because he was a traitor, and now prays that Oreste will also take her life. Oreste, trying to console

her, confesses his love for her and promises that if she agrees to marry him, he will arrange it so that Oronte will give up the war. She haughtily refuses to agree to his proposal. He says he will give her all day to make up her mind; if she does not agree, she dies. Angrily he leaves with his court. Althea weeps at her unhappy fate.

ALIDORO
ATTENDANT

At that moment, Alidoro enters with his attendant. He asks the cause of Althea's grief. She tells him of the betrayal of Oreste, his brother, in killing Bramante, her father, and that, moreover, he wants her to become his wife. Weeping, she goes in with her nurse. Alidoro asks his attendant the reason for the commotion and for the army of Oronte. The attendant informs him that Oronte, to make peace with himself, as Bramante was his brother-in-law, wanted to give Althea for wife to the Prince of Lidia. Since Oreste will never consent to that, Oronte will fight. Alidoro reveals that he himself is in love with Althea, that his love began when he was a page at King Bramante's court, and he reproaches his brother for his traitorous action. At that moment, trumpets sound.

ORESTE
PANTALONE
GRATIANO
PAGES

Oreste, the King, sits in tribunal; the ambassadors report King Oronte's wrath, saying that he drove them away. The King orders them to again arm the city with soldiers; then he orders his brother Alidoro to go to the senate and declare that Althea is his wife and from him they will have credentials as proof of the truth. Then they will await the help of the armada, which was Bramante's. He sends an attendant to tell Althea to make ready, for that night she will be married. The attendant goes. Alidoro leaves and all exit. Trumpets sound from far off.

ORONTE
CAPTAINS
SOLDIERS

Oronte enters, saying he does not want to attack the city that night but will hold off. He orders that a messenger be sent off to the kingdom of Mycena to report the death of Bramante and inform them that he is encamped to see the destruction of Oreste. He also orders that tents be pitched at the Gate of the Sun; then all leave.

ALIDORO
ALTHEA
NURSE
ATTENDANT

Alidoro enters with Althea, who appeals to him for help, having learned of the King's will. Alidoro reveals his love for her and promises all his help; she says she will marry him.

A MESSENGER

At that moment, a messenger, who has entered and overheard their conversation, leaves and goes to tell Oreste. Meanwhile Althea begs the favor of seeing Alidoro's brother Oreste dead and he, King of Sparta and her husband. They discuss how to inform

Oreste; Althea wants to write the letter to the Senate, but she wants Alidoro to be present. They plan that with her help, Alidoro is to come to her room to kill Oreste.

ORESTE PANTALONE GRATIANO COURT MESSENGER	At that moment, Oreste enters, having heard from the messenger of their conspiracy. Without revealing his knowledge, he orders his brother Alidoro into the castle; Alidoro obediently goes. Oreste then tells Althea that that evening they will marry; she pretends to agree. The attendant flees. Althea begs a favor of the King, that she be allowed to prepare for her wedding night in the manner of her country. Oreste agrees. She requests that the statue of Hymen be brought to her room and that she may pray until midnight; then she will do whatever he wishes.
A SOLDIER	At that moment, a soldier brings news that the army of Oronte is at the wall, and his tent is pitched. Oreste takes heart and leaves to prepare for battle and to arrange for someone to go to the Senate that night in place of his brother Alidoro. He goes, and Althea rejoices with her nurse.
THE ATTENDANT	The attendant returns and tells Althea that the guards have promised to let Alidoro leave at his own will from the castle. Althea orders him to tell Alidoro that she will be dressed as a waiting maid and to come to her room as soon as Oreste prays at the statue of Hymen. The attendant goes, and the women go in as night falls.
NIGHT	
CAVICCHIO	Cavicchio, a peasant, enters and says he lives in his cottage with his children, who work as seamstresses, while he plays and sings, rejoicing in his little family.
THE CAPTAIN SOLDIERS	At that moment, the Captain enters, making the rounds and visiting the corps of guards of the army.
CAVICCHIO	Just then, Cavicchio enters carrying a light, and he is frightened at seeing the Captain. He reassures him. Cavicchio calls his wife.
PASQUELLA CHILDREN	Pasquella comes out; Cavicchio plays his bagpipe and sings, and his children dance with gusto. Then they all hear the sound of trumpets and drums. The Captain wonders what is happening.
A MESSENGER	At that moment, a messenger rushes on who tells of the death of Oreste, King of Sparta, killed by the hand of his brother Alidoro, who, after killing him, presented the head of Oreste to Althea, and she, enraged, killed Alidoro with the same sword that killed Bramante, and cut his head from his shoulders. Then they hear again the sound of arms, of trumpets, and drums.

ORONTE SOLDIERS PAGES	At that moment, Oronte enters the city by the Gate of the Sun, with pages and lighted torches, all rejoicing at the victory; the Captain tells the King of the death of Oreste and of Alidoro by the hand of Althea. Oronte is aroused by the news.
ALTHEA	At that, Althea enters carrying the two heads, one of Oreste, the other of Alidoro. She presents them to Oronte, her uncle, who, enraged condemns her to death and has her taken away.
A SOLDIER	Then, a soldier brings news that a great army is coming against him. Oronte commands the army to regroup and wait for the attack.
PANTALONE GRATIANO PEDROLINO BURATTINO	At that moment, Pantalone, Gratiano, Pedrolino, and Burattino enter and beg pardon of Oronte, who gives them assurance one by one. At that, trumpets, discordant, sound. Then the executioner's cart, on which lies the body of Althea with the head cut off, passes and goes off. Oronte and the captain of the troops go out to gather the army to fight the coming enemy. Pantalone and Gratiano speak of the fickle turns of fortune. They hear sounds of battle and of drums and trumpets outside the city.
A MESSENGER	At that moment, a messenger enters and relates the death of Oronte, killed in battle by the enemy. Pantalone and Gratiano say that Sparta will now regain its ancient liberty. They speak of living in a republic; and thus ends the comical, pastoral, and tragical opera.

The Forty-third Day

ALVIDA *

A Royal Opera

ARGUMENT

*The King of Egypt had a very beautiful daughter named Alvida.
She was loved by Silandro, Prince of Persia. He came to the court
of Egypt in disguise, discovered himself to her, and she fell in
love with him. They were secretly married. She became pregnant
by him and told Silandro of it, whereupon he sent a secret
message to his father, the Sultan, asking him to send ambassadors
to the King of Egypt to ask for his daughter in marriage. Also, he
told his father what happened between him and Alvida. Meanwhile, a groom of the chamber, seeing the Prince go to the
Princess at night, told the King, who, finding them together, had
them thrown into prison. Then Silandro revealed himself to be the
Prince of Persia. This drove the King to greater rage and cruelty,
and he resolved to put both of them to death. The people, who
loved the Prince and Princess, were displeased at this sentence.
While things had come to this unfortunate pass, Silandro awaited
the ambassadors of his father, the Sultan. The Sultan, after hearing of his son's wishes, rejoiced and resolved to go himself to
honor his son's wedding. Learning of the coming of the Sultan,
the King of Egypt decided to put the two prisoners to death in a
forest near the royal city before he arrived. The deed was to be
done in great secrecy so that no one could warn the Sultan. That
very morning the Sultan, with a large number of horsemen, came
to the city and learned what was to take place. He, with all his
men, went to the forest. Meanwhile Alvida was freed by the very
men who were taking her to be killed, moved to compassion by
her prayers and her weeping. They promised to tell the King that
they had killed her. Silandro, with the help of a squire, freed
himself from the soldiers who were taking him to his death by
another road. Although he was badly wounded, he put them all to
rout; but those who escaped informed the King, who was so
enraged that he went off after him with a large body of soldiers
to capture and imprison him himself.*

* See Appendix p. 407.

333

The Sultan had a daughter, sister of Silandro, who, as a small child, was taken off by her nurse when she followed her husband, who had been banished for killing a man. Although she had had no news from him, she managed to find him, and the nurse and her husband eventually had come to live in that forest where the Prince and Princess were to be put to death. Here they bought a little land and a small cottage and lived the life of peasants, dressing the child as a shepherd. Every morning the girl visited a hermit, who lived a religious life of solitude, in order to learn to read and to be taught religion. For twelve years she lived under the name of Brandino. It came about that she saved her father from death, although he did not recognize her, and at the same time, fell in love with her own brother. The Kings made peace between them, Silandro found his Alvida again with her two babies, born in the forest, and with rejoicing on all sides, they married. The nurse and her husband were pardoned and afterward lived a life of happiness and contentment.

CHARACTERS IN THE PLAY

King of Egypt
Alvida, his daughter
Pantalone, attendant of Alvida

The Captain
Soldiers
Pages
Magician
Spirits

Sultan of Persia
Silandro, his son
Brandino, then his daughter at the end
Gratiano, attendant of Silandro
Durino, servant of Silandro

Captain
Soldiers

Pedrolino
Laura, his wife
Brandino, thought to be his son

Two new-born babies

A Hermit, dead

ALVIDA

Lion
Bear
Ass

A little girl, who speaks

PROPERTIES

Woods
Beautiful grotto
A large tree with a seat
Much armor
Much spoils
Long Turkish clothes
Crown
Hermit's habit
Short sword and shield
Rustic dress for Alvida
Sheepskins
Knotted club
An axe
A beautiful silver vessel
Caldron of water, rags, swaddling clothes, and fire, to bathe the babies

ACT ONE

EGYPT

ALVIDA   Alvida, Princess of Egypt, comes out of her grotto, expressing pity for those who by order of the King, her father, must die in the forest, praying heaven that she find the body of her dead Silandro. She says she is close to her time of delivery; she hears sounds of someone coming and goes into her grotto.

PEDROLINO   At that, Pedrolino enters with his ass and an axe to get wood; he ties the ass to a tree.

ALVIDA   Then, Alvida, frightened, comes out of the grotto. Pedrolino is amazed to see her emerge from the cave. She, with piteous words, begs him to go into the grotto with her, and they go in.

SILANDRO   Silandro, Prince of Persia, enters, covered with blood from wounds received while trying to save himself from those who were going to kill him. He prays heaven to let him find the body of Alvida, his dead wife. Feeling tired, he lies down under a tree.

DURINO	At that, Durino, servant of Silandro, enters with sword and buckler and weeps over the body of his Prince.
THE CAPTAIN SOLDIERS	Just then, the captain of the King of Egypt enters with soldiers, looking for Silandro. They see him and attack. Silandro with his club, and Durino with his sword and buckler, defend themselves. Finally, Silandro kills the captain, cuts off his head, and all the others flee. Then Durino binds Silandro's wounds and helps him mount the ass, and Silandro goes off. Durino, at Silandro's order, goes off with the head of the captain to take it to the King of Egypt.
ALVIDA PEDROLINO HERMIT	Alvida and Pedrolino enter carrying the dead hermit out of the grotto. Pedrolino despairs at not finding his ass. Alvida gives him her splendid clothes, asking him to bring her a rustic habit. Pedrolino says he will do that and carries the hermit off to bury him. Alvida enters the grotto to do penance for her sins.
BRANDINO LION	Brandino, that is, Hermione, daughter of the Sultan and supposed son of Pedrolino, enters, dressed in a shepherd's habit and fighting a lion.
ALVIDA	At that moment, Alvida, hearing the noise, comes running and stands to watch the fierce battle. The lion finally runs off, wounded. Alvida marvels at Brandino's valor. Brandino is amazed to see her in the grotto and from her learns of the death of the hermit and that Pedrolino has taken him off to bury him. She begs him to hasten to bring the rustic clothes, and hearing mourners coming, she enters the grotto. Brandino, weeping over the death of the hermit, his teacher, remains.
PANTALONE	Pantalone, attendant of Alvida, comes looking for her body.
GRATIANO	At that, Gratiano, attendant of Silandro, comes looking for the body of his lord. He speaks to Pantalone of the cruelty of the King of Egypt.
PEDROLINO LAURA	At that moment, Pedrolino enters with his wife, Laura, who brings a dress and a wicker basket with food in it for Alvida. Pantalone and Gratiano try to talk to them, but being suspicious, Pedrolino and Laura enter the grotto without replying to them. Pantalone and Gratiano remain. Then they hear a noise.
DURINO SOLDIERS	Durino enters, chased by many soldiers because he has the head of their captain. Durino defends himself against them, and Pantalone and Gratiano come to his aid.
BRANDINO	At that moment, Brandino, with his club, helps Durino, and they put the soldiers to flight. Safe and victorious, Durino leaves with the others; and the first act ends.

ACT TWO

A MAGICIAN SPIRITS	A magician enters, riding on a chariot drawn by four spirits. He orders them to go and do their work, that the two kings are coming to this forest. The spirits go off shrieking. The magician speaks of his profession, predicting that they would see wondrous things that day.
PEDROLINO LAURA	At that moment, Pedrolino and Laura come out of the grotto, saying that the young girl is having labor pains. They have Alvida's clothes and are going to get all that is necessary for the delivery. The magician informs them that today they will discover their misdeeds, and Laura will be the foster mother of an abandoned girl. They marvel at this. Then the magician gives a liquid to Pedrolino, explaining that with this he will cure a great prince. They again marvel at him and go off. The magician goes off to make incantations.
DURINO PANTALONE GRATIANO	Durino enters, telling them that Silandro might still be alive—relating the first event. Pantalone leaves to find the body of Alvida; and Durino, with Gratiano, leaves for the Sultan's camp.
ALVIDA	Alvida comes out of the grotto, saying that the time of delivery is near. She laments her sad state.
A BOY	At that moment, a boy enters astride a bear and leading a lion on a leash. He comforts Alvida, presenting her with a liquid, saying that he will send a very wise man to help her and she is to drink the liquid before delivery. Alvida kisses the boy, who leaves as he came; and she, rejoicing, goes back into the grotto.
PEDROLINO LAURA	Pedrolino and Laura enter with a caldron, water, wood, fire, rags, and other things for the woman's delivery, saying that they have healed the cavalier with the magician's liquid.
ALVIDA	At that moment, Alvida, within the grotto, screams from her labor pains, and they hurry into the grotto.
BRANDINO SILANDRO	Brandino enters with Silandro, healed by Pedrolino. Silandro thanks Brandino, who tries to discover who he is, but Silandro leaves without answering. Brandino discourses on his love for the cavalier who did not want to tell him who he was.
DURINO	At that, Durino enters asking after the cavalier. Brandino offers to tell him where he is if Durino will tell him who the cavalier is. Durino then relates the story of Silandro, which grieves Brandino; she shows him the path to her cottage, saying that the

cavalier is healed of his wounds. Durino is happy and goes. She leaves sorrowfully.

PEDROLINO	Pedrolino enters with a baby in his arms, crying, "It's a boy! It's a boy!"
LAURA	Laura enters with another baby, saying the same thing.
BEAR LION	At that moment, a bear and a lion arrive and catch between them Pedrolino and Laura, who are frightened; however, the wild animals lift themselves to reveal their teats filled with milk, showing signs of gentleness and of wanting to give milk. Pedrolino and Laura attach the babies to the teats of the pitying animals.
KING OF EGYPT SOLDIERS	At that, the King of Egypt enters, sees the wild animals and demands to know whose babies those are. Pedrolino replies that they are those of a hermit woman who stays in the grotto. The King tries to enter to see her, but the wild animals attack him and keep him from going in. Frightened, the King flees with all his men. Then the bear takes its child in its mouth and goes off; the lion also takes hers and goes off. Pedrolino and Laura determine to follow the wild animals to see where they take the babies. They go off after them; and the second act ends.

ACT THREE

SULTAN CAPTAIN SOLDIERS GRATIANO	The Sultan of Persia appears with all his men, looking for his son Silandro in the forest. He is accompanied by Gratiano. They are awaiting the arrival of a shepherd boy.
DURINO	Instead, Durino, servant of Silandro, arrives and gives the Sultan news that his son is alive and well. The Sultan rejoices and goes off with them to find him.
ALVIDA	Alvida enters, lamenting because her babies were taken away; she praises the liquid which the magician sent, without which she would have died.
PANTALONE	At that moment, Pantalone arrives, sees Alvida, marvels at her, and rejoices; hearing a great tumult, he runs into the grotto with Alvida.
BRANDINO	Brandino enters, saying she cannot live without the cavalier, and as she, being a commoner, cannot have him, she weeps with despair.

THE MAGICIAN	At that moment, the magician enters, comforts Brandino, and gives him a sword and buckler, saying that with these arms he must free his father from death. Then he goes, leaving Brandino astonished.
PEDROLINO	Then, Pedrolino enters, grieving for the loss of the babies, sees Brandino with arms, and asks him what he plans to do, and who gave them to him. Brandino tells him all, saying that she loves the cavalier whose wounds he cured. Pedrolino is suspicious of this marvel; then they hear the noise of arms.
SILANDRO SOLDIERS	Silandro enters, fighting with the soldiers of the King of Egypt. Brandino fights beside Silandro; Pedrolino does the same. They rout all the soldiers. Silandro marvels at the valor of Brandino. Pedrolino leads them toward his cottage offstage, and they go off.
THE KING OF EGYPT SOLDIERS	The King of Egypt, tired after so much traveling and fighting, says he wants to rest; he orders a guard to stand watch while he sleeps in the middle of the scene.
LION BEAR	At that moment, a lion and a bear enter with the babies in their mouths; the guard, frightened, runs away. The wild beasts place themselves and the babies on each side of the King.
ALVIDA PANTALONE	At that, Alvida enters with Pantalone, who is telling her that Silandro is alive. She sees the King asleep and the babies held by the wild animals. She is very frightened. Finally they kneel, one on each side of the King, whose wrath they fear, and weep for the poor babies. He is awakened by their weeping and sees Alvida and Pantalone, who speaks in their defense. The enraged King draws his sword to kill Alvida, but the wild animals leap on him.
SILANDRO	At that moment, Silandro, armed, enters and drives away the wild animals, frees the King, and embraces Alvida. Then they kneel before the King, begging his forgiveness. Overcome by love and pity, he forgives all and embraces them. Then the King picks up the babies and kisses them.
PEDROLINO	At that, Pedrolino, who has seen all, enters and kneels before the King and begs that they all go into his cottage to see what grace is to be offered. They go.
BRANDINO LAURA	Brandino enters and reveals to Laura her love for the cavalier. Then they hear the sound of an army, trumpets, and drums.
THE SULTAN SOLDIERS	The Sultan enters, fighting with the soldiers of the King of Egypt. The soldiers of the King of Egypt attack the Sultan, and they overwhelm and capture him. The soldiers are about to kill the Sultan when Brandino intervenes, fighting with sword and shield,

and saves the life of the Sultan, his father, who does not recognize him. The Sultan thanks the young shepherd, then asks who gave him those arms. Brandino tells him, and the Sultan is amazed. Then the Sultan orders all to bow to the young shepherd who saved his life. All bow, and then Brandino leaves.

SILANDRO
ALVIDA
KING OF EGYPT
SOLDIERS

Silandro enters, sees the Sultan, his father, and begs him to be reconciled to the King of Egypt, his wife's father. His father agrees, embraces the King of Egypt, and makes peace.

THE MAGICIAN
BRANDINO
PEDROLINO
LAURA

At that moment, the magician enters and bows before the King of Egypt. He declares he is the King's ancient minister of religion who worked many strange manifestations in his court. He went to the woods to find a remedy for all sickness, and here he still practices his magic, only to help and not to hurt others, and that on this day, with his potions, he healed Silandro of his wounds and saved Alvida during her delivery. He it is who gave the sword and shield to the young shepherd, who is not Brandino, as everyone thinks, the son of the peasant, but is Hermione, daughter of the Sultan and sister of Silandro. She was, the magician explains, taken off by Laura, her nurse, who followed Pedrolino, her husband, when he was banished from the city and came with him to live in the forest; also, he, the magician, has served everyone and even sent the wild animals to feed the children of Alvida and Silandro. He begs the King and the Sultan to forgive the nurse and her husband, which they do, and all become reconciled. Pedrolino and Laura bow before the Sultan, who says that to settle all problems, they will have to find a husband for Hermione. The magician announces that he has provided for this by his art and soon she will be royally attended. At once they hear the sound of a trumpet.

A MESSENGER

At that moment, a messenger brings the news that a great personage comes to speak to the King of Egypt; they send an emissary to meet him. Then all wait. Then again trumpets and drums sound.

THE AMBASSADOR

The ambassador of the King of Armenia enters and greets the King of Egypt, shows him his credentials, then asks for Alvida, in the name of his King, for wife. The King says he has already married her; then he turns to the Sultan and asks permission to marry Hermione to the King of Armenia in place of Alvida. The Sultan consents. The magician informs them that this is the husband provided by him through his art, offering to go himself to arrange the marriage contract. Thus all ends in accord, and they go to the city; and the royal opera ends.

The Forty-fourth Day

ROSALBA, ENCHANTRESS *

An Heroic Opera

ARGUMENT

*There lived on an island in the Aegean Sea a very famous
magician named Artano. He was lord of the Happy Island and
had a daughter named Rosalba who, like her father, practiced
magic. He had also a child of four named Hyacinth. The magician had an ancient enemy, another famous magician named
Arimaspo, who was lord of the Green Isle. His enemy killed him
and took away his child, whom he brought up until the age of
ten. As Hyacinth was very beautiful, Arimaspo wanted him to
see, by way of his art, that which was to be; thus Hyacinth saw
and understood that he would be the means of reconciliation
between Arimaspo and Rosalba, daughter of the murdered Artano. Whereupon, he brought it about that he would by chance be
brought to the court of the magician Rosalba, mistress of the
Happy Isle. In her court he was reared by his sister, who did not
know he was her brother but loved him dearly. She was likewise
loved by him. There was near the island another, larger and
richer, on which lived a lord, one Alicandro, Prince of the Isle of
the Sun. This prince had a daughter named Nerina who, at that
time, fell into such a deep melancholy state that no remedy could
be found to cure her. Having recourse to the magician Arimaspo
for a remedy and advice, he received the reply that he would have
no joy in his child if he did not send her to spend some time at
the court of Rosalba. Pleased with the advice, Alicandro told his
daughter and she was very happy at the prospect of being in the
company of the magician, her dear friend. Her father sent her with
beautiful companions to her friend Rosalba, having first informed
Rosalba by one of his jesters of Nerina's coming. Almonio, son of
the magician Arimaspo, loved Princess Nerina. Although he was
a courageous knight, she did not return his love but hated him as
a deadly enemy. Almonio, upon discovering that the lady he
loved had gone to the court of the magician Rosalba, his enemy,*

* See Appendix p. 408.

*resolved, regardless of the danger, to go in disguise with one
of his servants. And thus he did. His enemy the magician no
sooner laid eyes on him than she fell in love with him. With her
father's magic and by her commands, she made him leave off
loving Nerina and become inflamed with love for herself. After
many wonderful adventures, he revealed his identity and became
the friend and husband of his enemy; and Nerina, as soon as she
came to the Happy Isle, fell in love with Hyacinth, and discovering him to be the brother of Rosalba, married him. Thus, with
the help of Arimaspo's art, the lord of the Island of the Sun came,
with Prince Almonio, to celebrate both weddings.*

CHARACTERS IN THE PLAY

Rosalba, Magician and Mistress of the Happy Island
Hyacinth, her lover, then her brother
Ormonte, Captain of the Guard
Gratiano, Majordomo

Alicandro, Prince of the Island of the Sun
Nerina, his daughter
Pratilda, waiting maid
Burattino, his servant

Arimaspo, Magician, lord of the Green Island
Almonio, his son
Pedrolino, his servant

Arlecchino, servant of Nerina

Minister of the fire of truth
Servants

Shepherd musicians
Four spirits
Four nymphs
Four dwarfs

PROPERTIES

A beautiful Genoese chair
A silver vase with fire
Hot water
Four outfits for spirits
Four beautiful outfits for nymphs

A beautiful little book for Arlecchino
Nobleman's clothes for Arlecchino
Many silver vessels with gifts inside
A dummy full of straw
A suit of Ormonte's clothes
A large cistern on stage
A secret lantern
Four white torches, lighted
Trumpets and drums

ACT ONE

THE HAPPY ISLE

ROSALBA
Rosalba, magician of the Happy Isle, tells her friends that she awaits Princess Nerina of the Island of the Sun and that she wants to greet her with the greatest of honor. She jests with Ormonte, her captain, because she knows that he is in love with Pratilda, her chamber maid. Then turning to Hyacinth, she asks him the reason for his pensiveness. He replies that it is because she caresses Arlecchino so much. She smiles at that, saying that he shows he has a fine wit, and she does not know how to defend this new love, but she knows what she is doing and understands his secret glances. She is amazed that in such a noble soul such a strange thought should appear. Then she sends Ormonte, her captain, to call Arlecchino.

ORMONTE
ARLECCHINO
Ormonte enters with Arlecchino, nobly dressed. Rosalba caresses the jester as if he were her lover; then she gives him a little book of magic so that he might have whatever he wishes. She leaves Ormonte on guard and goes off with her court.

HYACINTH
Hyacinth, having seen from hiding how Rosalba treated Arlecchino, is dumbfounded and leaves. Ormonte tells Arlecchino he is a spirit imprisoned by the magician in that body. Arlecchino begins to be frightened, opens his mouth, and calls for help.

SPIRITS
At that moment, spirits infernal come forth screaming, "Command us! Command us!" Arlecchino tells them to beat Captain Ormonte. The spirits beat him; then they ask the jester if he wishes to give other commands. Arlecchino instructs them to bring him a beautiful sedan chair and to appear in comely and gentle form. The spirits go. Chastened, Ormonte humbles himself before Arlecchino.

NYMPHS
At that moment, nymphs enter with the sedan chair; Arlecchino steps into it and sits down, ordering Ormonte to go before as he has them take him off.

ALMONIO
Almonio, son of Arimaspo the magician, lord of the Green Island, enters. He is following Princess Nerina, who is coming to the Happy Island, because he is in love with her, even though it is dangerous for him to be there since his father killed the father of Rosalba, the magician. Pedrolino reminds him of the danger, but he retorts that he is not concerned about danger.

ROSALBA
GRATIANO
PAGES
At that moment, Rosalba, the magician, sees Almonio and immediately falls in love with him. She asks him who he is, and he answers that he is an adventurous knight. She takes him with her to the gate to welcome Princess Nerina, and they go off. Pedrolino remains, afraid for his lord.

ARLECCHINO
At that moment, Arlecchino enters, being carried by the nymphs in his sedan chair. He recognizes Pedrolino, who tells him that his lord, Almonio, has come after Nerina, whom he loves, begging him not to reveal it. Arlecchino promises. At that, trumpets sound within. Arlecchino, to discover the reason, opens his little book.

SPIRITS
At once, spirits come out, saying, "Command us! Command us!" Arlecchino, the jester, commands them to send him the most beautiful nymphs, with the most beautiful gifts to present to Princess Nerina. The spirits leave, then immediately return.

NYMPHS
Nymphs enter, carrying beautiful gifts. Arlecchino takes them from each. At that moment, trumpets and drums within sound the arrival of Nerina.

ROSALBA
NERINA
ORMONTE
PRATILDA
HYACINTH
BURATTINO
ALMONIO
PAGES
Then, Rosalba, the magician, arrives, leading Nerina by the hand. Arlecchino immediately gives the presents to the Princess. Then he becomes jealous of Ormonte, who gazes longingly at Pratilda, his love, who shows only contempt for him. Rosalba tells Nerina that she will send Arlecchino, whom she has deprived of his dear liberty, as her ambassador. Nerina gazes longingly at Hyacinth, and with amorous gestures, all go into the palace. Trumpets and drums sound for joy; and the first act ends.

ACT TWO

ROSALBA
NERINA
PRATILDA
Rosalba learns from Nerina that her troublesome melancholy has ceased ever since she arrived at Rosalba's court. Rosalba promises all the help of her magic and in jest tells her that Arlecchino is

her lover. Pratilda laughs, and Rosalba tells her to attend to her love for Ormonte, her captain.

HYACINTH
ALMONIO
ORMONTE

At that moment, Hyacinth, Almonio, and Ormonte arrive and greet the ladies. Rosalba again asks Almonio about himself and wonders if he is in love. Almonio replies that he is a knight of little merit and of poor fortune in love. He relates his story of what has happened to his lady love without naming her. Rosalba is moved by his feeling. Nerina asks Hyacinth about himself; he tells her of his love for Rosalba, and she is moved by his feeling. Ormonte expresses his love for Pratilda.

ARLECCHINO
PEDROLINO
BURATTINO

At that moment, Arlecchino arrives, and on being told that Ormonte loves Pratilda, his beloved, he is disgusted. Rosalba asks Almonio for his servant Pedrolino. Graciously he gives him to her, and she, in return, gives him Burattino. Then, fondling Arlecchino lasciviously, she reminds him to open his little book, which he does.

SHEPHERDS

At that, shepherds enter, playing on different instruments. Arlecchino takes Pratilda by the hand, whereupon Rosalba becomes more jealous of Arlecchino. Ormonte immediately removes Arlecchino's hand. Hyacinth takes Nerina. Almonio is scornful of him, but Rosalba cautions him not to be scornful because there are women who would dearly love to be the favorite of Hyacinth. Almonio, still scornful, leaves. Rosalba again asks Pedrolino about his lord. He says he knows him only as a servant and leaves. Rosalba, after discoursing on her love for Almonio, conjures demons to find out who he is.

A SPIRIT

At that moment, a spirit appears who informs his mistress that she cannot know about her knight if he does not choose to tell her about himself, that she runs the risk of death; but as she herself recovers, a lost treasure would also be recovered which would bring consolation to the Happy Island. Rosalba then wants to know why Nerina suffers. The spirit replies that she is in love with Hyacinth and departs. Rosalba is scornful of her art because it cannot tell her about Pedrolino's lord, and she goes off.

ARLECCHINO
PEDROLINO
BURATTINO

Arlecchino, Pedrolino, and Burattino enter. Having become jealous of Captain Ormonte, Arlecchino plots with the others to kill Ormonte and throw him into the cistern.

ORMONTE

At that moment, Ormonte arrives. Arlecchino proposes to him that at the second hour of night he be seated on the cistern, for he has some important things to talk over with him. Ormonte agrees to wait for him there and sends Arlecchino with Burattino to the Princess, and they leave. Pedrolino reveals to Ormonte the betrayal that Arlecchino has planned. They decide to put a dummy in his place. Then Ormonte leaves. Pedrolino remains. At that moment he sees Almonio and others coming.

HYACINTH NERINA PRATILDA ALMONIO	Hyacinth, Nerina, and Pratilda are about to arrive, but before them comes Almonio, who is jealous of Hyacinth because of his love for Nerina. He complains about Love. Pedrolino tells him he thinks Rosalba is in love with him; then, seeing people approach, they withdraw.
HYACINTH NERINA PRATILDA	Hyacinth, Nerina, and Pratilda enter. Nerina again asks Hyacinth about himself; he replies that as a small child he was brought to the magician Rosalba, and he relates the story as it is told in the Argument. Nerina reveals that she is in love with him, promising to be his forever when he knows his lineage. Then night falls among the lovers.
NIGHT	
ROSALBA	At that moment, Rosalba, having heard all, with her magic frees Hyacinth of her love and gives him to Nerina; then she turns to Almonio, and smiling, advises him to bear with patience the blows of fortune.
ARLECCHINO	Just then, Arlecchino arrives. Rosalba is contemptuous of him because he comes up close to the Princess. Then she instructs him to have light brought to that place, as it is dark. Arlecchino opens the book.
DWARFS	At that moment, dwarfs enter with four lighted torches and immediately there can be heard within the palace the music of many instruments. On hearing the music, and accompanied by the Dwarfs with their lights, they all go into the palace.
ORMONTE PEDROLINO	Ormonte enters with the dummy dressed in his clothes. He and Pedrolino place the dummy upon the cistern; then Ormonte hides behind it to make responses.
ARLECCHINO BURATTINO	At that moment, Arlecchino arrives, sees the dummy, and thinking it to be Ormonte, he and Burattino throw it into the cistern. Arlecchino then says he will enjoy the favors of Pratilda that night without her suspecting. He opens his book.
SPIRITS	At that, spirits appear and ask to be commanded. Arlecchino commands them to bring Pratilda to him. They go to fetch her.
PRATILDA	Pratilda is brought in by the spirits, and Arlecchino tries to embrace her.
ORMONTE	At that moment, Ormonte, pretending to be a spirit, takes Pratilda in his arms and carries her off. Arlecchino and Burattino,

frightened, flee. Pedrolino, laughing, goes to find Ormonte; and the second act ends.

ACT THREE

DAWN

ARIMASPO SPIRITS	Arimaspo, the magician, says it is the last day of his travail; he sends the spirits for Pedrolino while he remains.
PEDROLINO	At that moment, Pedrolino is carried in by the spirits. Arimaspo gives him a letter to bring to his son Almonio. Then he leaves. Pedrolino says he is afraid of his master the magician.
ROSALBA NERINA	Then, Rosalba, the magician, draws out of Nerina that she is in love with Hyacinth. Rosalba tells Nerina that she wants to find a way through her art to make him Nerina's husband, but she has not been able to discover who he is.
HYACINTH ALMONIO ARLECCHINO BURATTINO	At that, Hyacinth, Almonio, Arlecchino, and Burattino enter and greet the ladies. Rosalba asks Nerina to concur in whatever she says to make sport with Arlecchino—from whom she has removed the power of the book of magic. She shows herself to be very angry with him for having killed Ormonte, her captain. All protest they know nothing about it. Rosalba answers that she could find out the murderer by her art, but she wants each to swear upon the fire of truth. Arlecchino, afraid, opens the book to save himself, but no spirits appear, because the book no longer contains its singular power.
MINISTER SERVANTS	At that moment, the minister enters with a silver vase in which is the fire of truth. Rosalba makes each swear in turn as she touches them and finally touches Arlecchino to swear. She first makes him wash his hands—the water must be very hot—then swearing and putting his hands over the fire, he burns himself.
ORMONTE	Then, Ormonte, pretending to be a spirit, enters and says that Arlecchino killed him. Arlecchino and Burattino are frightened and run away. Ormonte chases after them, much to the amusement of all.
PEDROLINO	At that, Pedrolino arrives, laughing about Arlecchino. Rosalba again gives up Hyacinth to Nerina, saying that she may have her love because of the little wit he showed in thinking that she could be in love with Arlecchino; and on this day Hyacinth will learn his parentage.

ORMONTE PRATILDA	At that moment, Ormonte enters with Pratilda. Rosalba orders them to go to the temple, because they are to be made man and wife. All leave except Pedrolino, Almonio, and Rosalba. Rosalba sends Pedrolino away; then she reveals her love for Almonio, begging him to tell her who he is and whom he loves.
SPIRITS	As Almonio is about to tell her, spirits arrive, sent by Arimaspo. They take Almonio and carry him off. Rosalba falls into great despair; with an iron sword she is about to kill herself.
ARIMASPO	At that moment, Arimaspo, the magician, enters disguised as a woman, holds her, and consoles her, and putting her under a spell, makes her sit upon a chair. Rosalba immediately begins to laugh and to sing. Arimaspo leaves, and she remains under the spell, laughing and singing. Then a great noise is heard.
ORMONTE HYACINTH ALMONIO NERINA PRATILDA	Ormonte, Hyacinth, Almonio, Nerina, and Pratilda enter, all frightened and fleeing from the flame which pursues them. They see Rosalba singing and laughing and nearly out of her senses. They stand in wonder at her, and standing thus, they begin to dance.
PEDROLINO	At that moment, Pedrolino arrives and also begins to dance.
ARLECCHINO BURATTINO	Then, Arlecchino and Burattino come, and they too begin to dance; then they all hear trumpets and drums and stop dancing to form a circle on the stage and stand still as if enchanted.
ARIMASPO ALICANDRO ALMONIO PAGES	At that moment, Arimaspo, the magician, arrives with Alicandro, Prince of the Island of the Sun and father of Nerina. Arimaspo shows him his daughter, saying that they are under his spell. Alicandro begs him to undo the spell, and he does so. Then Arimaspo begs Rosalba to forgive him for the death of her father Artano, revealing that Hyacinth is her brother. She forgives him. Then Hyacinth marries Nerina; Almonio, Rosalba; and Ormonte, Pratilda; and all rejoicing, they go into the palace. Trumpets sound for joy.

THE INNOCENT PERSIAN

A Royal Opera

ARGUMENT

There was a certain Artabano, King of Persia, whose queen had twins, a boy and a girl. The boy was named Virbio, and the girl Teodora. It happened that while the King was vacationing at one of his seaside resorts, his son was kidnapped by a pirate named Dolone, taken on a ship, and carried off. The King, his father, was not able to get him back. After the death of Dolone, the child was abducted by a pirate named Alfeo. Alfeo took off the boy's pretty suit, and because of his beauty, put him in girl's clothes, and all thought him to be a girl. When the boy was about sixteen, Alfeo decided to send him as a gift to the King of Egypt, solely for the great price he would get in return. Therefore, he put the boy in the care of Arbante, his nephew, to take him safely to the King. With him he sent a servant who had been taken with Virbio and who was the son of the nurse who raised him. The servant would not reveal the identity of Virbio, who was raised by Alfeo to the servant's satisfaction and taken with him. It happened that on their voyage, Arbante, thinking Virbio a woman, fell in love with him, and when they arrived in Persia, tried to ravish him. When the servants of the King and the soldiers who accompanied him saw this, they tried to stop him, and while they fought, the sister, Teodora, arrived as an unknown knight, drew her sword, put all to flight, rescued Virbio, and took him away with her. Artabano, King of Persia, had driven away the nurse and attendant of his lost son and had made his daughter Teodora, ever since she was a small child, dress always as a boy and a knight; thus she had learned the art of war, in which she became a most courageous fighter. She came to be loved by Oronte, Duke of Persia, who made known his love through a third party. As a warrior, Teodora's thoughts were far from love, and she gave it no ear. The Duke, however, was determined to win by trickery what he could not win by love. He bribed a chambermaid to let him into her room at night. When he came, he was heard by Teodora and caught. She spared his life, and feeling wronged and scorned by her, he went away. Afterwards, in a short time, his love turned to hate. Then with the help of the same chambermaid and of one of his faithful servants, he made the King believe that his daughter Teodora was lying with a man by having him observe his servant climb down from Teodora's window at night. King Artabano had his daughter thrown in prison, and according to the ancient law of Persia, he gave her a certain time to live, within which time a knight would have to appear to defend her and fight her accuser. But because Duke Oronte was the strongest warrior in the kingdom of Persia, no one wanted to do battle with him. Meanwhile, when she saw the time assigned by her father passing away, she begged him as a favor to let her fight him herself to prove her innocence against the accuser. Oronte refused to agree to this; instead, he sent a chambermaid with a letter which said that if she agreed, he would find a way to get her father to pardon her. Teodora, with the help of the chambermaid, fled from prison; and from the kin of the maid, she gained possession of weapons with which to arm herself. Still holding onto the letter written by Oronte and taking the maid along with her, she freed her brother from the pirates and from the hands of his own father, who, not knowing him, was going to kill him. Teodora was found to be innocent, and Oronte, a traitor. She became the wife of Prince Adrasto of Egypt, who fell in love with her because of her fame and who risked great danger crossing the sea to find her.

CHARACTERS IN THE PLAY

Artabano, King of Persia
Teodora, daughter of the King
Lady of honor
Pages

Oronte, Duke of Persia

Counselor of the King
Court
Soldier, who speaks

Adrasto, Prince of Egypt
Burattino, his servant

Lioneo, merchant of Egypt
Many Egyptian passengers

Pasquella, nurse
Pedrolino, her husband
[A Soldier, their son]

Arbante, nephew of Alfeo
Persian soldiers
Virbio, in woman's clothes and thought by all to be a
    woman, then finally the Prince of Persia

A knight, who speaks
Many soldiers

PROPERTIES FOR THE ROYAL OPERA

Beautiful armor with helmets for three knights
Food
Persian clothes for a woman
Many Persian costumes for the entire cast
Trumpets
Drums
Writing paper

ACT ONE

A FOREST IN
PERSIA

LIONEO
BURATTINO
PASSENGERS

Lioneo, a merchant of Egypt with many Egyptian passengers, and Burattino, servant of Adrasto, Prince of Egypt, have escaped the peril of the sea. The passengers all take their leave. Burattino wants to stay with Lioneo because he has lost his lord in the storm, believing he saw him drown. They call at a cottage to ask for something to eat.

PASQUELLA
PEDROLINO

Pasquella and Pedrolino come out to see the poor wretches saved from the angry sea; they embrace them and prepare them a rustic meal; while they eat and while Lioneo recounts the shipwreck, Pedrolino recognizes Burattino as his brother. They rejoice at their reunion. Pedrolino offers to accompany Lioneo on the road to the city, and they go off. Pasquella and Burattino go back into the cottage.

ARTABANO
DUKE ORONTE
PAGES

Artabano, King of Persia, enters, angry at the flight of Teodora, his daughter, who escaped from prison. Oronte consoles him. The King declares they must reinforce the laws and that he is going to the oracle to learn what the gods have to say, and he goes.

ARBANTE
VIRBIO
PIRATES

Arbante, nephew of Alfeo, enters with Virbio, who is thought to be a woman. They were ordered to go by way of the river to take Virbio to the King of Egypt for a large ransom. Virbio had been given to Alfeo by Dolone, the pirate, who died when Virbio was a small child. Being in love with Virbio because he thinks he is a maid, Arbante tries to rape him, and as he does violence to him, Virbio cries out. The pirates come to his aid and turn on Arbante with swords drawn.

TEODORA   As they fight, Teodora arrives, armed as a knight. Virbio calls to her for help. With sword and shield she scatters them and puts them all to flight. Then, alone with Virbio, she asks the reason for all the fighting. Virbio, without revealing that he is a man, recounts the attempts of Arbante to ravish him and says he is being taken to the King of Egypt. He thanks the knight for helping him and offers him whatever is in his power to give.

PEDROLINO   At that, Pedrolino arrives and greets the two, whom he does not recognize. Teodora asks for lodging for the two of them so that they might rest. Pedrolino agrees to find them a place and calls at the cottage.

BURATTINO   Burattino comes out, and seeing Virbio, thinks him to be a damsel, and Teodora, his lover.

PASQUELLA   He calls Pasquella, who comes out, embraces Virbio, and receives him from the knight as a woman. Then Teodora takes Burattino with her to talk over some things. Pedrolino, Pasquella, and Virbio remain. Pasquella looks at Virbio and begins to weep. Virbio asks why she is weeping. She answers that his face is very like that of her lord, who was abducted as a small child. Virbio consoles her and they go into the cottage.

ADRASTO   Adrasto, Prince of Egypt, enters in his nightshirt, soaking wet from having saved himself from the shipwreck. He laments his misfortune at sea, for he lost Burattino, his servant; his arms; and his shield on which was depicted the image of Teodora, the Princess of Persia, whom he has fallen in love with through her fame, and for whom he left his kingdom.

PEDROLINO   At that, Pedrolino, who has heard part of his lament, enters, and talking to him, learns that he escaped from the shipwreck. Pedrolino consoles him, informing him that he is in the forest of Persia and near the city. Adrasto rejoices at this and asks for his help. Pedrolino calls at the cottage.

PASQUELLA   Pasquella comes and marvels together with Virbio to see a knight
VIRBIO   in such a wretched state. Virbio asks from what shipwreck the knight has come. He says he is not an ordinary knight. Virbio sighs.

TEODORA
BURATTINO
WAITING MAID

At that moment, Teodora enters with her faithful waiting maid, who brings her clothes. She is amazed to see the man so beaten about by the sea. Burattino, with rejoicing, recognizes his lord, who secretly commands him not to give him away. Teodora removes her helmet to cool her face. Adrasto, looking at her, sighs and falls into Teodora's arms; all pick him up and take him into the cottage to revive him, blaming the hardship of the sea for his condition; and the first act ends.

ACT TWO

TEODORA
BURATTINO

Teodora enters, asking Burattino to reveal the identity of his lord. Burattino says he is a great prince who fell in love with a princess because of her fame, and left his kingdom because of her, but he may not reveal the name of the one or the other. Teodora sends him to suggest that they dress Virbio in her clothes. Then remaining alone, she discourses on her being in love with the unknown knight and hints that she is a woman.

VIRBIO
ADRASTO
WAITING MAID
PEDROLINO

At that moment, Virbio enters, dressed in Teodora's clothes. Adrasto tells them that if he had arms he would accompany them, and if they wish, he could guide them even as he is, in his nightshirt. Teodora thanks him, asking him to wait there. She hopes soon to send him arms and the spoils of the greatest enemy she has, and, parting, says, "Wait, oh knight, for I go to avenge the innocence of the Princess of Persia," and she goes. Adrasto, suddenly angry, asks if they have heard anything of the Princess of Persia. They reply that they have heard nothing, and Adrasto leaves, despairing. Pedrolino asks Burattino who his lord is. Burattino tells him who he is and that he had come with him to that court because he knew he had a brother. Pedrolino begins to weep; then, when asked the reason, he tells the story of Virbio, who was abducted by pirates as a small child. Pasquella, his wife, was Virbio's nurse, and because of the abduction, they were driven away by Artabano, King of Persia. Then they had come to live in these woods and now make their living by selling wood and fuel. They go into the house.

KING ARTABANO
DUKE ORONTE
COURT

King Artabano enters, angry at the reply of the oracle. He commands the wisest sages of Persia be brought together to interpret the words of the oracle, which gave the following verse:

With the death of the culprit faithful in name
The truth will be known, your child will have fame.

Artabano then asks Oronte why he is thus armed out of his usual fashion. Oronte says he was frightened by a dream he had, and for that reason he is armed.

TEODORA
VIRBIO
WAITING MAID

At that moment, Teodora enters, armed as a knight with her visor over her face, leading Virbio, dressed in Teodora's clothes, and her waiting maid. She has them stand apart; then approaching King Artabano, she announces that she appears to defend the innocence of Teodora, whom she has with her, and to prove Oronte a traitor to his king. Oronte accepts the challenge, sends for the rest of his forces and plans to appear as he sees fit. The King, however, commands him to fight immediately and orders the soldiers to appear and seize Teodora when she is brought in by the knight. Then they go off. Teodora is left alone with Virbio. She reveals herself to be Teodora and asks him to bear patiently, for love of her, this inconvenience. Virbio is about to reveal that he is a man when they are interrupted by the sound of trumpets and drums.

DUKE ORONTE
SOLDIERS

At that, Duke Oronte returns armed, and immediately they are locked in battle. The Duke falls to the ground at the first exchange. Immediately all the soldiers come between them, and some seize Virbio, thinking he is Teodora. The waiting maid flees. Teodora goes off and they lead Virbio away, thinking he is the Princess.

PEDROLINO
BURATTINO

Pedrolino enters, telling Burattino that his lord appears to be possessed.

WAITING MAID

At that moment, a waiting maid comes running and shouting for help.

A KNIGHT

A knight comes chasing after her. She kneels before him and begs to be spared.

ADRASTO

At that, Adrasto enters with a big stick, beats the knight over the head, and knocks him to the ground. All jump on him and take him into the cottage to learn from him and the waiting maid the reason for the tumult.

TEODORA

Teodora enters, grieving at the capture of Virbio and at the little valor she showed because she did not have the courage to oppose the unknown knight. She removes her helmet, lamenting her bad fortune.

ADRASTO

At that, Adrasto enters, in despair at having heard from the knight and the waiting maid of Teodora's imprisonment. He vows he wants to go even thus unarmed to avenge her. She hears him out, then asks him who he is. Adrasto tells her, then asks the knight to tell him about himself. Teodora relates her story, of the betrayal of Oronte, and of the capture of the waiting maid. Adrasto kneels before her, swearing that because of her fame, he fell in love with her, left his kingdom to seek her, and thus made this long journey. Teodora raises him up and promises to be his when she returns to the good graces of her father.

BURATTINO
KNIGHT

At that moment, Burattino enters with the strange knight, from whom he has taken all arms. Teodora commands the knight to tell the King, her father, that she was the unknown knight who did battle with Oronte and soon she would make known her innocence. The knight leaves. They remain.

PASQUELLA
WAITING MAID
PEDROLINO

Then, Pasquella enters, and having recognized Teodora, falls to her knees before her, revealing that she is her brother Virbio's nurse, driven away by the King, her father, together with Pedrolino, her husband. Teodora promises to have them pardoned when she returns with her father, and they go in to make preparations in the cottage; and the second act ends.

ACT THREE

KING ARTABANO
COUNSELOR
COURT

King Artabano enters, angry at his daughter, and orders that she be brought before him to be condemned to the stake. The servants go to fetch her. The counselor reminds the King of what the oracle said and advises him to be prudent in all he does.

VIRBIO
SERVANTS

At that moment, Virbio is brought in by the servants of the King. He, seeing himself in great danger, reveals himself to be a man, explaining that the knight who accompanied him was Teodora, the King's daughter, and that Oronte is a traitor. Furthermore, the King is failing in his kingly duties by allowing this affront of Oronte's. Artabano, scornful, orders that he be burned immediately and has him taken away. Then he issues a new proclamation for the capture of Teodora. Again the counselor reminds him of the words of the oracle and that Teodora could not be guilty, having come in person to defend her innocence. Artabano, angered, says Teodora is guilty, and he knows very well that Oronte is true, and he goes off.

ADRASTO
TEODORA
BURATTINO

Adrasto enters, armed with the weapons of the knight whom he captured, saying he is going to the city to challenge Oronte and defend Teodora's innocence. Teodora declares she is going to share his fortune. They send Burattino with a letter they have written to King Artabano. Burattino goes. They remain, speaking of their armies. At that moment, they hear the sound of arms and men.

SOLDIERS	Soldiers enter, armed, come to fight them. They fight off the stage, and one of them is left wounded. Adrasto, in their midst, fighting, follows them off, saying he has wounded one of them who has fallen. Teodora lifts the wounded man from the ground, and asks him the reason for the present fight.
ADRASTO	At that moment, Adrasto returns.
PEDROLINO PASQUELLA	Pedrolino and Pasquella arrive; they all hear what the wounded soldier has to say. He tells them he is one of those who set out to take Virbio to the King of Egypt and had been long before with Dolone; then he relates how he had come to blows with Arbante, nephew of Alfeo, the pirate, for having caused the loss of Virbio, thought to be a woman, but who is truly a man. Here he gives his story as it is set down in the Argument, showing by way of proof the token he has on his breast. It reveals that Virbio is the brother of Teodora. Then the wounded man faints, and Pasquella weeps over him, saying that he is her and Pedrolino's son, who had been kidnapped with Virbio. They take him into the cottage and then declare they will go to the city to rescue Teodora's brother. They go off.
VIRBIO	Virbio appears on the tower of the prison, lamenting his evil fortune.
BURATTINO	At that moment, Burattino arrives, sees him, and recognizing him, bids him to have hope.
THE GUARD	Just then, the guard of the tower appears and shouts at him. Burattino shows him the King's letter, saying he is the ambassador invited by King Artabano.
DUKE ORONTE COUNSELOR	At that moment, Duke Oronte arrives. Burattino repeats that he is the King's messenger and that he has a letter for the King. Oronte asks for the letter; then having read it, he orders that Virbio be immediately put to death. The counselor orders that, before they leave, the knight speak to the King. Oronte, angered, leaves. Burattino threatens to expose him for having read the letter meant for the King.
THE GUARD VIRBIO CONSTABLES	The guard of the tower enters with constables leading Virbio, in chains, to take him to be executed, sentenced by King Artabano. Burattino weeps over the sad case of Virbio.
ADRASTO	At that moment, Adrasto enters with Teodora, armed. They see Virbio. Immediately they draw their swords, put the assassins to flight, and free Virbio. Then they ask the counselor to tell the King that two knights request an audience of his majesty for reasons of great importance. The counselor goes in. They remain,

consoling Virbio. Teodora finally reveals herself to be his sister. They embrace and greatly rejoice.

KING ARTABANO
DUKE ORONTE
COUNSELOR
COURT

At that moment, King Artabano enters to give audience to the two knights. He sits upon the royal tribunal. This done, Adrasto presents to the King the letter which Duke Oronte sent to Teodora when, falsely accused by him, she was put in prison. Artabano reads it and through it learns of Oronte's betrayal, and, angered with him, orders that he be seized and put to death on the spot. Teodora kneels before her father, who weeps over her, makes her rise, and kisses her tenderly. Adrasto turns to the King and asks that if he found for him a treasure that had been lost, could he beg a favor of him. Artabano replies yes. Adrasto then reveals his son Virbio, kidnapped by the pirate Dolone, and then taken from the hands of Alfeo, the very famous pirate. Artabano recognizes him by his face and by the feeling in his own breast. Then turning to Adrasto, he tells him to demand that which he wants. Adrasto relates his own story, and revealing his love for Teodora, requests her for wife. Artabano gives her to him. Teodora begs the fulfillment of the promise she made to Pasquella, Virbio's nurse, and to Pedrolino, her husband. Artabano rejoices that they are alive and pardons them.

PASQUELLA
PEDROLINO

At that moment, Pasquella and Pedrolino enter the city. Teodora gives them the pardon they were granted. They kiss the King's feet. Then they say that the wounded soldier, their son, was not badly wounded and that a worthy surgeon of those woods had dressed his wound. Artabano, reminded of his anger at Oronte, repeats the sentence of death. Oronte confesses his betrayal of Teodora, blaming it on his great love for her and his wish to make her his wife. Adrasto and Teodora plead for Oronte, blaming all on Love and on his bad fortune. Virbio does the same. Artabano is satisfied and pardons him. The counselor shows the King the truth of the Oracle's reply when it said:

> With the death of the culprit faithful in name
> The truth would be known, your child would have fame.

And here, with rejoicing, they propose to celebrate the wedding of Prince Adrasto with Teodora, daughter of King Artabano; and the royal opera ends.

The Forty-sixth Day

PART I

THE BEAR

A Royal Opera

ARGUMENT

Sileno, Prince of Cyprus, while sleeping often saw in his dream a beautiful nymph. He fell madly in love with her and visited his soothsayers to learn of his future love. They urged him to go to Arcadia, saying that there he would find a young shepherd descended from the god Pan through whom he would have his wish and be freed. He crossed the sea, arrived in Arcadia, and after many adventures, found his nymph; and in the clothes of a shepherd, he found Evrilla, Princess of Passo, who was enamored of him, and he happily took her for wife.

CHARACTERS IN THE PLAY

Priest of the Temple of Pan
Dorinda, nymph and his daughter
Elpina, shepherdess
Ergasto, an old shepherd
Many young shepherds

Nymphs, companions to Dorinda
Pan, god of the wood

Sileno, Prince of Cyprus

Evrilla, Princess of Passo, also the young shepherd

Gratiano
Pedrolino
Arlecchino, servants

Slaves

The bear, a ferocious animal

358

PROPERTIES

Trumpets

ACT ONE

ARCADIA IN
PELOPONESSIA

PRIEST YOUNG SHEPHERDS	The priest of the Temple of Pan enters with many young shepherds. They act as though it is dawn and they are on the top of a mountain. He greets the dawn with a devout and brief oration. Then with the shepherds he leaves to go to the Temple to pray to the gods to free Arcadia of the cruel bear who murders flocks of sheep and herds of cattle. They all go off.
DORINDA NYMPHS	Dorinda, a nymph, enters with many other nymphs, her companions. They cross over the mountain, and playing on different instruments, singing and dancing, they go to the Temple by the same path taken by the priest, and go off.
PEDROLINO	Pedrolino, servant of the Prince of Cyprus, enters dressed as a Cypriot. He sees the nymphs and calls after them just before they disappear. He talks with Dorinda, marveling at her strange beauty, and she learns from him that he was captured in Arcadia. She thanks him for this information and, with her companions, crosses over the mountain. Pedrolino remains. At that, trumpets sound from far off. Pedrolino leaves to tell the Prince, his lord, of the beauty of Dorinda and to tell him about Arcadia. He goes off.
PRIEST ERGASTO YOUNG SHEPHERD	The priest returns from the Temple with Ergasto by another path. The old shepherd asks the priest to tell him why he is sad. The priest replies that in a dream he saw Dorinda, his daughter, being led about by a dark cloud that then submerged itself under the ground, from which grew a tree loaded with beautiful fruit. Among the fruit was one who was crowned. Afraid he might lose his daughter, he became sad and now lives in melancholy. Ergasto consoles him, interpreting the dream as a good omen for his daughter and the priest. At that, trumpets sound from afar.
EVRILLA DAMSELS	Thereupon, Evrilla, Princess of Passo, enters, pursuing Prince Sileno, of whom she is enamored. She sees the priest, bows to him, and learns from him that she is in Arcadia. Then, to his question, she answers that she is a Cypriot but does not reveal that she is a woman, as she is wearing clothes that look more like a man's than a woman's.

DORINDA

At that, Dorinda arrives alone, greets her father, then seeing Evrilla and thinking her to be a man, immediately falls in love with her. At the command of the priest, she greets her and kisses her.

GRATIANO
ARLECCHINO
SLAVES

Just then, Gratiano, master of Evrilla's household, arrives with slaves who carry the Princess' things. They see her and greet her, addressing her not as a woman, but as a man, using a masculine name with great dignity. Then they greet the priest, who receives them with courtesy. He invites them, together with their lord, to accept his hospitality. Evrilla accepts his invitation, and thus all leave for the priest's house, and the first act ends.

ACT TWO

THE PRIEST
YOUNG
SHEPHERD

The priest speaks of the beauty and bounty of the strangers who came to Arcadia and who are now lodged together. He goes to meet the others and leaves.

DORINDA

Dorinda enters and reveals to Elpina, the shepherdess, that she is in love with the young stranger. Elpina says that for her part, she has fallen in love with the servant Arlecchino.

ARLECCHINO

At that moment, Arlecchino arrives and says immediately to Elpina, "I am yours, my heart." The nymphs are so embarrassed they leave, unable to say a word. Arlecchino remains wondering.

EVRILLA
GRATIANO
SERVANTS

At that, Evrilla arrives and commands all her servants to go about the island looking for Prince Sileno. She remains with Gratiano, to whom she confides that when she saw the Prince of Cyprus leave for Arcadia, she followed him because she loved him. Gratiano wonders at that. Then trumpets sound from afar.

ARLECCHINO

Thereupon, Arlecchino enters and tells Evrilla that he has heard from a page that there are many persons on their way to Arcadia. Trumpets again sound from afar, and all leave in the direction of the trumpet sounds.

SILENO
PRIEST
PEDROLINO
SERVANTS
YOUNG
SHEPHERD

Sileno, Prince of Cyprus, enters with the priest and servants. He asks the priest who he is and if in Arcadia there is any young shepherd who is a descendant of the King Pan, god of shepherds. The priest answers that in Arcadia there is not one, but many unknown shepherds. The Prince replies that he would like to see them. The priest leaves with all his people to find them. Sileno remains with Pedrolino, whom he tells why he has come to Arcadia as it is set down in the Argument. Pedrolino says he has seen a most beautiful nymph. They decide to find her and discover if she is the one whom Sileno loves, and they leave.

DORINDA ELPINA	Dorinda and Elpina enter, embarrassed still by the words of the servant Arlecchino.
EVRILLA	At that moment, Evrilla, the Princess, in the habit of a shepherd, enters and asks the nymphs if they have seen more strangers. Dorinda says no and sends Elpina to see if there is anyone about. Dorinda remains, reveals to the young shepherd that she is in love with him, and pleads for his love. Evrilla promises to love no other nymph than her.
GRATIANO	Just then, Gratiano hurries in, out of breath, and takes Evrilla off, with the permission of the nymph. Dorinda announces she will await the return of the young shepherd. She begins to lie down, pretending to be asleep.
SILENO	At that moment, Sileno, Prince of Cyprus, sees the nymph asleep; he takes her for the nymph he saw in his dream; he praises her beauty, every part of her.
EVRILLA	At that, Evrilla, who stands aside, sees and hears all, to her great sorrow. Then Dorinda awakes, and seeing the stranger, flees in fright. Sileno, seeing the young shepherd and thinking him to be a diviner, asks him to show him how he may win the nymph. Evrilla reveals herself to be the Princess of Passo and reproaches him for the little sense he shows in loving a poor nymph, as he is a great prince. Sileno excuses himself by telling her of the power of love and she, taking that opportunity, reproaches him, saying that because of the power of love she followed him to Arcadia.
THE PRIEST DORINDA ELPINA GRATIANO PEDROLINO	Then, the priest arrives with all his train. He sees the strangers and greets them. Pedrolino, seeing Evrilla dressed as a shepherd, recognizes her, but remains silent about who she is.
ARLECCHINO	Arlecchino enters, and while all stand exchanging pleasant talk, they hear a terrible screaming and shouting of nymphs and shepherds, "Look out for the bear! Look out for the bear!"
THE BEAR	At that moment, the bear lumbers in. He stands on his feet, as a bear does, and opens his mouth, begging for something to eat. Arlecchino and Pedrolino throw him apples, and together they tame him, caressing him. But suddenly the bear flings himself upon Dorinda, takes her in his arms, and carries her off. Everyone is frightened and runs off; and the second act ends.

ACT THREE

THE PRIEST ERGASTO SHEPHERDS	The priest enters, being consoled by Ergasto for the loss of Dorinda, his daughter. The priest commands that all Arcadia arm itself to kill the voracious bear.
ELPINA	At that moment, Elpina, shepherdess, arrives weeping, having seen the bear take Dorinda into his grotto. The priest, weeping, leaves with all the shepherds. Elpina remains alone. At that, there is a noise within of many voices, shouting, "Look out for the bear!" Elpina runs off.
THE BEAR	Just then, the bear enters, pulling a bloody corpse of some animal. He comes dragging it along, passes over the stage, and goes off.
ELPINA	Elpina enters weeping, thinking that the prey is part of the body of Dorinda.
ARLECCHINO	At that, Arlecchino enters, sees Elpina weeping, and he also begins to weep.
PEDROLINO	Then, Pedrolino arrives and weeps at their weeping.
GRATIANO	Gratiano enters and also begins to weep and learns from each of them of the slaughter of Dorinda by the bear. They are determined to kill him, and all leave filled with brave defiance.
SILENO	Sileno, the Prince, enters, railing against Love and Fortune, thinking that the bear has devoured Dorinda, his love. Falling to the ground in hopeless despair, he is about to kill himself.
EVRILLA	At that moment, Evrilla enters and stops him. She tries to console him and offers to be his wife. Sileno thanks her, but declares he wants to share the sepulchre of the bear's belly with his nymph, and enraged with grief, he leaves. Evrilla determines to stop him from fighting the bear and having Sileno and Dorinda entombed together, and also enraged, she goes off.
DORINDA	Dorinda then enters, rejoicing because she has discovered happiness by becoming the wife of one who is much in love with her; however, she does not name him.
THE BEAR	At that moment, the bear arrives and tamely caresses Dorinda. She appears to caress him. Then the bear rises to his feet, embraces her, and still embracing, they go off together, apparently very happy.

THE PRIEST ERGASTO SHEPHERDS	The priest, Ergasto, and shepherds enter, armed with spears, bows and arrows, slings, and other weapons to kill the bear and avenge the death of Dorinda.
EVRILLA GRATIANO PEDROLINO ARLECCHINO	At that, Evrilla enters with a knotted club intending to fight the bear; Pedrolino recognizes her and attempts to stop her. Gratiano and Arlecchino do the same. She vows she is going to go; then she kisses all, asking that they bring the news of her death to Passo. The priest apparently talks her out of it by saying that that revenge is his alone.
SILENO	Sileno then arrives and says that it is his job, not hers. Evrilla pleads with him because of her love for Dorinda, to let her be the first to fight the bear. Sileno agrees and withdraws.
THE BEAR	At that moment, the bear comes out as if ready to fight. Evrilla confronts the bear, and fighting with him, is wounded, and the bear runs away. She, weak from the loss of blood, calls Sileno, begging him that after her death he be kind enough to offer two tears and one sigh, at which piteous words Sileno, weeping, also weakens on the bosom of Evrilla. Then, as the priest, enraged, cries out, "Death, death to the voracious beast!" those with rustic instruments call the bear to battle. At that, a very loud noise is heard within and immediately a prospect opens to view, in which can be seen the cave of Pan and the deity himself sitting in tribunal.
PAN	Pan, god of the woods and of shepherds, demands peace and silence, decreeing that the beast will not die by their hands. The gods will that Dorinda and the bear couple so that by this conjunction will eventually be born heroes and demigods, and the vision of the priest, father of Dorinda, has no other significance than this conjunction. The tree with many fruits and one crown represents the many kings who will be born from this conjunction. Then he commands that Sileno marry Evrilla, she being that young shepherd spoken of in his prophecy and whom he had Sileno see in dreams again and again, in order to bring him to Arcadia where he would learn that his blood is descended from the ancient kings of Arcadia. They are not to seek any longer after Dorinda, for she lives happily as, in his time, he will arrange for them to see. When Pan ends his speech, immediately the prospect closes. Then the priest happily arranges the wedding between Sileno and Evrilla; and rejoicing, they all go the priest's dwelling to celebrate the rites of Hymen. Thus ends the first part, after which will follow the second, and then the third, to the end.

The Forty-seventh Day

PART II

THE BEAR

A Royal Opera

ARGUMENT

Trineo, Prince of Amatunta, went to visit Sileno, Prince of Cyprus and his very good friend. While crossing the sea, he encountered the armada of the Prince of Algeria who, being in love with Levina, Princess of Crete, abducted her. After making many dangerous assaults on the armada, Trineo rescued her and took her with him. Corebo, Prince of Denmark, to whom Levina was betrothed and sent by her father with a number of vessels, on hearing the news of the rescue, left his kingdom with a large armada and by chance was guided to Arcadia. He found Levina and the Prince of Trineo there together. They made peace, and he was given the wife promised him by the King of Crete.

CHARACTERS IN THE PLAY

Bear
Lion

Dorinda, daughter of the priest

Trineo, Prince of Amatunta
Arlecchino, his servant
Servants of Trineo

Levina, Princess of Crete
Pedrolino, her servant
Althea, waiting maid of Levina

Priest, father of Dorinda
Orsella, sister of the priest

Many young shepherds
Argeo, soothsayer

Corebo, Prince of Denmark
Gratiano, servant of Corebo
Servants of Corebo

364

Pastor Tubicina

Almonio, Grand Priest of Arcadia

Two new-born babies

Priests, who draw the chariot of Almonio

ACT ONE

ARCADIA IN
PELOPONESSIA

BEAR — A bear and a lion come out of the woods fighting.
LION

DORINDA — While they are biting and clawing each other, Dorinda arrives with a large knobbed club to defend the bear. The lion runs off. The bear caresses Dorinda, who weeps because every living creature conspires to kill her husband. They hear the sound of trumpets from afar. She is afraid for her husband, and together they go off into the woods.

TRINEO — Trineo, Prince of Amatunta, enters with Levina, Princess of
LEVINA — Crete, who thanks him for freeing her from the Prince of Algeria,
ARLECCHINO — who, because he was in love with her, took her by force while she
PEDROLINO — was on her way to her husband. They rejoice at the death of the fierce barbarian, and she says that Corebo, Prince of Denmark, her husband, will remain always in his debt. Trineo tells her that a year before he left Amatunta seeking Sileno, Prince of Cyprus, his very dear friend. Levina then asks when and where she is to rest. Trineo sends Pedrolino to the temple to call the minister or priest.

THE PRIEST — Pedrolino goes, then returns with the priest, who is suspicious at seeing so many people. Trineo reassures him and bows to him, asking for lodging for Levina. The priest leads Trineo away with him, leaving Levina, Pedrolino, her servant, and Arlecchino, his servant, behind. Levina, not being aware of Arlecchino, tells Pedrolino that she is aware that Trineo is enamored of her and fears for her honor; furthermore, she is pregnant by the Prince, her husband, having been made so by him when he was at her court in Crete. She weeps at her ill fortune. Pedrolino consoles her, saying that the god who freed her from the hands of Prince Mauro of Algeria would rescue her from the hands of this lord whom they do not know. Then he explains that he is a specialist in herbs and knows their properties; he has seen many in that place which he can use whenever she needs.

TRINEO ORSELLA SHEPHERDS	At that moment, Trineo enters with Orsella, sister of the priest, and with many young shepherds who bring food and drink for Levina, who was brought by Orsella and the young shepherds to her cottage while Pedrolino was away. Trineo learns from Arlecchino that Pedrolino is a herbalist and witch doctor and that they must keep an eye on him.
PEDROLINO	At that, Pedrolino, who had gone to the ship for some things for Levina and her maid, enters. He has heard what Arlecchino told Trineo. He declares he is going to take revenge. When he sees Trineo, he tells him he wants to go to the ship on an errand, and Trineo gives him permission. Pedrolino goes. Trineo and Arlecchino go off to pass the time.
LEVINA ORSELLA	Levina enters with Orsella, to whom she briefly tells her story, including that she is pregnant and near delivery. Orsella consoles her, telling her, in turn, of the loss of Dorinda, her niece, who is forced to live with a bear. Then they hear the sweet harmony of musical instruments in the temple at the top of the mountain.
ARGEO	Out of the Temple comes Argeo, priest, son of a grand priest who was killed by Apollo. Now, accompanied by a nymph, he remains in his father's stead as a soothsayer in the temple. Seeing Levina, he tells her that she will be happy in her delivery, to the great satisfaction of Orsella, and then he leaves. Orsella tells Levina that he is Argeo, the soothsayer.
PEDROLINO ALTHEA	At that moment, Pedrolino enters with Althea, Levina's waiting maid, who carries a little chest of silver given to her by her father to aid in time of need. In it are liquids and the quintessence to heal at once any infirmity. She greets Levina. They they hear the sound of trumpets.
TRINEO PRIEST SERVANTS	At that, Trineo enters and hears from the priest that Sileno, Prince of Cyprus, the friend he is seeking, left Arcadia nine months before, with Evrilla, Princess of Passo, his wife. Trineo rejoices to have word of his friend. At that, there is a great tumult of voices, shouting, "Look out! Look out!" Trineo draws his sword.
SHEPHERDS	Suddenly, shepherds run on, fleeing from the bear.
THE BEAR	The bear rushes on and attacks Trineo; they fight, and finally Trineo kills the bear.
ARLECCHINO	This done, Arlecchino arrives, bringing news of a great armada which comes toward port. They go to see it, leaving the dead bear.

DORINDA   Dorinda, frightened by the fight, enters and sees the bear, her consort. She weeps bitterly, and after a long lament, she swoons upon him, remaining there until the opening of Act Two; and thus Act One ends.

ACT TWO

THE PRIEST
LEVINA
ALTHEA
PEDROLINO

The priest enters with Levina, who begs him to make arrangements to keep Trineo from taking her out of Arcadia. He promises. He sees the dead bear and rejoices, but then seeing Dorinda, his daughter, and thinking her dead, he grieves and weeps. When Dorinda awakens and recognizes her father, she embraces him, begging him to allow her to entomb the bear, her husband, in his grotto. He agrees, and they drag the bear off.

SERVANT
ARLECCHINO

A servant of Trineo enters with Arlecchino, saying that Trineo is afraid of the armada that approaches the port, and he is going to leave and take Levina with him. He has been ordered to find her. At that, trumpets sound from afar and they leave.

PEDROLINO

Pedrolino, entering in haste, comes to take the little chest of precious potions by order of Levina to help Dorinda, who is about to give birth.

TUBICINA

At that moment, Tubicina, a shepherd, enters, playing an instrument and calling all the shepherds to come to the temple by order of the priest; then he goes off. Pedrolino remains, wondering.

SERVANT
ARLECCHINO

At that, a servant and Arlecchino enter and ask about Levina. Pedrolino sends the servant off by another path. Arlecchino wants to take Pedrolino to the ship, but he refuses to go and attaches to Arlecchino an herb that immediately makes him dumb; then he leaves. Arlecchino remains speechless, making gestures.

DORINDA

At that moment, Dorinda, within, in labor, screams.

ALTHEA

Just then, Althea enters and speaks of the great labor pains of Dorinda; however, she fears that they will not come so quickly to Levina. Then she sees Arlecchino, who is unable to speak, and wonders at him. She returns to the grotto, and Arlecchino leaves.

PEDROLINO
ORSELLA

Pedrolino enters with Orsella, with rags, swaddling clothes, wash basins, and other things for a woman about to give birth. From within come the screams of one in labor, and they go in. Trumpets sound for the arrival of Corebo, Prince of Denmark.

COREBO	Corebo, Prince of Denmark, asks the shepherd if there are any
GRATIANO	strangers in Arcadia. He answers yes but that he does not know
SERVANTS	them. Corebo asks for the temple of Apollo. The shepherd points
SHEPHERD	it out to him and leaves. Corebo tells Gratiano of the loss of his
	wife, Levina, the victim of Algerian pirates, and says he was by
	chance transported over the sea to Arcadia.

TRINEO   At that moment, Trineo enters, dressed as a shepherd. He remains hidden to hear all that is said. Corebo with all his train goes to the temple to pay homage. Trineo, having heard that this is Corebo, Levina's husband, says he is going to take her away as soon as possible.

ARLECCHINO   Then, Arlecchino arrives. Trineo asks about the women. Arlecchino, with gestures, tries to tell him that he can't speak. In desperation, Trineo takes Arlecchino with him.

DORINDA LEVINA   Dorinda and Levina, within, scream from the pains of delivery.

PEDROLINO   At that moment, Pedrolino enters, worried, with a white apron before him to take up the babies.

ALTHEA   Althea does the same. They ask each other for many things for the women; finally they hear the last screams, and they go in. At that, music is heard from the temple.

THE PRIEST SHEPHERDS   Then, the priest, with the shepherds, arrives at the temple, and hearing music, they wonder at this strange harmony. Then again they rejoice at the death of the bear.

ARGEO   At that, Argeo, soothsayer of the temple, enters playing and singing and announcing the birth of the two babies—one of Dorinda, and the other of Levina.

At that moment, music is heard again in the temple, and at the sound all enter the temple with Argeo; and the second act ends.

ACT THREE

PEDROLINO   Pedrolino enters with a new-born baby in his arms, shouting, "It's a boy! It's a boy!"

ALTHEA   At that, Althea enters with the other baby, shouting, "It's a boy, a boy!" At that moment they hear noise and the tumult of people. They wait to see.

ALMONIO PRIESTS   At that moment, Almonio, grand priest of Arcadia, enters on a beautiful chariot drawn by many priests. They appear when the music sounds from the temple and have returned on his orders that they take the two new babies. They do so. Almonio then suggests that when it is time, they announce throughout Arcadia the fortune of the two infants; then they pass over the stage to the sound of the music of the temple and leave. Pedrolino and Althea weep over the loss of the children.

ORSELLA · At that moment, Orsella learns what happened to the two babies; she weeps, then orders them to say they had been given to be brought up by two shepherds. Pedrolino leaves to find fresh eggs, pullets, and other things good for women who have given birth. He goes off. Orsella wonders at the miraculous powers of the potions in the silver casket and goes in with Althea.

ARLECCHINO · Arlecchino, dressed as a shepherd, enters saying that before crossing a river he took off his clothes; then, on the other side, he stole clothes from a shepherd who was bathing in the river, and immediately his speech returned.

TRINEO · At that moment, Trineo, dressed as a shepherd, sees Arlecchino, and asks about Levina and Althea. Arlecchino replies that he knows nothing about them. Trineo says he wants to trick Corebo of Arcadia into leaving and that Arlecchino is to follow him in all he does and says when the time comes.

COREBO · At that, Corebo enters and asks the two shepherds if they have
GRATIANO · seen two strange women, describing Levina and Althea, her
SERVANTS · waiting maid. Trineo begins to weep. Arlecchino does the same. Then Trineo tells him that by chance she was taken to Arcadia into the house of some woman, and thereafter, having been pregnant for nine months, she died in childbirth together with her child, having first ordered that should she die, her body was to be taken to Denmark; thus, not many days ago she was taken to that kingdom. Corebo weeps over the death of Levina, his wife, and thanking the shepherd for his information, goes with all his train to embark and return to his kingdom.

PEDROLINO · Then as Corebo is about to leave, Pedrolino arrives with things for the women. From a hiding place he recognizes Trineo and Corebo and runs off. Trineo and Arlecchino console Corebo and leave. Corebo remains with Gratiano, weeping again over the death of Levina. He said that she was pregnant by him, and little by little he is driven nearly mad; overcome by grief, he falls unconscious on the ground at the other side of the grotto.

LEVINA · At that moment, Levina, Dorinda, and Orsella enter, returned to
DORINDA · their former selves with the help of the precious potions from the
ORSELLA · silver casket. They desire to see their babies. Orsella replies that

they will see them soon and goes. The women remain. Then
Corebo returns to his senses, and as if mad, calls the name of
Levina again and again. Levina thinks he is the spirit of her
husband, and seeing her, Corebo thinks she is a ghost. He begins
to cry out. Afraid, the women flee. Corebo remains, frightened.

PEDROLINO   At that moment, Pedrolino enters, telling the priest what hap-
PRIEST   pened between Trineo and Corebo. They see Corebo and kneel
before him. Pedrolino tells him that Levina his wife is alive and
that the shepherd who told him his wife is dead is Trineo, the
Prince of Amatunta.

LEVINA   At that, Levina and Dorinda arrive, and after much fright Levina
DORINDA   and Corebo recognize each other as husband and wife. Corebo
then wants to avenge himself on Trineo, but Levina placates him
by telling him that Trineo had killed the Prince of Algiers who
had abducted her, and, rescuing her, had brought her here. At
that, trumpets sound as a sign of rejoicing.

ALMONIO   Just then, Almonio, the Grand Priest, arrives on foot with all his
PRIESTS   following, calling by name Corebo, Levina, and Dorinda. All are
SHEPHERDS   amazed.

TRINEO   At that moment, Trineo and Arlecchino enter, dressed as shep-
ARLECCHINO   herds. Almonio immediately calls Trineo by name, ordering him
to make peace with Prince Corebo; then he tells Dorinda that her
son is saved and that in time he will be married to the daughter
of Levina and be crowned king. As a sign of this truth, the poor
house in which the two infants were born would, by the will of
the gods, be transformed into a king's palace. At that, music of
various instruments is heard, after which a part of the scene falls
away opposite the house of Orsella, and in its place is seen a
beautiful palace, illuminated in many colors, decorated with beautiful pictures and other things which render it a marvelous sight.
All are dumbfounded. Then they are led by the Great Priest
Almonio to see the children of Dorinda and Levina; and here
ends the second part, after which will follow the third.

The Forty-eighth Day

PART III

THE BEAR

A Royal Opera

ARGUMENT

Ulfone, son of Dorinda and of the bear killed in the hunt by Trineo, Prince of Amatunta, grew up to be crowned King of Arcadia. To avenge the death of his father, though a bear, he besieged Amatunta with a great armada. After the victory, he hoped to lay siege to Algeria in Barbary to kill the King, father of that fierce barbarian, his son, who abducted Levina, mother of his wife. Lucella, sister of Prince Trineo, fell in love with Ulfone. Meanwhile, the Princess of Algeria, named Alvida, came to kill Trineo to avenge the death of her brother, who was killed at sea. After many strange events, Alvida became the wife of Ulfone, who was crowned King over three kingdoms.

CHARACTERS IN THE PLAY

Ulfone, King of Arcadia, camped at Amatunta
His soldiers

Trineo, Prince of Amatunta
Lucella, his sister
Silandra, his confidant

Squire
Ambassadors

Alvida, Princess of Algeria as an unknown knight

Maids
Squire

Captain of Ulfone's army

Captain of Tarisio's Army
Tarisio, Prince of Hungary, in disguise
Squire

Almonio, Grand Priest
Priests

Shepherds

Sentinels on the wall

ACT ONE

AMATUNTA	Trumpets sound; then the forecurtain opens, revealing in all his majesty Ulfone, King of Arcadia, surrounded by his soldiers.
ULFONE SOLDIERS [AMBASSADORS]	Ulfone, King of Arcadia, announces that they have laid siege to Amatunta and that before he raises the siege, he will kill Prince Trineo to avenge the death of his father. At that, trumpets sound. Then two ambassadors arrive from Trineo. The ambassadors announce that their prince asks for peace and offers his sister in marriage. Ulfone replies that he does not want peace, that he will not negotiate with him, that if he does not soon kill the Prince with his own hand, he will put the city to sword and fire. Then he will go to Algeria to conquer that kingdom to avenge one greatly deserving. The ambassadors leave and he, with all his train, goes off to review the army. Trumpets sound at his departure and go off.
LUCELLA	Lucella, Princess of Amatunta, appears on the wall; she tells her squire of her love for Ulfone, King of Arcadia, a brave knight, and that she lives in the hope that he will accept peace and take her to wife as her brother Trineo wishes.
A SOLDIER	At that, a soldier appears on the wall to give news to the Princess of the return of the ambassadors; happily, they go to learn the reply.
ALVIDA MAIDS SQUIRE	Alvida, Princess of Algeria and an Amazon warrior, arrives to avenge the death of her brother, killed by Trineo; the squire warns that he is guarded by many soldiers. She sends him for refreshment; then she lies down under the watchful eyes of her maids who bring her helmet, shield, and lance.
PRINCE TRINEO SOLDIERS	Just then, Prince Trineo appears on the wall, encouraging his battling soldiers. The enemy again attacks Amatunta.
LUCELLA SQUIRE	At that moment, Lucella hails her brother, the Prince, lamenting that Ulfone would not accept the offer presented by the ambassadors. The Prince goes off to review the attacks on his defense. Lucella, greatly saddened, gives her squire a letter to be delivered to King Ulfone. The squire goes. Lucella notices the knight sleeping under the watchful eyes of the maids. Then she leaves.

THE SQUIRE	The squire enters with Lucella's letter. He observes the beauty of the knight and the maids and speaks amorous words with them.
THE SQUIRE	At that, the squire of Alvida thinks that the other squire has attacked Alvida; he draws his weapons on him.
ULFONE	As they fight, Ulfone arrives, and he parts them. Alvida bows to him as King and Captain of the army, saying she is a knight of fortune. Lucella's squire gives him the letter. Ulfone reads it aloud, then states that he is obliged to keep his word to his mother and must avenge himself in the blood of Trineo, but that afterward he will treat Lucella with every knightly courtesy. The squire leaves. Alvida offers to be his knight, being already envious of Ulfone's success; he accepts her, saying he wants to lead her in the assault on Algeria. Alvida stands in admiration.
THE CAPTAIN	At that moment, the Captain of Ulfone's army enters with the news that some ships with black sails are coming, and more can be seen on the high seas—a great armada on the way. He fears that they come to help Trineo. Ulfone takes Alvida by the hand, and they go toward the sea to learn more about the approaching armada. Trumpets sound at the departing of Ulfone; and the first act ends.

ACT TWO

ULFONE ALVIDA SQUIRE SOLDIERS	Trumpets sound and Ulfone enters, saying that his spirit forebodes evil and strange events. He orders brought in the ambassadors who were with the black sailing ships. The soldiers go to get them.
AMBASSADORS SERVANTS	Then, ambassadors, dressed in mourning, enter, bowing to Ulfone. They present their credentials and tell him of the death of the Queen, his wife, and that Almonio, Grand Priest of Arcadia, has also come to pay tribute to him. Ulfone, grieved at this bitter news, swears that he will put the city of Amatunta to fire and sword. Then all leave.
THE SQUIRE	The squire of Lucella, having heard of the destruction he plans, goes off to tell Lucella.
ALVIDA MAIDS SQUIRE	Alvida rejoices at the death of the wife of Ulfone, hoping to win him for herself, as she is in love with him. The squire reproaches her for loving one who would destroy her kingdom.
LUCELLA	At that moment, Lucella enters, happy at what Ulfone has sworn to do, saying she wants him for her husband when she betrays her

brother Trineo and makes Ulfone lord of the city. Alvida, hearing what Lucella has said, is saddened and immediately considers ways of tricking Lucella, showing herself to be suspicious of her, and prays for strength. The squire informs Lucella that that is the beautiful knight who slept near the wall, that he and his squire want to come into the city to talk to Lucella. Lucella answers that she will give orders for them to be let into the city and goes. Alvida decides she will tell Ulfone of her love for him and of her obligation to the soul of her brother.

THE SQUIRE At that, the squire of Lucella appears at the gate, welcomes Alvida and her squire to the city, and they go in.

TARISIO Tarisio, Prince of Hungary, enters disguised; he has fallen in love
SQUIRE with Lucella because of her celebrated beauty and has asked Trineo for her hand. He has disembarked from his armada which has been wandering over the sea, afraid of Ulfone's armada, because he wants to enter the city and tell Trineo of his arrival, and of the armada brought to help him. The squire praises the undertaking.

THE GUARD They call the guard, who learns that they wish to hold a parley with Trineo.

LUCELLA Just then, Lucella enters, happy because the knight has promised
SQUIRE that Ulfone will be her husband. Tarisio is so impressed by Lucella's grace that he looks fixedly at her as if enchanted. She reproaches him for his bad manners in staring at her so and not greeting her. Tarisio begs her pardon and asks the favor of being allowed to go into the city.

ALVIDA At that moment, Alvida appears on the wall and asks as a favor that she be allowed to send her squire to the camp of the enemy. Lucella says that he may go. Tarisio beholds the beauty of the unknown knight, who asks Lucella to allow him to enter the city. Lucella gives the order and goes off with Alvida. Tarisio says he would like to know who that beautiful and gracious knight is.

THE SQUIRE At that, the squire and his servant enter on their way to the camp
SERVANT to bring Tarisio in. The servant leads Tarisio and his squire into the city. The squire of Alvida, holding the letter, speaks of the great danger his mistress is running. At that, trumpets sound the arrival of Ulfone.

ULFONE Ulfone enters, resolved to storm the city. The squire, at the
SOLDIERS command of Ulfone, announces that his lord is to enter the city, thinking he is in love with Lucella. The squire gives him the letter, explaining that while he was coming out of the city, a beau-

tiful maid gave it to him, begging him to give it into the hands of King Ulfone himself. Ulfone takes it and reads it. He finds it is written by the Queen of Algeria and tells him that she has come to that place to wreak her revenge. She offers him the kingdom of Algeria, without his having to conquer it. Ulfone wonders at this. Finally, he gives the signal for a general assault. Then all the squadrons get ready to storm Amatunta. Trumpets and drums sound the "To arms! To arms! To the attack! To the attack!"

THE ARMY	At that the army of Ulfone attacks the city with weapons and ladders.
TRINEO ALVIDA SOLDIERS	Then, Trineo appears with his army on the wall to fight the enemy. Alvida can be seen close to Trineo, looking for an opportunity to kill him. At that, trumpets sound the withdrawal of Ulfone's army. Trineo wonders why.
THE CAPTAIN	At that, the Captain of Ulfone enters and says he knows why the retreat was sounded. It was done because the armada which was on the way had entered the port to assault Ulfone's armada. Ulfone says the Captain did well to regroup the army, and all together they go to help Ulfone's armada.
TRINEO ALVIDA ARMY	Trineo and Alvida, thinking that Ulfone is fleeing with his army, cry "Victory! Victory!" They order the trumpets to sound. Trumpets and drums of Trineo sound, rejoicing at the victory; and the second act ends.

ACT THREE

THE SQUIRE	Tumult and great noise sound inside the city. At that, the squire of Alvida, with a bloody sack attached to his waist by a long cord, little by little scales the wall.
A SENTINEL	A sentinel sees him and draws his bow, but the squire, safe, runs off.
LUCELLA TARISIO SILANDRO SQUIRE	Lucella enters, weeping at the death of Prince Trineo, her brother. She does not know who killed him. Tarisio consoles her, saying that the killer has been caught; it is the beautiful unknown knight. Lucella is astonished at this.
SOLDIERS ALVIDA	At that moment, soldiers lead Alvida in, tied; she, without revealing who she is, confesses the murder and says she was sent by the Queen of Algiers to avenge the death of her brother who was killed by the hand of Trineo. Lucella, discovering that she is in love with Ulfone, is greatly angered and has her put in the tower prison to die.

THE SQUIRE The squire of Alvida, below the wall, hears all, and weeping, leaves. Lucella learns from the unknown knight, who is Tarisio, that it would be well if she remembered the help of Tarisio, Prince of Hungary, who loves her very much. She says she will decide nothing yet, that she is determined to see Ulfone face to face. She goes. Tarisio remains in despair with his squire.

THE CAPTAIN At that, the Captain of Tarisio, below the wall, recognizes Tarisio and gives him news that the armada of Ulfone, with the help of his army, has destroyed Tarisio's entire fleet. Tarisio, grieving, tells him not to reveal it and sends him away. Then he resolves to kill Ulfone, and should Lucella refuse to accept him as husband, he will, in desperation, kill her. He goes off to find her.

  Trumpets and drums of Ulfone sound for joy at the victory against the armada of Tarisio, Prince of Hungary.

ULFONE Ulfone and soldiers enter, rejoicing over the victory.
SOLDIERS

THE SQUIRE At that, the squire of Alvida presents the head of Trineo to Ulfone, telling him that this head was sent by the Queen of Algeria; then he tells him that his mistress had asked for him and wished to help him. Ulfone accepts the gift in the name of the Queen. Then he swears to vindicate the knight.

SILANDRO At that, Silandro, the Ambassador, asks audience for Lucella, his
SERVANTS Princess. Ulfone says that she certainly can come; they are expecting her.

LUCELLA At that moment, Lucella enters, dressed with great pomp, kneels
WAITING MAIDS before King Ulfone, and begs him to make peace with her and
TARISIO take her as wife with her entire kingdom as dowry. Ulfone raises her up, replying that he cannot give her an answer until the imprisoned knight who killed Trineo is brought before him. Lucella sends Silandro and the servants to fetch the knight. Meanwhile Ulfone asks Tarisio who he is. He responds that he is Hungarian, rescued from the wreckage of the armada. Ulfone asks about the Prince of Hungary and is told that he lived in the court of a princess whose beauty made him fall in love with her, but that she does not return his love. Ulfone remarks that that is too bad, since the Prince of Hungary is a knight of great merit.

SILANDRO At that moment, Silandro and servants lead Alvida in chains
SERVANTS before Ulfone, who does not recognize her as any but a knight.
ALVIDA He embraces her and consoles her. Then he turns to Lucella and informs her that he will make peace on the following terms: that first they find the Princess of Algeria or else force the knight to reveal where she is, and second, that he cannot take her as wife

without her own authority and without the authority of those from whom he descends. Lucella thanks him and agrees. Ulfone asks the knight about the Princess of Algeria, who reveals herself to be Alvida, comes to avenge the death of her brother. This she has done, and adds that whenever he wishes she will willingly be his wife.

ALMONIO
SERVANTS

At that, great tumult sounds from within. Then music of many instruments can be heard within, at which arrive Almonio, Grand Priest, upon his chariot drawn by the priests, and the shepherds, and others who bring three chests of gold within each of which is a royal crown with its scepter and its mantle. Ulfone, recognizing him, bows with all his train, asking the reason for his coming. Almonio announces he has come to fulfill the will of the gods, which is that Ulfone take to wife Alvida, Princess of Algeria, and that Tarisio, discovered disguised in that country, marry Lucella. Also the gods wish that Ulfone be crowned King of Arcadia, King of Algiers, and King of Denmark, the kingdom having fallen to Ulfone through the death of the King and of Corebo. Almonio then descends from the chariot, crowns Ulfone, and all bow before him. They perform the nuptials and make peace with the promise to restore the loss of the Hungarian Armada. Almonio mounts his chariot, and to the sound of the trumpets, all follow him off. Trumpets sound for joy; and thus ends the third part and the end of all three parts of *The Bear, A Royal Opera.*

The Forty-ninth Day

THE ENCHANTED WOOD *

Pastoral

ARGUMENT

Ergasto, an old shepherd of Erimanto, found he had a daughter named Fillide. She was in love with a shepherd of Arcadia named Sireno who at that time was exiled in the wood. The young man loved the nymph, but recalled suddenly by his father, he was forced to leave, promising to return soon to see his beloved nymph. It happened that an uncle of the shepherd, who was a magician and enchanter, made Sireno lose his memory so that he would not leave and would not again remember his beloved nymph. Seeing that her lover did not return, Fillide fled from her father and came to Arcadia under the name of Lesio, a young shepherd; and by chance she became mad, but Sireno regained his senses. Finally, after many adventures, with the help of another nymph, believed dead, and with the art of the magician, all ended happily.

CHARACTERS IN THE PLAY

Ergasto, father of Fillide, and
Carino, father of Sireno, Shepherds

Sireno, mad

Corinto, Shepherd

Fillide,
Clori, and
Timbri, nymphs

Lesio, young shepherd, that is, Fillide

Savage Shepherd

Sabino, Magician, brother of Carino
Two Spirits

* See Appendix p. 408.

Salvatico
Pedrolino, servant of Carino
Arlecchino, servant of Corinto

PROPERTIES

Painted wood for the transformation
Tree with growing apples attached
A sea shore which appears
Grotto for the Magician
Two fires that give off a scent
Greek pitch and many small candlesticks
Two streams of fire
Earthquake
Many skins for the shepherds
Garlands and clubs
Transformation for Arlecchino
Rod and book for the Magician

ACT ONE

ARCADIA

ERGASTO
CARINO

Ergasto, an old shepherd of Erimanto, tells Carino he is seeking his daughter Fillide, thinking he will find her in this wood. She has followed the shepherd Sireno, who, when he was in Erimanto, was called by his uncle back to Arcadia. Carino, hearing his son named, begins to weep, crying that Sireno has gone mad. Then they decide to find the magician Sabino, brother of Carino, to learn news of Fillide, and they go off.

CORINTO

Corinto, shepherd, enters playing his pipe and singing of his love for the nymph he saw hidden in a fountain.

CLORI

At that, Clori, a nymph, having heard his playing and his song, falls in love with Corinto and pleads for his love. Corinto urges her to love another shepherd, he being already in love and having given all his feeling to the nymph of the fountain. Singing and playing, he leaves. She laments, saying she would weep until she herself became a fountain so that her shepherd would the better know her love.

LESIO

At that, Lesio, a young shepherd, that is, Fillide, enters and consoles the nymph, promising to help her win her shepherd. Clori leaves, and Fillide remains, talking of the power of Love and the love of Sireno, thinking that he has feigned madness because he does not love her any more.

SIRENO
PEDROLINO

At that moment, Sireno, shepherd, enters and says many strange things, all nonsense and madness, to his servant Pedrolino. Then he sends him for something to eat. Pedrolino withdraws to see what Sireno will do. Lesio speaks with Sireno, recalling his name and his love. Sireno replies with nonsense and leaves. She, weeping, follows him. Pedrolino says he has heard all and knows that Lesio is a woman; he decides to play a trick on them, as he is in love with her.

ARLECCHINO

At that, Arlecchino, a herdsman, friend of Pedrolino, enters and tells him that he is in love with Lisetta. Pedrolino admits that he himself is in love with a young shepherd. Arlecchino laughs.

TIMBRI
CLORI

At that, Timbri, a nymph, enters with Clori, who comes speaking of the cruelty of her shepherd. Timbri laments that she is no longer loved by her woodsman. Pedrolino and Arlecchino greet the nymphs amorously. Finally Timbri, to pass the time with the herdsman, shows them the grotto of the magician, asking one of them to fetch from within a veil of silk and one of gold which she has forgotten. They are about to enter the grotto.

At that moment, flames of fire shoot out of the grotto again and again. Then, seeing the magician come out, the nymphs run off laughing. Frightened, Pedrolino and Arlecchino rush away.

SABINO
THE SAVAGE

Sabino, the magician, enters, reproaching the savage because of his love, reminding him of the evil that he bore out of love for him. On this day, he prophesies, because of love many strange things will happen, and because of his desire to help others, he will arrange a new meeting. He sends the savage into the grotto to fetch the goblets filled with the waters of Lethe. Sabino remains and calls on the spirits of winter.

THE SPIRITS

At that, the spirits appear with two copper goblets filled with scented fire. Sabino places them at opposite sides of the stage.

THE SAVAGE

Then, the savage comes out with the water of oblivion. Sabino has him sprinkle it all over the stage. Immediately thereafter, they hear a great deal of noise; then the prospect vanishes from their midst and instead there appears a sea shore on one side of the stage and a tree on the other. The tree bears beautiful apples. Sabino drives the demons off. Then he commands the savage that as he loves him, he is not to eat any of the apples or he will be sorry. Having said that, Sabino leaves. The savage speaks of his love for Clori and of his desire to eat some of the apples forbidden by the magician. As he is about to pick some, he hears the sound of music. He stops.

THE SPIRITS   At that moment, two spirits enter, dancing to the music. The savage also dances and thus all three, dancing hand in hand, go into Sabino's grotto; and the first act ends.

ACT TWO

SABINO   Sabino the magician enters with Carino, his brother, and Ergasto,
CARINO   who asks for help in finding his daughter Fillide. Carino begs
ERGASTO   him to make Sireno, his son, well. Sabino sends them to the temple to pray to the gods because it is better if the gods themselves discover their wishes. The old men leave, and Sabino enters his grotto.

LESIO   Lesio, that is, Fillide, enters grieving over Sireno's lost sanity.

THE SAVAGE   At that, the savage enters, having heard Lesio bewail her love and fortune and pray to the gods to send her death. Lesio, thinking it to be the will of heaven that the savage kill her, cries out for him to kill her right away.

SIRENO   At that moment, Sireno enters, and in his madness, embraces Lesio. The savage comes between them, and Sireno beats him. The savage, angered, picks him up and takes him into Sabino's grotto. Lesio is about to follow him. At that, flames from the grotto frighten her, and believing that the savage has killed Sireno, she weeps over his cruel death, then falls unconscious to the ground.

PEDROLINO   Then, Pedrolino enters, sees Lesio, and examining her all over, recognizes her to be a woman. He tries to kiss her, but she then awakens and flees, Pedrolino running after her.

SELVAGGIO   Selvaggio, a shepherd, formerly in love with the nymph Timbri, enters and discourses on his new love for Clori, a nymph.

CLORI   At that, Clori, a nymph, enters. Selvaggio confesses his love, but Clori tells him to return to his love Timbri and not to think about her because she does not love him, and she goes. Selvaggio, in despair, follows her.

ARLECCHINO   Arlecchino enters, urging Corinto to love Clori. He tells him to
CORINTO   leave off loving the nymph he saw in the fountain whom he does not know. Corinto laughs at him.

CLORI   Just then, Clori enters, hails Corinto, and pleads for his love. He answers that he cannot and does not wish to love her, and that she would do well to love Arlecchino, who is in love with her, and he goes off. Arlecchino makes amorous pleas to her.

THE SAVAGE   At that moment, the savage enters, sees his nymph, and tries to take her. Clori runs across the stage; unable to escape, she is transformed into a tree. The tree into which Clori has been transformed now appears. The savage says that this is the work of Sabino, who wants to interfere in his love. Angered, he goes off. Arlecchino weeps near the tree; then he goes off.

LESIO   Lesio comes again to the grotto to see about Sireno.

PEDROLINO   At that moment, Pedrolino greets her and reveals his love, saying that he knows she is a woman. Lesio wonders how he knows, then declares that if all day he does not speak a single word, she will then be his. Pedrolino immediately becomes mute, and making many amorous gestures, leaves. Lesio, seeing the apples, picks one to refresh herself, eats it, and immediately loses her memory.

ARLECCHINO   At that, Arlecchino enters and speaks to Lesio, who responds always with nonsense. Then, thinking he is her Sireno, she caresses him. Arlecchino, laughing, goes off, and Lesio follows after him, calling him her soul.

DEMONS   Demons enter, carry Sireno out of the grotto, then immediately
SIRENO   go back in. Sireno speaks simple-mindedly, sees the apples, picks one, eats it, and returns to his former state, remembering nothing of what passed.

PEDROLINO   At that moment, Pedrolino calls him master. Sireno marvels that he should do so. Pedrolino then speaks to him of many things, which Sireno insists he does not remember. Pedrolino asks him if he wishes to see his father. Sireno replies yes, and they go to find him.

ARLECCHINO   Arlecchino enters, saying that the young shepherd has gone mad. He walks around the tree, which is the transformed Clori, speaking abusively of Love.

SABINO   At that moment, Sabino, the magician, enters and scolds him for swearing at the gods. He summons the spirits.

THE SPIRITS   They enter, pick up Arlecchino, and by order of the magician, carry him into the grotto. Sabino returns to the tree, and speaking with Clori, informs her that she must remain in that shape until the blood of the most faithful and loved nymph of Arcadia is shed; then he calls the spirits to bring Arlecchino out.

THE SPIRITS   The spirits bring out Arlecchino transformed into a wild crane. The magician tells him that for having abused Love, he is to remain thus transformed for as long as Clori lives in the tree; then he goes. Arlecchino pleads with him, and weeping, stretches out his neck again and again. Thus he goes off up the path; and the second act ends.

ACT THREE

THE SAVAGE
: The savage enters, speaking of his love for Clori, turns again to the tree, weeps for the nymph, then picks an apple from the tree, eats it, goes mad, and leaves speaking nonsense.

CORINTO
SIRENO
: Corinto enters, rejoicing over Sireno's recovery; he confides to Sireno his unhappy love for a nymph whom he has seen once and never again. His story causes Sireno suddenly to remember his love for Fillide, whom he has left in Erimanto. Corinto then goes off, leaving Sireno lamenting that his father called him back so quickly to Arcadia.

LESIO
: At that, Lesio, that is, Fillide, enters and speaks nonsense to Sireno. Sireno recognizes her and tries to embrace her, but she flees. Sireno, weeping, follows her off.

PEDROLINO
: Pedrolino enters, frightened at having seen what happened to the savage.

ARLECCHINO
: At that, Arlecchino enters as a crane, stretching his neck again and again. Pedrolino becomes even more frightened.

THE SAVAGE
: Just then, the savage enters, speaking nonsense to Pedrolino; then the savage picks him up and carries him off. Arlecchino leaves.

SIRENO
CORINTO
: Sireno enters and hears from Corinto that the nymph that he saw in the fountain had a face like that of Lesio, the young shepherd. Sireno tells him that she is Fillide, daughter of Ergasto, the old shepherd of Erimanto. He begs him to go tell her father. Corinto goes, laughing about Sireno's mad love. Sireno now realizes it is his fault that Fillide has become mad, and he rails at himself.

SABINO
: At that moment, Sabino, the magician, his uncle, enters and consoles him, saying that it is true that he is the cause of Fillide's going mad, but that before the day passes all will be happy. He commands him to go comfort Ergasto and Corinto and then enters the grotto. Sireno obediently leaves.

TIMBRI
SELVAGGIO
: Timbri then enters, begging Selvaggio to love her. Selvaggio answers that he does not love her anymore, revealing that he loves another nymph; then he leaves. She remains, bemoaning the strange transformation of Selvaggio. Falling into despair, she

draws a knife, stabs herself in the breast, and falls onto the sea shore as if dead.

SIRENO
ERGASTO
CARINO

At that moment, Sireno, Ergasto, and Carino enter, rejoicing because of what they have discovered about Fillide.

CORINTO

At that, Corinto arrives and hails them. Then they see the nymph Timbri, whom they take to be dead, and they wonder about it.

FILLIDE

Just then, Fillide, that is, Lesio, the young shepherd, enters speaking nonsense. Sireno leads her to her father Ergasto.

SELVAGGIO

At that moment, Selvaggio rushes in, fleeing from the savage.

THE SAVAGE

The savage runs in, chasing him; then he bends over the body of Timbri, the nymph, and draws the bloody knife. They all hear a great tumult. At that moment, flames envelop the scene.

CLORI

The tree turns, and in it appears Clori, the nymph. Timbri rises to her feet.

ARLECCHINO

Arlecchino suddenly appears in his own form. As they all go toward the noise and the tumult, the flame continues, and from its midst the magician arrives.

SABINO

Sabino steps forward and stops all—the noise and the flame—and addresses them.

PEDROLINO

At that moment, Pedrolino enters and asks the magician if he can speak without harm from the nymph, for she has said that he, that is, Pedrolino, could not speak for the whole day. Sabino replies that he may, then cures Fillide, and finally relates all that he has done through his art and all that will take place: Sireno marries Fillide; Selvaggio marries Timbri; Corinto marries Clori, and so the pastoral ends.

The Fiftieth Day

THE FORTUNE
OF THE SOLITARY PRINCE OF MUSCOVY *

A Royal Opera

ARGUMENT

*The Prince of Muscovy, in love with the Princess of Poland, came
to her court as an unknown knight, having on his shield the
picture of a damsel, for which he was called the Knight of the
Damsel. She fell in love with him, he secretly married her, and
she became pregnant. At the same time, the King of Muscovy, his
father, fell ill; therefore, he was forced to return home, where he
was compelled by his father to take as wife a princess, a kins-
woman. The King of Muscovy recovered his health, and the
Prince, saddened, lived with his wife, who at the year's end died.
Whereupon the Prince, without saying anything, left alone in disguise, and while voyaging, was enslaved by the Turks. Without
revealing his identity, he lived thus in captivity for three years on
a ship of Turkish pirates, where he was put at the oar. He was
liberated by a Maltese galley and then captured in Poland, where
he found his sister. She had fallen in love with the famed Prince
of Poland, who wished his father to bring her there to marry her.
Meanwhile, the Princess of Poland, having heard of the wrong
done to the Prince of Muscovy and finding herself pregnant,
begged as a favor of her father the King, permission to live in
solitude far from the city, three or four miles away, with some of
her waiting maids. She was granted this favor, and later gave birth
to a child whom she sent to be nursed at a villa nearby. The
unhappy child, by a strange accident, wandered off, but after four
years was found again. The Princess finally won her husband, the
Prince of Muscovy, and the fugitive Princess became the wife of
the Prince of Poland.*

CHARACTERS IN THE HEROIC OPERA

Stefano, King of Poland
Giorgio, the Prince, his son

* See Appendix p. 411.

Giovana, the Princess, his daughter
Gratiano, Councillor
Pantalone, a male nurse of the Princess
Pedrolino, a Corporal
Many soldiers
Pages

Simone, Prince of Muscovy
Lucella, Princess, his sister
Arlecchino, his servant
Ambassadors of Muscovy

Cavicchio, a rustic
Pasquela, his wife
Foresta, orphan, believed to be his daughter

PROPERTIES

A royal chair
Two bundles of wood
Folded drapes of satin
Trumpets and drums
Hunting dogs
Horns and clubs
A letter
A small table with food
Beggar's clothes
Arms for the soldiers

ACT ONE

CROCOVIA

STEFANO   Stefano, King of Poland, sits on his throne and orders the ambas-
GRATIANO   sadors of Muscovy to be brought before him. Gratiano announces
PAGES   that the Prince, his son, will bring them in. At that, trumpets
sound.

GIORGIO   Then, Giorgio, Prince of Poland, arrives leading the ambassadors
AMBASSADORS   of Muscovy to his father, the King. After the ambassadors present
their credentials, they say that it is now four years that they have
been looking for the Prince who, unknown, is called by all the
Knight of the Damsel, and whose father, the King, lives in great
sorrow because of him. Stefano recalls that four years ago he
knew such a knight at his court, but he did not know he was the

Prince of Muscovy. The ambassadors explain to the King that their great King of Muscovy has a daughter of singular beauty who is sought after by many princes in marriage, but she declares she will not marry until her brother is found. They have many portraits of her; they show one of these to the King, who praises her beauty and receives it as a gift, presenting it to his son, who informs his father that he has arranged a great hunt for the ambassadors. The King says he will come if he feels well, but that his spirit is troubled because of the solitary life of Giovana, his daughter. Then all enter the palace. Trumpets sound on the entrance of the King into the palace.

LUCELLA

Lucella, Princess of Muscovy, dressed as a man, enters, having fled from her father because she is in love with the famed Prince of Poland and does not want to marry unless she can marry him. She says she has wandered through the forest, and being tired, must lie down.

PASQUELA
FORESTA

At that moment, Pasquela comes to gather wood with Foresta, believed to be her daughter. Each has a bundle of wood on her head. Pasquela, being old and weak and tired, sits down, calling upon death again and again to come deliver her from so much misery. Then Lucella awakes, saying, "I am here. What do you want?" Pasquela, thinking that she is Death, is frightened, saying that she called her in order that she could help her put the bundle of wood on her head. Lucella, to console her, reveals herself to be a woman, helps her carry the wood, and they all go together to Pasquela's cottage.

GUARD
ARLECCHINO

A guard on the tower appears to see if anyone approaches. He sees Arlecchino and shouts at him. Arlecchino approaches the tower.

PEDROLINO

At that, Pedrolino, corporal of the soldiers, comes out of the tower, demanding to know who Arlecchino is and what he is doing. Arlecchino gives many excuses.

GIOVANA

At that moment, Giovana, Princess of Poland, appears at the window of the tower and asks who the stranger is. Arlecchino replies he is a Muscovite. She orders him brought before her, and Pedrolino takes him inside, first lowering the drawbridge.

GIORGIO

Giorgio, Prince of Poland, enters, revealing that he has fallen in love with the portrait of the Princess of Muscovy and is thinking of many ways of going to find her.

THE SERVANT

At that, the servant enters and informs the Prince the hunt is ready. They go off together.

CAVICCHIO

Cavicchio, a rustic, with an ass carrying goods, comes from the market, grumbling about the unhappy life of a peasant.

SIMONE — At that moment, Simone, Prince of Muscovy, rescued from the Maltese galley, enters and asks Cavicchio what country this is. Cavicchio tells him that this is a forest of Poland, four miles from the city, and that in the tower dwells the Princess Giovana, in devout solitude, and that four years have passed since, with the consent of her father, she retired into that fortress. Speaking more of this, they go up the path. Then there is a sound of horns and trumpets for the royal hunt.

GIORGIO
AMBASSADORS
HUNTERS
— Out comes Giorgio, Prince of Poland, from the palace with the ambassadors, dogs, and hunters, blowing and shouting; they will go off to the hunt, and the first act ends.

ACT TWO

PEDROLINO
SOLDIERS
GIOVANA
PANTALONE
ARLECCHINO
— Pedrolino comes out of the fortress with the soldiers, who act as escort. After them comes Giovana, Princess of Poland, accompanied by Pantalone, her attendant, and by Arlecchino, who promises to return to her as soon as he finds his master; he goes off. Giovana takes Pantalone aside, and, weeping, tells him that the Prince of Muscovy is dead. Pantalone consoles her. The Princess says she would like to see her child. Pantalone promises she will see her.

SIMONE — At that moment, Simone, Prince of Muscovy, enters, begs alms of Giovana, and asks her why she weeps. Pantalone tells him she weeps for the death of a great prince, and hearing he is from Muscovy, asks him if he has heard news of his prince. Simone replies that all believe the Prince to be dead, but he does not believe it. Giovana orders Pantalone to take care of the beggar, and she goes into the fortress. Pantalone questions Simone, who claims he is the secretary of the Prince of Muscovy, and he tells Pantalone his story as it is set down in the Argument. Pantalone comments that he is well informed; then they hear the sound of the hunters.

GIORGIO
HUNTERS
— At that, Prince Giorgio arrives. He says the hunt is over and that the ambassadors have returned to the city. He wishes to visit Giovana, his sister. Then Pantalone goes in, and the beggar goes off up the path.

ARLECCHINO — Arlecchino enters, weeping because the hunters took him for a wild animal. The Prince is amused. Arlecchino says he is the squire of a disguised knight.

LUCELLA — At that moment, Lucella arrives. Arlecchino immediately runs up to embrace her, declaring himself her knight. Lucella asks the

Prince who he is that she might honor him. He answers he is the Prince of Poland. She looks closely into his face and faints in his arms. Then, regaining consciousness, she begs the Prince to be her servant. The Prince, because of her beauty, accepts. To find out if he is a Muscovite, she calls to the tower.

PEDROLINO
SOLDIERS
PANTALONE

Pedrolino, soldiers, and Pantalone come out of the fortress to receive the Prince and Lucella into the tower. Pedrolino and Arlecchino remain outside. They speak and recognize each other as brothers. Rejoicing, Pedrolino orders the soldiers to prepare the table outside the drawbridge for all to have supper together. They prepare the table with much good food and then call Pantalone.

PANTALONE

Pantalone comes out. Everyone sits down and begins to eat.

SIMONE

At that, Simone, Prince of Muscovy, enters, saying he is very hungry. He sees the soldiers eating and boldly begins to eat. A soldier scolds him and tries to strike him, but the Prince beats them all with his club.

GIORGIO
HUNTERS
LUCELLA

At that moment, Giorgio, Prince of Poland, enters and quiets them down. Then he asks the beggar where he comes from and who he is. Then the beggar describes for them the many parts of the world he has seen; he tells them he is a philosopher who goes seeking the truth about a supernatural event. The Prince takes him as his servant; then he has his sister called.

GIOVANA

Giovana comes out, and with the permission of her brother, asks for the young man as squire. He gives her Lucella, and Giovana goes in. Pedrolino and Arlecchino laugh at the beggar. Then all leave, and the second act ends.

ACT THREE

GIORGIO
[SQUIRE]

Prince Giorgio appears, gazing at the portrait of the Princess of Muscovy. He is full of ardor and inflamed with the desire to find her. Then the squire rouses him from his entranced gazing at the portrait, and Giorgio declares he is determined to go to Muscovy. He orders him to call the beggar, and the squire goes in and brings the beggar out.

SIMONE

Simone, Prince of Muscovy, enters in noble dress. Giorgio tells him he wants to go with him to Muscovy. Simone says he is much welcomed into that court. Giorgio asks him about the beauty of the Princess of Muscovy. Simone, perceiving the other's love, praises her and says he is a close acquaintance of hers. Giorgio, rejoicing, orders the squire to bring two or three horses so they can leave secretly from the fortress of his sister. Then Giorgio gives his seal to the beggar as a sign that he is to wait in the household of his sister.

SERVANT

At that, a servant calls Giorgio to his father, the King, and they go in. Simone thanks Love and Fortune, then leaves to go to the tower and reveal himself to the Princess.

GIOVANA
PANTALONE

Giovana and Pantalone come out from the tower, Giovana repeating her desire to see her daughter.

CAVICCHIO
FORESTA

At that moment, Cavicchio and Foresta arrive. Cavicchio has come to beg alms of the Princess. The Princess sees Foresta, embraces her, and asks if she is Cavicchio's daughter. Cavicchio says no, but that he keeps her as his child, saying that it is now four years since he found her barefoot in a stack of hay one night and took her to the villa to protect her from bandits that would do her some harm because she was swaddled in cloth of satin and gold. Suspicious, the Princess orders him to leave his daughter, saying she wants to see her face well. Cavicchio goes, leaving Foresta. Pantalone immediately kneels and recounts to Giovana that one night in the villa where he brought the baby to nurse her, he heard a great fight among bandits, and to save himself because one wanted to kill him, he placed the baby at the foot of a haystack and fled from the danger. Now he recognizes Foresta to be the daughter of Princess Giovana and of Prince Simone. They embrace Foresta and take her into the tower.

STEFANO
GIORGIO
PAGES

Stefano, King of Poland, enters telling the Prince, his son, he plans to visit Princess Giovana and dine with her that evening. They go to get their horses at the stable and go off up the path.

PEDROLINO
ARLECCHINO

Pedrolino enters, asking his brother what secret understanding he has with his master. Arlecchino confesses his master is a woman, the Princess of Muscovy, who ran away from her father because he wanted to marry her off; and because of Prince Giorgio's fame, she fell in love with him. Now she suspects that the beggar is her brother.

CAVICCHIO

Cavicchio enters with the swaddling clothes of Foresta. Pedrolino takes him to the Princess in the tower, and Arlecchino goes to find the beggar.

PRINCE SIMONE

Prince Simone arrives at the tower and marvels at the great constancy of the Princess Giovana, who placed herself in this solitude for him.

ARLECCHINO

At that, Arlecchino, who has heard part of what the Prince said, recognizes him.

PEDROLINO

Pedrolino stands at the window of the tower to listen to their conversation. Arlecchino kneels before the Prince, calling him by name. The Prince recognizes him and embraces him. Arlecchino begs him to pardon Lucella and himself, saying that she fled because her father wanted to marry her off, and that he is presently in the tower as a page of the Princess.

PANTALONE
PEDROLINO

At that moment, Pantalone comes in and learns from Pedrolino all that he overheard. They see the Prince; Pantalone recognizes him, greets him, and tells him all that happened to Princess Giovana, his wife, and his daughter, Foresta. The Prince has the Princess and his sister called to him.

GIOVANA
LUCELLA

Giovana comes out of the tower and joyfully embraces Prince Simone. Lucella begs pardon of her brother.

GIORGIO
THE COURT

Then, as they embrace again, Prince Giorgio arrives. Seeing his sister embraced, he draws his sword to kill the servant, but Lucella kneels before him, begging him not to do any harm, revealing herself to be the Princess of Muscovy, and the servant to be her brother and his brother-in-law; she also reveals that she has fallen in love with him. Giorgio calms down and is more than happy when he learns that Foresta is his niece.

CAVICCHIO
FORESTA

At that moment, Cavicchio and Foresta come out, and Foresta is embraced by her father and by her uncle.

STEFANO
THE COURT
PAGES

Then they hear the sound of trumpets, and afterward Stefano, the King of Poland, arrives and learns all that has happened. He rejoices and embraces all the princes. Then he orders that Giorgio marry Lucella and Simone marry Giovana. He embraces Foresta, and then all enter the palace for dinner; and the heroic opera ends.

The End of the Book

Philipin, Harlequin, and Il Segnor Pantalon. Seventeenth-century French engraving of a scene from a Commedia dell'Arte play involving these characters.

APPENDIX

All indications are that the English and French dramatists knew the commedia dell'arte *and knew it well. The following discussion of analogues, then,
suggests the extent to which the repertory of the* commedia dell'arte *companies pervaded the theaters of England and France during the sixteenth and
seventeenth centuries. It is by no means a comprehensive list and serves only
to point the way for further research in this area.*

Louis Moland in Molière et La Comédie Italienne *(Paris, 1867), I. A.
Schwartz in* The Commedia dell'Arte and Its Influence on French Comedy
in the Seventeenth Century *(New York, n.d.), and Kenneth N. McKee in*
The Theater of Marivaux *(New York, 1958) present many more analogues
of character, theme, and plot to be found in the French drama of the seventeenth and early eighteenth centuries. Indispensable for the study of English
drama's debt is Kathleen M. Lea's* Italian Popular Comedy: A Study in the
Commedia dell'Arte, 1560–1620, with Special Reference to the English
Stage *(Oxford, 1934).*

The Old Twins   FIRST DAY (1)

This situation of lost twins—lost parents in this case—parallels that of
Shakespeare's *Comedy of Errors*. There is much the same kind of farce and
comic confusion in both plays. The lost parents plot in *The Comedy of
Errors* is considered Shakespeare's own. Of course both Scala and Shakespeare
had a common source in Plautus' *Menaechmi*.

Flavio's Fortune   SECOND DAY (11)

Piero Rebora and Winifred Smith cite this scenario as the basis for the
mountebank scene in Ben Jonson's *Volpone*. A comparison of the two scenes
from both works indicates these similarities: the mounting of the stall by
the zanni under the window, the playing and singing of the zanni, the lady
at the window being saluted by a man in the street, the upsetting of the
mountebank's stall, and the dispersal of the crowd. The motivation for the

action is similar: the Captain in the scenario upsets the mountebank's stall because Arlecchino, who controls his lady, is standing on the stall; Corvino in *Volpone* upsets the stall because the mountebank is flirting with his wife. Smith suggests that Nano's song is very much like that of a zanni:

> You that would last long, list to my song
> Make no more coil but buy of this oil. (II, ii, 192–93)

Flavio Betrayed   FIFTH DAY (39)

There are several points of similarity between this scenario and Shakespeare's *Two Gentlemen of Verona*. Both open with two friends talking of love. Oratio's plan to betray his friend and win his friend's sweetheart, Isabella, begins almost immediately in the scenario with the false letter delivered by Franceschina to Oratio; whereas in Shakespeare's play the plan of betrayal does not begin until Act II, Scene iv. In the scenario, Isabella is betrothed to Captain Spavento; in *Two Gentlemen* Thurio is betrothed to Silvia. Proteus, as Oratio, goes to Silvia's father to try to further his suit against that of his friend, Valentine. The scenario uses letters and overheard conversation as devices. *Two Gentlemen* uses some overheard conversation, as when Valentine overhears Proteus reveal his disguise. In both *Flavio Tradito* and *Two Gentlemen* the treacherous friend begs forgiveness which is readily granted. Thurio, the intended husband of Silvia, is as chicken-hearted as Captain Spavento when forced to the wall, but not nearly so colorful a bluffer. Shakespeare reserves his farcical sequences for his servant clowns, Speed and Launce—the Pedrolino and Burattino of the scenario.

The Jealous Old Man   SIXTH DAY (47)

Among surviving Elizabethan plot outlines is one called *Dead Man's Fortune*. This outline was once thought to be a scenario of the *commedia* type, but there is not enough indication of plot action—not nearly as much as is to be found in Scala's scenarios, for instance—for these outlines to have served as a basis for improvised drama. It is more likely that they served as cues for the actors and were perhaps tacked up at stage entrances. *Dead Man's Fortune* has two plots—a tragi-comic plot involving noble characters, and a comic underplot with Pantalone, his servant Peascod, his young wife Aspida, and her lover Validore. This underplot bears striking resemblances to Scala's scenario: In both plots, Pantalone is apparently cuckolded by a young man with the help of the servant; in both plots music and dancing are the occasion for the young lovers to deceive the husband; in both there is a discovery of the young lovers and a uniting of them at the end. In *Dead Man's Fortune,* Pantalone has a chest brought in, apparently to bestow some sort of dowry upon the lovers.

Dead Man's Fortune, dated around 1589, is one of the first English dramas to contain a Pantalone character. The authorship of this plot is ascribed to Tarleton. Perhaps it is more than coincidence, then, that Tarleton dressed very much as the *commedia dell'arte* clowns—particularly like Arlecchino—according to descriptions by Tarleton himself and by contemporaries. In his *News out of Purgatory* Tarleton says:

As thus I lay in slumber, methought I saw one attired in russet, with a buttoned cap on his head, a great bag by his side and a strong bat in his hand, so artificially attired for a clown as I began to call Tarleton's wonted shape to resemblance. . . .[1]

According to Halliwell, this agrees with Chettle's description of Tarleton in *Kind-Harts Dream*, 1592. This costume is very like Arlecchino's with his cap, pouch, *bastone de bastonare,* and generally "artificially attired for a clown." There is another description of him that suggests the Bergamo peasant:

> . . . like a rogue in a foul shirt without a
> band, and in a blue coat with one sleeve,
> his stockings out at the heels and his head
> full of straw and feathers.[2]

Corvino in *Volpone* resembles Pantalone of this scenario. Like Pantalone, Corvino is married to a beautiful young wife whom he guards closely from the eager eyes of young men. Outraged at his wife's behavior toward the mountebank, Corvino identifies himself in his rage against the would-be cuckolder:

> What is my wife your Franceschina, sir?
> No windows in the whole piazza, here,
> To make your properties, but mine? but mine?
> Hart! ere tomorrow, I shall be the new christen'd
> and called the *Pantalone di bisogniosi* about the town.

The title for Pantalone used here by Corvino appears in many of Scala's scenarios, including this one.

John Chapman's *An Humorous Day's Mirth* also contains a Pantalone type in Count Labervele. The play opens with the old Count "in his shirt and nightgown, with two jewels in his hand" and he strews the jewels along his young wife's walk, hoping to compensate in gifts and verses for what he lacks in youth and romance. This is the Pantalone of *The Jealous Old Man* fearful of the rivalry of youth. Like Pantalone, the Count will not allow anyone access to his wife Florilla; like Oratio, the young Lemot plans to gain access to Florilla.

The Lady Who Was Believed Dead   SEVENTH DAY (55)

Thomas Dekker's *The Honest Whore,* Part I, contains the well-known plot of the supposedly dead sweetheart who turns out to have taken a draught of a strange potion which produced the death-like state. The best known such plot is in *Romeo and Juliet.* In *The Honest Whore* the plot is hatched by the heroine's father, the Duke, who does not want his daughter to marry the man she loves, Hippolito. The aim of the plot is to get rid of Hippolito as a result of his despair over his lost love. However, with the help of friends, Hippolito survives the Duke's scheme, finds Infelice, the heroine, alive in a convent and marries her. In the scenario, Flaminia, the daughter of Pantalone, loves Oratio, but her father wishes her to marry someone else, as in *Romeo and Juliet*. Thus she takes the potion. *The Honest Whore* opens, as does this scenario, with the funeral procession of the supposedly dead girl, who is being taken to the family sepulchre, and the young lover is mourning over the body of his dead sweetheart. Both plots turn out well for the lovers.

The Fake Madwoman　　　　　　　　　　　　　　　　EIGHTH DAY (60)

Madness, real and feigned, occurs in many Renaissance plays. Several of Scala's scenarios involve feigned, as well as real, madness. Shakespeare and his contemporaries employed madness as plot and theme in many of their plays. The subplot in Middleton and Rowley's *The Changeling* takes place in a madhouse. There is a fake madwoman who, like the woman in the scenario, is named Isabella. Antonio, a young man, assumes the disguise of an idiot in order to woo Isabella, who is the wife of the keeper of the madhouse, Doctor Alibius. Antonio never penetrates Isabella's disguise, and she remains faithful to her jealous husband, Doctor Alibius. There are two characters, as well as some plot, parallels: Both women are named Isabella; both young men feign madness for the same reasons; and Doctor Alibius and Doctor Gratiano are both charlatans, fools, jealous, and easily deceived old men.

This scenario was played in Paris in 1645 during Molière's early years in the French theater, and it was very successful.[3] It is no wonder, then, that the plot device of the woman who resorts to a stratagem to avoid marrying the man of her father's choice appears in a Molière play. In Scala, the woman pretends to be mad; in Molière's *Le médecin malgré lui,* she pretends to be dumb. In both plots, the women manage to marry the men of their own choice as a result of the stratagem.

Another French play, Quinault's *La comedie sans comedie* (1654) develops, in the third act, the Isabella-Pentalone-Doctor situation. Panfile, the father of Isabella, tries to marry her off to an old doctor while Isabella, as in the Scala scenario, loves someone else. Quinault is interested here in poking fun at the doctor as a charlatan, as do the *commedia dell'arte* and Molière.[4]

The Captain　　　　　　　　　　　　　　　　　　ELEVENTH DAY (78)

The scene in this scenario in which Pedrolino manages to get one hundred *scudi* from his master Pantalone on the pretext of ransoming his son Oratio from bandits has its analogue in Act II, Scene xi of Molière's *Les fourberies de Scapin*. Scapin, on the pretext of ransoming his son from a Turkish galley, gets five hundred crowns from the boy's father, Geronte. In this connection it is noteworthy that several of Scala's plots involve the kidnapping of parents and children by Turks and their being ransomed by friends and relatives from Turkish slavery.

The Dentist   TWELFTH DAY (85)

Thomas Middleton's *The Widow* contains a scene which could have come right out of Scala's *The Dentist*. Latracino, a thief, is a veritable Arlecchino in his tricks and disguises. In Act IV, Scene ii, Brandino takes Martino, who has a toothache, to Latracino, disguised as a dentist, to have his tooth pulled. While his confederate Occulto is pulling Martino's tooth and picking his pocket, Latracino is applying an eye cup to Brandino's ailing eye and picking his pocket. Latracino does not call out his profession as does Arlecchino in the scenario, but on his advertising banner he says he cures, among other things, "Breath that stinks beyond perfumer."

The Faithful Pilgrim Lover   FOURTEENTH DAY (99)

There seems to be an inconsistency in this scenario between what the Argument suggests about the plot and what happens in the play. The Argument indicates the Olivia-Viola situation of *Twelfth Night:* Flaminia falls in love with Isabella disguised as a male servant, Fabritio. The only hint of this in the scenario is Fabritio's cryptic response to Oratio that he can prove Flaminia does not love him. His proof would very likely be Flaminia's confession of love to Fabritio as suggested in the Argument. It is possible that in performance the actress, at some point, actually offered such verbal proof. However, this particular plot line is not followed through. Another possibility is that in actual performance the actors decided to drop this particular bit of complication. The full development of this plot is to be found in the scenario for the Thirtieth Day.

There is a parallel in this scenario and in Shakespeare's *The Taming of the Shrew* of the marriageable, contrary daughter who opposes any match proposed because she abhors marriage. Other features of the play suggest *commedia dell'arte* origins: Shakespeare's use of many Italian expressions and allusions throughout; the character of the pedant; and the scene between Lucentio and Bianca in which Lucentio and Bianca plan an intrigue under the pretext of a Latin lesson while Hortensio, an old suitor, sits nearby:

> LUCENTIO: I am Lucentio . . . son unto Vincentio . . . disguised thus to get your love . . . and that Lucentio comes awooing . . . is my man Tranio . . . bearing my post . . . that we might beguile the old pantaloon. (III, i, 31–37)

It is likely that the origin of the shrew plot is an Italian novella by Andrea Volpino called *Madonna Isota da Pisa,* published in Siena in 1581 and reprinted in Venice in 1583. The basic situation is the same as Shakespeare's: A wealthy merchant of Pisa named Marc Antony has a daughter, Madonna Isota, whom he would like to marry off, but she is a veritable demon who will obey no one and hates marriage. Another merchant, Jacob, has a son, Andrea, who loves the girl and would like to marry her. His father warns him against attempting to marry a girl who is such a shrew. But the marriage is arranged, and the husband immediately after subjects his wife to such cruel and harsh treatment that she learns to love and obey.

The Trials of Isabella   FIFTEENTH DAY (105)

Winifred Smith points out that the two old men in the scenario, Doctor Gratiano and Pantalone, talk of a "bona roba" much in the manner of Justice Shallow in Act III, Scene ii of *Henry IV, Part II*.[5]

Another character parallel from Shakespeare's play is Pistol. Pistol speaks and acts in the flamboyant and bombastic fashion of Captain Spavento. Like Spavento, Pistol is full of mythological bombast:

> I'll see her damn'd first, to Pluto's damned lake,
> by this hand, to the infernal deep, with Erebus and
> Tortures vile also. . . . (II, iv, 168–69)

Like Spavento, Pistol, upon rare occasion, speaks the truth. He harps upon the fact so strongly that he identifies himself:

> When Pistol lies, do this, and fig me like
> The bragging Spaniard. (V, iii, 125–26)

Here he makes the obscene gesture, the *fico*, so common in the *commedia dell'arte*.

The Twin Captains   SEVENTEENTH DAY (121)

Like Shakespeare's *The Comedy of Errors*, this scenario is based on the Plautine plot of the twin brothers and mistaken identity. As in *The Comedy of Errors*, one brother, Captain Spavento, is a native of the city in which the story takes place, and his twin brother, also a captain, is seeking his brother. The visiting captain brings his servant, Arlecchino, with him. Arlecchino, like Dromio, also confuses the two brothers. There is also, as in Shakespeare, some byplay about money, and there is the wife's confusion of mistaking the visiting twin for her husband. This scenario and *The Old Twins* contain the plot of the separated twins and the lost parents of *The Comedy of Errors*.

The Tragic Events   EIGHTEENTH DAY (128)

This scenario is a comic treatment of the Romeo and Juliet story. Bandello's tale was certainly available to both Scala and Shakespeare. Some of Shakespeare's comedy in the opening of *Romeo and Juliet* in which the servant Samson bites his thumb at Abraham, an insulting Italian gesture, suggests the clowning of the *commedia dell'arte* comics. It is interesting to note that the Tybalt character is played by Captain Spavento and the Romeo character, by Oratio. Tybalt's arrogance and pride in his ability as a swordsman find their appropriate parody in the person of Captain Spavento; Romeo's love-sickness and his impulsiveness are appropriately embodied in the young lover Oratio. The scenario dramatizes what is really the last act of *Romeo and Juliet*—the return of Oratio from banishment, the discovery of Isabella alive, and of his old enemy, the Captain, whom he thought he had killed. Scala works his happy ending by reversing two tragic events—the Captain, unlike Tybalt, is found to have survived the wound suffered in the duel, and Oratio, unlike Romeo, finds his beloved alive.

The first act of Scala's scenario, like the first act of Shakespeare's play, has an altercation between the two feuding houses. In Shakespeare, it is the servants who begin to fight; in Scala, it is the two old men themselves, Pantalone and Gratiano. Both Pantalone and Gratiano suggest the testy, loud, and overbearing character of Capulet.

The Jealousy of Isabella   TWENTY-FIFTH DAY (177)

It is likely that Scala and Shakespeare took the story of the discovery of the lover in the act of betrayal from Bandello. In Shakespeare's *Much Ado About Nothing,* Don John arranges to have Claudio observe Hero betraying him by having Claudio overhear Hero making love to her supposed paramour through her window. Scala reverses the roles: the young lady, Isabella, is deceived into believing that her lover, Oratio, is unfaithful to her when she sees and overhears, as in *Much Ado,* her lover exchanging amorous words with a servant, Franceschina, through a window. In both plays, the woman servant is used as part of the stratagem to trick the lovers.

Often, the attempt to identify the source of a disguise in Italian popular comedy is much like trying to find a particular harlequin at a Mardis Gras of harlequins. There are just too many of them, and most of them are very much alike. The disguise plot is certainly popular in Italian comedy, and particularly in the *commedia dell'arte.* Among Scala's fifty scenarios are no less than eighteen plots in which the *prima donna* disguises herself as a boy, usually to pursue her lover and to win him or to discover some mystery which is important to her. Among the eighteen are three plots which bear significant resemblances to *Twelfth Night: The Jealousy of Isabella, The Disguised Servants,* and *The Bear, Part 1.*

The Alexandrian Carpets   TWENTY-SIXTH DAY (184)

The opening scene of this scenario is a kind of caricature of the father-son situation exemplified by the Polonius-Laertes scene in *Hamlet* in which

Laertes is about to go off to Paris. The scene is, as a matter of fact, touched with irony against the father in both plays. In this scenario, Pantalone reprimands his son, Oratio, who has just returned from the university at Bologna. Polonius advises Laertes just before he goes to seek his pleasure in Paris. Both fathers are concerned about the son's behavior in chasing women, gambling, and generally pursuing a life of licentiousness. Undoubtedly when played, Pantalone's speech, like Polonius', was filled with platitudes and sententious advice. For such speeches, the *commedia dell'arte* had a term— *Zibaldone* (Medley) *di concetti*. For the scolding speech, the term used was *La Maledizione al figlio*. Polonius' scolding of Ophelia and warning her against any further concourse with Hamlet would be called *La Maledizione al figlia*. Polonius' advice to Laertes would be called *La Persuasiva al figlio*. Throughout the play, Polonius is treated by Hamlet as if he were Pantalone, and Polonius reacts to Hamlet as a pantaloon.

That Shakespeare was aware of the traditional view of Pantalone is amply attested by his allusions to "pantaloon," with a small *p*, in *As You Like It*, and *The Taming of the Shrew*. These allusions do not, either in their implicit or explicit suggestion, conflict with Hamlet's view of Polonius. Hamlet sees Polonius as a foolish and tedious dupe; as a spy and meddler; as a suspicious father; as bawdy and vulgar in his taste; as senile; as the butt of mockery. All of these fit the traditional view of Pantalone. And Polonius reacts toward Hamlet as a Pantalone. In his early judgment of Hamlet, Polonius reacts as Hamlet would expect him to react, as a suspicious old fool who expects every young blade to attempt to steal his daughter's honor and thus his own. "You'll tender me a fool," he scolds Ophelia, if she is too free in her affection for Hamlet. Later in the same scene he does Hamlet's character an injustice— the very injustice that a pantaloon would be guilty of:

> Do not believe his vows; for they are brokers,
> Not of that dye which their investments show,
> But mere implorators of unholy suits,
> Breathing like sanctified and pious bawds,
> The better to beguile. (I, iii, 127ff.)

The temptation is to add ". . . the old pantaloon" as in the allusion in *The Taming of the Shrew*. Hamlet's first words to Polonius are to call him a fishmonger (II, ii, 173), which epithet, as Malone states, is a cant term for *wencher*.[6] Throughout the scene Hamlet treats him as an old fool, giving him mock warning against the violation of Ophelia's honor, for Hamlet knows that this fear is uppermost in Polonius' mind. In one speech Hamlet characterizes Polonius as he sees him; it is the scene in which Polonius asks Hamlet what he is reading:

> . . . the satirical rogue says here that old men
> have grey beards, that their faces are wrinkled,
> their eyes purging thick amber and plum-tree gum
> and that they have a plentiful lack of wit, together
> with most weak hams. (II, ii, 195ff.)

Again the description neatly fits Pantalone. Hamlet ends the scene with the final phrase: "These tedious old fools!" In Act II the players appear and Hamlet requests the chief player to recite a speech; midway through the speech, Polonius interrupts:

POLONIUS: This is too long.

HAMLET: It shall to the barbers, with your
beard.—Prithee, say on; he's for a
jig or a tale of bawdry, or he sleeps. . . . (II, ii, 520ff.)

Hamlet is clearly characterizing both Polonius' taste and character. Whether or not Hamlet is joking, the fact remains that he does have such a view of Polonius in mind. Finally, toward the end of the scene, aware, perhaps, both of his treatment of Polonius before the players and of the inclination to treat Polonius as a buffoon, Hamlet says to the player: "Follow that lord; and look you mock him not." (II, ii, 518ff.)

In Act III, Scene i, Ophelia is set to decoy Hamlet while the King and Polonius, at Polonius' suggestion, listen behind the arras:

HAMLET: Where's your father?

OPHELIA: At home, my lord.

HAMLET: Let the doors be shut upon him,
that he may play the fool nowhere
but in's own house. (III, i, 132ff.)

Here Hamlet, whether or not he realizes that Polonius is behind the arras, characterizes Polonius as a suspicious and meddling old fool—a veritable peeping pantaloon. Again, in Act III, Scene ii, he treats Polonius as an old fool and Polonius reacts in kind. Polonius is the one who suggests he hide behind the arras in the Queen's closet; whereas in the older *Hamlet* the Queen made the suggestion. Hamlet's words over the discovered body sum up the sudden, tragic end of a *Pantalone de Bisognosi:*

Thou wretched, rash, intruding fool, farewell!
I took thee for thy better; take thy fortune;
Thou findst to be too busy is some danger. . . . (III, iv, 31ff.)

And the final epitaph:

Indeed this counsellor
Is now most still, most secret and grave
Who was in life a foolish prating knave. (III, iv, 213ff.)

Polonius, as Hamlet and, perhaps, Shakespeare saw him, is the widower Pantalone, with a son and daughter, old, senile, and meddling lover of things bawdy, suddenly caught up in tragic circumstances, peeping from behind the arras, and getting, not just a drubbing with a *bastone de bastonare,* but a deadly thrust of the sword.

The Faithless One   TWENTY-SEVENTH DAY (193)

In this scenario three names appear to be missing from the list of characters in the play: Gratiano, Captain Spavento and Arlecchino. Though other cast lists have occasionally omitted the names of minor characters, this is the first substantial omission. The omission of Gratiano is understandable since his is only a walk-on role in the play. But Captain Spavento and Arlecchino play their usual roles. In their case the omission is further strange in that both were very popular characters at the time. The omission is probably due to an editorial error.

Flavio, the Fake Magician   TWENTY-EIGHTH DAY (201)

Parts of John Marston's *What You Will* bear certain similarities to this scenario. Both are set in Venice and both contain similarities of character and situation. Marston's Albano, like Pantalone, is a rich Venetian merchant; also, like Pantalone, he has a young wife, Celia, who is besieged by suitors. In *What You Will,* Albano is reported drowned. When he returns, he finds himself face to face with Francisco, disguised as Albano. As a result of the other characters insisting that he, Albano, is really Francisco, he begins to doubt his own identity. This is an exact parallel to Flavio's disguising himself as Pantalone's ghost, and appearing before Pantalone, making him doubt his own identity.

Thomas Dekker's *Westward Ho* contains a situation like that involving Burattino, Pedrolino, and Franceschina of the scenario. In Dekker's play, Justiniano, an Italian merchant, suspects his young wife of being unfaithful and is determined to discover the truth. Like Burattino, Justiniano dresses up in his wife's clothes to see if the Earl has been cuckolding him. Also like Burattino, he finds that his wife has not been unfaithful.

The Faithful Friend   TWENTY-NINTH DAY (210)

The opening scene of this scenario of Pantalone, holding a lighted lantern, railing through the dark streets with his servant, Arlecchino, seeking his daughter who has fled, suggests Shylock raving through the streets of Venice seeking his daughter and his ducats. J. P. Moore, in an article in *The Boston Public Library Quarterly,* makes a case for Pantalone as the basis for the Shylock portrait in *The Merchant of Venice.* Moore's thesis is based on the following: The description of Shylock closely resembles the Pantalone of the scenario and of contemporary pictures and sketches; both are widowers whose domestic relations are treated satirically; Pantalone, like Shylock, invariably has a son or daughter who robs him and who elopes with a lover of whom he disapproves; both are avaricious and tight-fisted toward their servants; and Pantalone is invariably a merchant of Venice.

The Disguised Servants   THIRTIETH DAY (218)

This scenario also contains a disguise plot like that in *Twelfth Night.* Isabella, disguised as Fabritio, becomes a servant in the house of the man she loves, Oratio. This suggests the Viola-Duke Orsino relationship in Shakespeare's play. Her twin brother, Cinthio, wins over Flaminia as Olivia wins over Olivia, because she mistakes him for Fabritio, as Viola mistakes Sebastian for the disguised Viola.

The Pedant   THIRTY-FIRST DAY (227)

This scenario, from which Molière appears to have derived his basic plot for *Tartuffe,* has a fairly simple farcical situation but contains most of the germinal devices of the Molière play: Pantalone, the husband of a pretty young wife, Isabella, has, like Orgon, been completely taken in by the hypocritical Pedant. Just as Orgon cannot believe that Tartuffe is other than pious and good, so Pantalone cannot believe that the Pedant is a scoundrel. Pantalone's wife and son, like Orgon's wife and children, try to tell him what is the true character of the Pedant, but he will not hear the Pedant maligned. Ironically, as Orgon, he advises his son to follow the example of the Pedant. The young wife, Isabella, also tries to persuade Pantalone, but he refuses to listen. Finally, as in *Tartuffe,* the wife is forced to resort to a stratagem to expose the lecherous hypocrite. In the scenario the hypocrite is locked in the wife's bedroom and then exposed to all. Molière resorts to a funnier stage device: The husband hides under the table and is able to see the hypocrite in action trying to seduce his wife. At the end, the Pedant, exposed as a scoundrel, is threatened with castration and finally let off with a sound thrashing by the clown; Tartuffe, a stronger and more fully-realized character, must be removed by royal edict.

Another analogue in this play is the mountebank scene which is like that in *Volpone.* Corvino's wife dropping the handkerchief to the disguised Volpone is like Isabella dropping her handkerchief to the Captain. This scene and that from *Flavio's Fortune* contain all the essential details of the mountebank scene from *Volpone.*

John Chapman's *An Humorous Day's Mirth* contains a situation and disguise plot like that in *The Pedant.* As part of a plan to gain access to old Count Labervele's young wife, Catalian, the would-be seducer, disguises himself as a pedant. Soon after the young lover, Lemot, enters, presumably as a Puritan to test the wife's constancy. The similarity of the two names, Cataldo of the scenario and Catalian of Chapman's play, may be coincidental, but along with other resemblances suggest Chapman's familiarity with Scala. Lemot is at the center of the play's intrigue. His familiarity with Florilla turns out to be a plot to humiliate her as a Puritan. He invites the King to an assignation with Martia, and then tells the Queen of the assignation and of a fictitious plot to castrate the King. The castration story also suggests Scala's scenario.

Shakespeare's *Merry Wives of Windsor* contains one device that suggests Scala's plot. Mistress Ford, like Isabella, is wooed by Falstaff, and Mistress Ford conspires with her husband to trap and expose Falstaff, as Isabella conspires with Pantalone to trap and expose Cataldo. O. J. Campbell maintains that Shakespeare's play was a rewrite of the lost *Jealous Comedy* (1592–93) which, in turn, was based on Italianata farce, including *The Pedant* by Scala.[7]

The Two Disguised Gypsies   THIRTY-SECOND DAY (235)

Act V, Scene iii of Shakespeare's *The Winter's Tale* in which Hermione, supposed dead, is presented to Leontes as a marvelous statue, is a striking analogue to the last act of this scenario. In the scenario, Isabella, also believed dead, is led out, her eyes closed, and made to stand still in the center of the room. Her husband, Flavio, seeing her and believing her dead, wants to kill himself. Pedrolino draws a magic circle around Isabella and inscribes diabolical characters. Then he has Isabella move one arm, then the other; open one eye, then the other; and made to sing, walk, dance, and laugh. Finally, she, like Hermione, reveals herself to be alive and embraces him. All of this action is clearly paralleled in the following excerpts from Shakespeare's scene:

LEONTES: Would I were dead. . . . (63)

The fixture of her eye has motion in't. (67)

PAULINA: I'll make the statue move indeed, descend
And take you by the hand; but then you'll think,
Which I protest against, I am assisted
By wicked powers. (88–91)

Music, awake her; strike!
(Music)
'Tis time; descend; be stone no more; approach;
Strike all that look upon with marvel. (98–100)
POLIXENES: She embraces him.

CAMILLO: She hangs about his neck. . . . (111–12)

Isabella, the Astrologer   THIRTY-SIXTH DAY (265)

John Marston's Cocledemoy, a clowning trickster in *The Dutch Courtesan*, bears a keen likeness to Scala's Arlecchino. In this scenario Arlecchino is a pimp who serves itinerant merchants coming through Naples. Arlecchino names a number of courtesans of different nationalities from his long list and promises Pedrolino he will have one of the most beautiful for his master. Alone, Arlecchino then gives a long speech praising his profession. Cocledemoy in Act I, Scene ii of *The Dutch Courtesan* gives a speech which sounds like the very thing Arlecchino might say:

List them:—a bawd; first for her profession or vocation, it is most worshipful of all the twelve companies; for, as that trade is most honourable that sells the best commodities—as the draper is more worshipful than the pointmaker, the silkman more worshipful than the draper, and the goldsmith more honourable than both, little Mary, so the bawd above all: her shop has the best ware; for where these sell but cloth, satins, and jewels, she sells divine virtues, as virginity, modesty, and such rare gems; and those not like a petty chapman, by retail, but like a great merchant, by wholesale; wa, ha, ho! And who are her customers? Not base corn-cutters or sow-gelders, but most rare wealthy knights, and most bountiful lords, are her customers. Again, whereas no trade or vocation profiteth but by the loss and displeasure of another—as the merchant thrives not but by the licentiousness of giddy and unsettled youth; the lawyer, but by the vexation of his client; the physician, but by the maladies of his patient—only my smooth-gumm'd bawd lives by others' pleasure, and only grows rich by others' rising. O merciful gain, O righteous in-come!

The Just Punishment   FORTIETH DAY (303)

Scala's device of the husband pretending to be dead in order to test his wife's chastity occurs in John Chapman's *Widow's Tears*. The original source of this tale is Petronius' *Satyricon* 111. Oratio, in the scenario, discovers that his wife Flaminia, as a result of the stratagem, is faithful. In Chapman's play, the "widow" eventually succumbs to the wooing of the guard (the disguised husband) and is even willing to hang her husband's corpse as a substitute for the stolen corpse the guard is responsible for. The latest treatment of this tale is Christopher Fry's *A Phoenix Too Frequent*.

Alvida   FORTY-THIRD DAY (333)

The plot of Shakespeare's *Cymbeline* contains striking similarities to this scenario. *Alvida*, like *Cymbeline*, has a princess, Alvida, secretly in love with a member of her father's court. Silandro, Alvida's love, is a disguised prince of Persia. They are secretly married, as are Imogen and Posthumus. Whereas Posthumus is banished in *Cymbeline*, both Alvida and Silandro in the scenario are condemned to be slain in a nearby forest after the King, Alvida's father, discovers them together. Silandro and Alvida are saved by Silandro's father, the Sultan of Persia, and his soldiers. In the fight in the wood the captain of the King of Egypt's soldiers is killed by Silandro, and his head is cut off as Cloten's is in *Cymbeline*. In both plots, the husband and wife think the other is slain during the fighting in the forest. Alvida, like Imogen, drinks a liquor which puts her into a death-like sleep. Both heroines dress up as rustics and seek shelter in a cave. There is also the plot of the reunion of father and offspring: The Sultan of Persia is reunited with his child whom he thought to be dead but who was saved by a servant;

Cymbeline's sons, whom he thought to be dead, are reunited with him, having been saved and brought up by Bellarius. Whereas the villainy in *Alvida* results from the anger and rashness of Alvida's father, the King of Egypt, the villainy in Shakespeare's *Cymbeline* results from the machinations of the Queen, Imogen's step-mother. In the end, the King of Egypt, like Cymbeline, forgives all, and all are united.

Rosalba, Enchantress   FORTY-FOURTH DAY (341)

There are several *commedia dell'arte* scenarios which contain remarkable analogues to Shakespeare's *The Tempest*—all of which were played years before *The Tempest* was written. (See the discussion of *The Enchanted Wood.*) This scenario, which has a very complicated plot, contains several likenesses: the island itself, called the Happy Isle; the plotting of the clowns, Arlecchino, Pedrolino, and Burattino suggest the plotting of Caliban, Trinculo, and Stephano; the sudden appearance and disappearance of the summoned spirits; and the clowns caught in an enchanted circle near the end. One other Shakespearean analogue is suggested by the strange love of Rosalba, the magician's daughter, for the clown Arlecchino; it is reminiscent of the strange love Titania has for Bottom in *A Midsummer Night's Dream.*

The Enchanted Wood   FORTY-NINTH DAY (378)

There are many important features of *The Tempest* which, as Kathleen Lea points out, are unexplained and which suggest the *commedia dell'arte.*[8] These features are the two groups of shipwrecked survivors, stranded on a strange island; the magician who rules the island by fear and magic; the relationship of the magician to the strangers upon whom he has reason to revenge himself; the tormenting of the strangers and native shepherds by spirits; the plot to kill the magician and take over his rule; the structural unity by way of the magician's foreseeing the end of his rule and the renunciation of his art. All of these can be found in at least one, sometimes in several, of the Arcadian masks of the *commedia dell'arte.* There are seven of these scenarios which will be referred to here. Five of the masks were printed by Ferdinando Neri in his book, *Scenari della Maschere in Arcadia.* These include *La Pazzia di Filandro, Il Gran Mago, La Nave, Li Tre Satiri,* and *Arcadia Incantata.* One appears in Scala's collection—*L'Arbore Incantato;* and the other, *Pantaloncino,* is a mask of the same type, though the setting is Frascati rather than Arcadia.

Four of the above scenarios have two groups of shipwrecked survivors. In *The Great Magician,* Zanni, in Act I, relates the story of his being shipwrecked in Arcadia with his master's children whom he has brought up as shepherds. Then another group of newly arrived shipwrecked survivors, Pantalone, Gratiano, and Burattino, enter calling for their companions. All

are famished and kneel before the temple of Bacchus and beg for food. Also
in this scenario there is shown a shipwreck at sea in which a Captain and the
Queen sink into the sea with the ship. In *The Three Satyrs* Pantalone enters
and tells of the shipwreck and loss of his companions. He is lost and afraid
of wild beasts. He calls out to his friends Gratiano, Zanni, and Burattino.
After he talks to himself awhile, he sees an apparition of a sea with ships and
boats. Pantalone shouts but gets no answer. The boats disappear and a whale
appears, vomiting Burattino onto the coast. Later Gratiano and Coviello enter
and talk of their misfortune—the loss of their companions, their hunger, etc.
In *The Enchanted Wood* the magician, like Prospero, announces the arrival
of strangers. Then follows a scene of a stormy sea with a sinking ship.
Pollincinella, from the sea, talks of the tempest passed and the wreck and
loss of his companions. Coviello enters from the other side and repeats
Pollincinella's tale. They see each other and, after playing *lazzi* of hearing
and touching, realize they have been saved and talk of the loss of master and
companions. Tartaglia and the Dottore enter from the opposite side, each
giving an account of the loss of his companions. They also play *lazzi*, then
notice each other and play the scene of being scared among the four. Finally,
all realize that they have been saved and recount their adventures.

The ruling magician appears in all the scenarios mentioned. However, four
of the scenarios contain the idea of the magician's foreseeing the destruction
of his rule. In *Pantaloncino* the magician fears his daughter, imprisoned because he has foreseen by his art that she will dip her hand in his blood. In
The Three Satyrs, the magician in Act II discourses on his art, and seeing
a rock and tree disenchanted, is surprised that the Fates should have foreseen
all so soon. In *The Ship* the magician—the only one of them who is apparently evil in his actions—says he must prepare against certain danger that,
ironically, he believes lies in wait for the native shepherds. It turns out,
however, that he himself is in danger. At the end he is turned into stone as
a result of Pantalone's, Gratiano's, and Zanni's prayer to Jove to punish the
magician for his evil ways. In *The Great Magician* the magician tells of his
powers and his wisdom and says that he has foreseen that he will lose all
if he cannot find the necessary remedy.

Three of the scenarios contain plots against the magician. The plot in *The
Great Magician* is hatched by Pantalone, Burattino, and Gratiano who decide
that all the transformations—Pantalone into a mule, Burattino into a frog,
and Fillipa into a tree—are the work of the magician whose magic they will
attempt to counter. The plot in *The Three Satyrs* involves Pantalone and
Zanni, who steal the magician's book and decide that they will take over the
rule of the island. The magician is forced to counter the conspiracy by spells.
Like Prospero, he draws a magic circle, into which the conspirators are
lured; then they are forced to dance without stopping. The magician upbraids
them for plotting against him and releases them for the return of the book.
In *The Ship,* the Captain rides onto the island on a dolphin's back to save
the Queen who is in the magician's power. This plot against the magician

is the only sympathetic one, since the magician in this scenario is considered evil.

Aside from these plots against the magician, several of the scenarios contain farcical situations very like those involving Caliban, Trinculo, and Stephano. In *The Madness of Filandro* there is a farcical sequence in Act II in which Gratiano, lost, enters and recounts his shipwreck experience and has *lazzi* concerning his hunger. He does not know whether beasts or men inhabit the place. Meanwhile Coviello and Zanni enter from the opposite side. Gratiano then has *lazzi* about Zanni, saying he does not know whether he is man or beast. It has a head, he says, and legs, but so has an ass. Later, in Act III, Coviello and Zanni enter talking drunkenly, find Lidia tied to a tree, and play the *lazzi* of wanting to make water against her. Coviello, Gratiano, and Zanni are scolded for their drunkenness. In *The Three Satyrs,* Gratiano and Coviello enter lost and hungry, see a sleeping nymph, admire her, and say they will enjoy her, and do so in a dumb-show pretense. The magician tells them to leave her alone; they insist on doing as they please. The magician raises his rod and invokes Jove. Then he strikes the ground and flames appear. Gratiano and Coviello flee in terror. All of this sexual farce suggests the relishing of the violation of Miranda by Caliban, Trinculo, and Stephano.

The Prospero-Caliban relationship is suggested in *The Three Satyrs,* in which Zanni has been turned into a rock by the magician because Zanni would not obey him. In *The Ship,* the magician warns Zanni to leave Nespola alone. Zanni only laughs, plays *lazzi,* and goes, obviously defying the magician's warning.

Various enchantments and spells, reminiscent of those in *The Tempest,* also occur in the scenarios. The appearance and disappearance of food to the hungry strangers occur in several scenarios. In Act I of *The Enchanted Wood* the Dottore, Tartaglia, Coviello, and Pollincinella notice a fruit tree and as they pick the fruit, flames arise, and the fruit vanishes. Music and dancing spirits in magic spells occur in nearly all the scenarios. In *The Enchanted Wood,* as the savage attempts to pick the forbidden fruit, music is heard, and the savage stands perfectly still. Then spirits come dancing to the music, and taking the savage by the hand, dance him into the grotto. In *The Ship,* Bacchus appears in song and dance. The magician makes himself invisible, as does Prospero in Act III, Scene iii, in Scala's scenario: The magician, invisible, puts a magic garland, which causes the beholder to see the wearer as the beloved, on each of four characters in turn, causing some amusing confusion among the four. Prospero's magic circle can be found in *The Three Satyrs* in which all the characters are lured into the circle and made to dance. Like Prospero, the magician reveals all to those in the circle and reunites each parent to his proper child. The scenario ends in merrymaking, all ready to set sail for Venice. Prospero's method of breaking up the Stephano-Trinculo-Caliban plot by having spirits, hunters, and dogs chase them about, is roughly paralleled in *Pantaloncino* in which the magician breaks up a plot to kill Pantalone by having a lion scare off the plotters, Zanni and Burattino.

The magician in the scenarios resorts to various methods, as does Prospero, to torment strangers and plotters alike. However, whereas Prospero has his Ariel, undoubtedly Shakespeare's own creation, the magician in the scenarios has unidentified spirits or satyrs do his bidding. Like Ariel, they are made to prevent mischief among the strangers, to enchant and to carry off whatever the magician asks. Ariel, of course, has his attendant spirits to do most of the hard labor.

There is even a suggestion of the Ferdinand-Miranda story in one scenario —*Pantaloncino*. In Act II, Fausto seeks the nymph of his dream. He meets Filli, and it is love at first sight. She begs her father, the magician, to take him into their home. The magician takes him into the grotto to tell him about the country. Filli is left to say that she has learnt the power of love at the sight of Fausto and has lost her heart to him.

The final analogue in which the magician lays down his art, throws his book and rod away, as Prospero declares in Act V, Scene i, occurs in *Pantaloncino*. In Act V of this five-act scenario, the only one in this group, the magician says that he does not wish to practice his magic art any longer, but that he will live with the people of the island; then he throws away his rod and his book, thanking Jove for all, and thus ending the play. All of the action of these scenarios takes place within the space of a day.

The Fortune of the Solitary Prince of Muscovy   FIFTIETH DAY (385)

Shakespeare's *The Winter's Tale* contains an analogous theme of the high-born child brought up by peasants. Pantalone, entrusted to leave the child in the nearby village (Shakespeare's Perdita was left in the woods.), deposits her at the base of a haystack where Cavicchio, a rustic, finds her swathed in silk and gold, very much as the Shepherd and Clown in Shakespeare find Perdita in Act III, Scene iii of *The Winter's Tale*. There is also a parallel in the prince who disguises himself to woo the girl he loves, although Giovana is not a princess in disguise as is Perdita.

[1] James O. Halliwell, ed., *Tarleton's Jests and News out of Purgatory* (London, 1844), p. 54.

[2] Jacob Isaacs, "Shakespeare as a Man of the Theatre," *The Shakespeare Association* (London, 1927), p. 114.

[3] Louis Moland, *Molière et La Comédie Italienne* (Paris, 1867), pp. 173, 175.

[4] I. A. Schwartz, *The Commedia dell'Arte and Its Influence on French Comedy in the Seventeenth Century* (New York, n.d.), p. 122.

[5] Winifred Smith, *The Commedia dell'Arte* (New York, 1912), p. 198n.

[6] H. H. Furness, *Hamlet* (Variorum Edition; Philadelphia, 1877), I, 145n.

[7] O. J. Campbell, "The Italianate Background of *The Merry Wives of Windsor*," *Essays and Studies in English and Comparative Literature* VIII, (Ann Arbor, 1932), 81–117.

[8] Kathleen M. Lea, *Italian Popular Comedy*, II (Oxford, 1934), 443.

The Stuart Editions

J. Max Patrick, *series editor*

ALREADY PUBLISHED

The Complete Poetry of Henry Vaughan

EDITED WITH AN INTRODUCTION, NOTES, AND VARIANTS
BY FRENCH FOGLE

An Anthology of Jacobean Drama, VOLUMES *I & II*

EDITED WITH AN INTRODUCTION, NOTES, AND VARIANTS
BY RICHARD C. HARRIER

The Complete Poetry of Ben Jonson

EDITED WITH AN INTRODUCTION, NOTES, AND VARIANTS
BY WILLIAM B. HUNTER, JR.

The Meditative Poem: An Anthology of Seventeenth-Century Verse

EDITED WITH AN INTRODUCTION AND NOTES
BY LOUIS L. MARTZ

Short Fiction of the Seventeenth Century

SELECTED AND EDITED BY CHARLES C. MISH

The Complete Poetry of Robert Herrick

EDITED WITH AN INTRODUCTION AND NOTES
BY J. MAX PATRICK

The Psalms of Sir Philip Sidney and the Countess of Pembroke

EDITED WITH AN INTRODUCTION BY J. C. A. RATHMELL

The Complete English Poetry of John Milton

ARRANGED IN CHRONOLOGICAL ORDER WITH AN
INTRODUCTION, NOTES, AND VARIANTS
BY JOHN T. SHAWCROSS

The Complete Plays of William Wycherley

EDITED WITH AN INTRODUCTION, NOTES, AND VARIANTS
BY GERALD WEALES